THE PSYCHOPATHIC MIND

ORIGINS, DYNAMICS, AND TREATMENT

THE PSYCHOPATHIC MIND
ORIGINS, DYNAMICS, AND TREATMENT

J. REID MELOY, Ph.D.

Jason Aronson Inc.
Northvale, New Jersey
London

1997 Softcover Printing

Copyright © 1988 by Jason Aronson Inc.

10 9 8 7 6 5 4

Library of Congress Cataloging-in-Publication Data

Meloy, J. Reid
   The psychopathic mind : origins, dynamics, and treatment / J. Reid
Meloy.
     p. cm.
   Bibliography: p.
   Includes index.   88-3454
   ISBN 0-87668-311-1
   1. Psychology, Pathological. 2. Psychiatry. 3. Psychotherapy.
I. Title.
RC454.M37 1988
616.89-dc19

Printed in the United States of America on acid-free paper. For information and catalog write to Jason Aronson Inc., 230 Livingston Street, Northvale, New Jersey 07647-1731. Or visit our website: http://www.aronson.com

About the Author

J. Reid Meloy, Ph.D., is a diplomate in forensic psychology of the American Board of Professional Psychology. Former Chief of the Forensic Mental Health Division for San Diego County, he now devotes his time to a private civil and criminal forensic practice, research, writing, and teaching. He is an associate clinical professor of psychiatry at the University of California, San Diego, School of Medicine, and an adjunct professor at the University of San Diego School of Law. He is also a Fellow of the Society for Personality Assessment, and is currently President of the American Academy of Forensic Psychology. In 1992 he received the Distinguished Contribution to Psychology as a Profession Award from the California Psychological Association.

Dr. Meloy has authored or co-authored over one hundred papers published in peer-reviewed psychiatric and psychological journals, and has written or edited four books: *The Psychopathic Mind* (1988); *Violent Attachments* (1992); with Dr. Carl Gacono, *Rorschach Assessment of Aggressive and Psychopathic Personalities* (1994); and *Contemporary Rorschach Interpretation* (1997). His fifth book, *The Psychology of Stalking*, will be published in 1998. He is a sought after speaker and psychological consultant on various civil and criminal cases throughout the United States, most recently the Madonna stalking case and the Polly Klaas murder case. In June 1997, he completed work as the forensic psychologist for the prosecution in the *United States v. Timothy McVeigh*.

To William D. Wilkins, Ph.D.,
psychologist, humanitarian, mentor, friend

Contents

PART II
STRUCTURE AND DYNAMICS

PART III
VIOLENCE, PSYCHOSIS, AND RELATED STATES

Malingering and Dissembling
Psychotic Modes of Aggression
Drug-Induced Psychosis
and Psychopathy
Mental Retardation and Psychopathy

PART IV
TREATMENT

Acknowledgments

The publishing of this book marks the celebration of an intellectual communion: a communion of thought with those I have known personally, and with those I have known by way of their writings. This book, in a real sense, has come from me and through me. Much of the thinking is original, and much of it is an elaboration and extension of others' intellectual findings.

I would first like to thank those whom I have admired and respected through their writings. Those individuals, of course, are listed in the reference section.

On a more personal and collegial level, Drs. Jim Grotstein and Bill Wilkins have been mentors for me, invariably supportive, encouraging, and challenging of my intellectual pursuits. I will always be grateful to them for their faith in my capacities.

Drs. Carl Gacono, Judith Meyers, David Feinstein, Joan Roth, Edward Calix, Katherine DiFrancesca, Ansar Haroun, Gregg Michel, Gerard Neuman, Lloyd Droske, Ben Bensoul, William Vargas, Raymond Cameron, Tom Heaven, and Linda Helinski have all been delightful and stimulating thinkers with me during my writing of this book.

Drs. Phil Erdberg and Deborah Zambianco, my Rorschach teachers and friends, both made major contributions to the refinement of the Rorschach Appendix and are always a pleasure to work with.

Ms. Sue Moritz, Ms. Annette Lau, and Mr. Eugene Schiller extended to me their attention and critical thought in the review of several portions of the book, and I am grateful for their kindness. Ms. Joyce Eisen was always a loyal and attentive friend during the final phases of the book; and Ms. Rosslyn Morrison and Ms. Janet Rasco have earned my deepest respect for assisting me by keeping the daily tasks going so that the long-term dreams could be realized.

I want to thank all the professional and clerical staff of the Psychiatric Security Unit, and other members of the Forensic Mental Health Services division, for their competence in working with some of the most difficult patients anyone could encounter. To those patients, I also owe a debt of gratitude for being the guiding lights, and the ominous shadows, of this book.

I thank Larry Siegel, Janet Houts, and Denise McGuire for their wise counsel; and a special thanks to David Hawkins for his polemics in matters pecuniary.

I also want to thank Drs. William Cox and Harold Mavritte, of the County of San Diego Department of Health Services, for their support and their permission to use clinical and forensic case material from my public work. (All opinions and interpretations expressed in this book are mine and do not necessarily reflect those of the County of San Diego Department of Health Services.)

Dr. Jason Aronson, Ms. Norma Pomerantz, and my production editor, Mr. Nicholas Radhuber, are consummate publishing professionals, and their guidance from contract signing to finished product has been immensely helpful.

I reserve my most important debt of gratitude for last. My wife's daughters, Nancy and Kitty, and my lovely step granddaughter, Katie, gave me the caring and respect to be able to think and write in silence. This was a gift of inestimable importance.

Finally, in the deepest sense, I want to thank Sally, my best friend and lover, who also happens to be my wife, for her multitudinous showings of love, caring, and respect throughout the writing of this book.

The author gratefully acknowledges permission to reprint the following material:

"Marin Killer's Conspiracy Theory," by Erik Ingram and Kevin Leary. Copyright © San Francisco Chronicle, 1986. Reprinted by permission.

Excerpts from *The Boston Strangler*, by Gerold Frank. Copyright © 1966 by Gerold Frank. Reprinted by arrangement with New American Library, New York; Jonathan Cape Ltd., London; and Gerold Frank.

Excerpts from *Two of a Kind: The Hillside Stranglers*, by Darcy O'Brien. Copyright © 1985 by Darcy O'Brien. Reprinted by arrangement with New American Library, New York; and William Morris Agency, New York.

Excerpts from *The Only Living Witness*. Copyright © 1983 by Stephen G. Michaud and Hugh Aynesworth. Reprinted by permission of Linden Press, a division of Simon & Schuster, Inc.

Excerpts from *Confessions of Son of Sam*. Copyright © 1985 by David Abrahamsen, M.D. Reprinted by permission of David Abrahamsen.

Excerpts from "Concept and Percept Formation in Object Relations Theory," by J. Reid Meloy. *Psychoanalytic Psychology 2,1:36,43.* Copyright © 1985 Lawrence Erlbaum Associates, Inc., Hillsdale, New Jersey.

Foreword

The spotlight of current clinical and academic research seems to be settling its focus on the personality trait disorders. Of these, the antisocial personality is one of the most troubling, most paradoxical, and most elusive of personality conceptualizations.

Psychopathy is now being sorted out from its enmeshment with the narcissistic and impulse disorders, and its deeper nature is becoming better understood thanks to new contributions on the subject, especially this one by Dr. Meloy. He believes that psychopathy constitutes a continuum of clinical disturbance and can be understood as an aggressive subcategory of narcissistic personality disorder for diagnostic and theoretical purposes. According to the author, low levels or the absence of empathy, as well as sadomasochistic interactions based on the motif of power rather than attachment, characterize this condition.

Dr. Meloy has emerged from many years of intensive, full-time experience with psychopathic patients in jails, hospitals, and ambulatory settings, to offer us the rich harvest of his experience with and reflections on these patients. He prefers the term *psychopathic* to *sociopathic* or *antisocial* because of its historic provenance and broad associations on the one hand, and its signification of distinct psychopathology on the other. In regard to the latter, the author proffers a conception of the etiology of this disorder that spans psychobiological and psycho-analytic dimensions. He writes, "Psychopathy is psychobiologically predisposed, but there are necessarily deficient and conflictual primary object experiences that give it phenotypic expression."

With this dual-track orientation in mind, the author takes us on a tour in which we visit a wealth of relevant, up-to-date contributions from neurobiology and neuropsychology. We are then presented with a rich, extensive, and in-depth survey of a broad range of psychosocial and psychoanalytic formulations. The author is at his best in explicating the object relations point of view, and he is careful to distinguish between the contributions of the British and American schools of ego psychology.

One of the more impressive contributions Dr. Meloy makes is his distinction between affectively evoked aggression, which is more common in all of us, and predatory aggression, which seems to be the hallmark of the psychopath. Another yield from this work is the finding that psychopathic patients experience a characteristic hyporeactivity of their peripheral autonomic nervous system; to compensate they may pursue aggressive affective displays. "Predatory aggression," Dr. Meloy writes, "although not androgen-dependent, may be socially disinhibited due to the psychopath's pursuit of heightened autonomic arousal and affective aggression." Along this line, the psychopath may engage in violent behavior to enhance his sexual arousal. This autonomic hyporeactivity also seems to be the culprit in the psychopath's difficulty in learning from experience and in developing insight. He lacks the requisite anticipatory anxiety that ordinarily develops in the presence of negative experiences.

One of the most interesting contributions to the theory of abnormal personality development in recent years is that of the "mad, omnipotent self," a construction by Herbert Rosenfeld, which became modified by Otto Kernberg as the "grandiose self" typifying narcissistic personality disorders. The grandiose self is comprised of the real self, the ideal self, and the ideal object. Dr.

Meloy builds upon these constructs and uses them as a basis for his conception of the altered narcissistic personality disorder typical of the psychopathic personality.

The author has already made an important contribution to the literature; he has distinguished between intrapsychic selves and objects as *perceptual* and *conceptual* representations. The psychopath, like the narcissist, introjects abnormal *conceptual* images of the object, and, like the narcissist, develops a pathological grandiose self comprised of real self, ideal self, and ideal object *concepts*, but not necessarily *percepts*. Unlike the narcissist, however, the psychopath has an ideal self composed of a "stranger selfobject," an archetypal preconceptual object, a notion I hypothesized was the legacy of uncontained stranger anxiety. The psychopath, according to Dr. Meloy, fundamentally identifies with the stranger selfobject as a "hard" ideal object that is no longer persecutory because of his identification with it. The author's construction is a more complex variant of Anna Freud's "identification with the aggressor," but one in which a perverse grandiosity has taken hold of the personality.

This book represents the confluence of many streams of thought and addresses the interest of the whole mental health field in a way in which few others have.

—James S. Grotstein, M.D.

There are moments, psychologists tell us, when the passion for sin, or for what the world calls sin, so dominates a nature, that every fibre of the body, as every cell of the brain, seems to be instinct with fearful impulses. Men and women at such times lose the freedom of their will. They move to their terrible ends as automatons move. Choice is taken from them, and conscience is either killed, or, if it lives at all, lives but to give rebellion its fascination, and disobedience its charm. For all sins, as theologians weary not of reminding us, are sins of disobedience. When that high spirit, that morning-star of evil, fell from heaven, it was as a rebel that he fell.

Callous, concentrated on evil, with strained mind and soul hungry for rebellion, Dorian Gray hastened on. . . .

—Oscar Wilde,
The Picture of Dorian Gray

Part I

ORIGINS

1

Introduction

P sychopathy is a deviant developmental disturbance characterized by an inordinate amount of instinctual aggression and the absence of an object relational capacity to bond. Psychopathy is a process: a continuous interplay of factors and operations that are implicitly progressing or regressing toward a particular end point (Frosch 1983a), a fundamental disidentification with humanity.

Psychopathy represents both a category or class of disorders for diagnostic purposes, and a continuous psychological disturbance that may vary in terms of treatment from one individual to another in kind and degree. Hence the clinician will find individuals in outpatient mental health settings with mild psychopathic disturbances and individuals in inpatient and custody settings with moderate to severe psychopathic disturbances. Psychopathy will also distort other psychological problems, and will interact with and shape certain biochemical disorders, such as schizophrenia and bipolar illness.

I want to emphasize both the categorical *and* the continuum approach because psychopathic individuals, by virtue of their behavior, evoke countertransference reactions in others that compel classification and exclusion. It is much easier to deny psychopathy in one's psychotherapy patient, or precipitously to label an individual as a psychopath in a forensic diagnostic evaluation, than to ferret out the nature and extent of psychopathic disturbance in each case.

I have also chosen the term *psychopathy* for some important reasons. Although currently not in diagnostic vogue (American Psychiatric Association 1980, 1987), the word conveys a disturbance of character that has important historical and clinical implications: most notably the growing body of research that supports a psychobiological dimension to psychopathy (Hare 1986, Reid et al. 1986). My theoretical and clinical hypothesis is that psychopathy is psychobiologically predisposed, but there are necessarily deficient and conflictual primary object experiences that determine its phenotypic expression. The American Psychiatric Association's (1980, 1987) antisocial personality disorder criteria are too descriptive, inclusive, criminally biased, and socioeconomically skewed to be of much clinical or research use.

The Psychopathic Mind begins with the building of a psychobiological foundation and then proceeds to develop object relations constructs, in the tradition of Klein, Jacobson, Mahler, and Kernberg, that expand this nomological network. My hope is that such a task will lend construct validity to both lines of research that, with few exceptions, are generally kept disciplines apart.

Before I recapitulate the historical development of psychopathy as a diagnosis and a process, I want to risk a further sociological hypothesis. It is my impression, and fear, that psychopathy, and psychopathic disturbance, is a growing clinical and, therefore, sociocultural phenomenon. I cite only two statistics among many for support: the higher proportion of stranger homicides in the past decade (Riedel et al. 1985) and the increasing frequency of serial murder in the past several decades (Leyton 1986). These are facts illustrative of extreme and statistically rare violence, and citing them may betray my own ethnocentrism by being limited to the United States, but I am fearful this is not the case. Gardner (1986) postulated that children reared in a predominantly image-based, nonlinear, multimedia, briefly attentive society may not develop the deeper, unconscious levels of identity and meaning and therefore manifest a low level of empathy and a higher level of generalized anxiety. Perhaps the analytic focus upon narcissistic psychopathology during the past two decades will need to shift to understanding the varieties of psychopathic disturbance as we approach a new century.

HISTORICAL ANTECEDENTS

Millon (1981) noted the historical vacillation between clinical understanding and social condemnation of the psychopath. Pinel (1801) first observed and documented a certain group of patients who behaved in impulsive and self-destructive ways yet evidenced no defects in reasoning ability. He termed these patients' disorders *manie sans delire* (insanity without delirium). A decade later, the American physician Benjamin Rush (1812) characterized Pinel's diagnostic group in a morally reprehensible light and foreshadowed the writings of the British psychiatrist Prichard (1835), generally credited as the originator of the term *moral insanity* and the leader of generations that have contaminated scientific objectivity with moralizing. Millon (1981) noted the striking similarity between Lombroso's exposition (1872–1885) of the psychopath's behavior, Gouster's (1878) list of symptom clusters, and the contemporary *Diagnostic and Statistical Manual of Mental Disorders*, third edition, description of the antisocial personality disorder (American Psychiatric Association 1980).

The German psychiatric community introduced the term *psychopathic inferiority* (Koch 1891) and attempted to define a physical basis for a group of disorders whose discriminative validity had become unmanageable because of the wide cluster of symptoms that it attempted to embrace. Meyer (1908) separated psychopathic cases, which he called "constitutionally psychopathic inferior types," and psychoneurotic cases, which he believed were primarily psychogenic in origin. Likewise, Kraepelin, in successive editions of his psychiatric text (1887, 1889, 1896, 1903–1904, 1915), developed the theory of psychopathy as both biogenic in etiology and degenerative in moral stature.

Birnbaum (1914) introduced the term *sociopathic* and emphasized the psychogenic nature of the disorder, a product of social learning and deficient early environmental influences. Despite his focus, predominate clinical opinion espoused the biogenic and inferior nature of psychopathy through the first quarter of the twentieth century.

The psychoanalytic theorists entered this arena of thought with two major currents of scientific philosophy in motion: first, a contamination of neutral observation and inductive theorizing by moral judgments, and second, the divergence of two essentially convergent, legitimate, and complementary lines of inquiry into the behavior of the psychopath, the biogenic and the psychogenic.

THE PSYCHOANALYSTS

Freud had little to say about the psychopath, although his comments pointed to the psychopath as an exception to the majority of criminals: "Among adult criminals we must no doubt except those who commit crimes without any sense of guilt, who have either developed no moral inhibitions or who, in their conflict with society, consider themselves justified in their actions" (Freud 1916, p. 333).

Freud's thoughtful paper "Some Character Types Met with in Psychoanalytic Work" (1916) stimulated Alexander to write several papers spanning a decade that investigated the "robust, expansive, instinctual life" (Alexander 1935, p. 279) of the psychopath. He elaborated both the psychogenic and biogenic origins of psychopathy, although he preferred to conceptualize his discussion along four rather general levels of psychopathology that he labeled *neurosis, neurotic character, psychosis,* and *criminality* (Alexander 1923, 1930, 1935). Aichhorn (1925) published his seminal text *Wayward Youth* during this same period and developed an understanding of psychopathy that centered upon oedipal configurations, narcissism, and the failure of early identifications. Coriat (1927) and Partridge (1927) postulated that infantile, oral fixations explained the psychopath's behavior.

Wittels (1937), Karpman (1941), and Levy (1951) developed simple typologies of psychopathy based upon psychoanalytic constructs. Wittels (1937) suggested that neurotic psychopaths feared their bisexuality, whereas the simple psychopath indulged it. Karpman (1941) discriminated between the idiopathic psychopath (the true guiltless criminal) and the symptomatic psychopath (the neurotic character described by Alexander [1935]), the latter synonymous with the individual motivated by unconscious guilt (Freud 1916). Levy (1951) foreshadowed current object relations theory and its understanding of narcissistic pathology in his differentiation of the deprived and indulged psychopath. Millon (1969) respectively termed these the *aggressive* and *narcissistic* psychopathic types.

Cleckley published the first edition of *Mask of Sanity* in 1941 and psychodynamically attributed psychopathy to a concealed psychosis. He introduced an alternative term, *semantic dementia,* to account for the pathological lying of the psychopath and to delimit the use of the term *psychopathy,* but it did not take hold. Most important, he described sixteen behavioral criteria for psychopathy, some of which had clear psychodynamic implications, such as a lack of remorse or shame, poor judgment and failure to learn from experience, pathologic egocentricity and incapacity for love, general poverty in major affective reactions, and specific loss of insight. These criteria have been empirically defined and measured most recently by Hare (1980). Later edi-

tions of Cleckley's book (1976) reflected an evolution of his
thinking about the psychopath that was more closely allied with
Kernberg's (1984) borderline level, rather than psychotic level, of
personality organization; more specifically, structural criteria
defined the psychopath's identity integration, defensive operations, and reality testing. Cleckley wrote,

> My concept . . . postulates a selective defect or elimi-
> nation that prevents important components of normal
> experience from being integrated into the whole
> human reaction, particularly an elimination or attenu-
> ation of those strong affective components which ordi-
> narily arise in major personal and social issues. . . .
> Even his splendid logical faculties will, in real life
> situations, produce not actual reasoning but that imi-
> tation of reasoning known as rationalization. [Cleckley
> 1976, pp. 230–231]

Horney (1945), Fenichel (1945), and Reich (1945), in published editions of their books the same year, made further significant contributions toward understanding the unconscious life of
the psychopath.

Horney (1945) commented on the interpersonal exploitation
of others by the psychopath that lessens "his own sense of
barrenness. When he defeats others he wins a triumphant elation
which obscures his own hopeless defeat" (pp. 206–207). Thus the
psychopath perpetuates his emotional states and reinforces his
feelings of omnipotence. Bursten (1973a) further refined this
psychodynamic as "putting something over on someone." The
shameful, worthless selfobject is expelled and projected onto the
actual victim; and the psychopath is subsequently exhilarated
during this perceived victory as the fantasied grandiose self is
cleansed and glorified. Libidinally a reparative introjective-
projective cycle with both anal-eliminative and phallic-exhibitionistic themes was suggested.

Fenichel (1945) emphasized the inconstancy of the object in the psychopathic character and the consequent deficits and distortions in early identifications. In what he called "instinct-ridden characters," the isolation of the whole superego could result:

> Experiences with the persons whose incorporation created the superego have made it possible for the ego to feel the conscience in one place at certain periods . . . but to be relatively free from the inhibiting influences of the superego, when tempted by the irresistible urge of strivings for instinctual gratification. [Fenichel 1945, p. 374]

Psychopaths were seen as managing their self-esteem by answering narcissistic wounds with simple denial and a consequent, protective increase in narcissistic tone, or "felt quality of perfection" (Rothstein 1980, p. 4). Instinctual behavior could resonate with the superego's demands in unusual childhood milieus, or there might develop a "contradictory parasitic double" (Fenichel 1945, p. 504) of the normal superego in subsequent social-learning environments for the individual. Fenichel kept reiterating that identifications were essential for the development of any character.

Reich's (1945) contribution to psychopathic psychodynamics was his libidinal formulations concerning the phallic-narcissistic character. This character type was seen as self-assured, sometimes arrogant, elastic, energetic, often impressive in his bearing. He anticipated impending attacks with attacks by himself. There was an absence of reaction formations to his openly aggressive and sadistic behavior, and he expressed a typically derogatory attitude toward women. There was pride in the phallus and strong phallic aggression. Mother, as an internalized object, was retained only with narcissistic attitudes and impulses of revenge. The sexual act constituted a piercing or destroying of the woman. This character was continually defending against regression to more passive and anal stages of development. There was an unconscious attitude of revenge toward the internalized, yet persecutory, heterosexual object representation. Reich linked this character type to the sex murderers, or what I would call the sexual psychopaths or serial murderers, of his period.

In 1949 Eissler edited an important compilation of scholarly papers entitled *Searchlights on Delinquency.* Four of those papers made notable contributions to the psychodynamics of psychopathy. Eissler (1949) emphasized the alloplastic nature of the psychopathic personality and hypothesized that destructive acting out functioned intrapsychically as a reparative attempt to bolster self-esteem and maintain reality testing. He also noted the actual, concrete injustices that the delinquent often suffered as a child, interfering with appropriate identification processes and disinhibiting subsequent aggressive impulses. Schmideberg (1949) shifted her focus to a disturbance in object relations, rather than superego development, in the psychopath. She emphasized the role of anxiety and depersonalization in the activities of the antisocial individual. The behavioral absence of emotional ties, implying an intrapsychic distortion or deficit of appropriate identifications, and subsequent object representations of an unstable and predominately anhedonic tone, prevented the development of a strong, yet flexible, superego.

Anna Freud (1949), drawing from both drive theory and object relational hypotheses, centered on the first year of life and the transition from primary narcissism to object love. When the mother failed to be a stable and reliable source of emotional supplies, what Mahler (1968) would later call the ordinary devoted mother, adequate identifications did not occur and the transformation to object libido failed. Such deprivation was seen as leading to the inadequate binding of aggressive impulses and their consequent splitting off, or dissociation, from consciousness. These impulses would intermittently return in aggressive and antisocial behavior, rather than channeled, neutralized, and sublimated with the development of higher-level defenses during the oedipal period.

Johnson (1949) introduced the term *superego lacunae* to circumscribe the selective deficits in superego functioning of most psychopaths. In her clinical experience she found that the child's superego deficits often corresponded with the parents' and that the latter gained vicarious satisfaction from the child acting out the parents' unconscious antisocial impulses. Johnson hypothesized an intergenerational and sociogenic inheritance of such superego deficits and noted that treatment failures occurred most readily when the superego deficits were more global.

OBJECT RELATIONS

The clinical and theoretical works of Klein (1957, 1964), Mahler (1968, 1979), Jacobson (1964, 1971), and Kernberg (1975, 1976, 1980, 1984) have provided a rich conceptual basis for the further psychodynamic understanding of the psychopath. Of these four psychoanalytic thinkers, Kernberg has referred explicitly to the psychopath as a severe variant of the narcissistic personality disorder (Kernberg 1975). Both Mahler (1979) and Jacobson (1964), moreover, have elucidated empirically based theories that invite retrospective hypotheses concerning the etiology of the psychopath. It is my intent to apply their work to understand the experiential process of the psychopath, and to formulate both structural and functional hypotheses regarding the psychopath's dynamic configurations. Other psychoanalytic theorists that have largely influenced my thinking include Searles (1960, 1965, 1979), Grotstein (1978, 1980b), Modell (1968), Frosch (1983a), Meissner (1978), and Volkan (1976).

Psychodynamic theorists must seek empirical validation from within and without if they are to have scientific respectability. Recent work by a few psychoanalytic researchers is notable

(Reiser 1984, 1985, Silverman 1985). I will not only illustrate the psychopathic process with clinical cases, a time-honored tradition in psychoanalysis, but will also support these formulations with current neuropsychological and neurophysiological research concerning the psychopath. Such construct validation should anchor these psychodynamic hypotheses in an economical and consistent fashion.

I also will pay close attention to an area of empirical research that is newly emerging yet promises to bring to object relations theory a needed scientific objectivity. I am referring to work regarding the empirical measurement of object relations phenomena with the Rorschach (Kwawer et al. 1980, Kissen 1986).

This book is divided into four sections and eight chapters, and they may be read either sequentially or according to the reader's interest. Each chapter should stand on its own merits and is not wholly dependent on formulations from preceding chapters.

2

Dynamic and Biologic Origins

P sychopathy describes an intrapsychic process that has both structure and function. This process, although vulnerable to various physiological and emotional states, is characterized by enduring patterns, or traits, that are behaviorally expressed in interpersonal relations over time. The structure and function of psychopathy, both being necessary, and by themselves insufficient measures of the personality disorder, are describable in both metapsychological (primarily structural) and clinical (primarily functional) terms. Although psychoanalytic metapsychology has come under intense fire in recent years (Schafer 1976, Holt 1985), inferred structures of the mind are amenable to construct validity if carefully induced from clinical behavior; and moreover, hypothetical metapsychological constructs can help one deduce specific clinical behaviors.

The weight of clinical research supports the hypothesis that psychopathic personality organization is one subtype of narcissistic personality disorder, albeit an extreme and dangerous variant. Likewise, narcissistic personality disorder represents personality function and structure at a relatively higher developmental level of borderline personality organization. I am referring here to Kernberg's (1984) three levels of personality organization—neurotic, borderline, and psychotic—and his differentiation of respective structural criteria into identity integration, defensive operations, and reality testing. Borderline personality organization is evidenced by the lack of an integrated identity, the predominance of primitive defense mechanisms, and the maintenance of adequate reality testing.

The lack of an integrated identity refers to the maintenance of ego boundaries. A perceptual discrimination between self and others and a conceptual distinction between internalized representations of self and others exist, yet constancy of these internal images has failed and they remain "multiple, contradictory, affective-cognitive representations" (Kernberg 1984, p. 12). This is postulated to be the result of severe early aggression that has been activated.

The predominance of primitive defense mechanisms refers to the use of splitting and other related defensive maneuvers. Contradictory representations and affects concerning self and others are actively dissociated, or kept apart, in consciousness, and are alternately experienced. Other defensive derivatives of splitting include primitive idealization, projective identification, projection, introjection, denial, omnipotence, and devaluation.

The maintenance of reality testing refers to the "person's capacity to evaluate appropriately the reality of phenomena going on around and within him" (Frosch 1983a, p. 335). It is not to be confused with reality sense, although the latter appears to support the development of reality testing (Ferenczi 1913). The psychopathic individual, for instance, may have the reality sense of being physically larger and intellectually more astute than he or she actually is, yet his or her capacity to distinguish between interoceptive and exteroceptive stimuli is quite adequate. Reality testing is the *sine qua non* for differentiating between borderline and psychotic personality organization.

Narcissistic personality disorders are differentiated from borderline personality organization by a relatively smooth social functioning, better impulse control, and what Kernberg (1975) has called a pseudosublimatory potential, that is, a capacity for consistent, active work in some area that permits gratification of personal ambition and admiration from others. On an intrapsychic level, the distinction arises in the presence of an integrated but highly pathological grandiose self, the capacity for evocative memory of object representations (Rinsley 1982), and the failure to integrate ego ideal and superego (Volkan 1976). This "omnipotent mad" self (Rosenfeld 1964) is a pathological condensation of aspects of the real self, the ideal self, and the idealized object. In the case of the psychopathic character, the result would be a primary identification with the aggressor and a renunciation of weaker, more benign, and perhaps more nurturing object representations.

Psychopathic personality organization, as a variant of narcissistic personality organization, is distinguished from the latter by the following characteristics:

1. The predominance of aggressive drive derivatives and the gratification of aggression as the only significant mode of relating to others.
2. The absence of more passive and independent modes of narcissistic repair.
3. The presence of sadistic or cruel behavior, inferring the activation of primitive persecutory introjects, or "sadistic superego precursors" (Kernberg 1984, p. 281).
4. The presence of a malignant ego ideal with developmental roots in a cruel and aggressive primary parental object.
5. The absence of a desire to morally justify one's behavior, which would imply the presence of superego precursors of a more socially acceptable ego ideal.
6. The presence of both anal-eliminative and phallic-exhibitionistic libidinal themes in the repetitive interpersonal cycles of goal conflict with others, the intent to deceive, the carrying out of the deceptive act, and the contemptuous delight when victory is perceived (Bursten 1973a).

7. The emergence of paranoid ideation when under stress, rather than a vulnerability to depressive affect.

BIOLOGICAL SUBSTRATES

Psychic structure and function are built upon the biological substrates of the human organism, which are largely determined prior to and independently of the early parenting environment. Kernberg referred to these substrates as "biologically determined inborn affect dispositions together with inborn perceptual and behavior patterns" (Kernberg 1980, p. 108).

Psychodynamics, of course, do not exist in an intrapsychic vacuum, and Kernberg is scientifically correct, if rather brief, in acknowledging the biological influence upon all intrapsychic and interpersonal behavior. Two important questions follow Kernberg's acknowledgment: Are there specific biological substrates that predispose the development of a psychopathic character? If so, what are those substrates? I would certainly answer *yes* to the first question, although specifying what those biological variables are can be only tentatively addressed.

The empirical research presents us with an additional problem by mixing independent variables according to psychopathy, criminality, or aggression. Therefore, two other assumptions need to be questioned before the empirical data in this area can be summarized. The first assumption is that there exists a significant relationship between criminality and psychopathy. This is supported by research data that indicate psychopathy as a personality disorder positively correlates with criminality as a social and legal concept (Wilson and Herrnstein 1985, Hare 1981). The second assumption is that there exists a significant relationship between psychopathy and aggression. This is also supported by research data that indicate a positive correlation between psychopathy and violence (Hare 1981). Psychopaths generally commit more crimes than nonpsychopathic criminals (Hare and

Jutai 1983); they are more prone to recidivism (Ganzer and Sarason 1973); and they engage in more violent and aggressive behaviors than other individuals, including nonpsychopathic criminals (Kozol et al. 1972, Hare and McPherson 1984).

Beginning with these empirically based assumptions that positive and significant correlations exist among psychopathy, criminality, and aggression, I will analyze research findings according to neuroanatomical structure, genetic predispositions, neurochemical set, hormonal influences, and autonomic re-activity.

Neuroanatomical Structure

I have not found any studies that prospectively address the relationship between early infant neuroanatomical structure and the later development of psychopathy. The obstacles to such a lengthy and tedious study are obvious. Retrospective studies of habitually violent individuals using electroencephalogram meas-ures as a means of inferring neuroanatomical irregularities are available. Results suggest that the prevalence of EEG abnormal-ities among violent individuals ranges from 25 to 50 percent (Mednick et al. 1982). EEG abnormalities among normal popula-tions range from 5 to 20 percent (Kooi et al. 1978). EEG activity in habitually aggressive individuals is characterized by an excess of slow activity (theta range, 4 to 7 Hz) or fast activity (beta range, 13 to 40 Hz), a seemingly bimodal distribution (Mednick et al. 1982).

A few prospective studies addressing the relationship be-tween EEG activity and later criminality have been done. Med-nick and colleagues (1981) examined 265 Danish children, age 11 to 13 years, for EEG patterns. Seven years later the cohort was divided into three groups: noncriminal, one-time offender, and multiple offender. The multiple offenders exhibited slower alpha frequencies than either of the other two groups. The researchers then parceled out seventy-two subjects who had psychiatrically disturbed parents; statistical analysis of the remaining subjects with normal parents found that slow alpha EEGs afforded greater predictability of delinquent behavior among normals than among boys with psychiatric involvement. An independent study of twenty-two recidivist property offenders in Sweden replicated Mednick's results (Mednick et al. 1982).

Utilizing neuropsychological measures of brain functioning, which allow inferences concerning localization and lateralization of dysfunction, Yeudall (1977) found that approximately 91 percent of psychopaths exhibited significant neuropsychological impairment. His findings, and those of others (Bach-y-Rita et al. 1971, Blumer et al. 1974) implicate frontal and temporal area brain dysfunction. Attempts to establish a relationship between violent behavior and lateral dysfunction have been more ambiguous (Fitzhugh 1973, Flor-Henry 1979, Andrew 1980).

Genetic Predispositions

The differentiation of genotypic and phenotypic influences is best approached through the use of twin and adoption studies. Twin studies allow for the measurement of concordance between pairs and the comparison of identical (monozygotic, MZ) to fraternal (dizygotic, DZ) twins across a particular variable or set of variables. In this case, most of the work has addressed the variable of criminality, the identification of an individual as criminal through the perusal of prison, police, and court records. Wilson and Herrnstein (1985) pooled the data from eight studies of criminality concordance (Christiansen 1977a) and found that for MZ twins it was 0.69 and for same-sex DZ twins it was 0.33. This supports the hypothesis of a substantial genetic loading in criminal behavior. The most well-designed study of twin concordance for criminality used the national criminality register in Denmark and studied all twins ($N = 3,586$) born in a well-defined area between 1881 and 1910 (Christiansen 1977b). It reported 35 percent concordance for male MZ pairs and 13 percent concordance for male DZ pairs. Although Christiansen's results account for less of the criminality variance than the pooled data, the presence of some genetically determined biological variable is suggested.

Adoption studies provide an even more robust method for the separation of genetic and environmental influences. Schulsinger (1977) identified fifty-seven psychopaths from a sample of 5,483 Copenhagen adoptees by studying both psychiatric records and police files. He matched them with fifty-seven nonpsychopathic adoptee controls for gender, age, social class, neighborhood of rearing, and age of transfer to the adopted family. Among biological relatives of both groups, he found the psychopathic adoptees' relatives, socially unknown to the adoptees, manifested the most psychopathy.

In the largest systematic adoption study to date, Mednick and colleagues (1984) drew a sample of 14,427 male and female adoptees from all adoptions in Denmark between 1924 and 1947. A cross-fostering analysis of the 4,065 adopted males in the final sample found that the highest proportion of adoptees with one criminal conviction came from the group with both biological and adoptive criminal parents; the next highest proportion of males with one conviction came from the group with only biological parents who were criminal. This study strongly supported the hypothesis that biological contributions to criminality were more important than environmental contributions. I found several of the other findings particularly interesting: About a quarter of the adoptees were placed in their adoptive homes immediately after birth, another half by the end of the first year, and another 13 percent by the end of the second year. The age at placement exerted no effect on the strength of the relationship between biological parent and male adoptee criminality. The time at which the biological parents committed their crimes (before or after the birth of the child) also had no effect on the adoptee's criminality.

Both twin and adoption studies strongly support the hypothesis that an unknown genetic factor predisposes an individual to engage in criminal behavior. I assert that psychopathic character organization also has a necessary but not sufficient genetic loading, the specifics of which are not yet known. Mednick and colleagues (1982) defined this biosocial interaction:

> Where the social experiences of an antisocial individual are not especially criminogenic, biological factors should be examined. The value of the biological factors is more limited in predicting antisocial behavior in individuals who have experienced criminogenic social conditions in their rearing. [p. 55]

Neurochemical Set

Considerable research evidence supports the notion that differences in emotionality are inherited (Hall 1941, Broadhurst 1957, Wilcock 1968, Valle 1970, Valzelli 1981). Environmental factors interact with and modify the biologically determined emotional predispositions of the individual (Masur 1972, Henderson 1973, King and Appelbaum 1973, Russell and Williams 1973, Archer 1974). Emotionality and its clinical presentation called *affect* differentiate mammals from reptiles and appear to motivate such uniquely mammalian behaviors as parenting, the acquisition of material goods in anticipation of future consequences, and social behavior.

Neuronal circuits that biologically define the parameters of all behavior utilize a variety of neurotransmitters, which in turn biochemically interact with one another (Blondaux et al. 1973, Kostowski and Valzelli 1974). The most salient behavior that provides us with a link between psychopathy and neurochemical set is aggression.

Many attempts have been made to classify aggressive behavior, the most notable being Moyer's (1968) seven categories: predatory, intermale, fear-induced, irritable, territorial, maternal, and instrumental. Such a wide range of aggressive behaviors can be alternately classified as either *affective* or *predatory* aggression, two general categories of aggression with distinct neuroanatomical pathways and controlled by different sets of neurotransmitters (Eichelman et al. 1981).

Affective aggression is the result of external or internal threatening stimuli that evoke an intense and patterned activation of the autonomic nervous system, accompanied by threatening vocalizations and attacking or defending postures. Many of the pathways are tied closely to the spinothalamic tract and the periaquaductal gray.

Predatory aggression is directed toward the destruction of prey, usually for food gathering in subhuman species. It involves minimal autonomic arousal and vocalization and no elaborate behavioral rituals. There may be a selective suppression of other sensory input and species-specific killing patterns. Neuroanatomical pathways appear to project from the hypothalamus into the ventral midbrain tegmentum (Eichelman et al. 1981).

When a household cat is cornered and threatened, the neurochemical set produces a display of affective aggression: hissing, hair standing on end, dilating pupils, active clawing, arching back. When the same cat is stalking a bird in the backyard, predatory aggression dominates: quiet stalking of the prey, the absence of ritualistic display, and focused attention on the target.

Predatory aggression is the hallmark of the psychopathic individual, whether it is a primitive act of violence against a stranger or a technically sophisticated act of revenge against a business associate. I will explore in detail this mode of aggression of the psychopath in a subsequent chapter, but my focus here is the neurochemical set of predatory aggression and its emergence as a possible biological substrate of psychopathic character organization.

Four neurotransmitters appear to play a major role in aggression. Serotonin, the catecholamines norepinephrine and dopamine, and acetylcholine each correlate in a distinctive manner with behavioral displays of affective and predatory aggression.

Serotonin appears to correlate with the inhibition of both predatory and affective aggression (Valzelli 1981). Circadian (daily) and ultradian (seasonal) rhythms in whole-brain serotonin level have also been described (Valzelli 1978).

The catecholamines norepinephrine and dopamine appear to correlate positively with affective aggression and negatively with predatory aggression. The differential effects of these neuroregulators on two forms of aggression could reflect the separate action of neuronal groups releasing an identical regulator or a difference in receptor sites in discrete brain regions (Eichelman et al. 1981).

Acetylcholine, or activation of the cholinergic system, appears to positively correlate with both predatory and affective aggression (Eichelman et al. 1981, Valzelli 1981). The modulation of brain acetylcholine by both dopaminergic and serotonergic projections has also been demonstrated (Butcher et al. 1976).

Table 2-1 summarizes the correlations described among these four neuroregulators and two general forms of aggression.

The results noted above are generalized from an accumulation of animal research. Few comparable human research studies

Table 2-1
Correlations between Four Neurotransmitters and Affective-Predatory Aggression

	Affective	Predatory
Serotonin	−	−
Norepinephrine	+	−
Dopamine	+	−
Acetylcholine	+	+

are available. Among those that have been done, however, the results validate the animal neuroregulation research. Greenberg and Coleman (1976) found that in 83 percent of their patients studied, hyperactive and aggressive behaviors were associated with a fall of blood 5-hydroxyindoles (serotonin metabolites). Brown and colleagues (1979) reported statistically significant correlations of cerebrospinal fluid biogenic amine metabolites with independently scored aggression rating scales in a sample of personality-disordered military personnel. Results indicated aggressiveness negatively correlated with 5-hydroxyindoleacetic acid (serotonin) and positively correlated with 3-methoxy-4-hydroxyphenylglycol (norepinephrine); 80 percent of the variance in aggression scores was accounted for by the serotonin metabolites in the cerebral spinal fluid.

Hormonal Influences

Hormones are the slow behavioral cousins of the neuron. They may function as neuromodulators by setting the biochemical tone for synaptic activity (Eichelman et al. 1981). The biological fact that the "neurological system for aggression is sensitized by hormones derives from evidence that a reduced androgen level raises the threshold for aggressive displays" (Valzelli 1981, pp. 114–115). All forms of aggression in animal studies, with the exception of predatory aggression, appear to be androgen dependent and sustained by sex-specific gonadal hormones (Valzelli 1981).

Aggression in humans is also a male-dominated activity and appears to be one of the few biological differences between the sexes. Maccoby and Jacklin (1980) reviewed thirty-two studies of children under six years of age and found no instances of girls as a group manifesting greater aggression than boys as a group. Aggressiveness appears to be gender-related prior to the full impact of socially learned, imitative behavior of parents or peers.

Olweus (1975) found that levels of aggression in nursery school predicted aggressive behavior throughout childhood and adolescence. Mednick and colleagues (1982) hypothesized that circulating blood levels of testosterone influence aggression in adults, and prenatal circulating androgens biochemically predispose the fetal brain to later heightened aggression.

Testosterone levels and aggression do correlate in adult samples, but are confounded by the variable of social dominance, particularly during adolescence and young adulthood (Persky et al. 1971, Kreuz and Rose 1972, Ehrenkranz et al. 1974, Rada et al. 1976, Scaramella and Brown 1978). Persky and colleagues (1971) attempted to differentiate between "trait" and "state" aggression, highlighting the production rate of testosterone in their subjects compared with the periodic secretory "bursts" of testosterone that may trigger momentary feelings of hostility.

In female samples the premenstrual period may result in actual irritative aggression. Prison records that have been studied indicate a significant increase in violent crimes during the premenstrual week (Dalton 1961). The premenstrual period is characterized by a fall in progesterone level (Hamburg et al. 1968) and a concentration of estrogen (Bardwick 1971). Elevated prolactin levels coupled with low progesterone levels may also contribute to anxiety or irritative aggression (Carroll and Steiner 1978).

It is precipitous, however, to assert an empirical relationship between psychopathic character organization and a hormonal substrate such as elevated circulating levels of testosterone, despite my hypothesis of predominant aggressive drive derivatives in the psychopathic character. Predatory aggression does not appear to be androgen-dependent in animal studies; there is no empirical evidence linking circulating fetal hormone levels to later displays of aggressive behavior that would rule out the influence of social learning; and there are no studies, to my knowledge, that have differentiated psychopathic from nonpsychopathic prisoners and subsequently investigated the relationship between their social dominance and testosterone levels.

Yet a strong correlational relationship would seem to exist. Interpersonal dominance and aggression play primary roles in the object relations of the psychopathic character. Psychopathic processes may predominate among males if the correlations among psychopathy, criminality, and aggression are valid and reliable. Other forms of aggression that involve affective displays and autonomic arousal are endogenous to the psychopath, and such individuals may vigorously pursue these to compensate for their autonomic hyporeactivity, as I will elaborate in the next section. Predatory aggression, although not androgen-dependent, may be socially disinhibited as a result of the psychopath's pursuit of heightened autonomic arousal and affective aggression.

The sexual psychopath, whether a sadistic rapist (Groth 1979) or a serial murderer, engages in violent behavior that enhances his sexual arousal. The neurological proximity of the sexual and aggressive centers within the hypothalamus and the shared influence of the androgens appear to be implicated (Zillmann 1984). The sexual arousal and intense pleasure that sexual psychopaths feel during the commission of violent acts is ubiquitous in the case studies of their subjective experiences (Krafft-Ebing 1965, Abrahamsen 1985, O'Brien 1985). Likewise, castration has been reported to be effective in controlling certain violent criminals (Bremer 1959, Campbell 1967). Estrogens and other antiandrogenic drugs, such as cyproterone and medroxy-progesterone, appear to reduce both aggression and some sexual offenses (Chatz 1972, Laschet 1973). More empirical research with well-defined psychopathic samples is necessary to test these hypotheses.

Autonomic Reactivity

During the past twenty-five years a number of researchers have investigated the relationship between peripheral measures of autonomic nervous system functioning and behavioral measures of psychopathy. Research findings have strongly and consistently supported the hypothesis that psychopathic individuals are autonomically hyporeactive, at an electrodermal level, when compared with other nonpsychopathic population samples.

Peripheral autonomic functioning may appear, at first glance, to be a distant cousin of psychopathic character pathology, but if it is viewed as a psychophysiological mediator of emotionality and emotional responsiveness to self and others, its link to personality disorder becomes more tenable. Furthermore, autonomic hyporeactivity holds crucial implications for the individual's capacity to learn from experience, that is, the development of insight; his capacity to develop anticipatory anxiety in the face of negative experiences; and his propensity to lead a sensation-seeking, extroverted life-style.

Measures of autonomic baseline and reactive levels have most commonly used skin conductance, or galvanic skin response, as an electrodermal indicator of autonomic arousal. It is a reliable and valid measure, and there is a sizable methodological literature for its use (Venables and Christie 1975). Most of the research concerning autonomic measurements of the psychopath have used galvanic skin response as the indicator of arousal.

The psychopathic character's emotionality and emotional responsiveness has been inferred by studying his autonomic baseline when compared with other matched samples; his spontaneous autonomic reactivity in the absence of external stimuli; and his autonomic reactivity to external stimuli, mostly of a noxious or unpleasant variety.

The autonomic baseline activity of the psychopath has been found to be consistently lower than other nonpsychopathic samples, but the difference is not always significant (Hare 1978a). One prospective study (Loeb and Mednick 1977) did find that significantly lower autonomic baselines in a small group of Danish adolescents did predict a record of delinquency ten years later.

Spontaneous autonomic reactivity in the absence of external

stimuli occurred to a lesser, but not significant, degree in psychopathic prisoners when compared with nonpsychopathic prisoners (Hare 1978a). The replication of these studies with the addition of nonprison control groups might produce significant differences.

Autonomic reactivity to external stimuli, usually unpleasant, has been found to be consistently and significantly less in psychopathic groups when compared with nonpsychopathic groups. Although most of the studies were retrospective in design, that is, the individuals' psychopathic histories and behaviors occurred prior to measurement of their autonomic functioning, the electrodermal hyporeactive hypothesis appears to be quite reliable (Hare 1972, Schalling et al. 1973, Hare and Craigen 1974, Hare 1975). One prospective study (Loeb and Mednick 1977) found that the mean response amplitude of seven young adolescent subjects contributed to the prediction of delinquency records a decade later. The amplitude of their autonomic reactivity to stimulation was five to ten times less than the nondelinquent controls. A prospective finding such as this adds great validity to the retrospective body of research and supports the notion that autonomic hyporeactivity may *predispose* an individual to antisocial behavior, rather than *result from* the aversive consequences of such behavior.

The psychopathic individual also shows significantly less autonomic arousal when anticipating a negative experience. Laboratory-induced negative events are usually the infliction of pain, shock, loud noise, or exposure to photographs of injured or mutilated people. There is a reliable body of research supporting this hypothesis when the aversive stimulation will be felt by the self (Lykken 1957, Hare and Craigen 1974, Wadsworth 1975, Hare 1978a) or perceived that it will be felt by others (Sutker 1970, Hare and Craigen 1974, House and Milligan 1976). Wadsworth (1975) designed one of the few prospective studies in this area and found that significantly slower increases in pulse rate when anticipating a negative experience in a group of 11-year-old boys contributed to the prediction of their delinquency records ten years later. This research supports my psychodynamic inference that the psychopathic character feels significantly less anticipatory anxiety when faced with an unpleasant, or even traumatic, situation; and even more important, it points toward an autonomic correlate, or biological substrate, for the psychopath's lack of empathy, the incapacity to identify with another's emotional pain. On the other hand, the psychopath gains autonomic support for his object relational and defensive inclination to detach from, or disidentify with, the emotional experience of his victim.

The autonomic hyporeactivity of the psychopath led Mednick and colleagues (1982) to develop a biosocial theory to explain why the psychopath fails to learn from punishment. He hypothesized that a reduction of fear of punishment powerfully reinforces the inhibition of aggression in the nonpsychopathic individual. Psychopathic individuals do not inhibit their aggressiveness because the reduction of fear as a negative reinforcer is diminished or absent. They have an inadequate fear response, only mildly anticipate a fearful event, and, most significant, dissipate what fearful response they experience in a slower manner.

The slow dissipation of fear was inferred by the slower "skin conductance recovery" of the psychopath. This peripheral measure of autonomic activity implies that psychopaths return to their autonomic baseline much more slowly than normal individuals once they have reacted to stimuli.

Mednick's biosocial theory prompted several researchers to analyze their data again and measure skin conductance recovery within their psychopathic and nonpsychopathic groups. The significantly slower autonomic recovery of the psychopath was found to be quite reliable (Siddle et al. 1973, Hare 1975, Hare et al. 1978). Hare (1978b) found a significant correlation between skin conductance recovery and the prediction of recidivism in a study of psychopathic and nonpsychopathic prisoners.

The learning failures of the psychopathic character disorder appear to be limited to autonomic nervous system mediated negative consequences. The psychopath appears to respond normally to both autonomically mediated positive conditioning and other learning tasks that do not involve autonomic or emotional arousal (Schmauk 1970).

Despite the autonomic hyporeactivity at a peripheral level, it appears that psychopaths show normal cardiovascular reactivity to both pleasant and aversive stimuli (Hare and Quinn 1971, Hare and Craigen 1974, Hare et al. 1978). Hare (1986) has interpreted these findings by drawing on a model proposed by Lacey and Lacey (1974) that heart-rate acceleration and increased carotid pressure are associated with decreased cortical arousal and sensory rejection, a "defensive response" to the environment. In other words, cardiovascular reactivity plays an important role in the modulation of sensory input. This pattern in the psychopath may reflect an active coping mechanism and, as a consequence, the inhibition of fear arousal. Venables (1985) argued that this sequence of events is physiologically tenable; that is, cardiovascular reactivity can occur quickly enough to inhibit electrodermal reactivity to a significant degree.

The psychodynamic implications of these findings are formidable. First, the psychopathic individual's anticipation or experience of unpleasant, negative affect will have little or no behavioral consequence. Second, insight may be imitated and quickly learned, but will exist without an affective dimension such as shame, guilt, or remorse. Third, predominant aggressive-drive derivatives will be less inhibited by the psychopathic personality despite their aversive consequences for the individual and others. Fourth, subsequent positive affect may strongly reinforce these aggressive-drive derivatives. And fifth, punishment of the psychopathic criminal exists only as a public projection.

A body of research that validates the autonomic hyporeactivity hypothesis, but is less well known in psychoanalytic circles, is the work of experimental psychologists with the personality construct extroversion (Claridge 1967, Eysenck 1967, Gray 1972).

Extroversion has been established as an independent dimension of personality that is both genetically loaded and highly reliable (Eysenck 1947, 1957, 1967, Shields 1962, Scarr 1965). The traits of sociability and impulsiveness have been identified as subfactors in extroversion and appear to correlate about 0.50 with each other (Eysenck and Eysenck 1963).

Eysenck proposed a biological construct to explain this personality dimension, based upon findings that extroversion correlated positively with lower cortical arousal, higher stimulant thresholds, and lower sedative thresholds (Eysenck 1967). Subsequent research supported his hypothetical construct (Claridge 1967, Gray 1972).

Based upon his own research, as well as that of MacLean (1960) and Gellhorn and Loofbourrow (1963), Eysenck (1967) hypothesized that differences in extroversion were related to differential thresholds in various parts of the reticular formation. Differences in "neuroticism," an orthogonal personality dimension that he empirically defined, were produced by differential thresholds within the visceral brain, or limbic system.

Eysenck proposed a corticoreticular loop in which ascending afferent pathways projected into the cortex and the reticular formation; the latter would send arousal messages to the cortex, and the cortex would respond with more arousal or inhibition messages back to the reticular formation. In the same manner, a visceroreticular loop provided information processing between the limbic structures and the reticular formation. Thus autonomic activation, seated in the hypothalamus, was partially dependent on diffuse cortical arousal through the corticoreticular loop. Cortical arousal, however, might occur without autonomic activation. Activation equaled arousal only under extreme stimulus conditions, whether internally or externally cued (Eysenck 1967). Eysenck further postulated that introverts would tend to have a higher level of inherent cortical arousal than extroverts; and extroverts would have a higher inherent level of cortical inhibition than introverts. Conditionability, or learning, was demonstrated to occur more quickly in introverts than extroverts (Eysenck 1962).

Drug experiments to test Eysenck's theory of cortical excitation clearly validated the inherent arousal differences between extroverts and introverts. His drug postulates stated that depressant drugs would have an extroverting effect on behavior through reduced cortical arousal. This was inherently lower in extroverts and thus would occur more readily. Stimulant drugs would have an introverting effect on behavior through increased cortical arousal. This was inherently higher in introverts and thus would occur more readily. Psychopharmacological research supported the introverting effects of the stimulants and the extroverting effects of the depressants and the differences in cortical arousal between extroverts and introverts (Franks and Trouton 1958, Rachman 1961, Holland 1963, Sinha 1964).

Gray (1972) modified Eysenck's theory by asserting that the reticular formation, the medial septum, the hippocampus, and the orbital frontal cortex were all part of the central nervous system determinants of extroversion and that conditionability among extroverts and introverts should be understood as susceptibility to punishment. He proposed that introverts had a more reactive septohippocampal "stop system" and extroverts had a more reactive medial forebrain bundle and lateral hypothalamic "go system" (Gray 1972).

Studies confirmed that extroverts have higher pain thresholds (Haslam 1967), may be less sympathetically responsive (Meikle 1970), condition less readily to words (Gupta 1970); and have smaller pupillary responses to taboo words (Stelmack and Mandelzys 1975).

Prisoners as a group are significantly more extroverted than adult normal populations (Eysenck and Eysenck 1968). Eysenck proposed a strong positive correlation between psychopathy and extroversion. Aspects of his definition of the extrovert have high face validity for the psychopath: "He craves excitement, takes chances, often sticks his neck out, acts on the spur of the moment and is generally an impulsive individual . . . tends to be aggressive and to lose his temper quickly . . . not always a reliable person" (Eysenck and Eysenck 1968, p. 6). Extroversion also appears to positively correlate with sensation-seeking (Farley and Farley 1967).

Extroversion in adults appears to be a highly reliable trait. The Minnesota Multiphasic Personality Inventory Scale 0 (Social Introversion) has high temporal reliability in adult populations (Dahlstrom and Welsh 1960). The most closely related index in the Rorschach to extroversion is the *erlebnistypus* (EB). This indicator, a ratio of movement to weighted color responses, reflects the manner in which a person's resources are used and may not correlate with behavioral indices. Nevertheless, the extratensive individual habitually manifests affect to his or her world more routinely than does the introversive and is inclined to gratify basic needs via external objects rather than through internal experience (Exner 1986a). Psychopathic character disorders would appear to be more extratensive in interactional style. The EB is remarkably stable in adult population samples in both psychiatric and normal groups (Exner 1986a).

Extroversion, as a behavioral reflection of lowered central nervous system arousal in the psychopath, has several psychodynamic implications. First, it validates the autonomic hyporeactivity hypothesis and may correlate with the dampening of peripheral autonomic baseline measures and reactivity potentials at a primitive and vegetative level. Second, conditioning and learning problems, particularly in relation to punishment, are increased by the degree of extroversion. Third, extroversion appears to contribute to a lack of psychological mindedness, or capacity for insight, and may manifest in an extratensive style of dependency on external objects for gratification. Fourth, extroversion correlates with a sensation-seeking interactional pattern to compensate for lowered reticular arousal during the individual's waking hours. Fifth, extroversion will correlate with a preference for sympathomimetic drugs, such as methamphetamine and cocaine, rather than central nervous system depressants. The psychopath's propensity to abuse alcohol (Schuckit 1973), a depressant, is probably due to its initial disinhibiting, and highly reinforcing, effects.

SUMMARIZING THE BIOLOGICAL MATRIX

I am certain that a necessary, but not alone sufficient, biological substrate must exist for the development of a psychopathic character disorder. The five dimensions that I have explored retrospectively support psychobiological differences within the psychopathic personality that correlate with, and undoubtedly influence, early developmental experience with significant objects.

First, neuroanatomical variances are suggested in the psychopath through electroencephalographic and neuropsychological measures of localized frontal and temporal area dysfunction. The few prospective studies that have been done, however, reach back only to adolescence; and there is, as yet, no data supporting neuroanatomical differences prior to the separation–individuation stage of development.

Second, twin and adoption studies reliably support the hypothesis of a genetic loading for criminality. This genetic predisposition appears to affect more of the variance in later criminal and psychopathic behavior when early parental or social conditions are not particularly criminogenic. On the other hand, the lack of an opportunity for the child to internalize appropriate superego constraints, perhaps because of the absence of available parenting, would appear to override the child's predisposition to resist such internalizations and subsequent superego integration.

Third, although no empirical data exist specifically linking psychopathy and neurotransmitters influencing aggression, the relationship is quite tenable and needs further research. I am especially intrigued by the predominance of predatory aggression in the psychopathic process and its cholinergic substrate in the peripheral and central nervous systems.

Fourth, a strong and positive correlational relationship would seem to exist among the psychopath's aggression, social dominance, and testosterone levels, especially during late adolescence and young adulthood. But no retrospective, or prospective, research with carefully defined psychopathic samples has been done.

And fifth, I have constructed a nomological network that links the psychopath's autonomic hyporeactivity, lowered central nervous system arousal, extroversion, sensation-seeking, perceived lack of empathy, and abuse of sympathomimetic drugs. There appears to be strong construct validity for such a psychobiological and psychodynamic model. Both retrospective and prospective studies from early adolescence lend empirical support.

3

Developmental Origins

The developmental origins of narcissistic object relations, and psychopathy in particular, cannot be understood without differentiating concept and percept formation within the mind (Meloy 1985). Perception is a primary, immediate, subjective, and bimodal activity that organizes interoceptive and exteroceptive sensory-neural impulses and the contact-linking barrier between the two. Percept formation developmentally and phenomenologically precedes concept formation. Grotstein (1980b) emphasized the primary role of the perceptual background in his construct, the "background object of primary identification."

The mother provides the perceptual background as a primary object of identification for the infant prior to any conceptual knowledge of the "mother" by the infant or any idea of separateness from her. Percept formation provides for the infant a beginning, subjective sense of "I." The concept of self, thrust to the interpersonal foreground by the verbally assertive toddler, represents the birth of a conception that becomes limited and defined as a foreground experience. The conceptual sense of self is the foreground dependent upon the primary background perceptual experience of a sense of "I," which, in turn, is the perceptual heir to the "background object of primary identification," the biological mother.

Concept formation is the process that objectifies experience. It may have perceptual properties, but these are not
necessary. It is an active process that is central to the secondary
autonomous ego functions of memory, symbolization, judgment,
abstraction, comprehension, and insight. In the context of object
relations theory, concept formation objectifies and limits the
perception of self and other. It is not a bimodal experience; it is a
modal "frame of reference" for the self and object that has both
form and value (Spiegel 1959).

Concept formation is free to be wedded to percept formation
at a concrete level of thought or imagery; or it can be divorced
from perceptual experience at an abstract or symbolic level of
thought. The distinguishing criterion between concept and percept formation is the capacity of the former to proceed without
sensory-perceptual data. Because of this capacity for autonomous functioning, concept formation represents a developmentally higher, yet secondary, level of cortical functioning. Perception, attention, sensory-motor integration, and skin-boundary
cohesion are biological-perceptual factors that precede the formation of self and object concepts (Mahler 1958, Ornitz and Ritvo
1968a, 1968b, Ornitz 1969, 1970, Grotstein 1980a, 1980b).

The preverbal and preconceptual experiences that contribute to the psychopathic process are highly speculative, yet
the presence of early physical and emotional abuse in the case
histories of psychopathic individuals is common (Morrison 1978).
The early sensory-perceptual experience of the psychopathic
individual can be characterized as one of premature psychological
birth.

Tustin (1981) noted that one of the earliest integrations that
needs to occur is that between "hard" and "soft" sensations. Soft
sensations correspond to that which is pleasurable and comfortable; hard sensations correspond to that which is displeasurable
and uncomfortable. Optimal holding and suckling of the infant at
this time results in an integration of receptivity ("taking in,"
softness) and entering ("thrusting," hardness) and the germina-

tion of adaptability and resiliency in the infant, a beginning sense of psychological well-being.

Precocious separation, or "twoness," accompanied by a predominance of "hard" or uncomfortable sensations, could result in the excessive projection of "hard not-me" sensations outside the nascent self-boundary. The primitive skin boundary separating interoceptive and exteroceptive stimuli could become precociously aligned with the excessively vulnerable "soft me" inside the skin boundary and the "nameless dreads" (Bion 1984) of the "hard not-me" outside the skin boundary. In other words, "the child has experienced 'twoness' too harshly, too early, too suddenly for him" (Tustin 1981, p. 190).

This precocious separation may not be solely the responsibility of the parent figure. The infant's autonomic hyporeactivity or innate aggressiveness may render the mother's enveloping symbiosis less potent, less caretaking than she would like it to be. On the other hand, the mother's discomfort with symbiosis may compel her to hold on and then push the infant precipitously into autonomy (Mahler 1967).

This harsh sensory-perceptual experience with the mother may combine with an atavistic fear of predation and predispose the formation of a narcissistic shell that will callous over the excessively vulnerable "soft-me." Herein may lie the skin-boundary precursor of character armor as described by Reich (1945), more specifically, the phallic-narcissistic character structure of the psychopath.

It is also probable that such early sensory-perceptual predispositions may catalyze the use of persecutory introjects as "ad hoc scaffolding" to form an outer defense perimeter against malevolently perceived others. These persecutory objects would serve as a "form of stimulation and painful sensory immediacy" (Grotstein 1982, p. 62) for the infant.

An organismic distrust of the environment subsequently unfolds. Basic trust (Erikson 1950) of the holding environment (Winnicott 1962) is weakened as a result of the absence of a consistent, predictable, and predominantly nurturant mothering experience.

The relative presence or absence of trust of the holding environment, begun at a primitive sensory-perceptual, skin-boundary level of pleasure–displeasure, also provides the emotional color for the subsequent processes of internalization. The presence of a safe and trustful containment by the mother allows, and perhaps catalyzes, the internalization of more hedonically toned, nurturant, and benign objects, both as introjects and identifications. The absence of safety in containment, or a lack of adequate containment, will foster the internalization of more anhedonic, aggressive, and malevolent objects or constrict the internalization process itself (Gardner 1986).

INTERNALIZATION

Hartmann (1939) called the process of internalization an evolutionary and phylogenetic transfer of functional-regulatory mechanisms from the external world to the internal world of the organism. Schafer (1968) defined internalization as "all those processes by which the subject transforms real or imagined regulatory interactions with his environment, and real or imagined characteristics of his environment, into inner regulations and characteristics" (p. 9).

It is my hypothesis that the psychopathic process is fundamentally a virtual failure of internalization. There appears to be a paucity of deep and unconscious identifications with, initially, the primary parent figure and ultimately the archetypal and guiding identifications with the society and culture and humankind in general.

The failures of internalization begin, as mentioned above, with the organismic distrust of the sensory-perceptual environment. Throughout this early sensorimotor period (Piaget and Inhelder 1969), and corresponding to the symbiotic phase of

Mahler and colleagues (1975), occur early incorporative failures. I am using Schafer's (1968) definition of incorporation as a specific and wishful primary process ideation of taking in the actual object through the mouth or other body orifice. It expresses the primitive wish to introject the other person within the self, and therefore carry on a relationship, or the wish to modify the self through union with the part of the object that is perceived, the process of identification. Incorporation is the developmental heir to empathy, and with early incorporative failures, the ground is fertile for subsequent failures and distortions of the internalization process and its twofold expression through identification and introjection.

Let us pause here briefly and clarify the use of the terms *identification* and *introjection*. Identification is "that modification of the self which is caused by union with an object" (Grotstein 1982, p. 74). Schafer (1968) similarly defined identification as the modification of the self or behavior to increase resemblance to the object. In my words, it is the nascent self-representation becoming like the perceived object.

Introjection is a process by which perceived objects are internalized as representations yet continue to carry on a relationship to the self. I am inclined to agree with both Schafer (1968) and Volkan (1976) that introjections are likely to occur in times of distress and crisis for the infant when object supplies are urgently needed but not available. Volkan (1976) rightfully cautioned that the metaphorical implication of the term should not be forgotten, despite its obvious use in conceptualizing what the patient experiences as an internal presence separate from the subjective sense of "I." I would classify the term *introject* as an "object percept" that is often experienced as a visual image "seen" in the mind, or as an auditory sound "heard" in the mind, yet that is subjectively experienced as "not-I" (Meloy 1985). An introject is both primitive and relational and is oftentimes confused with an auditory hallucination by both patient and doctor unless care is taken to locate the "sound" and describe its perceptual characteristics. This appears to happen quite often with patients when there is disagreement concerning the proper diagnosis of severe borderline psychopathology or schizophrenia.

The failure of incorporation in the psychopathic process, however, is not complete or even obvious. The incorporative failure is due to a predominance of "hard" objects that are experienced as painful by the infant, such as ill-timed or unduly rough feeding and holding experiences. A predominance of unpleasant incorporative orifice experiences, beginning orally, yet tactilely experienced over the entire skin boundary as a hostile envelope, leads to a dearth of soothing internalization experiences. The absence of actual soothing experiences and later the distrust of available soothing experiences because of the anticipation of malevolence in others, contributes to an unconscious disavowal of the need for soothing internalizations, whether identifications or introjects.

What occurs instead is the infant's identification with the *stranger selfobject* (Grotstein 1982), a preconceived fantasy that helps the infant anticipate the presence of the predator in the external world, or the prey to whom the infant is to eventually be the predator. Grotstein (1982) viewed this selfobject as an *a priori* representation that "designates the unconscious pre-awareness of the enemy which is believed to be both within ourselves and to have an external counterpart" (p. 63). It is most obvious in its projected form during the infant's experience of stranger anxiety, of which there are tremendous variations in timing, quality, and quantity (Mahler et al. 1975).

But in the psychopathic process, the stranger, or predator, selfobject as a narcissistic identification is the predominant, archetypal internalization of the infant. It will later shadow the development of the grandiose self-structure, within which is the child's identification with the aggressive parent. The stranger selfobject will be interpersonally expressed in the asocial, if not antisocial, behavior of the psychopath as an adult, unknown to others on an intimate level, yet feared because of a conscious lack of a need for affection and attachment to others.

This *identification* with the stranger selfobject, reinforced by the actual experience with the parent as a "stranger" and predisposed by more aggressive and autonomically hyporeactive biological characteristics in the infant, is distinctively different from the borderline patient's internalization of the stranger selfobject as a persecutory *introject*, an internal object to which the borderline individual relates in a fearful and, at times, rageful fashion. In the psychopathic process, the stranger selfobject becomes an integral part of the child's self-esteem, whereas without the psychopathic process the stranger selfobject is experienced by the borderline individual as a source of anxiety and terror and is projected onto the environment and behaviorally expressed as persecutory fears of others. The narcissistically disordered adult will also show strong identifications with the stranger selfobject, but in a more independent, benign, and less aggressive manner than the psychopath.

GRANDIOSE SELF-STRUCTURE

Kernberg (1976) distinguished the narcissistic personality from the borderline personality by the presence in the former of a pathological grandiose self. This condensation within the developing ego structure is composed of the *real self*, the "specialness" of the child that is supported by early experiences; the *ideal self*, compensatory self-percepts that the small child has formed to balance severe oral frustrations, rage, and envy; and the *ideal object*, perceptual images in the child's mind of an ever-loving and accepting parent, in contrast with the actual behavior of the parent.

I consider the self to be a supraordinate and structural entity, in disagreement with Kernberg's view that the self is a substructure of the ego (Kernberg 1982). I am in agreement with Meissner's (1977, 1981, 1983, 1986) theoretical formulations that the self must involve personal agency and subjectivity. It is a vehicle for the articulation of qualities that reflect complex integrations of substructural components of the personality organization, one such quality being the formation and functioning of values. Internalizations, carrying with them some functional aspects of all the psychic systems, are primarily relevant to the organization of the self.

I also want to note the difference between self as structure and as representation (Boesky 1983). In the context of the psychopathic process, I would assert that the grandiose self, as structure, is inherently unconscious; that is, it cannot be observed by the personality as the representations within it can. The actual self-representations, ideal self-representations, and ideal object representations within the grandiose self-structure can be observed and reflected upon, but they are not agents of action. These self-representations within the grandiose self-structure would correspond to the self-as-object in Schafer's (1968) usage. The grandiose self-structure, as personal agent, is only consciously experienced as an affective state, known derivatively, but not internally imaged, as expansive, omniscient, and omnipotent.

In contrast to Kohut's (1971) view that the grandiose self is a fixation of an archaic, but normal, primitive self, Kernberg hypothesized the structural origins of the grandiose self as a pathological process distinctively different from normal infantile narcissism:

> Idealized object images which normally would be integrated into the ego ideal and as such, into the superego, are condensed instead with the self-concept. As a result, normal superego integration is lacking, ego–superego boundaries are blurred in certain areas, and unacceptable aspects of the real self are dissociated and/or

repressed, in combination with widespread, devastating devaluation of external objects and their representations. Thus, the intrapsychic world of these patients is populated only by their own grandiose self, by devaluated, shadowy images of self and others, and by potential persecutors representing the non-integrated sadistic superego forerunners, as well as primitive, distorted object images onto whom intense oral sadism has been projected. It needs to be stressed again that these developments occur at a point when self and object images have been sufficiently differentiated from each other to assure stable ego boundaries, so that the pathological condensation occurs after the achievement of the developmental stage which separates psychotic from nonpsychotic structures. [Kernberg 1975, p. 282]

I generally agree with Kernberg's analysis of the origins of the grandiose self, but must note several contradictions in his statement. First, the pathological condensation of the grandiose self precludes the blurring of ego–superego boundaries, because developmentally there is no superego. There is no clear differentiation between ego and superego structures at the borderline level of personality organization because this assumes at least a partial resolution of the Oedipus complex. Kernberg is correct, however, in noting the presence of "sadistic superego forerunners," which precede the fusion of ideal self- and ideal object representations to form the integrated ego ideal, the second broad layer of superego formation described by Jacobson (1964). The precursors of superego formation in the narcissistic personality, and in the psychopathic process, contribute to the formation of the grandiose self and interfere with later development of the superego as a third layer of internalization, namely the realistic, demanding, and prohibitive aspects of the parents during the oedipal period (Jacobson 1964).

Second, I would contend that unacceptable aspects of the real self are only dissociated, and not repressed, since there is no repression as a defense in the narcissistic, or psychopathic, personality structure. Moreover, there is no differentiation between the ego and the id as structures since there is no repression (Kernberg 1980). This is fundamental to the work of both Kernberg and Jacobson, although often overlooked in attempts to reconcile, or at least juxtapose, a dyadic theory of self- and object relations with a tripartite theory of personality structure. It is implicit in their work that there is no tripartite structure to the personality of the child until repression as a defense signals the differentiation between ego and id and the integration of ideal self- and ideal object representations as the ego ideal signals the differentiation between ego and superego. When one speaks of the structural characteristics of the preoedipal personality, one is referring *only* to dyadic self- and object representations that are either condensed (as in the formation of the grandiose self) or displaced somewhere else (as in the defensive process of splitting). Condensation and displacement, as the genotypes of the primary process, also appear to link self- and object representational maneuvers and the phenotypic expressions of formal thought disorder (Meloy 1986b).

My third criticism of Kernberg's structural origins of the grandiose self begins with a fundamental contradiction: How can "self and object images (that) have been sufficiently differentiated from each other to assure stable ego boundaries" (Kernberg 1975, p. 282) become condensed whereby the boundaries are lost in the grandiose self yet remain differentiated?

I do not think this is necessarily a contradiction if a distinction is made between the percept and the concept of the self- or object representation (Meloy 1985). The distinction between percept and concept formation, as I defined earlier in this chapter, offers the hypothesis that self- and object percept differentiation in the narcissistic personality disorder is normal. How then do I explain the condensation of self- and object representations within the grandiose self-structure? *Precisely because the fusion occurs between self- and object concepts and remains divorced from the developing and separate self- and object percepts.* In other words, the distinction between the subjective and primarily background sense of "I" and "not-I" is perceptually clear. The manner in which the self and its relation to others is conceived, however, is distorted and exaggerated, reflecting the fusion of self- and object concepts. The conceptual other becomes a psychological extension of the conceptual self.

The fused selfobject concepts remain an insular, autonomous psychic process within the grandiose self that becomes clinically evident in fantasies of achievement, power, admiration, perfection, and entitlement—fantasies that will be acted out by the more aggressive psychopath. As one 40-year-old male patient said to me in the face of personal bankruptcy, "I don't aspire to greatness; I claim it."

Achievement for the narcissistic personality disorder can proceed relatively unhampered since the differentiated self- and object percepts support ego skills that are socially and financially rewarded in the nonintimacy of the workplace: decisive and autonomous judgments, emotional detachment, objectivity, "coolness," high self-regard, and pragmatism.

The fused self-object concepts within the grandiose self-structure become most problematic when issues of intimacy disrupt the life of the individual with narcissistic personality disorder, or the psychopathic variant. Suddenly good reality testing, that is, self- and object *percept* differentiation, is not enough. Sustained intimacy requires empathy, an acknowledgment of worth of the other, and a realistic appraisal of one's self-concept in relation to others in the world. The fused self-object concept of the narcissist, which has heretofore remained submerged as an exaggerated yet inherently supportive self-representation, now intrudes into intimate relationships as an "I" that is entitled, angry, and grandiose. The fused selfobject concepts within the grandiose self necessitate that others remain without separate worth and empathic regard. The presence of value in others must be denied or enveloped to be, in a Piagetian sense, assimilated by the fused selfobject concepts of the narcissistic personality disorder (Piaget 1954).

But is there a distinction between the grandiose self within the narcissistic personality structure and its more severe and aggressive variant, the psychopathic personality? Clearly, there is. First, the real self-concept within the grandiose self-structure is the "specialness" of the child who is precociously experienced as "twoness" and is synonymous with separateness. Second, the ideal self-concepts within the grandiose self-structure, the selfobjects of the future or destiny (Grotstein 1982), are formed through identifications with the stranger selfobject. Instead of these identifications forming a primitive layer for the development of the superego structure, separate from the ego structure, they contribute to the conceptual confusion, as it were, within the grandiose self-structure. The ideal self-concepts, therefore, are representational modifications of the self to be like the stranger selfobject, an internalization of the actual cold, distancing behavior of the primary parent, instinctually fueled by an atavistic fear of predation, or attack, from others outside the skin boundary. This sensory-perceptual experience at the skin boundary, however, has receded in psychological importance as internal structuralization becomes more apparent during the separation-individuation phase of development. Third, the idealized object within the grandiose self-structure is an aggressive introject to which the real self and the ideal self form an intrapsychic relationship. But since the ideal self is fundamentally the stranger selfobject and is representationally quite similar to this aggressive introject, this hypothesized relationship within the grandiose self-structure becomes a conceptually fused *identification*.

This intrapsychic identification between the ideal self and the idealized object is interpersonally expressed as identification with the aggressor (A. Freud 1936). It is an intensely bound identification for the psychopathic character, since any clinical attempts to modify the ideal self in a more socially adaptive or affectional direction would cause a disidentification with the idealized object and a reactivation of the idealized object as an aggressive introject within the grandiose self-structure. This would phenomenally be experienced by the psychopathic character as a subjective sense of being under attack, as the aggressive introject would then be *in relation to*, rather than *identified with*, the real and ideal self-concepts. Psychotherapeutic maneuvers would be quickly thwarted, and identification between ideal self and the idealized object would be reassured by projecting the aggressive introject onto the clinician. Anxiety would lessen, and the grandiose self-structure would refuse, having warded off a regressive threat to its equilibrium. This may be the fundamental psychodynamic within the psychopathic process that impedes psychotherapeutic change.

I want to reiterate that the fusion, and refusions, within the grandiose self-structure are conceptual, not perceptual, self- and object representations. Perceptual distinctiveness at an intrapsychic level, expressed in the psychopathic personality's capacity for adequate reality testing, is developmentally preserved despite the fusion of real self-, ideal self-, and idealized object representational concepts. At lower levels of borderline personality organization, self- and object percepts may be somewhat undifferentiated and could be clinically measured by poor form level responses to the Rorschach (Sugarman 1986). Borderline patients closest to a psychotic level of perceptual distortion are prone to respond with quite primitive confabulations to the Rorschach. For example, to Card X:

> two blue crabs . . . almost looks like they have human
> faces . . . and you know how a scorpion has a long claw,
> it's like a mixture of parts of a monster. . . .

Higher-level borderline patients would be more likely to evidence fabulized combinations, such as "a man with wings" to Card

I (Smith 1980). I have found that contaminations, the most serious of perceptual distortions within the Rorschach process (Johnston and Holzman 1979), are very unusual in the psychopathic process unless a psychotic disorder is also present. The conceptual fusions within the grandiose self-structure usually become clinically evident in the transference relationship with the psychopath.

ATTACHMENT

The psychopathic process crystallizes toward the later subphases of separation–individuation with the failure of object constancy and a primary narcissistic attachment to the grandiose self-structure. A specific dysfunctional direction of development (Eagle 1984) coalesces in the child's deactivation of a need for attachment (Bowlby 1980) and his or her narcissistic choice of the grandiose self to subserve individual survival.

Bowlby (1969) wrote that attachment is mediated through five instinctual behaviors: sucking, smiling, clinging, crying, and following, organized and maintained through proximity-seeking behavior toward the mother. From an evolutionary perspective such behavior enhances species survival by protecting the child from predators. Bowlby (1973) argued that attachment to the mother is primary, and anger is a response to separation. The experience of the mother figure as an aggressive predator, or more benignly as a passive stranger, leaves the child no choice but to disavow a primary emotional attachment to an actual object outside the child's skin boundary. Willock (1986) termed one facet of this child's narcissistic vulnerability "the disregarded self" and postulated that much of this child's aggressive and antisocial behavior can be understood as an attempt to cope with and defend against hurt, anxiety, and anger associated with this primitive, internalized object relational paradigm.

Other researchers have noted that most hyperaggressive

children have experienced some degree of emotional abuse or neglect (Field 1940, Redl and Wineman 1951, Bandura and Walters 1958). Tooley (1974, 1976) studied a sample of mothers of aggressive children and noted their nonresponsiveness; they would sit impassively and gaze vacantly while their children sought attention. Minuchin and colleagues (1967) observed alternations in mothers' behavior between enmeshment and disengagement in delinquent families. At the point when family tensions and stress were highest, mother was most prone to abandon her role as parent to protect her own emotional equilibrium. They also observed that mother and child often felt a complete lack of connection when they were not directly interacting.

I must note, moreover, the reciprocal nature of the parent–child relationship and the ways in which the child can contribute to parental neglect and detachment. Willock (1986) argued that both excitability and nonconsolability (Aleksandrowicz and Aleksandrowicz 1976) in the infant, psychobiological factors that would aggravate parents' attempts to console and infants' attempts to soothe themselves, could grossly interfere with attachment or bonding. Stott and colleagues (1975) postulated that a distinctive feature of aggressive, antisocial children was an overreacting temperament. This inhibitional impairment would impel the parents to attack the child or distance themselves in an extreme and inappropriate fashion. A child who is behaviorally aggressive and autonomically hyporeactive could easily fail to resonate with parents genuinely committed to a protective, holding environment, and capable of providing such an environment for a less aggressive, autonomically normal child. On the other hand, an aggressive, psychopathic parent would only exacerbate the psychobiological propensities of the child.

The psychodynamic marker of successful, normative attachment behavior is object constancy. It is "the capacity to feel and use the psychological presence of the primary love-object even when he or she is not present or, if present, not approving" (Solnit

1986, p. 2). Object constancy is the process by which later oedipal and postoedipal identifications take place; it is the bedrock of socialization. Object constancy implies an affective, libidinal investment in the object, which reinforces the evocative recall of the object concept. It is dependent upon object permanency, the perceptual-mnemonic characteristic of the infant to evoke a memory of the actual object in its absence (Rinsley 1982) and to differentiate actual objects from the manipulation of them (Piaget 1954). Object constancy is the intrapsychic paragon of safety for the child. It is more closely allied to the conceptual-affective sphere, rather than the perceptual sphere, of self- and object relations. In the midst of overwhelmingly frightening or rageful feelings within the self, the child is aware of a loving, constant, approving presence. It is the tearful child's diminishing need to ask, "Mommy, do you still love me?"

Object constancy enables the young child to complete the passage through separation–individuation with an emotionally available and inherently supportive primary parent. Psychopathic character formation infers the absence of such a figure. Instead of the child's emergence into the third and fourth year of life with internally stable, affectively gratifying, and clearly delineated self- and object representations, the fused self- and object concepts within the grandiose self-structure help the child defensively maneuver through the blighted landscape of deficient parenting.

When the primary parent is physically or emotionally sadistic, the child will usually establish a sadomasochistic primary attachment (Solnit 1986). In borderline individuals the developmental struggle for object constancy may be associated with a provocative, pain-inflicting constant object:

In these instances, tension reduction is preceded by sudden storms of painful aggression as compared or contrasted to gradual tension reduction associated with object constancy in which the love object representation is predominately cathected with affectionate, pleasurable, self-esteem-promoting libidinal energies. These theoretical inferences ... are useful in explaining the strong, life-threatening attachment behavior displayed by children who are violently abused physically and/or sexually. [Solnit 1982, p. 210]

Donald Lunde, in his preliminary research with a small sample of sexual psychopaths who engaged in serial murder, noted the close association between violence and eroticism in their early childhood histories. In one example, the child was physically beaten by his father after school, whereas his mother would fondle his penis in an eroticized, soothing gesture after he went to bed.[1]

A fuller understanding of psychopathic structuralization is gained by applying a dual-track theory of development (Grotstein 1980b). The infant is subject to two modes of experience, one of total separateness and one of continuing primary narcissism or identification. What Mahler and colleagues (1975) referred to as periods of autism and symbiosis can be conceptualized as *permanent* stages consisting of physiological rhythms and drives that coexist with states of separation–individuation throughout the life cycle. The normal infant is in contact with the reality principle and the pleasure principle from the beginning, and the two optimally work in harmony as well as dialectically (Grotstein 1980b).

The psychopathic process is an extreme and deviant variation of the dual-track theory of development. On the one hand, primary narcissism and identification are conceptually glorified in the grandiose self-structure; on the other hand, states of relatedness are aggressively and sadomasochistically pursued to find the heretofore missing constant object.

---

[1]This case was presented at the California State Psychological Association Annual Convention, San Francisco, March 2, 1986.

These coexisting processes of sadomasochistic attachment, or aggressive attempts to bond, and profound detachment from one's own and others' affective experience, telescoping back from adulthood to suggest paranoid-schizoid (Klein 1957) issues in early infancy, are often clinically apparent in the psychopathic character:

> R was a 30-year-old black male charged with murder and "special circumstances" following an armed rob-bery in which he shot and killed the proprietor of the store in front of the proprietor's wife and child. He was admitted to our acute forensic inpatient unit following several suicide threats and one attempt while in cus-tody. Psychological testing revealed an individual with a full-scale IQ of 80. The Rorschach indicated a severe borderline personality organization with much aggres-sive and primary process thought content. R's thinking was pervaded with the belief that he would be "gassed or electrocuted," and therefore he should commit sui-cide. This paranoid belief persisted despite his knowl-edge that no one in California had been executed for a crime in over a decade, and he would probably not be the first. He showed virtually no affect while on the inpatient unit except for a teasing smile when he would explain to the nursing staff his latest plan for suicide. He was quite asocial, and had no verbal interchanges with other patients. He would delight in handing over various pieces of string, metal, and bandages to the nurses that he reportedly had not decided to use in a suicide attempt. Following his conviction for first-degree murder without special circumstances, and prior to his transport to prison, he stated to me, "My unconscious wants to terminate my life but my con-scious wants to prolong it." Not once during his two-month inpatient stay did he mention the victim or the victim's family.

This case illustrates both the paranoid and schizoid processes in the psychodynamically quite transparent and intellectually below-average psychopathic personality. R's paranoia, or sado-masochistic pursuit of attachment, was evident in the totally unwarranted and sadistic killing of his victim and his resolute belief that he would be "gassed or electrocuted." His schizoid characteristics, betraying a profound detachment from the affective experience of self and others, were evident in his benign indifference to self-inflicted pain, his lack of any expressed emotion, and his absence of empathy toward the victim or his family.

CONCLUSIONS

The developmental origins of the psychopathic personality are characterized by a precocious separation from the primary parent during the symbiotic phase of maturation; failures of internalization that begin with an organismic distrust of the sensory-perceptual environment; a predominate, archetypal identification with the stranger selfobject that is central to the conceptual self and object fusions within the grandiose self-structure during the period of separation–individuation; a failure of object constancy and a primary narcissistic attachment to the grandiose self; and states of relatedness (separate from the *traits* of primary narcissistic attachment) that are aggressively and sadomasochistically pursued with actual objects. This coexistence of benign detachment and aggressively pursued, sadistically toned attempts to bond is pathognomonic of the psychopathic process.

These five developmental themes coalesce in the psychopathic personality structure to distinguish it from a more benign narcissistic disturbance. Developmental origins of the psychopath, however, should still be conceptualized within the range of borderline personality organization (Kernberg 1984).

Part II

STRUCTURE AND
DYNAMICS

4

Affective Life and Death

David Berkowitz, known to himself and millions as "Son of Sam," was convicted of the serial murdering of five young women and a man in New York City from 1976 through 1977. He was initially diagnosed as paranoid schizophrenic, but careful evaluation revealed that he was malingering much of his psychotic symptomatology, and he was more appropriately diagnosed as a psychopathic personality with paranoid and hysterical traits (Abrahamsen 1985).

He confided to David Abrahamsen, M.D., at Kings County Hospital:

> I was literally singing to myself on my way home, after the killing. The tension, the desire to kill a woman had built up in me to such explosive proportions that when I finally pulled the trigger, all the pressures, all the tensions, hatred, had just vanished, dissipated, but only for a short time. I had no sexual feelings. It was only hostile aggression. I knew it when I did it it was wrong to do it. I wanted to destroy her because of what she represented . . . a pretty girl, a threat to me, to my masculinity, and she was a child of God, God's creation. I couldn't handle her sexually. [Abrahamsen 1985, p. 178]

The emotional experience of the psychopathic personality is a baffling, and at times shocking, phenomenon. It compels the psychoanalytic thinker to understand both the absence of affect when its presence would be predicted in a more socialized, empathic individual and the presence of intense, unmodulated affect that is dramatized by its unpredictability and capacity to arouse an atavistic fear in others.

My attempt to understand the emotional dynamics of the psychopathic character begins with two questions: First, what is the psychopathic personality's biological capacity for emotion? Is it conceivable that biochemical and neuroanatomical abnormalities in the deep limbic structures of the brain could predispose an individual to a "reptilian" state of mind and a subsequent absence of capacity to experience any emotion? And second, what is the psychopathic personality's conscious experience of emotion or affect? I must pause here to note that any deductive attempts to conceptualize emotions do not do justice to the idiographic subtleties of individual emotional experience; but I will delineate common characteristics of the most salient affects within the psychopathic process, such as boredom, envy, exhilaration, contempt, sadistic pleasure, sexual sadism, anger, and the vicissitudes of depression.

REPTILIAN STATES

The common denominator among mammals, including humans, for the experience and expression of emotion appears to be the limbic system. First called the "great limbic lobe" by Broca (1878) and later defined by MacLean (1952) as the limbic system, it is a phylogenetically old cortex that surrounds the brainstem structures. This diverse group of brain structures forms the medial edge of the cerebral hemispheres as well as the subcortical telencephalic areas that partially envelop the deep gray matter of the basal ganglia (Damasio and Van Hoesen 1983). Beginning with Papez's (1937) theory of emotion and MacLean's (1949) reformulation of it, the functional importance of the limbic system is its high level of integration of interoceptive and exteroceptive inputs, sensations, perceptions, and affects (Valzelli 1981). Although arguments have continued over the validity and heuristic value of the limbic system concept (Brodal 1981), the central role of the limbic structures in emotions and affects appears to be a reliable and valid clinical observation (MacLean 1952, 1973, Penfield and Jasper 1954, Damasio and Van Hoesen 1983).

More recent studies have supported the hypothesis that parts of the limbic lobe project not only to areas of the motor system, but to the primary and secondary associational areas of the cerebral cortex (Pandya et al. 1981). It also appears that key elements of the limbic structure receive a large proportion of their input from associative areas of the cerebral cortex (Herzog and Van Hoesen 1976). It is highly probable that the limbic structures are affected not only by immediate associational responses to sensory stimuli, but to *memories* of events that have influenced the organism in the past. This, of course, would provide psychobiological support for an aspect of the psychoanalytic concept of transference.

It is beyond my intent and capability to review in detail the structure (see Valzelli 1979) and function (see Livingston and Horneykiewicz 1978) of the limbic system. The articles cited contain further explication. I do want to emphasize, however, the fundamental role the limbic system plays in both conscious affective experience and the capacity for emotional relatedness.

Although shared among mammals (Papez 1958), limbic structures subserving the expression and modulation of affect are generally absent in reptiles. The reptilian cerebrotype, described by MacLean (1976) as the first evolutionary step in the development of the human triune brain, is centered primarily on the striatal complex and neuroanatomically supports several basic and genetically transmitted behaviors, such as home site selection, establishment and defense of territories, hunting, feeding, mating, competition, dominance, aggression, and imitation (MacLean 1962, 1964, 1972). The latter imitative behaviors are generally repetitive, compulsive, highly ritualized, and automatized. What is absent in the reptilian cerebrotype is a parental response to its offspring, hoarding, and social behavior.

The parental or maternal drive is one of the most strongly motivated behaviors in mammals (Stone 1942). It is absent in most reptiles and is one of the distinguishing behavioral characteristics between mammals and reptiles (Cockrum and McCauley 1965). As I have noted earlier, parental abuse or neglect is ubiquitous in the childhood histories of psychopathic individuals.

Hoarding, a distinctively mammalian behavior, is the storage of food in excess of immediate needs. It is absent in reptiles and implies a capacity to project into the future and anticipate aversive consequences. The psychopathic individual is autonomically hyporeactive when anticipating negative consequences, and this, in turn, appears to lead to deficits in new learning.

Social behavior—the interpersonal expression of the individual's early internalizations, successful attachments, and developing capacity for empathy—is the consummate failing of psychopathic individuals in the eyes of others. They are the embodiment of the antisocial personality, the stranger in our midst. They share with the reptilian cerebrotype an inability to socialize in a consciously affectionate and genuinely expressive manner.

In animal studies, removal of the hippocampus and ablation of the neocortex appear to extinguish nest building, grooming, and social behavior (Kolb and Nouneman 1974, Shipley and Kolb 1977). Valzelli (1981) called this a reptilelike behavioral regression that is due to the functional prevalence of the reptilian brain structures.

Although there is absolutely no neuroanatomical or neurophysiological research to support a correlation between psychopathic behavior and the functional prevalence of the reptilian cerebrotype, the conceptual parallels are striking. I would hypothesize that the term *reptilian state* describes the functional psychobiology of certain primary, psychopathic characters. The etiology of such behavioral regression, or perhaps genetically predisposed limbic dysfunction, is, however, unknown.

I first had contact with T. G. when he was brought to psychiatric "sick call" in the local custody facility. Sick call took place in a six by eight foot room within which the psychiatrist, nurse, deputy, and myself stood around a small table. When T. G. entered the room he filled it. He was a 24-year-old Caucasian male, six feet four inches tall, and probably weighed 280 pounds. He wore no shirt, and his large, fat chest and abdomen cascaded in sweaty folds down toward his cotton pants. His wrists were cuffed and attached to a metal chain around his waist. His legs were shackled in chains so he walked with a decided shuffle. T. G. had his head shaved and wore a Fu Manchu moustache.

As soon as he sat down he began hounding the psychiatrist for Valium. When this didn't work, he tried Librium and Restoril. He finally settled for Thorazine.

As I learned more about T. G. I began to develop a clinical picture of a young man who could be described as a "walking impulse." He was housed in an individual cell and always moved in restraints because of his extremely poor impulse control and unmodulated affect. In fact, he was more instinctual than affective. If he felt aggressive he would physically assault others; if he felt sexual, he would attempt to rape whatever animate object was available. He was the raw expression of primitive libidinal and aggressive drives. He showed no capacity for affection, or even an inclination to mimic emotional relatedness that I found in more intelligent psychopaths. He showed no symptoms of psychosis, but his social judgement was virtually absent and his intelligence was estimated to be mildly retarded (full-scale IQ 55–70). His personality, without formal psychodiagnostic testing, appeared to be organized at a borderline level. His thoughts were marked by projection and denial. He showed no motivation or capacity to even rationalize his behavior. T. G. had been taken into custody by the state shortly after his birth and his mother's failure to provide basic maternal care. He was contained by various homes and institutions throughout his childhood, and began contact with various criminal justice and psychiatric systems in adolescence. He was a biogenic and sociogenic tragedy who now presented a continuous danger to others.

The other clinical observation, or perhaps more specifically a countertransference reaction, that supports the hypothesis of a reptilian state among certain primitive psychopathic characters is the absence of perceived emotion in their eyes. Although this information is only intuitive and anecdotal, it is my experience in forensic treatment and custody settings to hear descriptions of certain patients' or inmates' eyes as cold, staring, harsh, empty, vacant, and absent of feeling. Countertransference reactions from staff to this perception of the psychopath's eyes have included, "I was frightened . . . he's very eerie; I felt as if he was staring right through me; when he looked at me the hair stood up on my neck." This last comment is particularly telling since it captures the primitive, autonomic, and fearful response to a predator. I have rarely heard such comments as these from the same experienced inpatient staff during highly arousing, threatening, and violent outbursts by other angry, combative patients. It is as if they sensed the absence of a capacity for emotional relatedness and empathy in the psychopathic individual, despite his lack of actual physical violence at the moment.

Although the perception of eyes, or the sense of being watched by eyes, is pathognomonic of paranoid mechanisms during projective testing, I have found little in the research literature, either theoretical or empirical, that attempts to understand this act of visual predation in the psychopathic process (Webbink 1986, Hymer 1986).

The popular media, both fictional and nonfictional, is quite adept, however, at capturing the reptilian, predatory, and emotionless stare of the psychopath. The reader is encouraged to study newspaper and magazine photographs of such contemporary sexual psychopaths as Charles Manson, Theodore Bundy, and Richard Ramirez.[1] Steven Railsback's portrayal of Manson in the film "Helter Skelter" was an exquisite capturing of the reptilian stare. Other popular film actors such as Clint Eastwood, Charles Bronson (artistically representing morality and justice), Bruce Dern, Anthony Perkins, and Rutger Hauer (personifying evil) have successfully exploited the larger-than-life visual image on the screen to convey the absence of emotion and the presence of more primitive instinct through their eyes.

The reptilian, predatory eyes are, in a sense, the antithesis of the affectionate mirroring of the infant in the eyes of mother. The nascent self is reflected as an object of prey, rather than an object of love. The fixated stare of the psychopath is a prelude to instinctual gratification rather than empathic caring. The interaction is socially defined by parameters of power rather than attachment.

---

[1] Richard Ramirez is alleged to be the "night stalker" responsible for fourteen murders in California in 1985. At the time of this writing, he is standing trial in Los Angeles County Superior Court and is individually incarcerated in the Los Angeles County Jail in a "high power" area. Custody officials have used the words "manic psychopath" [see Chapter 7] in describing his observed behavior to me.

Scoptophilia, the sexualization of the sensation of looking, may be a predominant component of the reptilian stare. The psychopathic character may want to see in order to destroy the object in a fantasied, sexually sadistic manner. The unconscious fantasy of incorporation through the eyes may also be present (Fenichel 1945).

Condensed sexual and aggressive instincts communicated through the eyes of the psychopath will induce not only fear but shame in the perceived victim. The individual subjected to such a stare may feel physically caught by it, yet ashamed and not wanting to be seen. He or she may hide or avert the stare, suggesting the magical belief that anyone who does not look cannot be looked at (Fenichel 1945); a physical sensation of heat may wash over the face and body.

In another paper, Fenichel (1935) emphasized the oral sadism of the staring eye; it is not only actively sadistic in the folklore sense of "casting a spell" (Elworthy 1895), but is passively receptive to the fascination of the victim, who is at risk of metaphorically being turned into stone or salt. This latter danger finds its mythological roots in the legend of Medusa and the biblical story of Lot and the destruction of Sodom. The physiological basis for such a legendary transubstantiation appears to be the muscular rigidity that may overwhelm a person who suddenly sees something, or someone, terrifying.

> As the sun rose over the land and Lot entered Zoar, Yahweh rained on Sodom and Gomorrah brimstone and fire. . . . He overthrew these towns and the whole plain, with all the inhabitants of the towns, and everything that grew there. But the wife of Lot looked back, and was turned into a pillar of salt. [Genesis 19:23–26]

The original Sicilian fear of the "evil eye" is analogous to the visual act of predation. It is mentioned by Mahler and colleagues (1975) in reference to a child not wanting people to see his baby sister, thus acting out his wish that the baby be invisible and perhaps warding off his own wish that the baby be afflicted by the "evil eye." Freud (1900) referred to his mentor Ernst Brucke's "terrible blue eyes. . . . No one who can remember the great man's eyes . . . and who has ever seen him in anger, will find it difficult to picture the young sinner's emotions" (p. 422). Later, Freud (1919) theorized that the functional significance of watching or being watched in manifest dreams was a product of superego formation. Peto (1969) asserted that this representation of archaic superego elements by the threatening eye was a remnant of the earliest phases of childhood sensory-perceptual experience. In a thoughtful argument incorporating the work of others (Hartmann 1924, Hermann 1934, Szekely 1954), he stressed the significance of the Cyclopean glaring eye, specifically the primary perception of a red glowing eye, for the subsequent structuralization of anxiety in a biologically determined real danger situation for the infant. This external traumatic agent becomes internalized as a parental introject, or in my terms, an object percept (Meloy 1985). Regression to the psychotic level of elementary visual hallucinations of red (Hartmann 1924) or the archaic primary perception, *urwahrnehmungen*, the red glow of the retaliatory parental eye (Hermann 1934), is illustrated in the following case of a nonpsychopathic patient:

> F.C. was a 20-year-old Hispanic male in an acute schizophrenic psychosis when admitted to our forensic inpatient unit. He was charged with the murder of a 52-year-old female prostitute. He responded rapidly to neuroleptic medication, and subsequent psychodiagnostic testing and clinical observation revealed a hysterical character organized at a borderline level of personality. F. C. quickly developed a strong emotional attachment to the staff and the other patients. During the course of psychotherapy he recalled that a week prior to the murder he had seen a dog with glowing red

eyes which chased him and barked at him. The patient delusionally believed the dog was an agent of Satan. On the day of the murder, F. C. met an older woman who invited him to her apartment. Once they were undressed she taunted and teased him about the size of his penis. As he became more ashamed and angry, he noticed her eyes were glowing red. He was convinced she was also a demon and proceeded to stab her repeatedly with a kitchen knife.

The psychopathic individual, in the absence of psychosis, is able to unconsciously project an annihilatory stare that is intuitively felt by others receptive to a predatory introject to be omniscient and omnipotent. The absence of modulated emotion warns of behavior devoid of empathic constraint and suggests the functional prevalence of the reptilian cerebrotype.

CONSCIOUS EXPERIENCE OF EMOTION

The psychopathic process allows the conscious experience of emotion, but emotion is structured by severe narcissistic psychopathology, more specifically, the grandiose self-structure. Emotions felt in the presence of others are, by necessity, contaminated by selfobjects that provide the projective-introjective medium through which actual others are perceived, and subsequently defensively conceived, as extensions of the grandiose self. The particular selfobject that is activated is dependent upon certain characteristics of the actual person that is perceived; for instance, an actual woman may behave in ways that remind the psychopathic individual of his teasingly erotic, yet abandoning mother with whom he identified as a child for defensive purposes and internalized as a wished-for and idealized selfobject concept.

Emotions consciously felt by psychopaths when alone are still intensely narcissistic but are activated and directed by more grandiose and less defensively motivated fantasies; they are no longer constrained by the perceptually quite accurate, and reality-bound, perceptions of others in their presence. David Berkowitz, the sexual psychopath, wrote, "I always hope to be the first one to go to heaven, one of the first fruits. I do feel more important to God than other people. This is probably why I am alive today because, despite my anger towards God, he still loves me the most" (Abrahamsen 1985, p. 173).

But how does one reconcile the "reptilian state" hypothesis with my seemingly contradictory assertion that the psychopath consciously experiences emotion?

The reptilian state is not a characterological trait. It is a functional psychobiological state that momentarily may exist with its object relational and instinctual correlates. The enduring psychopathic process, or structured psychopathic character, predisposes the individual to psychodynamically, and psychobiologically, assume a reptilian state of mind. At other times, in less behaviorally regressive and instinct ridden situations, the psychopathic character may manifest a wide range of modulated, consciously felt emotion, but it never progresses beyond an intensely narcissistic developmental stage. In a sense both ontogeny and phylogeny are evident in the psychopaths' shift between the reptilian and mammalian cerebrotypes and their individual emotional vacillations with their limiting narcissistic envelope. There undoubtedly exist, however, certain primitive psychopathic characters who do not experience emotion as we know it; in other words, the reptilian state is actually an enduring trait. T. G., described earlier, may be such an individual. Such case studies are the exception to the hypothetical rule.

Pleasure

The conscious experience of pleasure in the psychopathic process is distinguished by the absence of empathy and affectional bonds, an inability to repress painful affect, the absence of love for the anticipated pleasurable object, and, if alone, difficulty overcoming a predominately tense, anhedonic state without overt behavior that contains an aggressive or sexual dimension.

Pleasure is distinguished by the presence of dominance–submission behavioral patterns, the use of dissociative defenses such as splitting to ward off painful affect, gratification of sadistic impulses through the intentional infliction of emotional or physical pain upon others, sexual and aggressive "fueling" of the pleasurable event, and sensation seeking. Psychopaths do not experience pleasure by empathically responding to the joy in others. Their perception of others' pleasure arouses only envy and greed in themselves.

Sexual sadism, the conscious experience of pleasurable sexual arousal through the infliction of physical or emotional pain on the actual object, is characteristic of the sexual psychopath. Attempts to categorize and understand such behavior have generally been limited to descriptive and behavioral paradigms (Krafft-Ebing 1965, Groth 1979, Revitch and Schlesinger 1981).

The etiology of such behavior is unknown, but I have posited that the neurological proximity of the sexual and aggressive centers within the hypothalamus may provide the biological substrate for early conditioning or limbic dysfunction that results in the expression of sexual psychopathy as an adult (Meloy 1988). I mentioned earlier the verbal report of Donald Lunde concerning the temporal proximity of eroticism and violence in the childhood histories of several sexually psychopathic "serial murderers." Such case examples, and the unconditioned, reflexive nature of sexual arousal, support my notion that classical conditioning (Pavlov 1927) may explain the first pairing of violent behavior and sexual arousal in these individuals.

If the child passively observes violence in the home that is habitually accompanied by sexual acting out, he or she may later be genitally aroused when witnessing only violence. More specifically, if the child is physically or emotionally abused by a parent and then in the midst of consciously felt fear, rage, shame, or actual physical pain, is "soothed" by the parent fondling or caressing the child's genitals, the pairing of these interoceptive sensations will not easily extinguish with more highly differentiated hormonal development. With such a classical conditioning paradigm the later experience of violence (the conditioned stimulus) in the absence of direct sexual stimulation (the unconditioned stimulus) becomes sexually arousing (the conditioned response) as a result of the early temporal pairing of both stimuli.

Frank (1966) wrote of such experiences in the childhood of Albert DeSalvo, the Boston Strangler:

> "My father," DeSalvo spoke dully. "We used to have to stand in front of him, my brother Frank and me, every night and be beaten with this belt. I can still to this very moment tell you the color of the belt and just how long it was—two inches by 36—a belt with a big buckle on it. We used to stand in front of him every night and get beaten with that damn thing—every night, whether we did anything wrong or not. We were only in the fourth or fifth grade. . . ." "My father used to go around with prostitutes in front of us . . . my sisters always had black eyes . . . When you're under the environment of sex all day long . . . you go up on the roof of our building and there'd be a couch up there. . . . They'd give you a quarter and say, 'Beat it, kid.' . . . Always in the bedroom something being done. . . ." [pp. 316–317]

Abrahamsen (1985) noted the voyeurism and fantasy that may precede actual sexual sadism. As the sexual psychopath becomes a more conscious actor in gratifying his impulses, rather than a victim of classical conditioning as a child, an operant conditioning model (Skinner 1953) becomes conceptually more relevant. The individual begins to experiment with the infliction

of physical pain and finds himself intensely gratified, or positively reinforced, by his own interoceptive feelings of sexual
arousal and his perception of the victim's fearful, enraged affective state. Operant conditioning has taken over, and the sexual
psychopath is likely to repeat his behavior with increasingly
greater frequency as a result of the intermittent or variable
reinforcement schedule of his antisocial and clandestine acts
(Hilgard and Bower 1975).

Such conditioning models are, of course, most germane to
the relationship among instinctual, visceral, and affective states;
they are probably less relevant when considering important
linkages among internal representations of self and others at
higher cortical perceptual and conceptual levels. For instance,
the sexual psychopath, during an act of violence and increasing
sexual arousal, may become psychotic at an object concept level
and actually conceive his victim as a ragefully devalued "mother"
introject that internally taunts and criticizes him. Yet at an
object percept level he is not psychotic; he can perceptually
distinguish between his actual victim and his actual mother, and
there is no loss of reality testing between interoceptive and
exteroceptive sensations.

In contrast is the violent paranoid schizophrenic who may
be quite psychotic at a sensory-perceptual level of experience,
perhaps delusionally believing that his actual victim is his mother
while at the same time experiencing the introject of her as an
auditory hallucination due to a collapse of ego boundaries; in
other words, her taunting is heard as an actual voice coming from
outside his mind and is believed to originate from the actual,
biological mother. This is a very important diagnostic distinction
in assessing the state of mind of a psychopathic versus psychotic
individual during the commission of a violent act.

The psychopath's experience of pleasure through somatosensory stimuli appears to be devoid of more affectionate yearnings and is linked to more highly charged and circumscribed
sexual sensations. Sexual psychopaths appear to prefer acts of

violence that necessitate skin contact with the actual object (Levin and Fox 1985). This may momentarily represent a point of adhesive identification (Bick 1968, Meltzer 1975) between the sexual psychopath and victim wherein he projectively identifies at their now common skin boundary and briefly gratifies a symbiotic wish for reunion with the precociously separate mother; yet the violence, and its accompanying affects, ward off any primitive fear of engulfment by the mother as a not-to-be-trusted stranger selfobject.

The texture (T) response to the Rorschach represents a compelling somatosensory analog of the affective experience of emotional or dependency needs (Exner 1986a). The T response is the interpretation of the shading features of the inkblots as representing "tactual" stimuli. The elaboration carries with it such tactual features as soft, hard, smooth, rough, silky, grainy, furry, cold, hot, sticky, or greasy. Implicit in the T response is the perceptual representation of somatosensory stimuli.

Klopfer and colleagues (1954) suggested that it was related to needs for affection and dependency. T also appears to correlate with the presence of a childhood transitional object (Exner et al. 1980, Exner and Chu 1981). Other research has supported the hypothesis that the absence of T means the affective experience of emotional or dependency needs has become "neutralized," and if this occurs, it seems to take on a durable characteristic (Leura and Exner 1976, Pierce 1978, Exner 1986a).

Although there is currently no available data on the prevalence of T among psychopathic subjects, I would hypothesize that such a carefully selected sample would produce predominately "T-less" (see Appendix III) protocols. Exner's (1986a) normative sample and psychiatric reference groups lend support to such a hypothesis as illustrated in Table 4-1. The "character problem" sample is undoubtedly the most psychopathic of all four groups. It is composed of 121 males and 79 females, ranging in age from 18 to 47. The protocols were all collected in outpatient settings, and the majority (124) had histories of drug and/or alcohol abuse;

Table 4-1

Comparison of Texture (T) Responses among Four
Sample Groups (Exner 1986a)

Texture (T) Responses	Mean	S.D.
Character problems ($N = 200$)	0.44	0.67
Inpatient schizophrenics ($N = 320$)	0.49	1.15
Inpatient depressives ($N = 210$)	0.93	1.42
Nonpatients ($N = 600$)	1.16	0.80

113 had been involved in at least one legal dispute. No subject in this sample was hospitalized more than ten days, and the majority were single, separated, or divorced.

As suggested, the character problem sample averages the least number of texture responses and has the smallest variance of T responses. Such data lend support to my suggestion that the psychopathic individual is devoid of affectionate yearnings, and does not seek pleasure through the gratification of dependency needs or, more specifically, the expression of affection and caring through somatosensory stimulation.

The conscious experience of pleasure in the psychopathic process is inextricably linked to either sensation-seeking or sadistic impulses. Careful analysis of the psychopath's pleasure seeking and pleasure gratification will usually uncover one or both as motivational factors. The MacDonald triad (MacDonald 1963, Hellman and Blackman 1966) identified bed wetting, fire setting, and cruelty to animals in childhood as predictive of adult criminality. Although not as empirically reliable a predictor of psychopathy as was hoped (MacDonald 1968), fire setting and cruelty to animals in the childhood histories of some psychopaths suggest respective motivational dynamics of sensation-seeking and sadism as avenues to pleasure. Revitch and Schlesinger (1981) noted that specific cruelty to cats was often prognostic of the sexually motivated compulsive murderer who targeted women as victims. They asserted that cats are symbolic of the feminine and oftentimes represent the displaced matricidal wishes and oedipal conflicts of this endogenously motivated murderer. Feltous and Kellert (1986) found a significant association between a pattern of substantial abuse of vertebrate animals in childhood and later recurrent, protean personal violence in adulthood. They suggested that variety of cruel acts, variety of species victimized, and inclusion of socially valued species, such as cats, are meaningful areas of investigation in the clinical assessment of aggressive adults.

Anger

The conscious experience of anger in the psychopathic process is distinguished by the predominance of projective mechanisms that, at times, may be characterized as delusionally paranoid. Meissner (1978) noted that the paranoid hostility of the psychopath is usually more general and diffuse than the hostility of the paranoid personality disordered individual.

> H. V. was arrested for driving under the influence and reckless driving. He was a 25-year-old Turk who had the misfortune of being arrested several days after the American bombing of Libyan targets on April 14, 1986, during a heightened public fear of terrorist reprisals by radical Arabic individuals in the United States. Despite his incarceration in a maximum security setting surrounded by mistrustful, and sometimes overtly hostile, law enforcement personnel, H. V. would continually scream obscenities at the staff. Despite his physically small stature and fractured left knee, he would threaten to kill any person he saw in a uniform, arrogantly insist he had done nothing wrong, and hurl invectives at anyone who passed by his individual cell.
> Our initial evaluation of H. V. did not reveal any

systematic delusional thought content. His rage was diffuse, yet the obvious projective mechanisms were refractory to any verbal interventions. His judgment and insight into his behavior were absolutely lacking, despite the absence of any psychotic or affective disorder diagnosis.

Contact with H. V.'s relatives revealed a quite arrogant and irresponsible young man who had immigrated to the United States in 1981. He was the youngest of four siblings, and they felt he "had been spoiled" by his middle-class Turkish parents. He had no prior psychiatric history, yet had not been able to hold a job since his arrival and had lived intermittently with friends and cousins until they asked him to leave.

After three days of raging, with no diminution of affect, H. V. was involuntarily treated as a danger to himself with chlorpromazine. The neuroleptic succeeded in sedating, and therefore modifying H. V.'s behavior. Within a week H. V. was very compliant, no longer sedated, and at times obsequious toward psychiatric and security personnel. He would occasionally, however, challenge other patients, security guards, and even his attorney to fight for no apparent reason.

Psychopathic anger is also contaminated by an attitude of righteous indignation that betrays the felt "specialness" and entitlement of the grandiose self. It is here that the narcissistic core of the psychopathic process is most readily apparent. Typical countertransference reactions to such infantile displays, if one is physically safe from the individual, include annoyance at the behavior, an impulse to aggressively retaliate, or a passive-aggressive desire to withhold further gratification.

The aftermath of anger in the psychopathic process, with the diminution of autonomic arousal, is accompanied by the use of rationalization as a defense. Perhaps the most plebeian rationalization following the expression of such rage is "They had it coming." Although not limited to the psychopathic process, such a statement implies an attribution of malevolence to the object, a devaluing attitude that implies the rage was deserved. Psychodynamically a past innocuous event, a small insult may provide the seed that the psychopath fertilizes with paranoid ideation. The insult and its originator become intrapsychically a part of a more diffuse conspiratorial grouping, perhaps only defined as "they" but condensed and identified with sadistic introjects that provide a projective lens through which actual persons are perceived as familiar yet conceived as malevolent, attacking objects deserving of the psychopath's rage. Angelo Buono, one of the two "Hillside Stranglers" responsible for the rape, torture, and strangulation of ten young women in Los Angeles from October 1977 to February 1978, remarked, "Some girls don't deserve to live" (O'Brien 1985, p. 119).

The conscious experience of anger in the psychopathic process has a greater probability of resulting in violence because of the absence of superego structuralization and appropriate modulation of intensely felt affect. Such affective violence will be studied in detail in Chapter 6, particularly in contrast with predatory violence, a more focused, intentional, and goal-directed behavior with distinct neuroanatomical pathways and neurochemical catalysts (see Chapter 2 for a biochemical introduction to this distinction). I would hypothesize that such affective violence in the psychopathic process could be usefully conceptualized as "episodic dyscontrol" (Monroe 1981), especially if remorse is absent following the violent event.

The assessment of episodic dyscontrol if primarily defined as a neurological impairment through a self-report questionnaire in prison samples (Monroe 1981) has virtually no validity. The higher prevalence of psychopathy in prisons and the propensity of psychopaths to project responsibility for their behavior onto other people and things, such as neurological impairment, renders such an instrument almost useless. A sample of questions from the Monroe Scale (Monroe 1981) will illustrate my point:

1. I have had the experience of feeling confused even in a familiar place.
4. I do not feel totally responsible for what I do.
5. I have lost control of myself even though I didn't want to.
8. My speech has been slurred.
9. I have had blackouts.

Such self-report measures, in the absence of objective neuropsychological data, only validate the projective defenses within the psychopathic process. I would advocate the use of the term *episodic dyscontrol* to describe violence that results from affective arousal and a lack of developmentally appropriate superego formation. I would differentiate a subgroup within this dyscontrol syndrome that had a primary neurological trigger only on the basis of neuropsychological or neurological indices. Reliability among self-report measures and between self-report and clinical-behavioral measures in criminal populations is very poor (Hare 1985a).

Consciously felt anger may be used in the psychopathic process to control or dominate the actual object in a manipulative fashion. Higher-functioning psychopathic individuals, as measured by both intelligence and stability of the grandiose self-structure, may recognize their ability to control others with their anger and may be quite talented mimics of rageful behavior when it is not genuinely felt. In contrast with this is the consciously felt anger of the nonpsychopathic adult, which in an attachment-affectionate context, carries with it the fear of retaliation or abandonment by the actual object at whom the anger is targeted. This close autonomic-sympathetic and psychodynamic link between anger and fear, supported by higher-level repressive defenses, is common in everyday experience in the hesitancy of openly expressing anger toward someone of emotional value; value as defined by emotional attachment, rather than dominance-submission. The psychopath's conscious intent is to put something over on someone (Bursten 1972) by using anger as an affective and effective controlling mechanism of the other's behavior. The paradigm of power and control, rather than attachment and bonding, is center stage.

> P. C. was transferred to the acute forensic inpatient unit following an assault against another patient at the local Veteran's Administration Hospital. P. C. had struck the patient with his forearm cast and had seriously injured the victim. Three weeks prior to the assault, P. C. had attempted suicide by trying to cut his femoral arteries, his throat, and his left forearm artery. P. C. had been a paramedic prior to his series of hospitalizations, wherein he had been diagnosed as paranoid schizophrenic.
>
> P. C. presented himself as a 25-year-old Caucasian male, tall in stature, mesomorphic, and quite handsome. His first words to the attending psychiatrist and to me were, "I'm a paranoid schizophrenic." In a very lucid and coherent manner, with no indications of formal thought disorder, P. C. told us of his multiple hospitalizations since age 20, his two years in the service, and his pending 100 percent VA disability claim. He was in quite good contact and control, showed no indications of systematic delusions, and was bright–normal in intelligence. His singular presenting symptom was complaints of auditory hallucinations commanding him to hurt himself and others. We noted that despite his subjective complaints of depression his mood was quite expansive and his thought content was generally grandiose. He denied illicit drug use, but

reported "having tried" methamphetamine and cocaine.

The VA hospital transfer notes, despite the nursing staff's written skepticism, indicated that the resident psychiatrist diagnosed P. C. as paranoid schizophrenic.

The attending psychiatrist and I conferred, and we concluded that the young man was not paranoid schizophrenic, but quite psychopathic. We informed the patient that he would be placed in full restraints and seclusion due to his imminent danger to self and others, but that all neuroleptic medications would be stopped. P. C. greeted this news with a somewhat surprising indifference. He was instead prescribed Benadryl as a p.r.n. for anxiety or agitation and was allowed one phone call before he was restrained.

Within thirty minutes I received a telephone call from the patient's father, whose opening comment was a rageful, "How dare you discontinue my son's medication! That is medical incompetence!!" His tone and telephone demeanor were openly sarcastic, caustic, and threatening. I was used to such encounters, however, and reassured the father that, in our judgment, we were behaving quite competently, and, of course, it was our decision what his son's treatment would be.

The father's voice suddenly became calm and controlled, and he asked me to please spell my full name and the name of the treating psychiatrist, along with our addresses and type of professional licenses. I felt an immediate surge of anxiety, but knew that my reaction was symptomatic of a psychopathic attempt to manipulate and intimidate the wished-for-victim, in this case, myself. I had been telling my students for several years that the subjective feeling of actually being under a patient's thumb was oftentimes diagnostic of the psychopathic process: a countertransference reaction to the repetitive dominance–submission ritual of the psychopathic personality.

P. C.'s father assured me that I would hear from him again and calmly ended the conversation. Within several hours I had received three phone calls from three separate administrative-political authorities that exercised power and control over my direction of the forensic program; each agency, because of their historical trust of my judgment, asked only for hints as to managing this irate father who was incessantly calling their offices and complaining of his son's treatment by our program.

P. C.'s complaints of auditory hallucinations rapidly diminished once we explained to him that, in our opinion, he was not genuinely hallucinating and was not paranoid schizophrenic. He did not assault anyone on the unit following his initial restraint and seclusion for twelve hours and our admonition that if he did, he would immediately be returned to isolation. His expansiveness, grandiosity, and demands for attention persisted. His thoughts turned to worry lest he not be granted the VA disability pension that both he and his father were anticipating. He wondered if one acute inpatient unit's assessment of him, so drastically different from the multiple diagnoses of paranoid schizophrenia he had already received, would jeopardize his chances for the guaranteed income.

Due to the lack of repression in the psychopathic process and the predominance of more primitive defense mechanisms, rage may be dissociated, or "split off," from conscious experience. This has been described in higher-functioning sexual psychopaths as a "compartmentalizing" of the perverse and violent acting out: The sexual psychopath may lead a quite normal and routine life with the appropriate social accouterments such as job, spouse, and family, yet unbeknownst even to his spouse he is surreptitiously carrying on his sexually violent activity. Albert DeSalvo, the Boston Strangler, spoke of his secretiveness with his wife, Irmgard:

> "What did I tell her?" DeSalvo asked himself aloud. "Did I tell her I was going fishing? No . . ." Then: "That's it! I know." He was employed at the time by Russell Blomerth's construction firm as a maintenance man, and it was his job to keep kerosene heaters burning over the weekend at construction sites so that newly poured cement would not freeze and crack. "I volunteered to go down and keep them lit – this was in Belmont. I'd go out early Sunday to Belmont, get the burners going, then shoot into Boston. I came to this building . . . it all happened before 8 A.M. I was home before 9 A.M." Then again, as if to himself: "Why did I do it to her? She treated me like a man." He looked up . . . he seemed on the verge of tears, but he controlled himself and was returned quietly to his cell. [Frank 1966, p. 293]

And following DeSalvo's strangulation-murder and necrophilic rape of Joann Graff, age 23, in Lawrence, Massachusetts, his twelfth victim,

> "I had supper, washed up, played with the kids until about eight o'clock, put them to bed, sat down and watched TV – it came over about her . . . I knew it wasn't me. I didn't want to believe it. It's so difficult to explain to you. I knew it was me who did it, but why I did it and everything else – I don't know why. I was not excited. I didn't think about it; I sat down to dinner and didn't think about it at all." [Frank 1966, p. 302]

The dissociation of rage may also be apparent prior to and during the act of sexual sadism. Sexual psychopaths may have no conscious experience of anger during the stalking, or predatory, period prior to their actual assault on the victim; and subsequent physical contact with the victim, although highly autonomically arousing, may still not precipitate consciously felt anger. Yet the atrocious degree of violence acted out on the victim betrays the intensity of the dissociated affect. The predatory and affective modes of aggression as mutually exclusive psychobiological constructs for understanding violence (see Chapter 6) appear to interact with defensive processes in ways that remain hypothetical, yet are strongly correlated.

Again Albert DeSalvo evokes the experience of dissociated rage in his own words:

> It was all the same thing, always the same feeling . . . You was there, these things were going on and the feeling after I got out of that apartment was as if it never happened. I got out and downstairs, and you could of said you saw me upstairs and as far as I was concerned, it wasn't me. I can't explain it to you any other way. It just so unreal . . . I was there, it was done, and yet if you talked to me an hour later, or half hour later, it didn't mean nothing, it just didn't mean nothing. . . . [Frank 1966, pp. 307–308]

> If I did this—well, for a sex act, or hatred, or for what reason . . . I think I did this not as a sex act, but out of hate for her—not her in particular, but for a woman. After seeing her body, naturally the sex act came in. [Frank 1966, p. 292]

Implicit in this acting out of dissociated rage through sexual sadism is the absence of superego structuralization that could inhibit, or at least modulate, the behavior once the impulse was felt. This paucity of internal structure is endemic to the psychopathic process and accounts for the gross failures of inhibition, binding, and neutralization (Holt 1967) of primitive sexual and aggressive impulses in the psychopath. As a genotype of primary process, condensation may also be used to conceptually understand the psychodynamic blending, the confusion, of sexual and aggressive feelings in socially unacceptable ways by the psychopath (Gill 1967, Meloy 1986b).

What is most striking is the psychopathic individual's inability to consciously feel anger in any empathic sense. Witnessing the physical or emotional abuse of another, the violation of someone else's rights or the degradation of their dignity, evokes no feeling of righteous indignation in the psychopathic character. This is symptomatic of early failures of internalization and a consequent inability to spontaneously identify with the plight of another.

The more intelligent psychopathic individual, however, may be able to simulate such anger, most publicly apparent in expressed allegiance to a particular political or ideological group representing an oppressed segment of a society. The psychopath, hidden behind a facade of ideological commitment, may therein find intensely gratifying, sensation-seeking experiences. International terrorist groups who target civilian populations will provide certain violent psychopathic characters with outlets for the expression of sadistic impulses if they can tolerate the ideological fervor and ritual (Cooper 1978, Post 1984, Shaw 1986).

Psychopathic individuals within an extremist political group will disinhibit others through their risk-taking and violence. Their absence of superego constraints, aggressiveness, grandiosity, paranoia, and capacity to disidentify with any victim provide a powerful characterological template for uncharacteristic modeling behavior by other group members.

The risk to the extremist group, however, is the probability that such psychopathic individuals will ascend to a leadership position and threaten both the ideology and physical safety of their followers. They are overtly aggressive variants of the pathologically narcissistic leader whose internalized object relations evoke "in the network of the organization a replication of his internal world of objects populated only by devalued, shadowy images of others and by images of dangerous potential enemies" (Kernberg 1980, p. 364).

Once they have encouraged adulation and required submissiveness from their followers, yet remaining vulnerable to feelings of intense envy toward those they perceive as challenging their leadership, psychopathic leaders will aggressively defend their position without reference to values or empathic constraint. The transference illusion that they compel in their followers is that they do care for their welfare and are ideologically committed to their cause.

The end result of psychopathic leadership is destruction of the group. Followers are aggressively controlled to function as gratifying selfobjects and sources of narcissistic mirroring. Splitting within the group will occur as those who refuse to carry the grandiose projections of the psychopath begin to challenge his leadership and are perceived, perhaps quite accurately, as persecutory and malevolent forces by the psychopath. The primitive defenses of the psychopathic process are acted out in the group behavior, rather than higher-level compromise of opinion and modulation of affect that a less pathological leader could facilitate. The complete absence of internalized values and emotional attachment to the group members may result in utterly cruel and ruthless acts by the psychopathic leader toward both his submissive followers and perceived enemies. The psychopathology of Reverend Jim Jones and events leading to the collective suicide of hundreds of his followers and the murder of several perceived enemies is a horrific example of this group behavior (Reiterman and Jacobs 1982).

Depression

The conscious experience of depression as an affect within the psychopathic process probably does not exist. It is psychodynamically improbable for the psychopathic character to consciously feel depressed for the following reasons: first, depression necessitates a failure of denial, an operative defense without which the psychopathic process does not exist. Second, depression necessitates a discrepancy between actual self- and ideal self-representations that, by definition, does not exist within the grandiose self-structure. Third, depression is linked to a capacity to mourn for lost object or self-representations (Jacobson 1971) that must be perceived as partially whole, integrated, and the source of both goodness and badness. Such combining of opposite-valence self- and object percepts is not possible with a predominance of dissociative defenses, most generically splitting, in the psychopathic process. Without the appearance of ambivalence and a beginning capacity for repression, the affect of depression, and its more mature, object-directed emotions such as concern, guilt, and mourning, are impossible to achieve.

> The synthesis of internalization systems with contradictory affect valences promotes drive neutralization which, in agreement with Hartmann, Kernberg sees as providing the most important energy source for repression. Thus, the developmental relationship between splitting and repression is reflected in their metapsychological relationship: splitting keeps opposite valence introjections apart, which prevents neutralization, thereby depriving repression of the continuously flowing energy source which it requires. This leads to a weakened ego, which falls back on more primitive splitting defenses. [Greenberg and Mitchell 1983, p. 333]

Fourth, anaclitic depression (Blatt 1974) as a primarily oral form of childhood deprivation necessitates a valuation of the object for its capacity to provide need gratification. The predominance of devaluation as a clinical phenotype of splitting within the psychopathic process has "emptied the world of people and of values" (Kernberg 1980, p. 146). The appearance of symptoms of anaclitic depression in a heretofore diagnosed psychopathic character would, by definition, raise questions concerning the validity of the diagnosis or signal dramatic therapeutic progress. For these reasons I would disagree with Blatt and Shichman (1981) that the psychopath is an extreme variant of anaclitic delinquency.

And fifth, introjective depression (Blatt 1974) in the psychopathic process is fundamentally a contradiction due to the necessity of higher-level defenses, the consolidation of the phallic-urethral phase, and at least partial resolution of oedipal conflicts for this type of depression to manifest. Introjective depression involves feelings of being unworthy, unlovable, guilty, and having failed to live up to others' expectations (Blatt 1974). These are explicit and reality-based superego demands that do not exist in the psychopathic process. At most, the psychopathic character will consciously feel attacked by primitive sadistic introjects, but the response is always one of persecutory anxiety and rage, rather than profound dysphoria.

Yochelson and Samenow (1977) described a "zero state" within the criminal personality that is composed of a self-deception of worthlessness, a belief that thoughts and feelings are transparently real to others, and a belief that the state is permanent. They also noted that it is usually accompanied by an increase, rather than a decrease, in psychomotor activity. They wrote, "Depression in the criminal is basically an angry state in which he blazes at the injustice of the world" (p. 270). This conscious experience of the "zero state," or inner feelings of emptiness, is the closest the psychopathic character will come to the experience of depression. Moreover, this sense of emptiness appears to be an actual interoceptive derivative of the ongoing devaluation process that is occurring both consciously as habitual cognitions (one psychopath perseverated, "It's the middle-class fuckin' wi' me") and unconsciously as defense process.

This devaluation of actual objects, or introjects outside the grandiose self-structure that are not identified as "I" and that may be complained about as hallucinations (particularly if the psychopathic individual has been admitted to an acute inpatient hospital) both adapts to and perpetuates this internal sense (zero state) of emptiness. The adaptation is the unconscious fantasy, occasionally consciously expressed, that there is nothing of value to internalize. This is also supported by the fused representations within the grandiose self-structure of the originally idealized and identified stranger selfobject.

Devaluation perpetuates the emptiness by warding off any new attempts by actual objects to empathize with the plight of the psychopathic character. But why must the psychopath continually devalue? If the devaluation does not occur, the individual is vulnerable to conscious feelings of both envy and greed and may be compelled to both incorporate and destroy the actual object. The unleashing of such oral rage and aggression is likely to be accompanied by sadism and may result in the actual destruction of the object. Such a loss, if the object was conceived as whole, could lead to depression and mourning, and paradoxically improved reality testing. Invariably, however, the psychopathic character will fall back to a psychodynamic position of devaluation once the object, whether actual or fantasized, has been destroyed.

This intrapsychic phenomenon is most vividly illustrated by the sexual psychopath who will ward off others by continually devaluing them, yet quite predictably will be endogenously motivated (Revitch and Schlesinger 1981) to seek out an initially idealized target. Once contact with the victim is made, the incorporative greed and envy will usher in both rage and sadism and the victim will be injured or killed as the intrapsychic devaluing process once again establishes a primitive and defensive equilibrium.

But depressive anxiety is not attained (Klein 1935). There is no concern for the fate of the object as a genuine expression of love and regret. There is no attempt at reparation of the object through restorative fantasies or behaviors. Fantasized omnipotence is not used in the service of love and repair (Greenberg and Mitchell 1983). Omnipotent fantasies occur only as memories to gratify recurrent desires. David Berkowitz, when asked about his sexual dreams, stated in 1980 after his conviction and imprisonment, "They are restless dreams, when I wake up the cover is off. In my dreams I see a couple of my victims. The girl looks very attractive . . . I feel alright afterwards" (Abrahamsen 1985, p. 182).

Suicidal attempts within the psychopathic process are affectively triggered by the commingling of acute dysphoria and narcissistic rage, oftentimes precipitated by the psychopath's perception of being unjustly contained by a malevolent authority. This authority is commonly the criminal justice system, perhaps legal sanctions against the individual, or sudden, unexpected arrest and jailing. Invariably these affective states are intentionally denied to the examiner, but do appear to be consciously felt by the psychopathic individual. I have never had psychopathic characters describe suicidal gestures in words that imply a dissociative experience; my questioning of the event is usually answered with words that suggest gross projection and denial, for example, "It was an accident . . . I don't know what happened . . . somebody did it to me" (see also Appendix I).

This sudden containment by punitive external sanctions placed upon the grandiose self may cause splitting between the ideal self- and ideal object representations (the stranger selfobject) within the grandiose self-structure. Such splitting renders a heretofore identifying and stabilizing process an introjective and destabilizing process, wherein the aggressive, stranger selfobjects are now experienced as internal persecuting thoughts not belonging to "I" that are condensed with other sadistic introjects outside the grandiose self-structure, projectively identified with the actual external authority, and may precipitate self-destructive behavior.

Ironically the internal world of the psychopath during these brief periods of self-concept fragmentation will be much more immediately punishing than reality-based civil and criminal sanctions. This is due to the absence of higher-level and modulated superego structures (Jacobson 1964) in the psychopathic process, in contrast with the presence of such moderating "due process" variables in the procedures of the publicly sanctioned criminal justice system.

Accidental death during self-mutilation or suicidal gestures by psychopaths betray outrageously poor reality testing at a conceptual level, supporting psychopaths' grandiose belief in their own immortality and their lack of capacity to appreciate the vulnerability of their physical selves.

> R. B. was diagnosed as both paranoid schizophrenic and antisocial personality disorder. He had a lengthy history of felony incarcerations, usually for assault against a police officer. He was extremely ambivalent toward any form of psychiatric treatment and would take prescribed neuroleptics only for very brief periods of time. When clinically at his worst, R. B. would exhibit extremely paranoid thought content, but without the fantastic elaboration of paranoid schizophrenia. It was usually directed toward law enforcement, contained a kernel of truth due to their suspicion of him when out of custody, and was usually accompanied by rageful, but controlled, affect. He showed mild indications of formal thought disorder at times. His body was covered with self-inflicted wounds and scars; usually there were recent cigarette burns and scabs where he had attempted to remove old tattoos. Prior to his last arrest he had cut off his ear lobes to "alter his identity," as he expressed it.
>
> R. B. was a 30-year-old British male who had been born and raised in Liverpool. He was fostered in var-

ious juvenile and institutional settings and had an unverifiable and rather confusing psychosocial history. His biological family's history remained unknown to us, and he had no stable employment history or local social support system.

R. B. would occasionally consent to voluntary inpatient treatment and would acquiesce when involuntary treatment was forced upon him following episodes of self-mutilation. His most consistent effort at treatment was attending a twice-weekly psychotherapy group whenever he was in custody.

R. B.'s object relations indicated a consistent idealization of women and a devaluation of male authority figures. He showed some indications of intense, but ambivalent, attachment to females, and would treat them with a curious deference and politeness. This behavior aroused rather strong countertransference feelings in the female nursing staff to help and nurture R. B., attempts that were usually met with polite rejection. His devaluation of male authority figures was most evident in his verbalized hatred of "cops," his paranoid condensing of "their" attitude toward him, and his frank expression of homicidal intent toward them. When I would confront his aggressive sadism and its accompanying pleasurable affect, R. B. would initially deny my perceptions and then slowly smile with contemptuous delight during my empathic interpretation of the pleasure he felt in moments of physical violence.

During one group psychotherapy session, he placed his lit cigarette against his forearm in a moment of verbalized anger. I found myself reacting in a suddenly angry and parental manner, admonishing him that he was not to do that again – that there were other less physically destructive ways to manage emotion.

R. B.'s last arrest followed an alleged attempt to cut the throat of a female companion. He was psychiatrically evaluated several hours after his arrival in custody and it was determined that he did not need involuntary treatment; he refused voluntary treatment. Several days after his arrest, R. B. asked to see the psychiatrist, but assured the floor deputy he was not intent on suicide. He was scheduled to be seen at 1300; he was found dead at 1200, having hung himself with a sheet in his cell.

Despite this patient's exceedingly dangerous behavior and threats, and my relief that no one else had died with him as he had predicted, his death evoked sadness in me. There was a sense of tragedy surrounding this individual, an expressed vulnerability that endeared him to others, yet a capacity to engage in extreme sadomasochistic behavior toward himself and others.

By any diagnostic criteria he was psychopathic, yet there was a cyclothymic component to his self-esteem, the affects supporting his grandiose self-structure. He would rapidly oscillate between feelings of depression and rage, the latter supported by grandiose self-concepts and paranoid projections onto the law enforcement body. There was also an active, but highly ambivalent, seeking of dependency toward females. He never presented as a stable and well-defined psychopathic character, whose grandiosity and aggressiveness would shield him from more depressive and masochistic impulses. I would speculate that his suicidal act was the result of sadistic introjects outside the grandiose self-structure overwhelming the latter, perhaps consciously rationalized as a wished for and idealized final peace.

Klein (1935) postulated that anxiety about the fate of the object and attempts to make it whole again through love become the predominate force within the personality. Yet the psychopathic process prevents the depressive position, as the metapsychological construct for all subsequent depressive symptomatology, from unfolding.

> The attempts to save the love object, to repair and restore it, attempts which in the state of depression are coupled with despair, since the ego doubts its capacity to achieve this restoration, are determining factors for all sublimations and the whole of the ego-development. [Klein 1935, p. 290]

Exhilaration and Contempt

The conscious experience of exhilaration and contempt, which are usually simultaneous affective states in the psychopathic process and which may clinically appear as contemptuous delight, is a distinctive feature of psychopathy.

Bursten (1972) described this affect state as one of several steps in the intentional manipulative behavior of the psychopathic individual, destined to continually "put something over" on the actual object. First, there is a goal conflict with the actual object. Second, the psychopathic individual intends to influence the other through the use of deception. Third, the deceptive act is carried out. And fourth, the psychopath experiences a conscious sense of exhilaration, a contemptuous delight, if the deception is successful. This latter affect state distinguishes the psychopathic process from other situation-specific behaviors that nonpsychopathic individuals, from time to time, might choose. Like the psychopathic pattern, an individual might progress through the first three stages of the manipulation; but unlike the psycho-

pathic pattern, any momentary feelings of exhilaration and delight would be quickly overshadowed by feelings of guilt, shame,
or remorse. The presence of these emotions, of course, implies
some level of superego structuralization and capacity for empathy that is absent in the psychopath.

The tone of contemptuous delight is illustrated in the following portion of a letter written by a psychopathic individual to
his girlfriend:

> After a few weeks (in jail module 3B) I tied my sheet
> around the light fixture, then nervously sat down to eat
> a pack of oatmeal cookies, a Milky Way, a Baby Ruth
> and two fruit punch drinks, as I listened for the sound
> of the deputy's keys. When I heard the deputy ap-
> proaching my cell, I quickly sprang to my feet, grabbed
> the dangling end of the sheet and proceeded to tie a
> noose, as I repeatedly knock against my cell door to
> assure attracting his attention. When asked what I
> thought I was doing, I replied, "I have nothing to live
> for, so I'm going to die," as I got the noose around my
> neck and began climbing up the cell bars. As I had
> planned the deputy rushed in, placed me in hand cuffs
> and I was taken to the Psychiatric Security Unit . . .
> where I was seen by a psychiatrist. I, in all the drama
> of depression, inform him "I just want to be left alone,
> so I can die." He order (sp) that I remain in the Psy.
> Security Unit at the County Jail, for two weeks obser-
> vation and take an anti-depressant twice daily.
>
> Well my plan had worked. I was taken to the Psy. S.
> U. . . with twenty-two certified crazies . . . daily ses-
> sions with the quack psyc. (sp) . . . and plenty of atten-
> tion from a host of unqualified staff.

Joseph (1960) described this affective state as a "mocking, controlling attitude" (p. 528). Inherent in this feeling is a devaluing of

the actual objects and an enhancement of the psychopath's grandiosity and felt superiority.

Abrahamsen (1985) described the deception and contemptuous delight of David Berkowitz during the time of his serial killing:

> He never aroused any suspicion. At the Post Office, for instance, where his co-workers often discussed Son of Sam and whether or not he was insane, Berkowitz never told them Son of Sam was insane. "I was only a casual listener. Sometimes I asked, 'What do you think of the guy? Is he crazy or what?'" With a triumphant voice he added, "Nobody really figured out that I was Son of Sam."
>
> He played his double role with incredible coolness: "I would walk into work at the Post Office one day after a shooting. I would see the faces of confusion and fear. Then I would say 'What happened? Gee, that's too bad. I hope they catch the bastard.'" [Abrahamsen 1985, p. 189]

The contemptuous delight of the psychopath restores his pride. The manipulative cycle both enhances his narcissism and protects his vulnerability. It is necessarily repetitive because the threat of intrapsychic rupture within the grandiose self is always present; more specifically the identifications among the actual self-, ideal self-, and ideal object representations within the grandiose self-structure are most vulnerable to the sadistic, "bad" introjects, affectively toned by envy and rage, outside the grandiose self that are warded off by varieties of vertical, or dissociative, defenses. Bursten (1973a) described this as a purification process. The bad objects are projected onto the victim of the manipulation, an anal-eliminative purging of the shameful selfobjects within the mind occurs, and consequently a reunion, or reidentification, among the actual self-, ideal self-, and ideal object representations is ensured. Bursten (1973b) described this as the characteristic mode of narcissistic repair of the psycho-pathic process.

Frank (1966) portrayed strikingly similar behavior in Albert DeSalvo, the Boston Strangler:

> "This is going to be comical," he was saying. "We're all at a New Year's Eve party, the family, see? Well, I find out one of my sisters is taking judo to protect herself—against the Strangler! She and her friends, they all get together and they're taking lessons at a gym. I says, 'Sure you can handle the Strangler if you get him?' She says, 'Oh, I'm pretty well prepared for him.' I says, 'What would you do if he got you in this hold?' And before she knew it I had her in that hold. She couldn't do nothing. She says, 'Well, I'm learning.' "
>
> He looked up with his boyish grin. "Her husband has eleven sisters, all beautiful—fabulous! I tried to make all eleven of them."
>
> He began to chuckle. "One of them says to me one day, 'You know what I think you are? I wouldn't be surprised if you ain't the Boston Strangler. The way we remember you as the Measuring Man, and how fast and sharp you are with all those women, and now this guy is operating the same way . . . Bah, it can't be you!' " Hugely delighted, he mimicked her. [Frank 1966, p. 296]

Albert DeSalvo had an extensive juvenile record and was once committed to Lyman School, a well-known institution for juvenile delinquents in Massachusetts. In 1958 and 1959 he was arrested for numerous breaking and enterings. In 1961 he began posing as a representative for a modeling agency and would visit college-age girls at their apartments in the Cambridge area. Invariably they would allow him to physically measure their breasts, waists, and hips: hence, the police label "the measuring man." DeSalvo was arrested on March 17, 1961, and, at that time, was married with two small children and living in suburban Malden, Massachusetts. He was psychiatrically examined at Westborough State Hospital and was diagnosed as a sociopathic personality. On May 4, 1961, he was sentenced on conviction of Assault and Battery, brought by some of the women he had measured, and Attempted Breaking and Entering. Due to De-Salvo's good behavior in custody and his attorney's plea that his family needed him, he served eleven months and was released in April, 1962. Two months later DeSalvo killed and raped his first victim, 55-year-old Anna Slesers (Frank 1966).

I have already written of the relationship of envy and greed to devaluation, the defense necessary to ward off unconscious fantasies of oral rage and destruction. Devaluation both adapts to and perpetuates the interoceptive feeling of emptiness, but at great affective cost to the psychopath.

More commonly the psychopath will repetitively navigate this unconscious affect-impulse-defense triad (envy-greed-devaluation) through the conscious pursuit of behaviors that result in feelings of exhilaration and contempt. But what is the psychodynamic relationship between unconscious envy and greed and conscious exhilaration and contempt?

Joseph (1960) wrote of the psychopath, "What he gets he spoils and wastes; he feels frustrated and deprived and the greed and demands start again" (p. 527). Envy is commonly assumed to be a derivative of oral aggression (Kernberg 1980) and contains within it the infant's hatred of the actual object as actively withholding supplies. This hatred creates wishes to destroy the object, which, in turn, would eliminate the envy. Klein (1957) understood the importance of envy as hatred of the *good* object, in contrast with the infant's immediate dislike of unpleasant sensory-perceptual experiences, which would be internalized and eventually conceptualized as *bad* objects. Greed, a desire rather than an affect, was a wish to have all the contents of the good object. Destruction was the motive of envy and the consequence of greed. Klein (1957) used the infant's sensory-perceptual awareness of the mother's breast and the impulse to suck as the metaphor for understanding the infant's envy and greed. Despite the mother's breast as being an inherently satisfying sensory-perceptual experience and the supplier of warming and filling interoceptive sensations, sooner or later it would be withheld and this would frustrate.

Paralleling the infant's actual relationship to the mother was the internalization of objects and their demarcation into pleasant and unpleasant, frustrating and gratifying representations. Yet at times the good object representations were felt as actively withholding, and thus were envied and hated. The infant wished to both have and spoil the pleasant (later conceptualized and valued as "good") object representations, but at a great price. The defensive process of splitting was undermined by envy because it destroyed the good object representations. A consequence of such representational destruction was a decrease in the mnemonic traces of good object experiences, decreased conscious feelings of protection and safety that were unconsciously supported by a net of satisfying internalizations, and increased persecutory anxiety. In a real sense, "envy destroys the possibility of hope" (Greenberg and Mitchell 1983, p. 129) because object and self-representational development is dependent on a predominance of perceptually satisfying and later conceptually "good" internalizations.

Envy is most apparent in patients who hate goodness itself. Psychotherapeutic interpretations will be turned into useless and hurtful experiences. It is as if the patient must destroy hope because the sense of hopefulness is too painful. Psychopathic individuals who never enter psychotherapy are paradigms of this hatred of goodness. Perhaps the envious destruction of their meager supply of "good" internalizations early in their development foreshadows their characterization by others in adult life as destroyers of goodness, in other words, as evil.

I must reiterate that envy is usually not consciously felt in the psychopathic process. It is warded off, dissociated, and defensively protects the grandiose self-structure from oral rage. Behind the envy is the rage toward that which is idealized but cannot be possessed. But a product of this split-off envy and greed is a compulsion to "put something over on someone." In other words, envy is the destructive motivation for behaviors that initiate Bursten's (1973a) sequence and lead to conscious feelings of exhilaration and contempt.

Implicit in envy is an idealization of the actual object or projections of the ideal object within the grandiose self that are carried by an actual object, projections that must be reintrojected, or brought back into the grandiose self-structure, to restore the narcissistic equilibrium that is always threatened by sadistic introjects outside its boundaries. Thus Bursten's (1973) sequence begins with an idealization of the actual object, which is projectively identified with the ideal object within the grandiose self; continues with the envious and greedy spoiling of the actual object to reintroject the ideal object projections; and ends with the contemptuous devaluation of the actual object as sadistic introjects that continually threaten the grandiose self are projected onto it. It is an aggressive taking in and throwing out, incorporative and eliminative, cycle that begins with the conscious thought "I must have" and ends with the conscious thought "it was not worth having." As Kernberg (1980) noted, what appears as distance and uninvolvement on the surface in the narcissistic personality disorder is underneath an active process of devaluation, depreciation, and spoiling. The actual object must be devalued after it has been spoiled to ward off feelings of depression, mourning, and a wish to repair. Such reparation in the normal child, fostered by mother's willingness to be consoled, leads to a toleration of guilt and eventually a capacity for concern (Winnicott 1965).

The defensive use of Bursten's (1973a) manipulative cycle to ward off the conscious feeling of envy, and subsequently the expression of oral rage, poses an important question: If the psychopathic individual cannot repetitively, and compulsively, act out this manipulative cycle and experience the highly valued feelings of exhilaration and contempt, what can be predicted?

I hypothesize that the inhibition of such conscious behavior, for whatever reason, would eventually precipitate both conscious envy and rage and appreciably lower the psychopathic threshold for violence. David Berkowitz again provides a cogent example in his own writing:

> I have often noticed just how unobservant people are. It's been said that parents are the last to know. This may be true in my case, for I wonder how I, at ages nine, eleven, thirteen, etc., managed to do so very many negative things and go unnoticed. It is puzzling, indeed. And I think you will agree it is sad. [Abrahamsen 1985, p. 202]

Deprived of the affective experience of contemptuous delight as his deeds appeared to go unnoticed, he writes,

> It took me 24 years to erupt, to explode like a volcano. It took me 24 years before I reached the ultimate destiny – murder. This is the ultimate climax – murder. I reached this point . . . where I couldn't keep it in – I wanted to, but I couldn't. So I gave up resisting. [p. 206]

> The desires to do it, to kill, had filled me up to such explosive proportions, it caused me such turmoil inside, that when it released itself, it was like a volcano erupting itself, and the pressure was over, for a while anyhow. [p. 204]

Boredom

The conscious experience of boredom in the psychopathic process is a complex affective state that is a product of object relational, perceptual, and biological factors within the personality. It is a restless, anhedonic feeling that is acted out through aggressive, hypomanic activity. Boredom in the psychopathic process is virtually identical to boredom in the narcissistic personality in general, but is coped with more aggressively in the former.

Svrakic (1985) conceptualized boredom at two different structural levels in the narcissistic personality disorder. First, boredom is felt at a primary, or deeper, level as a mild, pervasive sense of restlessness and emptiness. It is continually present, felt as "a small distant part of (oneself) . . . the clinical trace of the real self existing deep inside the narcissistic personality" (p. 722). This pervasive, although mildly sensed, mood of boredom is the primary emotional dimension of the actual self-representations within the grandiose self-structure. The structural shell of the fused ideal self- and object representations both insulates and isolates the actual self-representations from the immediacy and novelty of genuine emotional interaction. What once was intolerable as an infant is predicted to occur again as an adult, hence the shell, the character armor of the grandiose self, and the boredom of the imprisoned core self.

At a secondary level, boredom is felt more intensely, although intermittently, during "idle intervals," Svrakic's (1985) expression for the moments when narcissistic personality disordered individuals have exhausted all existing narcissistic supplies without and are left within themselves. These feelings of intense boredom, in contrast to the pervasive, primary, but milder mood of boredom, originate within the grandiose self-structure as a product of the defensive interplay between the fused ideal selfobject representations and the actual objects that carry the projective-introjective material during cyclical modes of narcissistic repair. When external objects are unavailable, or existing ones are spoiled and devalued, the narcissistically disturbed individual must wait for replenishment; the psychopathic process, however, transforms this idle interval into a more aggressive pursuit of narcissistic supplies where the absence of superego restraints is more disinhibiting of behavior.

A correlate of this secondary, manifestly more intense, boredom is Svrakic's (1985) "pessimistic mood," closely paralleling Yochelson and Samenow's "zero state" (1977). It is the affective result of narcissistic decompensation, the recognition that desired grandiosity is illusory and self-satisfaction through omnipotent strivings is unreachable. Svrakic (1985) described five characteristics of this mood state: futility, the absence of grandiosity as a value criterion of meaningful life, paradoxical displays of superiority and arrogance despite one's felt mood, intrusiveness toward others in attempts to establish omnipotent control over the environment, and dysphoria with intervals of subjective relief. This pessimistic mood is most apparent in the psychopathic process during long periods of incarceration when there are few actual objects upon which to project and introject psychic material that will support the illusion of grandiose striving.

Theodore Bundy, a contemporary sexual psychopath convicted of several murders and awaiting execution on Florida's Death Row, revealed his grandiose strivings in his own words,

> I know a lot of guys wonder what I might do if pushed far enough . . . I had this one man who put his arm around a woman and escorted her past my cell . . . She was just scared to death! Other people have this fascination, too. They stand and look at me. I can look in my television and see their reflections. They all cluster around in big groups; not one at a time, but four or five at once. Then I turn around and they scatter! [Michaud and Aynesworth 1983, p. 277]

Boredom motivates an attentional search for something of interest within or without. The narcissistic, or psychopathic, individual is hampered in this task because actual objects are never perceived in an objective, empathic sense; they function only as containers of projected and devalued representational contents. Consequently, familiar actual objects are perceptually dulled; there is nothing fresh or novel about a familiar and devalued actual object. Instead of noticing and feeling a sense of anticipated pleasure in the sensory-perceptual fit of an actual object of love, the psychopathic character is bound to the pursuit of continual novelty in perception and relinquishes any hope of an enduring emotional attachment. This pursuit, moreover, is initially enhanced by the idealizing defenses, yet is quickly eroded by the devaluation that follows. Again, the perceptual distinctiveness between self- and object internalizations remains, yet the conceptual fusion and envelopment of the occasionally novel actual object as an extension of the grandiose self-structure is omnipresent (Meloy 1985).

Hartocollis (1983) noted that boredom, more than any other affect, is experienced as a disturbance in the sense of time. There is an impatience with the sense of self and the environment, a sense of dissatisfaction, and a vague want of something ideationally unknown. Fenichel (1953) described boredom as the presence of instinctual tension, but the absence of instinctual aim. Bibring (1953) theorized that boredom, depression, and depersonalization all represented states of mental inhibition, but only depression involved a reduction in self-esteem. Hartocollis (1983) took issue with this, and distinguished boredom from depression according to the experience of time; "the subjects, describing their discomfort either as boredom or depersonalization, find it difficult to experience time as either past or future. They experience themselves in a slow-moving, almost immobile present, which they obviously do not enjoy, yet find preferable – 'safer' – than either a past or a future orientation" (p. 70). Grinker and colleagues (1968) described boredom as an "affectless" depression.

Narcissistic, and specifically psychopathic, individuals are prone to boredom because of the insulation of the actual core self, the aggressive devaluing of actual objects during cyclical modes of narcissistic repair, and the predominance of "idle intervals" when additional supplies outside the self are not forthcoming.

Nonpsychopathic, higher-functioning individuals are not imprisoned by the idle moment. They will project into the future through the use of purposeful daydreaming (Schafer 1954) or reflect upon intentionally evoked memories. In both cases the absence of narcissistic gratification from without is met with a smoothly turning inward to thought that will evoke pleasant or unpleasant affect that is, in a sense, timeless, but can be reexperienced to fill the moment.

The need for immediate libidinal or aggressive gratification in the psychopathic process imprisons individuals in the present. Brenda Spenser, a psychopathic adolescent living near Cleveland Elementary School in San Diego, California, was the subject of this reporter's file:

> A 16-year-old girl fired a shotgun from the window of an upper floor apartment, killing and wounding several adults and children on the grounds of an elementary school below. She calmly told a newspaper reporter by telephone that she was "doing it for fun." He quoted her as saying: "I don't like Mondays. This livens up the day. I just started shooting for the fun of it." The reporter said the girl's voice carried no apparent remorse or sorrow. "She was obviously a kid," he wrote. "She was calm. She was not laughing." When he asked, "Do you realize that you almost shot two or three people?" she replied, "Is that all? I thought I shot twelve." [*The New York Times*, January 30, 1979]

The psychopathic individual, as a variant of the narcissistic personality, is most vulnerable to chronic feelings of boredom because he or she aggressively empties the world of meaningful relations to ward off feelings of envy and greed. Ironically, this need to devalue is only matched by the hunger for direct instinctual gratification through narcissistic supplies from without; when these are unavailable, "their world becomes a prison from which only new excitement, admiration, or experiences implying control, triumph, or incorporation of supplies are an escape" (Kernberg 1975, p. 218).

If psychopathic individuals are consciously aware of their heightened sense of boredom when compared with others, they render it acceptable by redefining it as a superior attribute of their personality. Others may be characterized by them as leading sedentary or mundane lives, yet their benchmark is always risk taking through overt behavior, rather than satisfaction through emotional experiences within themselves and with others. Emotional relatedness is sadly absent in the psychopathic process; and consequently psychopathic individuals are unable to experience loneliness, the longing for and awareness of the possibility of emotional closeness.

The prevalence of boredom in the psychopathic process finds psychobiological support in the work of several researchers. Electrodermal differences between psychopathic and nonpsychopathic subjects (Hare 1970) may be associated with lower levels of central nervous system arousal that are both state specific and trait generic. Hare (1970) and Quay (1965) both argued that the psychopath's behavior is the result of cortical underarousal and pathological sensation-seeking.

Zuckerman (1978) discussed the psychopath as a sensation-seeker, needing higher levels of sensory stimulation to reach comparative levels of cortical arousal in the nonpsychopathic individual. Eysenck (1967) postulated a biological theory of extroversion (see Chapter 1) that correlates personality trait with reticular formation arousal. The extroverted individual is continually seeking external stimulation to compensate for lower levels of cortical arousal. Much of Eysenck's work has been validated by pharmacological research (Claridge 1967, Gray 1972).

Boredom as a phenomenological experience appears to be closely linked to the behavior of sensation-seeking and the personality trait of extroversion (Farley and Farley 1967). I hypothesize that the psychopathic paucity of whole self- and object representations, an intrapsychic precipitant of boredom and its behavioral corollary sensation-seeking, may, in part, be due to cortical underarousal. This psychobiological difference would validate the dynamic and structural characteristics that predispose boredom as both a mood and an affect in the psychopathic process.

I have noted three factors in the production of boredom in the psychopathic process: first, decreased levels of central nervous system arousal; second, habitual devaluation of actual objects that results in perceptually dull exteroceptive experiences and a conceptually inflated reality sense; and third, a dearth of whole self- and object representations within the mind that could, if available, provide stimulation during idle intervals.

This last factor, however, is somewhat paradoxical if one reflects on the grandiose proclivities of the psychopath. Why would representations of self and others within the mind, if capable of such grandiose elaboration, be so limiting and unsatisfying?

To paraphrase Kris (1952), the psychopath's grandiose imagery is regression in disservice of the ego. Representations of self and others are grossly distorted, polarized, and flat; even if conceptually idealized, they are shorn of the variety and complexity of actual affective and representational experiences tied closely to reality. New experiences likewise are stripped of their potential for colorful and rich elaboration of memory and fantasy. This must occur for both devaluing and defensive purposes to ward off envy, greed, and oral rage that is dissociated from the grandiose self-structure. In a real sense psychopaths are easily bored with their own grandiosity, yet are conscious of no other way to recreate themselves.

As the psychopathic individual ages, his memory becomes a defensive idealization of the past with a lessening of grandiose strivings for the future. In the same way, evocative memory is subject to splitting and collapsed into a one-dimensional progression of idealized and devalued events (Grotstein 1978, Meloy 1984). But even the idealized memories are not experienced as safe, for they conjure up feelings of envy for "the person who once was" and therefore must be devalued to ward off oral aggression.

The aging psychopath may yearn for an early death as he realizes the cumulative failures of his emotional life and the incessant cycles of greed, spoiling, and devaluation prompted by boredom. The young psychopath may idealize death and commingle it with his own grandiose strivings, wishes that defend against the fear of an empty, futureless life. As I began this chapter with a quote from David Berkowitz, I will let him end it in his own words:

> As a child I had tremendous fascination with death. When I thought about dying, I thought of being transported into a world of bliss and happiness. . . . When I arrived at Stratford Avenue [in the Bronx] I used to stand looking out our window with a fantastic view. Throughout the year, rain, snow, or cold, I would look out the window and pray to God to kill me, that I would be hit by lightning. I begged to God for death, I used to sit on the fire escape and thought of throwing myself down, wanting to jump. . . . After Pearl's death, after my [adoptive] mother died, I never had these suicidal thoughts. I still wanted to die, but with heroism, with honor. I wanted to die while saving lives, battling a blaze. This is why I wanted to become a fireman, helping people, rescuing them, and being a hero, or possibly dying in the blaze. [Abrahamsen 1985, p. 31]

> I do love death. I've always loved it. I've wished for it, and tried to understand it. Death is fascinating . . . its power, its hold; it is wonderful. [Abrahamsen 1985, p. 88]

CONCLUSIONS

The psychopathic process is not devoid of conscious affect, but it is emotionally colored in intensely narcissistic hues. Psychopaths may be quite aroused by others, but they do not emotionally relate to them in an empathic, caring sense. Their affect is experienced in relation to the grandiose self-structure, wherein others are perceptually distinct, but conceptually are only extensions of their expansive sense of self. The psychopathic character has no empathic capacity, but has an exquisite ability to malignantly identify with the actual object and if intelligent enough, can sensitively manipulate the actual object by resonating with its more nefarious, and pathologically narcissistic, characteristics. Psychopathic individuals know well within themselves these feelings of righteous anger, sadistic pleasure, contemptuous delight, sudden dysphoria, and, deep within, a profound, disquieting boredom.

5

Unconscious Defense and Conscious Choice

T he psychopathic process brings into relief a larger question that has both theoretical and clinical ramifications for the psychoanalytic researcher: What is the relationship between conscious choice and unconscious determination in human behavior? Psychodynamic theory attempts to probe the latter dimension of intrapsychic activity, but the reality of conscious choice, at least as a phenomenological experience, is difficult to reconcile with a purely deterministic view of human nature. Free will and determinism also describe the fundamentally different premises of legal scholarship and psychological science in general, American jurisprudence and psychoanalytic thought in particular.

An interesting clinical example of this issue is a case that was decided by the United States Supreme Court, *Colorado v. Connelly* (No. 85-660) in which the respondent, a diagnosed paranoid schizophrenic, argued that the state's use of his spontaneous and incriminating statements made in a noncustodial setting, or its use of incriminating statements made subsequently by him following waiver of his "Miranda" rights, violated the due process clause of the Fourteenth Amendment because he was acting in response to auditory hallucinations commanding him to confess. The American Psychological Association submitted an *amicus curiae* brief on March 14, 1986, and wrote, in part,

". . . Behavioral science does not use or rely upon the concepts of 'volition' or 'free will.' Accordingly, Dr. Metzner was not testifying as a scientist when he testified that respondent's command hallucinations impaired his 'volitional capacity.' Furthermore, even if Dr. Metzner only meant to testify that command hallucinations are, in a statistical sense, coercive, his testimony finds no support in the professional literature, and is contrary to clinical experience" (Ennis 1986, pp. 25–26). The Supreme Court ruled that the Miranda warning was designed only to protect suspects from coercive tactics of the police, not from any internal psychological pressures.

The psychopathic process is clinically relevant to this question because of the commonly held belief, oftentimes correct, that psychopaths lie a lot. Their deceit is consciously and intentionally chosen. Most clinicians with whom I have discussed this question vigorously defend this "conscious choice" hypothesis, simply because they have observed psychopaths' ease with which they can choose, given the correct interpersonal determinants, *not* to lie, or more dynamically, to also undo a lie.

One psychopathic patient told me an elaborate reconstruction of a distressing childhood event that he felt explained much of his current behavior. When I challenged the credulity of it, he laughed and said, "Well, doc, would you believe this?" and proceeded to unravel an equally compelling tale of woe.

In a forensic setting the complex interplay between conscious choice and unconscious defense is most apparent when questions of malingering are asked. There is not, as yet, any psychological technique to detect malingering with any reasonable certainty, but several researchers (Beaber et al. 1985, Brandt et al. 1985, Schacter 1986b) have begun to analyze this perplexing clinical phenomenon.

Conscious choice and unconscious defense are also implicit in the historical differentiation between malingering and factitious disorder in descriptive psychiatry. The DSM-III-R (American Psychiatric Association 1987) postulated conscious intent in the former and unconscious, compulsive repetition in the latter, more closely allied with a severe personality disorder.

My purpose in this chapter is to explore the existence of both conscious choice and unconscious determinants, particularly defenses, in the psychopathic process. It is my hope that the acknowledgment of such a dialectic will pay homage to the relationship between conscious and unconscious topography in the mind and will avoid the excommunication of one in sacerdotal devotion to the other (Shapiro 1981). An excellent example of this dialectical argument when applied to expert testimony is to be found in Bonnie and Slobogin (1980) and Morse (1982).

I will analyze the interdependence and interrelationship of conscious choice and unconscious defensive structuring of the personality in the psychopathic process. I have suggested this blending of cognitive style and dynamic motivation in the previous chapter with my analysis of conscious manipulation by the psychopath and its unconscious motivation as a defense against envy and oral rage.

Likewise I hope to address a more general question. What constellations of defenses render emotional experience unconscious, outside of awareness, in the psychopathic personality? Instead of simply reviewing the nature and extent of defenses within the narcissistic personality (Kernberg 1975), I will focus on the idiosyncratic role of several of these defenses in the psychopathic process and their relationship to conscious thinking, emotion, and behavior.

Several avenues of inquiry will be pursued. First, what is the relationship between unconscious denial and conscious deception? Second, what is the nature and extent of consciously imitated and unconsciously simulated (Glasser 1986) affect? Third, what role does projective identification play in the capacity of the psychopathic character to be both exquisitely charming and sadistically violent? And fourth, what are the varieties of dissociative defenses, such as splitting, that pervade the psychopathic process; and how do these unconscious dissociative maneuvers help us to understand hysteria, dissociative states, and malingering in the psychopath?

DENIAL AND DECEPTION

Deception is ubiquitous within the psychopathic process. It is a necessary stage in the carrying out of the manipulative act (Bursten 1973a) because contemptuous delight as a wished-for affect cannot be felt unless deception has established within an external object the fertile ground for shaming and devaluing. In other words, the conscious act of deception "sets up" the actual object to receive and contain the purged psychic material that threatens to devalue the grandiose self if not projected. This continuous process of deception, to facilitate the unconscious purging cycle, is endogenous to the psychopathic character. It has virtually no relationship to situational factors and will recur regardless of the degree of therapeutic efficacy or secure control of the psychopath's environment. It is, in a sense, a compulsion that the psychopath may actively overcome only by risking the development of anxious and hypochondriacal symptoms. Such endogenous deceptive behaviors should be distinguished from exogenous deception; both types are conscious behaviors, but the latter, tied to situational factors, is more intentionally chosen by the psychopath when he desires improvement of circumstances. This exogenous deception would most likely result in a diagnosis of malingering in a clinical context:

> E. D., a 22-year-old Caucasian male, was admitted to our forensic unit with symptoms of major depression. Perusal of his clinical record indicated no prior history of treatment for depression, but an extensive history of criminal activity, usually involving drugs and property offenses, and a disruptive family history. E. D.'s expressed reason for his depression was his family's

ouster of him from their home and his mother's terminal cancer and impending death. The patient, however, refused to sign a release of information that would have allowed us to discuss his clinical situation with his parents.

E. D. showed little response to pharmacological and psychotherapeutic treatment. The characterological nature of his depression became more obvious to the inpatient staff. After two weeks of inpatient care, E. D. announced, with much tearful affect, that he had been told in a phone conversation with his father that his mother had died. He wished that we could help him with arrangements, through his attorney and the Superior Court, to attend her funeral.

The clinical staff became increasingly skeptical of E. D.'s verbiage. The treatment plan was reformulated, and the patient was told that since much of his current distress, by his own report, was due to family trauma, it was imperative that he allow us to talk with his father by telephone; otherwise we would no longer treat him. E. D. reacted with intense anger, but within hours admitted that his mother did not have cancer and had not died. Shortly after that he began threatening suicide if he was discharged from the inpatient unit.

Deception within the psychopathic process is characterized by intent, goal direction, and a facility to change both the logical content and the target of the deceit as necessary. Logical content describes the false information and rationalizations that are used by the psychopath to consummate the deceptive act; clinically speaking, however, the deceptive act may appear quite illogical, but only in reference to motivation, not content. The motivation is particularly baffling in endogenous deceit when the psychopath may appear to have everything he wants, yet continues, quite predictably, to commence the manipulative cycle. Here the logic of the motivation can be understood only if the unconscious dynamics are seen (refer to Chapter 4). The logic in exogenous deceit, both as motivation and as content, is much more easily comprehensible, as in the case of E. D. noted above.

The target of the deceit may be either an animate or an inanimate object, but in both cases is "possessed" as an extension, on a conceptual level, of the grandiose self-structure and is devalued of all attributes except those that facilitate the projective-introjective cycle. A loss of perceptual distinctiveness along with the conceptual fusion of self- and object representations would render the individual psychotic. This is pathognomonic of both a psychopathic character disorder and a psychotic disorder, the coexistence of which will be discussed in Chapter 7.

Denial, in contrast with deception, is an unconscious process. It is not consciously chosen or intentionally employed by the individual, and it is, by definition, a theoretically deterministic construct rather than a product of free will.

Freud spoke of denial within the neuropsychoses of defense (1894), as a defense within the psychoses (1911, 1924a), as analogous to repression to facilitate the ego's detachment from external reality (1924b), as different from negation (1925), and as a distinctive mechanism within the splitting of the ego (1938) that should be separated from defenses against internal instinctual demands. Throughout his writings he emphasized that denial was a defense against objective, external sources of anxiety and displeasure.

Anna Freud (1936) reiterated her father's position and specified that denial occurred through fantasy and through word and act. She emphasized that an inherent incompatibility existed between denial and reality testing as the child developed, since denial through word and act meant a reversal of real situations. Such reversals could not exist without a disturbance of reality testing. In other words, the capacity to test reality was inconsistent with the maintenance of denial, a position also taken by Freud (1938). Anna Freud (1936) noted another characteristic of denial in word and act that is especially relevant to both narcissistic and psychopathic pathology:

> The method of denial in word and act is subject to a second restriction, which does not apply to denial in fantasy. In his fantasies a child is supreme. So long as he does not tell them to anybody, no one has any reason to interfere. On the other hand, dramatization of fantasies in word and act requires a stage in the outside world. So his employment of this mechanism is conditioned externally by the extent to which those around him will fall in with his dramatization, just as it is conditioned internally by the degree of compatibility with the function of reality testing. [p. 91]

Such is the case of the psychopathic character, an aggressive variant of the narcissistic personality disorder wherein "word and act" are more familiar than "fantasy" as products of denial. The narcissistic individual, as I have noted earlier, will choose more benign and independent modes of repair. Denial in fantasy of real-life situations, and the concomitant elaboration of idealized fantasies that do not exist in reality, are more easily utilized than expressions through word and act. The psychopathic process, however, compels a more alloplastic expression of denial through word and act. The most common expression I have heard in forensic settings is "I am not a criminal . . . I do not belong with these individuals." But such words and actions are restricted by the nature and extent of acquiescence by others, and challenges to this overt and grandiose conceptualization of self are usually met with righteous anger or quiet disdain by the psychopath. Perhaps the most familiar example of this psychodynamic in public life was the phrase uttered with great frustration and anger by then President Richard Nixon in 1974, "I am not a crook!" His expression and words have been parodied by countless individuals, made all the more appalling by the existence of actual evidence to the contrary obviously known to him at the time and consciously hidden from the public.

Jacobson (1957, 1971) viewed denial as a primitive and archaic mechanism directed against both internal and external reality. She accomplished this theoretical broadening of the defense by hypothesizing a regression to a "concretistic infantile stage" in which external and internal were treated in the same manner. Because of primitive introjective and projective mechanisms, unacceptable inner realities could be treated as if they were external. In other words, the boundary between internal and external reality was lost, therefore the distinction between denial as a defense against instinctual threat or actual external event became irrelevant.

> Although neurotic denial may involve processes of disconnection, isolation, and collective joining of psychic elements, which turn them into quasi-concrete, imagelike units, the latter do not lose the quality of being psychic in nature. The line of demarcation between internal and external reality is maintained, even in view of such introjections and projections. . . .
>
> In psychotics, however, the pathological process leads to a real fragmentation, splitting, a concretization, and externalization of psychic manifestations, to the point of lending them truly concrete qualities. Consequently we find an equation between what is abstract and psychic and what is concrete and physical in nature. [Jacobson 1971, pp. 133–134]

Frosch (1983a) also noted that denial in the psychotic is much more concrete than denial in the neurotic. It is in the service of self-preservation and restitution and is coeval with a massive loss of reality testing.

I am in partial agreement with Jacobson's formulations, but do not believe they are clear enough in distinguishing between denial as a defense at the borderline and psychotic levels of personality organization. In the former, subserving both narcissistic and psychopathic character formation, perceptual distinctiveness is maintained between internal and external reality, and thus intrapsychically between self- and object representations. What is confused, and thus vulnerable to projective-introjective cycling, is the psychic material contained in either the self or object, internal and external. The boundaries of the psychic container remain intact, yet the thought and affective contents within and without are subject to exchange.

Bion's (1977a) metaphor of the container and contained is most germane to understanding this distinction. In psychotic personality organization, the container is lost, while in borderline personality organization that which is contained oscillates between self and object on both an intrapsychic and interpersonal level. The notion of concept and percept formation in object relations (Meloy 1985) is somewhat analogous to the contained-container metaphor; that is, the conceptual extension and distortion of the contents of the grandiose self to embrace actual others as gratifying selfobjects through projective identification (the contained) proceeds without necessarily a loss of sensory-perceptual boundaries (the container).

But is denial expressed in more primitive and mature forms across a developmental continuum? I believe that this is the case, denial representing a genotypic defense that is developmentally expressed through a variety of phenotypic forms, ranging from mild to grossly psychotic distortions of reality. Lichtenberg and Slap (1972) saw a developmental continuum wherein denial "becomes progressively refined to more subtle disavowals of the drive derivatives and of the memory links associated with the percept" (p. 785). At the most primitive level there is a complete denial of distressing sensory-perceptual stimuli. Denial would both precede and assist repression at a higher level of neurotic organization and be phenotypically expressed through negation, isolation, detachment, and rationalization through fantasy, or word and act. At a borderline level denial would be expressed through splitting and other derivative forms, such as dissociation, devaluation, and idealization. At a psychotic level denial would be expressed through the infantile, concretistic symptoms of delusions and hallucinations. Implicit in this latter symptomatic expression of psychotic phenomena is the disavowal, or *verleugnung* (Sandler and Freud 1985), that the psychotic symptoms do not actually exist in external reality.

M. came to me for individual psychotherapy when he was 30 years old. He was a young man of superior intelligence who was beset with obsessional thoughts of violence and lingering fears that at any moment he would lose control. When treatment began, M. was ingesting 10 to 15 mg of diazepam daily, but intentionally withheld this information from me until he "confessed" approximately three months after we initiated treatment. He also deceived me into thinking that he managed an avocado grove in a small town near the clinic; after several months he admitted that the grove was owned by his father, and he was "allowed" to live on the property in a small cottage if he did some of the daily property maintenance.

M. had no prior criminal record or psychiatric treatment. He had reportedly never been violent toward anyone. He had received a bachelor's degree with honors in music and composition from a major local university.

M. spent three years in weekly individual psychoanalytic psychotherapy with me and very slowly was able to understand the dynamics of his obsessive-compulsive personality, organized at a borderline level. His defensive functioning matured as he explored the vicissitudes of his inner life, heretofore very frightening for him, and its links to his early childhood experiences.

M.'s parents were both alcoholics. His father also appeared to have many antisocial, psychopathic traits in his characteristic business dealings and marital deceptions. M.'s early memories consisted of watching his mother and father physically assault each other late at night, seeing his mother unconscious on the floor, and witnessing his father burn his mother with cigarettes. His early experiences, similar to his sister's, were marked by familial violence, intense fear, and preoedipal rage.

His personality structure had been shaped by these events in ways that allowed him to deny much of his emotional life. He was able for years, through the combined effects of minor tranquilizers and borderline defenses, to detach from, dissociate, ward off, negate, and most fundamentally, deny painfully unpleasant affective states. Fortunately for him his defensive structuring was not completely impervious, and obsessional fears of becoming violent drove him to seek psychotherapy.

Early childhood memories for M. became more accessible in treatment, and the unpleasant affects accompanying these object and self-representations resurrected from his memory were reexperienced and understood in a more developmentally mature form. But a curious phenomenon began to occur: M. sought out corroboration from his sister that these early violent childhood events had actually happened, and she completely denied them. As other family members in the area joined in this collective denial and railed against M.'s memories, he began to question their basis in reality and ruminated as to whether they were only products of his "fantastical, psychotic mind."

M. had now been living away from his parents for one year and determined to demonstrate to me that his

memories were real, even though I had never questioned them. He enlisted his girlfriend to "stake out"
the parents' home with him to hopefully witness a
reenactment of the violence he remembered as a young
boy.

M. asked me one day if his girlfriend could accom-
pany him to a psychotherapy session. I consented, and
the hour was spent with both M. and his girlfriend
recounting a violent episode between his parents that
they had both witnessed late at night while surreptitiously observing the household. M. passionately told
of the assault he had now observed as an adult, relieved
that he was "not as crazy as everyone thought." Such
actual recapitulation of a childhood trauma–memory in
adulthood allowed M. to further separate, with his
reality testing intact, from his highly pathological
family.

M.'s case illustrates the varieties of conscious deception and
unconscious denial that can exist both intrapsychically and
within a highly disturbed family system. His initial deception
with me was exogenously motivated by a desire to appear more
in control, characteristic of his compulsive personality structure,
which was, at that point, quite dysfunctional. His conscious
deceptions quickly gave way to the gradual exploration of his
borderline manifestations of denial: polarized, split-off representations of his father's badness and his mother's goodness, and his
own self-representation as a violent monster who must, at all
costs, be kept under control. He would deny intense affective
states quite apparent to me and, for a period of time, was able to
dissociate the rage he felt toward his parents that would then
only return in his obsessional and violent fantasies toward
strangers. M. experienced through fantasy what his parents, and
entire family, continued to deny through word and act.

As M. developmentally matured in psychotherapy, there
was no further need for deception. Denial, moreover, became

phenotypically expressed at a higher, neurotic level: M. would negate the need for further treatment and for brief periods would cancel sessions; he would rationalize his parents' behavior and attribute some of their acting out to his behavior as a child; and he would continue to ruminate about ways he could detach from his affective life and literally "not feel."

As M. progressed, his family's pathology intensified, particularly as he confronted them both individually and as a group with their fabrications. Their primitive denial mechanisms also became more apparent to him as he was able to use his keen sense of analysis and circumspection in an adaptive, rather than defensive, fashion. Although his father was psychopathic, M. never felt a desire to act out this process as his father had. Once his fears of such self-explosiveness dissipated, he was content to experience, and creatively shape, his violent fantasies, now considerably diminished, in ways that allowed him both passive-aggressive entertainment and genuinely new insight.

Kernberg (1975), discussing denial from the perspective of Edith Jacobson, characterized denial as a broad group of defensive operations within borderline personality organization. He did not distinguish between denial as a defense against external threat or unconscious affect, and further emphasized the mutuality implicit in denial when two emotionally independent areas of consciousness took their turns being considered irrelevant by the patient, despite persistent memory of each:

> Denial in the patients I am considering may also manifest itself only as simple disregard for a sector of their subjective experience or for a sector of the external world. When pressed the patient acknowledges his intellectual awareness of the sector which has been denied, but again he cannot integrate it with the rest of his emotional experience. [Kernberg 1975, p. 32]

Rinsley (1982) noted, however, that evocative memory is impaired or deficient in the borderline personality and is not so in

the narcissistic personality. He attributed this important diagnostic difference to the degree of obsessional character organization in the narcissistic personality disorder and its reliance on
affective-isolative defenses:

> Whereas the future borderline personality is threat-
> ened with a cut-off of essential libidinal supplies, that
> is, with abandonment, if he pursues separation-
> individuation, the future narcissistic personality is so
> threatened only if separation-individuation compro-
> mises the integrity of the symbiotic selfobject (i.e., the
> tenaciously introjected pathogenic maternal part-
> object). In this latter case, an obsessional character
> organization develops as a defense against the regres-
> sive wish for symbiotic reunion or refusion. Basic to
> this character organization is the prematurely evolving
> capacity for evocative image recall, which is dissoci-
> ated from the affect linked to the pathogenic maternal
> introject. [pp. 165–166]

What is theoretically expectable and clinically evident is the
borderline patient's inability to evoke the memory of a particular
thought, percept, or affect while in the midst of a discordant, and
oftentimes completely opposite, affective state. Verbal
prompting by the psychotherapist redefines the task as one of
recognitive memory, and the borderline patient is able to remember. Kernberg himself shifted the mnemonic task from evocation
to recognition in the paragraph quoted above, expressed in his
words, "when pressed." The expectable correlate in the borderline personality is that developmentally more primitive uses of
denial will be accompanied by increasing evocative memory
problems.

The narcissistic personality, in particular the psychopathic
character, has a much greater capacity for evocative recall of
discordant or opposite ego states, yet their emotional irrelevance

to the individual is just as striking, if not more so, because of the absence of affect and the presence of an apparently coherent, "adultomorphic" false self without evocative memory problems (Winnicott 1960, Rinsley 1982).

Because of the development of this grandiose self-structure, and implicit within it the refusion and identifications among the real self, ideal self, and idealized object (in the psychopath, the more aggressive stranger selfobject), a curious clinical phenomenon has occurred: Denial as an unconscious defense is readily used, even in a very primitive manner by grossly denying large segments of external reality, yet at the same time evocative recall shows little impairment. The psychopathic process allows the individual to cultivate varieties of denial, developmentally ranging from almost psychotic forms to higher-level rationalizations, while at the same time showing no abnormal evocative memory impairments at the lower end of this continuum.

How can this patient show no evocative memory impairment yet evidence such primitive forms of unconscious denial? The answer appears to lie in the grandiose self-structure and its defensive capacity to ward off, through varieties of dissociative mechanisms, highly unpleasant and persecutory introjects, and their accompanying affect states, which could interfere and disrupt evocative recall. Even if intensely unpleasant affect is clinically apparent, the grandiose self-structure provides an isolative, perhaps in some cases obsessional, shell within which the secondary autonomous ego function (Hartmann 1958) of memory is sustained and even perhaps precociously developed. I think these higher-level isolating defenses, forms of denial if one uses the latter in a genotypic sense, are most apparent in the intelligent, socially adaptable, and interpersonally facile psychopathic character.

Appendix I is a detailed and cogent example of a psychopathic individual whose use of unconscious denial and conscious deception is vividly illustrated during a five-month period prior to his recommitment to a state hospital. I have included in the appendix my psychological evaluation, which addresses the question of current dangerousness, and portions of the court hearing transcript during which a determination was made as to whether the patient constituted a danger. I invite the reader to analyze the ways in which exogenous deceit, endogenous deceit, and unconscious denial interrelate in this psychopathic character of superior intelligence.

Forms of conscious deception and unconscious denial pervade the psychopathic process because there is always an external threat; projected aspects of the superior and deprecatory attitude of the individual's grandiose self-structure are perceived in those who are needed (Kernberg 1980). The psychopathic character is haunted by the shadow of his own grandiose self, for the ways in which he induces shame and humiliation in others may always be done to him.

IMITATION AND SIMULATION

The psychopath is an imposter (Greenacre 1958). Shorn of any deep and abiding identifications with others and primarily identified, if at all, with only the stranger selfobject of an aggressive, narcissistic parent, much of his subsequent behavior as an adult involves the conscious imitation and unconscious simulation of other people's thoughts, affects, and activities.

Unlike the person with narcissistic personality disorder who consciously feels, at times, a sense of being a fake (Kernberg 1975), the psychopathic character has no awareness of this "false self" (Winnicott 1960) or the "as-if" quality (Deutsch 1942) of his phenomenal experience. He does not merely play the role, observing the limits of his character, but lives the part, sometimes oblivious to the deceptions promulgated by his behavior.

The psychopath makes widespread use of these pseudoidentification processes. Glasser (1986) called the processes *simulations* and defined them as the unconscious modeling of attitudes or behaviors on that of the object, whether external or introjected, without any change in the structure of the self. A simulation is located on the continuum of internalization processes between intentional copying, or imitation, juxtaposed with introjection, or the internalization of an object that remains possessed but in relationship to the self, and before identification, or the modification of the self-representation to be like the originally incorporated object (Schafer 1968, Meissner 1970, 1971, 1972). It is fundamental to the defensive structure and dynamic functioning of the psychopath.

I am using the term *imitation* to describe the intentional, conscious mimicking of another person's attitudes or behavior. Despite the unique and rather idiosyncratic ways imitation has been defined by others (Gaddini 1969), I am in agreement with Glasser (1986) that this term conjures up choice, intent, and conscious mental activity; and to avoid ambiguity and confusion, I will retain this common-sense usage. Furthermore, if I associate imitation and simulation, once again there emerges the complex interplay of conscious choice and unconscious activity, or defense, that is so important in understanding the psychopathic, if not all psychopathological, processes.

Gaddini's paper "On Imitation" (1969) should not be dismissed, however, as just an unusual understanding of the term *imitation*. If I dare take the liberty of reading *simulation* instead of *imitation* throughout his important analysis, the developmental and dynamic basis of the process can be better understood.

Gaddini (1969) noted that simulations represent and are only concerned with unconscious, omnipotent fantasies, the latter a clinical marker in most character disturbances. They also seem to be originally connected with perceptions, and in my schemata would be closely linked to both self- and object percepts (Meloy 1985). These simulations, and their mnemonic traces, have their prototypes in the "hallucinatory image" (Rapaport 1951) that the infant experiences as reality in the absence of the actual gratifying object and for the purpose of ending emotionally or viscerally painful interoceptive experiences. This "primordial psychic (simulation)" (Gaddini 1969, p. 476) establishes itself in the absence of the object and its aim seems to be magical and omnipotent fusion between the self- and object percept.

On the other hand, introjective processes that are concurrently operative with simulations and begin in the symbiotic phase of development (Mahler et al. 1975) represent what one would like to possess, rather than what one would like to be (Freud 1925). These parallel processes also represent the twofold attitude taken toward the object:

> The primitive (simulative) perception seems to lead to the hallucinatory image, to the phantasies of fusion through modifications of one's own body, and to (simulations), in the direction of the wish *to be* the object. Oral incorporation seems to lead to the phantasies of fusion through incorporation and to introjections, in the direction of *having*, of *possessing*, the object. [Gaddini 1969, p. 477]

The affects of envy and rivalry, pervasive in narcissistic disturbances, also become more comprehensible if rivalry is understood as the affective expression of the simulative-perceptive model, what one would like to be; and envy is understood as the expression of the incorporative-introjective model, what one would like to possess.

Gaddini (1969) viewed identifications as a higher developmental station in which the simulative phenomena of the sensory-percepts and the introjective phenomena of the oral libidinal zones become integrated in the service of reality and the processes of ego adaptation. Gaddini's (1969) understanding of simulations, which predominately obey the pleasure principle and are the sensory-perceptual precursors of identifications, the latter adhering to the reality principle, seems eminently sensible.

I find in simulations the prototype of the narcissistic relationship in which the object percept, and later the object concept, is experienced in the service of the self-representations, whether perceptual or conceptual. Furthermore, simulations, or pseudoidentifications, function as regressive, or perhaps fixated, defenses against actual identification with the object.

This actual identification with the primary parental object and subsequently with other actual objects throughout early development and perhaps the life cycle is impeded because of the "core complex" (Glasser 1986). This central and coherent structure is comprised of a longing for intimate gratification and security, persecutory and annihilatory anxiety, and aggression that has been transposed into sadomasochistic behavior toward the object.

Longings for gratification and security within the mother are characteristics shared by all infants, but in the "core complex" are met with parental responses that are perceived as intrusive, enveloping, or noxious. The infant, in short, is caught on the horns of a sensory-perceptual dilemma. On the one hand, the parental object is the sole source of his gratification; yet on the other hand, it is threatening annihilation and must therefore be negated. One solution is the early sexualization of aggression. Aggression, as a self-preservative response to any physiological or psychological threat to the infant's homeostasis, is converted to sadism, wherein the attitude toward the object has as its aim the infliction of suffering. The intent to destroy, or negate, the object is transformed into a wish to hurt and control the object.

The object is preserved and the viability of the relationship is maintained, but in sadomasochistic terms. The object can then be intensely engaged on the condition that intimacy and union are never experienced (Glasser 1986). The prospect of momentary intimacy brings with it intense annihilatory anxiety, which is quickly warded off by engagement in sadistic acts toward the object to hurt and control, and thus the self remains safe from engulfment.

Governed by these "core complex" anxieties, the psychopathic process impedes identifications because they are experienced as something invasive or possessive, potentially annihi-
lating the self-representations. Any characterological traits
beyond the grandiose self-structure, which is fundamentally a
narcissistic defense against annihilation, are built upon simulation and its conscious, facilitating counterpart, imitation.

The paradox in the adult psychopathic character is that he
has a limited capacity to form any genuine identifications and has
developmentally struggled against identification (Greenson 1954)
with the stranger selfobject; and yet he hungers for, and easily
develops simulations, or pseudoidentifications, with actual objects that he attempts to engage in sadomasochistic relationships. The more deeply identified the psychopath is with the
stranger selfobject, the less rapid and arbitrary the simulations
appear to be.

Greenacre (1958) noted several characteristics in her clinical
cases of imposturing, a form of simulation: a dominant and
dynamically active "family romance," that is, fantasies that have
in common a relationship to the ancestry of the person creating
them (Freud 1909); an intense and circumscribed disturbance in
the sense of identity; an infarction in the sense of reality characterized by a sharp and quick perceptiveness, yet a failure to
protect against detection; a strong sense of exhibitionism and
voyeurism; pathological development of the superego; a compulsive urgency to perpetuate fraud; and a polymorphously perverse sexual organization characterized by sadomasochistic excitement. Most of these characteristics are evident in the
psychopathic process and suggest both failures of oedipal identification and defenses against maternal annihilation:

> The study of the lives of these versatile gentlemen has
> led to the conclusion that sustained imposture serves
> two important functions in the life of the pretenders. It
> is the living out of an oedipal conflict through revival of

the earliest definite image of the father. In so far as the imposture is accomplished, it is the killing of the father through the complete displacement of him. It further serves to give a temporary feeling of completion of identity (sense of self) that can be more nearly achieved in this way than in the ordinary life of an individual so impaired from having been psychologically incorporated by his mother.[Greenacre 1958, pp. 370–371]

The psychopathic process may be characterologically expressed in individuals whose simulations would be best described as schizoid, the "as-if" personalities of Deutsch (1942). In Chapter 3, R. is a clinical example of the schizoid and psychopathic personality. Patients similar to R. manifest a pervasive sense of emptiness and lack of individuality in both their emotional life and moral structure. They are quite suggestible, and despite their obvious antisocial behaviors, they often act in a passive-aggressive manner. In a rather primitive example of this behavior, one such patient, suffering from intermittent nose bleeding, would wipe his blood on one of the walls of the forensic inpatient unit, rather than secure tissues readily available to him. The objectless, affectively deficient internal life of these psychopathic individuals is most apparent in their absence of internal distress and the invariable presence of conflict that they create in the external environment; the hallmark event being the sudden, sadistically violent act that will result in arrest and custody, immediately followed by a quiet return to a passive-aggressive and schizoid mode of existence.

The psychopathic process may also be expressed by individuals whose simulations are so adept, whether they be cognitive, affective, or behavioral, that there is absolutely no suspicion whatsoever that pseudoidentifications may be occurring. This is especially difficult to assess in the socially engaging and intelligent psychopath because of the transient nature of his or her relationships. Any successful assessment of the nature and gen-

uineness of identifications in these individuals must be largely
dependent upon corroborative information from relatives, family, acquaintances, and other clinicians.

> T. D., a probationer, was a 16-year-old Caucasian male
> of superior intelligence. He was currently held in juve-
> nile custody, but was allowed certain day trips with his
> probation officer to facilitate planning and placement
> upon his release. On one such day trip the probation
> officer was amazed and pleased to find out that T. D.
> shared with her an interest in metaphysics. In fact, he
> displayed a remarkable intellectual command of the
> writings of Alfred North Whitehead, one of her most
> favorite philosopher-theologians. They conversed for
> several hours while riding in her automobile, and sub-
> sequently the probation officer found herself much
> more closely identified with and sympathetic toward
> the plight of T. D. His intellect also became a personal
> strength that she noted with high regard in her written
> recommendation to the court.
>
> Several weeks following these events, the proba-
> tion officer learned from a colleague that T. D. had
> specifically inquired of others to find out her personal
> interests; and when he learned of her metaphysical
> avocation, he acquired numerous books which he read
> in preparation for his encounters with her. She later
> found out that he was asking questions about his new
> resident manager with ostensibly the same purpose in
> mind. The probation officer consciously felt hurt and
> angry toward T. D., but also acknowledged to me her
> continuing admiration of his prowess and intellect.

T. D. imitated the probation officer's intellectual interests to
pursue his own ends. There was no coincidental, reciprocal sense
of emotional resonance and intellectual exchange between them.

The well-honed, imitative, and mirroring aspects of T. D.'s behavior, in this case in the intellectual sphere, enhanced the probation officer's self-esteem. Her narcissistic admiration of her own metaphysical knowledge increased as she identified with, and consciously admired, the metaphysical understanding of T. D.

This case illustrates a process that I call *malignant pseudoidentification*. It is the process by which the psychopath consciously imitates or unconsciously simulates a certain behavior to foster the victim's identification with this individual, thus increasing the victim's vulnerability to exploitation. Malignant pseudoidentification involves transference and countertransference phenomena wherein the psychopath simulates the more subtle narcissistic characteristics of the victim at an earlier, and unconscious, developmental level.

Mental health and legal professionals are most vulnerable to malignant pseudoidentification during work with the psychopath when the interactional content concerns their competency, autonomy, or knowledge. The goal of the psychopathic character is to increase the professional's genuine empathy for the individual's plight through pseudoidentification with the professional's narcissism.

The most common example of this is the client-patient who will compliment the professional for his competency or knowledge. On a more subtle level the psychopathic individual will simulate affects and mannerisms of the victim, and both mirroring and twinship (Kohut 1971) transferences will be acted out in an alloplastic, or destructive, manner. It is not unheard of for defense attorneys, enamored by the perceived helpfulness and competence of intelligent psychopathic clients, to find themselves considering ethical violations, and perhaps even illegal behavior, in the service of their defendants. Again, the victim's felt quality of perfection (Rothstein 1980) is enhanced, and a strong empathic bond is developed with the psychopath through his imitation and simulation of the victim's narcissistic investments. The victim will oftentimes be deluded into thinking that the psychopath shares this feeling of identification and bonding. In a legal setting the adversarial roles that attorneys play will foster ongoing processes of intrapsychic splitting so that twin-ship alliances between attorney and psychopathic defendant may render whole sectors of reality testing unavailable to the attorney-victim.

Individuals who deny their own narcissistic investments and consciously perceive themselves as being "helpers" endowed with a special amount of altruism are exceedingly vulnerable to the affective simulation of the psychopath. Empathy is fostered in the victim through the expression of quite visible affects that infer a transference dependency on an original object. The pre-sentation of tearfulness, sadness, longing, fear, remorse, and guilt may induce in the "helper" a strong sense of compassion, while unconsciously enhancing the "helper's" narcissistic invest-ment in self as the embodiment, or at least a whole representa-tion, of goodness. The psychopathic expression of such simulated affects may be quite compelling to the observer and difficult to distinguish from deeply cathected emotion. It can usually be identified, however, by two events: First, the clinical observer who has analyzed the narcissistic roots of his own empathic responses will feel little or no compassion during this outpouring of emotion by the psychopath. In fact countertransference ele-ments of a sadistic nature may be felt by the observer, tele-scoping back to hateful feelings of the biological parent toward this once vulnerable child. Second, the psychopath will recom-pensate much too quickly following such affective expression, leaving the clinical observer with the impression that the play has ended, the curtain has fallen, and the imposture, for the moment, is finished.

The psychopath, in brief, has no capacity for empathy. But there is an exquisite capacity for simulation and imitation of others' narcissistically invested self-concepts, whether they be expressed through ideation, affect, or mannerisms. The adeptness and social facility of such simulation and imitation appear to correlate with the psychopath's intelligence.

PROJECTIVE IDENTIFICATION AND OBJECT CONTROL

The role of projective identification as a defensive and intrapsychic process in psychopathy undergirds simulative and imitative dynamics. It is a process in which affective and ideational components of the individual are attributed to another, while at the same time the other actual person is controlled, or attempted to be controlled. Projective identification, by necessity, implies both false attribution and object control.

In a more precise sense in the psychopathic process, I must speak of projective *pseudo*identification or simulation. The projective-introjective cycle is a recurrent one involving repetitive simulations, and it is closely tied to incorporative and expulsive libidinal themes. The psychic content involved in projective pseudoidentification comes from within and without the grandiose self-structure.

From within the grandiose self-structure, ideational and affective material from the various fused self- and object concepts may be subject to projective identification. This material is potentially more easily available to consciousness because it is more ego syntonic for the psychopath and is characterized by attitudes of perfection, grandiosity, and power. This form of projective identification with the actual object is more easily tolerated and hedonic for the psychopath because, in a sense, it is psychic bathing under the narcissistic light that is also illuminated and extended through the shadow of the other.

From without the grandiose self-structure, projective identification may mobilize anxiety and discomfort during the psychopathic process. Ideational and affective components from this ego dystonic sphere of psychic life originate from the persecutory, and oftentimes sadistic, introjects that continually threaten the homeostasis of the grandiose self-structure. Such material is characterized by attitudes of envy, greed, rage, sadism, acute dysphoria, contempt, and arrogance. There is usually a paranoid theme present. This is projected as a means to attain psychic distance, yet must be controlled through pseudoidentification with the aggressor to prevent its monstrous exaggeration in the mind of the psychopath as a fearful predator.

A compelling example of such use of projective identification was found in the case of a 34-year-old sexual psychopath, whom I evaluated following thirteen years of hospitalization as a mentally disordered sex offender in California. He had been originally committed for the bondage, forced oral copulation, rape, electrocution, and strangling to death of a 15-year-old female stranger. These are excerpts from my report:

> Hitchhiker # 3 was the victim. C. V. stated that he picked her up with the intent of "getting sex" but he also felt awkward and shy. She came to his apartment and they shared two joints and engaged in small talk. . . . She then asked him to leave with her to attend a concert with several of her friends. V. reported feeling very paranoid after smoking the joints . . . he stated, "We merged by the front door, I kissed her impulsively . . . she pushed me away . . . I snapped . . . I was watching myself, I was possessed by this pure evil, I couldn't do anything about it and I dragged her back into the room."
>
> Although V. does not consciously feel his dissociated affect, he is prone to projecting it; that is, attributing it to other people and places. Several weeks ago he commented to his mother that he felt "a lot of evil" while in jail. He also reported to Dr. A. that he had "sensed evil" in his one-room apartment several weeks prior to the offense. This reasonably establishes a

thirteen-year history of dissociated affect that is still present yet consciously unknown to him. These emotions were once expressed in a violent and sadistic manner, yet, in a sense, remain timelessly alive and are now felt by V. in a projected form that assumes for him the meaning of "evil."

In both cases, from within and without, the psychopath attempts to resonate with the actual object, and in this process may unconsciously manipulate for a particular identified goal. The unconscious motivation is to maintain the homeostasis of the grandiose self-structure, which is always tenuous because of the necessity of continuous externalizing and internalizing of psychic content. Stability of psychic content, which is not available to the psychopath, appears to follow stability of psychic structure in normal development.

Is conscious imitation easier for the psychopathic individual because of the predominance of projective pseudoidentification? I think that it is. The young toddler very smoothly simulates with little conscious effort and no conscious awareness. The varieties of vertical dissociability (Kohut 1971), what I genotypically refer to as splitting, allow for the compartmentalizing of alternative means of interpersonal expression, which find their roots in discrete affective and ideational components. Practicing, or the "elated investment in the exercise of the autonomous functions" (Mahler et al. 1975, p. 69), is an easier process for the toddler precisely because of the dissociative flexibility of consciousness at that subphase of separation–individuation. Conscious imitation in the defensively more mature adult is more difficult because of the predominance of horizontal (repressive) rather than vertical (splitting) defenses (Kohut 1971).

There is no repression, or horizontal defensive operation, in the psychopathic process; paradoxically there is thus no potential for the interfering emergence of this preconscious, or unconscious, repressed material during periods of imitation or simula-

tion. The pathological residue of separation–individuation difficulties allows the psychopath to continuously practice varieties
of ideational and affective states through pseudoidentification
and projective pseudoidentification. The verticality of defenses is
most helpful when alternative, and perhaps very contradictory,
affects and ideations are imitated or simulated; for there is no
conscious sense of ambiguity or contradiction in the psychopath's
phenomenal experience of self. This may account for the chameleonlike effect of certain psychopathic individuals (Bauder 1985).

The distinction between projection and projective identification is that the latter involves a controlling relationship between the individual and the object of the projection. The concept
reflects combinations of Klein's work (1946) concerning projective and introjective processes between mother and child and
Bion's (1955) elaboration of her work through his metaphor of the
"container" into which psychic content can be placed. Finell (1986)
noted that the term *projective identification* has quasi-magical
overtones and "describes the mysterious interplay of two psy-
ches around projection and introjection, merger, and telepa-
thy. . . ." (p. 103). Whipple (1986) quite persuasively argued that
projective identification is only a metaphor, and to write as if
psychic contents are actually put into someone else, that one
literally becomes a container for an evacuated product, is reifica-
tion (Dorpat 1983). Grotstein (1981) hypothesized that projective
identification is the defensive process by which feelings are
communicated that are too primitive to be verbally expressed.
He wrote, "I have come to the belief – and insist upon the definition – that all projection is projective identification, from the
vantage point of the projector" (p. 202).

The psychopathic process that is predominately expressed
through sexual sadism on the part of a male toward a female
provides a compelling illustration of projective identification and
the sequential shift that occurs prior to, during, and following the
sexually sadistic act. The victim who is characteristically targeted is initially selected for her stereotypical and perceptual

"goodness of fit." During this beginning period of predation she is conceptualized as a representational object that is ideally loved and capable of expressing ideal love. The victim is projectively identified with traits of the ideal object within the grandiose self-structure, which, by virtue of the fusions that have occurred within the grandiose self between the real self-, ideal self-, and ideal object representations, are experienced as an extension of "I."

Again, I want to reiterate that this is not a psychotic identification or a mergence of ego boundaries that implies a loss of perceptual separation between self and object. The identification, or more precisely, the malignant pseudoidentification, is between *conceptual* representations of ideal self and object within the grandiose self-structure. The sexual psychopath at this point of initial projective identification will consciously feel expansive, exhilarated, and in omnipotent control of his behavior and that of the victim being stalked. This experience may be enhanced by the use of cocaine hydrochloride or methamphetamine hydrochloride, psychostimulants that pharmacologically fuel this sense of expansive pleasure.

At the moment of physical contact with the victim, idealized attributions with which the psychopath projectively identifies are suddenly challenged by the reality test of the victim's actual verbal or physical resistance. The victim may be a stranger, and affects associated with the stranger selfobject (Grotstein 1982) such as envy, rage, and persecutory fear are mobilized within the psychopath. The projective content then shifts to psychic material outside the grandiose self-structure that is persecutory and oftentimes sadistic. Affective tones of envy and oral rage emerge as the need for omnipotent control intensifies in the face of an actual physical struggle with the victim. Intrapsychically the persecutory introjects, the "not-I" content of the mind, are being projected onto the victim, and the stranger selfobject within the grandiose self-structure is being identified with to preserve the conceptual fusions and homeostasis of the grandiose self.

Interpersonally the victim is now perceived as a devalued and highly threatening actual object because she now carries the persecutory introjects of the psychopath. Psychodynamically the sexual psychopath has identified with the aggressor, the stranger selfobject, and a tremendous amount of sexual aggression is mobilized to protect himself from the perceived "monster" that he must omnipotently control and devalue at all costs. The violence that follows must shame, humiliate, degrade, and perhaps destroy the actual victim to sufficiently devalue the intrapsychic material that has threatened the grandiose self-structure.

Whereas the victim began as an idealized conceptual extension of the grandiose self, she is transformed into a monstrous object that carries the persecutory projections of the psychopath and therefore must be devalued to be controlled. When projective identification shifts from within to without the grandiose self- structure, sexualized aggression is mobilized and expressed to defend against the predominately unconscious affects of envy and greed. In a sense, the violence of the sexual psychopath reconstitutes the grandiose self-structure in the face of annihilatory and persecutory fear. Projective identification returns to a more ego-syntonic defensive operation within the grandiose self-structure once the actual victim has been devalued.

Other narcissistically disordered individuals will use projective identification in a similar manner, but usually only in fantasy. The aggressive, alloplastic expression of projective identification in a violent form is the sole province of the psychopathic process. The affective dimension of such an intrapsychic defense grows exponentially because interpersonal reality is engaged.

But does the sexual psychopath become psychotic at any point in the sequence that I have hypothesized? This question also has important ramifications in forensic evaluations concerning the temporary insanity of the sexual psychopath.

If we define psychosis as a loss of reality testing (Frosch 1983a), I think not. I have had the opportunity to clinically explore in detail with several dozen sexual psychopaths the sequence of their conscious thoughts, affects, and behavior during episodes of violence. In those individuals, I did not see complete loss of reality testing. In the absence of psychotic content, such as hallucinations and delusions, there is, instead, the striking presence of altered structure during these events, most clearly described as varieties of splitting or dissociability of consciousness. I will explore this in detail in the next section of this chapter. Suffice it here to say that self- and object concepts are radically altered during violence, most notably in the sequential idealizing and devaluing of the victim as a conceptual extension of the grandiose self, and then as a conceptual extension of the persecutory introjects. But the perceptual distinctiveness between self and other, both at a representational level and an interpersonal level, is never lost. The victim, for instance, may assume the monstrous characteristics of the sexual psychopath's mother, but she never becomes the mother, as may be the case in the "sudden murder" (Lunde 1975) of the paranoid schizophrenic.

John Wayne Gacy, Jr., was arrested on December 21, 1978. He had lived quietly in a small house at 8213 Summerdale in Norwood Park, an unincorporated area north and west of Chicago. During the six years prior to his arrest Gacy sadistically assaulted, raped, and murdered thirty-three boys, and buried the majority of them in the crawl space underneath his house.

During his trial, Richard Rappaport, M.D., a private forensic psychiatrist, gave expert testimony linking Gacy's sexually psychopathic behavior and projective identification and placed them in the larger context of a borderline personality organization:

> In the scenario, "he brings . . . young boys to his home," where he can star in a play scripted by himself, and the play itself is an example of the second primitive ego defense common to borderlines: projective identification. "First," Rappaport said, "he begins to act as a

father to them . . . acts tenderly . . . tries to show them that he has a fatherly instinct and they are boys he can take care of. As I mentioned, these are . . . young men and boys who are at the height of the oedipal themselves, who have the characteristics of the developed phallus . . . they are boys . . . he can identify with, who he recognizes as having qualities that he feels. . .

"Now, he'd get these boys and he would begin to project onto them the qualities that he had inside himself and that he didn't like . . . He could say that they are selling themselves, as he sold himself to try and impress his father. He could say that they were degraded . . . dehumanized as his father made him." He begins to feel it is not himself he is hating, but the young men.

At first, Rappaport said, Gacy would have been at least unconsciously aware that the familiar hatred he sensed in the boys actually existed within him. But "at some point in the scenario that he goes through" Gacy would progress from simple projection to projective identification. "He then feels that these qualities . . . exist in the other person. They are no longer a part of him. They are in this other person and he feels expunged or cleansed . . . Now he sees these persons as . . . bad . . . homicidal . . . threatening. . .

"He is then the father in identifying with the aggressor, and these victims, these boys, are then himself. He can . . . kill them . . . and in a way rid himself forever of these qualities that are inside of himself: the hostile threats and frightening figures that pervade his unconscious. He is so convinced that these qualities exist in this other person, he is completely out of touch with reality . . . and he has to get rid of them and save himself . . . he has to kill them." [Cahill 1986, pp. 339–340]

SPLITTING AND DISSOCIATION

D. W. Winnicott wrote in 1964, "It is not possible to conceive of a repressed unconscious with a split mind; instead what is found is dissociation . . . it is not possible for a split mind to have an unconscious" (p. 453).

Satinover (1986) noted that Jung (1907, 1916) was the first to attempt to conceptualize psychic dissociability through self-analysis of his own narcissistic and preoedipal difficulties. He called these "personified autonomous complexes" and they were always demarcated into stereotyped opposites (Jung 1916).

Freud (1938) articulated the difference between psychic dissociability and repression, the former more commonly termed *splitting.* Kohut (1971) crystallized this distinction by conceptualizing vertical, rather than horizontal, splits in the psyche of the narcissistic personality. He wrote that there is

> a specific, chronic structural change to which I would like to refer in a modification of Freud's terminology as a *vertical split in the psyche.* The ideational and emotional manifestations of a vertical split in the psyche — in contrast to such *horizontal splits* as those brought about on a deeper level by repression and on a higher level by negation — are correlated to the side-by-side, continuous existence of otherwise incompatible psychological attitudes *in depth.* [pp. 176–177]

> . . . We are not dealing with the isolation of circumscribed contents from one another, or with the isolation of ideation from affect, but with the side-by-side existence of cohesive personality attitudes with different goal structures, different pleasure aims, different moral and aesthetic values. [p. 183]

Kernberg, although viewing primitive splitting as a defensive process rather than a regressive deficiency as Jung and Kohut did, similarly wrote,

... What are completely separated from each other are
complex psychic manifestations, involving affect, ideational content, subjective and behavioral manifestations ... actually, we might say that there exist alternating "ego states," and I use the concept "ego state" as
a way of describing these repetitive, temporarily ego
syntonic, compartmentalized psychic manifestations.
[1976, p. 20]

There appears to be a general consensus in the psychoanalytic literature that one of the fundamental features of borderline
ego functioning is the presence of unconscious dual or multiple
identity processes (Fast 1974, Searles 1986). In fact, the term
borderline itself may hold within it the metaphor of dual or
multiple lines of demarcation that separate distinguishable
states of mind: intrapsychic experiences of self and object that do
not interpenetrate opposite valences, but instead vertically de-
scend as "psychological deep structure" (Ogden 1986) to a primitive psychotic core. This so-called psychotic core is quite clinically
apparent in transient psychotic states (Singer 1977), mild formal
thought disorder (Singer and Wynne 1965), and indications of
primary process structure and content in the borderline personality disorder (Urist 1980) because of an absence of horizontal
defenses to protect conscious "ego states" from an upsurge of
psychotic material.

Interpenetration occurs, instead, among these hypothesized horizontal levels, such as the absence of a distinction
between ego and id, since without repression the latter cannot
exist (Jacobson 1964, Kernberg 1980). And specific to the psychopathic process, the fusions that occur within the grandiose self-
structure between real self-, ideal self-, and ideal object representations preclude a horizontal demarcation between real self
and ideal selfobject representations as forerunners of superego
development (Jacobson 1964, Kernberg 1980). Such varieties of
dissociability, or vertical splits in the psyche, and horizontal

fusions are pathognomonic of borderline ego functioning in general, narcissistic conditions and the psychopathic process in particular.

Dissociation is, in my view, a phenotypic defensive process that expresses the genotypic defensive operation of splitting; it is ubiquitous in the psychopath. Note, however, that I am not just referring to a dissociative state, such as depersonalization or derealization; neither am I implying that amnesia is necessarily present as a product of the dissociative defense.

Yet varieties of dissociability in the psychopathic process, pathognomonic of borderline ego functioning and aggressive narcissism, invite several intriguing questions whose answers shed further light upon the psychopathic individual. First, if dissociative experiences, such as derealization and depersonalization as defined in DSM-III-R (American Psychiatric Association 1987) are extreme clinical manifestations of dissociation as a common defensive process in psychopathy, are these clinical experiences found in the phenomenology of the psychopath? And, if so, when? Second, if dissociative experiences are common to hysteria in its many forms (hysterical conversion reactions, hysterical personality, histrionic personality, somatization disorder, Briquet's syndrome), is there an empirical relationship between psychopathy and hysteria? And third, if varieties of splitting, or dissociability, are common to the subjective experience of the psychopath, could a more intelligent psychopathic individual malinger multiple personality, an extreme form of dissociative state with its attendant amnesic periods, to avoid responsibility for his or her intentional acts?

Depersonalization and Derealization

Dissociation as a defensive process is, by definition, ego syntonic because of its developmental role in character formation. Dissociative experiences such as depersonalization and derealization are usually clinically identified by their ego-dystonic nature. The individual phenomenally experiences an alteration in the sense of reality (Frosch 1983a) without a concomitant loss of reality testing. There is an intrapsychic change in the self-percepts (depersonalization) or the object percepts (derealization) that is *unusual*. "The symptom of depersonalization involves an alteration in the perception or experience of the self in which the usual sense of one's own reality is temporarily lost or changed" (American Psychiatric Association 1987, p. 275). Likewise, derealization is manifested "by a strange alteration in the perception of one's surroundings so that a sense of the reality of the external world is lost" (American Psychiatric Association 1987, p. 276).

The intrapsychic boundaries between self- and object percepts are not lost, which would render the individual psychotic; instead, the boundaries are distorted and are phenomenally experienced as a change of temporal or spatial contiguity, both interoceptively and exteroceptively. Dissociative experiences are transient sensory-perceptual states that do not necessarily affect self- or object *concepts*.

Ego-dystonic dissociative states are accorded a place in the diagnosis of borderline personality disorders (Kernberg 1975, Gunderson and Kolb 1978, American Psychiatric Association 1980, 1987). Dissociative states, however, are noted to occur in 30 to 70 percent of the normal population (Lehman 1974, American Psychiatric Association 1980, 1987) and should be diagnosed as a psychiatric problem only when they impair individual or interpersonal functioning.

Noting this considerable overlap between normal and pathological groups, Ludolph (1983) compared two samples of borderline and normal subjects for the presence of dissociative states, the adaptive value and affective intensity of the experiences, and the psychopathology of the reported experiences. She found that 73 percent of the control group ($N = 24$) reported at least one dissociative event, while only 41 percent ($N = 18$) of the inpatient borderline subjects reported dissociative states. The borderline sample, however, was much more likely to have chronic dissociative experiences if they admitted to any at all, and the dissociation was more likely to be intense, painful, and maladaptive, sometimes severely impairing reality testing or causing a life-threatening loss of impulse control. Of the borderline sample, 22 percent reported a completely discontinuous sense of self, feeling at times that they became an entirely different person. Additionally important was the finding that one third of the borderline sample adamantly denied any dissociative experiences. They expressed this extreme defensiveness against such experience in an anxious or angry manner. Ludolph (1983) hypothesized that these "extreme defenders" could be the most pathological dissociators and could represent one of two bimodal distribution points of dissociation among borderline personality disorders; that is, one group exhibits chronic and highly dysfunctional symptoms of dissociation and another group rigidly defends against such impending experiences. She found virtually none of these characteristics in the normal sample and, in fact, determined that 40 percent of the controls described dissociative states that were largely adaptive. Ludolph (1983) concluded,

> Borderlines plagued as they are with difficulties in the transition from narcissistic to objective reality, from symbiosis to separation, would experience the dissociative tendency as highly disorganizing, threatening to pull them back into psychotic or near psychotic disorganization. Borderline personalities do not have a sure enough grasp of reality to play with or electively suspend their sense of what is real. [p. 14]

It appears to me that normals maintain the integrity of whole self- and object percepts during dissociative experiences; but at the level of borderline personality organization dissociative states contain highly valenced part self- and object percepts that are, in a sense, experientially magnified and therefore are affectively felt as threatening, anxiety provoking, and potentially psychotically disorganizing.

Dissociative states also appear to correlate with high levels of affective or autonomic arousal. The psychopathic process is peculiarly suited to dissociative states for several reasons. First, the psychopath has a proclivity to seek sensation, or high arousal, because of general peripheral autonomic hyporeactivity (see Chapter 2). Second, the impaired capacity to form attachments and deeply internalize objects of identification renders conscious experiences of dissociation, or separateness from self or reality, unusual but quite tolerable. Dissociative states enhance and exaggerate the psychopath's normal feelings of detachment or removal from actual objects or surroundings. Dissociative states would accelerate the propensity of the psychopath to disidentify with his or her external reality.

Third, during periods of actual physical violence, the victim would be perceived as a two-dimensional, perceptually flat, stereotyped object, rather than a whole, multidimensional human being. In certain cases, the dissociative state may even be partially controlled to ensure that the victim remains derealized and flat, without emotional depth, usually by preventing or minimizing conversation between the psychopath and the victim. And fourth, memories of dissociative experiences can be used as rationalizations for avoiding responsibility for one's actions and choices, or they may support denial of certain events because of their dreamlike, unreal quality. This latter phenomenon illustrates the way in which dissociative states may dynamically support splitting and other dissociative defenses. The unusualness of a memory renders it easily compartmentalized as, perhaps, a dream that did not actually occur in reality at all. An attenuation in the sense of reality impairs the individual's ability to test reality in memory.

Derealization and depersonalization in the psychopathic process are most clinically evident in descriptions of subjective experience by the psychopath during periods of predation or actual violence.

The following case material illustrates depersonalization, derealization, and dissociative defenses in an individual who had forcefully orally copulated, raped, electrocuted, and strangled to death a 15-year-old female stranger. I evaluated this individual thirteen years after the crime during his civil trial to consider release from hospital commitment. He had originally been found to be a mentally disordered sex offender in 1973 in California (Penal Code Section 6316 et seq., repealed in 1982). This is the same case I used to illustrate projective identification earlier. Here I excerpt other portions of my evaluation to the court:

> He stated, "I was watching myself, I was possessed by this pure evil, I couldn't do anything about it and I dragged her back into the room."
>
> V. became increasingly tearful at this point and began to cry. I encouraged this, and he began to sob deeply and uncontrollably. He stated again that he has had problems talking, that it feels like a drug, a pain-killer, when he tries to talk.
>
> With my insistence he returned to his memory of the crime. He stated that he had his hand around her mouth and waist, and they fell on the bed together. She lay on her stomach, and he tied her hands with a string from her halter top. She said in a terrified voice, "please let me go." He remembered getting a rope from his chest of drawers, and felt scared and panicky, like he was "in a dream." He tied her legs spread-eagled to the bed, and then had the thought, "you stupid dummy . . . you don't even know how to rape a person right." He felt humiliated, untied her legs, took her jeans off, and retied them to the bed. "The demonic person was taking control." He reported that he then performed

cunnilingus on her, and she kept saying, "Please let me go. I won't tell." He stated to me that [the victim] was symbolic of other women, and there were "elements of degradation and humiliation there, but not to [the victim] herself." He straddled her waist, and told her to lick and kiss his penis, which she did. At this point he reported his first conscious feelings of sexual arousal, and his penis became erect. He penetrated her vaginally and reached orgasm. "The orgasm came quick, her vagina was small, lots of feeling."

V. began to sob again, "I felt disgust, regret, the dark side of me liked it." He expressed at this point what I consider deep remorse and emotion for the victim, her family, and his family.

"I began to panic, she was crying, my mind was racing. I went to the kitchen to get a cord. The dark side is telling me, 'kill her, kill her.' I couldn't do anything about it. I put a pillow over her face, attached alligator clips to her nipples, and plugged the cord into the wall. The radio was playing, I couldn't hear anything. I was thinking, 'kill her quickly.' She was still breathing when I removed the pillow. Her chest was moving, so I strangled her." V. then reported that as he was straddling and strangling her, he looked in the mirror and saw his face. He said it was "evil, contorted, demonic, another personality took over and I was watching this, but I couldn't control it." He stated that he heard his own voice speak, but it did not sound like him. It only matched his face in the mirror. His voice then said, "Oh, boy, you're going to get the gas chamber now."

Objective personality profiles like V.'s have a probability of being associated with an alcoholic father, and of having been physically abused by him. Such individuals are inclined to develop a dissociative response as an adaptation to the stress of violence when they were young children. . . . At a deeper, intrapsychic level, V. is usually quite detached from his own affective, or emotional, experiences. He feels personally isolated from others, and sees himself as alien and different from other people. He has great difficulty consciously managing his feelings when they do surface, and will experience them as overwhelming, frightening, and controlling.

His emotions are not well controlled at all by his thinking process, and he will feel led by them. He will deal with early, primitive oral aggression by distancing from it, making it static or depersonalized, and will reestablish control by focusing on details in his external surroundings.

V. oftentimes feels an impending sense of loss of control which is due to unconscious affects of a sexual and aggressive nature that remain largely unknown to him. Because of this, he is not able to read affectively charged situations very well, and may arrive at surprisingly inappropriate interpretations of reality following these situations. V. dissociates, or wards off to an extreme, early and intense feelings of hostility and rage toward his parental figures. He has no conscious insight or understanding concerning this dissociated affect and continues to understand it as the "darker, evil side" of him. He blandly characterizes his early family experience, and has little insight into connections between his instant offense, his poorly formed representations of his mother and father in his mind, and pathological rage toward his parents. Again, these feelings are not consciously felt, but remain a part of his psychology in a highly-charged and dissociated state. . . .

V. is generally inept at securing his affectional

needs in a socially appropriate manner. When faced
with his own ineptitude, he will devalue both himself
and the person from whom he is seeking affection, and
at that moment may become vulnerable to the rage
against the affectional object that he usually succeeds
in dissociating completely from his consciousness. Any
antisocial behavior that would result from the loss of
control of these dissociated affects would be reactive
rather than proactive. This is illustrated by the initial
sequence of events prior to the murder. The young girl
orally gratified him with her marijuana cigarettes, he
sought further direct sexual gratification, her rejection
of his advances became his mother giving and denying,
and, in his own words, disinhibited by the marijuana,
he "snapped."

Despite V.'s contention that the crime was due
partly to difficulties with girlfriends, he described carrying on an active sexual relationship with a neighborhood girl right up until days prior to the crime. Concurrently with this normal sexual activity and dating, V.
developed a subterranean fantasy life involving sadomasochism, and also began to act it out with hitchhikers. This concurrent activity, extremely compartmentalized and separated in real life, is another indication
of the dissociative and splitting aspects that are highly
prevalent and pathological in compulsive murder. . . .

This case graphically illustrates the ways in which unconscious defensive operations of a dissociative nature lend support
to the ego-dystonic experience of a dissociative state during
actual violence.

Theodore Robert Bundy is, perhaps, the quintessential serial murderer and sexual psychopath. A veritable cottage in-
dustry has sprung forth on the lecture circuit and in the popular

press around this man who probably sexually molested and murdered several dozen young women in the states of Washington, Utah, Colorado, and Florida between 1974 and 1978. He currently awaits execution on Florida's Death Row.

Michaud and Aynesworth (1983) accumulated extensive tape-recorded interviews with Theodore Robert Bundy that capitalized on his inclination to dissociate and ironically revealed much of his dissociative psychopathology. They interviewed Bundy at Florida State Prison following his conviction and death sentence for several murders he committed on January 15, 1978, in the Chi Omega sorority house, Florida State University.

Michaud and Aynesworth (1983) enticed Bundy to discuss with them during the course of their interviews the hypothesized psychopathology of a compulsive murderer. The condition of their discussions rested upon the use of the third person so that Theodore Bundy could not be personally implicated through any untoward use of the manuscript. Such a journalistic arrangement was wholly conducive to the detachment and disidentification of the psychopathic process. I have taken excerpts from the transcripts in Theodore Bundy's own words to illustrate elements of the dissociative process, both as unconscious defense and clinical event:

> ... But the significance of this particular occasion was that while he stayed off the streets and vowed he'd never do it again and recognized the horror of what he had done and certainly was *frightened by what he saw happening* [italics added], it took him only three months to get over it. ... (p. 110) What happened was this entity inside him was not capable of being controlled any longer ... at least not for any considerable period of time. It began to try to justify itself, to create rationalizations for what it was doing. Perhaps to satisfy the rational, normal part of the individual. One

element that came into play was anger, hostility. But I don't think that was an overriding emotion when he would go out hunting, or however you want to describe it. On most occasions it was a high degree of anticipation, of excitement, or arousal. It was an adventuristic kind of thing. . . .

The fantasy that accompanies and generates the anticipation that precedes the crime is always more stimulating than the immediate aftermath of the crime itself. He should have recognized that what really fascinated him was the hunt, the adventure of searching out his victims. And, to a degree, possessing them physically as one would possess a potted plant, a painting, or a Porsche. Owning, as it were, this individual. [p. 111]

Bundy spoke of the hypothetical conversations between the psychopath and his victim:

There'd be some. Since this girl in front of him represented not a person, but again the image, or something desirable, the last thing we would expect him to want to do would be to personalize this person . . . [p. 115] But once the individual would have her in a spot where he had, you know, security over her, then there would be a minimum amount of conversation which would be, you know, designed to avoid developing some kind of a relationship [pp. 128–129] . . . to remove himself from the personal aspects of the encounter, the interchange. Chattering and flattering and entertaining, *as if seen through a motion picture screen* [italics added]. He would be engaging in the pattern just for the purpose of making the whole encounter seem legitimate. . . . [p. 125]

He commented on the use of alcohol to disinhibit and perceptually dull the experience:

> Well, drinking has an effect on both parties. . . . on the one hand, the more intoxicated he became, the more repressed his normal codes of behavior. And the more she drank, the more she would lend herself to stereotypes. . . . [p. 126]

The victim was derealized from a whole object deserving of empathy to a part object for narcissistic gratification:

> They wouldn't be stereotypes necessarily. But they would be reasonable facsimiles to women as a class. A class not of women, per se, but a class that has almost been created through the mythology of women and how they are used as objects. [p. 118]

In his own handwriting Bundy scribbled the following notes during the January 7, 1980, jury selection for his murder trial of 14-year-old Kimberly Leach:

> I'm getting writer's cramp which is a small price to pay for missing the proceedings. I just looked up and heard some guy with moon-crater cheeks say that he had formed an opinion of my guilt, but that he would put it aside. Now Africano [Bundy's attorney] is questioning the man. His personal opinion is that Mr. Bundy is guilty. Blah. It's just entertainment. I will feel and act like an interested bystander. None of this has anything to do with me. [p. 282]

Psychopathy and Hysteria

The empirical evidence for an association between psychopathy and hysteria has been accumulating for nearly a century. Moravesik (1894) reported a high prevalence of criminal histories among hysterical subjects, and Kraepelin (1915) noted the frequent mingling of antisocial and hysterical traits in his patients. Psychodynamic links between the two disorders were constructed by several writers (Rosanoff 1938, Vaillant 1975, Chodoff 1982).

Hysterical conversion reactions and somatization disorders, as variants of the generic hysterical process, have also been empirically correlated with psychopathy (Robins et al. 1952, Guze 1964, Robins 1966, Cloninger and Guze 1970, Maddocks 1970, Guze et al. 1971a, 1971b, Spalt 1980).

Psychopathy and somatization disorder appear to be familially related. Several studies (Ljungberg 1957, Arkonac and Guze 1963, Woerner and Guze 1968) found a high prevalence of psychopathy among the first-degree relatives of their hysterical patient sample. Cloninger and Guze (1975) reported that mothers of female criminals had high rates of hysteria and that hysteria was present in more than 75 percent of the daughters of psychopathic fathers. Cloninger and colleagues (1975) were the first to propose a multifactorial threshold model of shared genetic liability among female hysterics and male and female psychopaths. Adoption studies have also supported an association between the two disorders (Cadoret 1978, Cloninger et al. 1984).

With the advent of DSM-III (American Psychiatric Association 1980), a descriptive typology emerged that differentiated somatization disorders, dissociative reactions, and histrionic personality disorder. Briquet's syndrome, hysterical conversion reactions, and hysterical personality are included, respectively, in these three diagnostic groups.

Lilienfeld and colleagues (1986) completed a landmark study to attempt to replicate the association between antisocial personality disorder and somatization disorder, clarify the role of gender as a moderator variable, and explore the relationship of histrionic personality disorder to both somatization disorder and antisocial personality. Drawing from a sample of 250 psychiatric patients in a variety of inpatient, outpatient, and consultation settings, they reported the following significant findings: first, somatization disorder and antisocial personality disorder were significantly correlated ($p < .001$) within both male and female subjects; second, somatization disorder and histrionic personality disorder were significantly correlated ($p < .001$) within individuals; third, a significant correlation ($p < .001$) within individuals was found between antisocial personality disorder and histrionic personality disorder; and fourth, alcoholism showed a significant correlation ($p < .001$) with both antisocial and histrionic personality disorders, but not with somatization disorder. They hypothesized that "an individual with histrionic personality is likely to develop either antisocial personality or somatization disorder, with the outcome dependent primarily on the sex of the patient. Antisocial personality and somatization disorder may thus constitute sex-typed alternative pathways for the expression of histrionic personality" (p. 721).

In related neuropsychological research, Flor-Henry (1974) argued that left-hemisphere (dominant) dysfunction may be a factor in psychopathic male behavior and hysterical female behavior. Tucker (1981) proposed a model of specific and lateralized arousal systems in the brain to explain the differential cognitive capacities of the two cerebral hemispheres. He proposed that the hemispheres may be specialized for both the type and valence of emotion and may reciprocally inhibit each other. Noting the poor left hemisphere contribution to the intellectual performance of psychopaths, Tucker (1981) suggested that the hypothesized inhibitory and self-regulating function of verbal and sequential ideation is deficient in these individuals. Low arousal of the left hemisphere is accompanied by the absence of anxiety and rationality and an exaggeration of the right hemisphere's role in emotion.

Tucker (1981) further suggested that the left hemisphere is

underaroused in both psychopaths and hysterics and cited etio-
logical and dynamic studies that support a similar cognitive-
behavioral style between the two: little overt anxiety, excessive
somatic complaints, egocentricity and sexual provocativeness,
theatrical or play-acting behavior, exaggerated emotionality,
and social imperturbability (Shapiro 1965).

Fedora and Fedora (1982) noted that psychopathy may also
be associated with an underarousal of the dopaminergic system,
citing evidence for the lateralization of the dopaminergic arousal
system to the left hemisphere. They hypothesized that Tucker's
model provided a more specific central nervous system substrate
for the hyporeactivity theory of Hare (1970).

Such a hemispheric laterality theory that associates hysteria and psychopathy to left hemisphere dysfunction and, con-
versely, obsessive-compulsive disorders to dysfunction of the
right hemisphere does not account for the clinical presence of
obsessional and compulsive features in a variety of psychopathic
individuals, most evident in the compulsive murderer (Revitch
and Schlesinger 1981). Such a theory of laterality would also
contraindicate the prevalence of obsessional character organization and its affect-isolating defensive structure, which allows the
psychopathic individual to dissociate from the pathogenic maternal introject (Rinsley 1982).

Despite the shortcomings of the laterality theory, there is a
growing empirical basis for the hypothesis that some varieties of
dissociative states are significantly related to psychopathy and
that psychopathic and histrionic personality disorders are significantly correlated. Such research supports my psychoanalytic
construct that varieties of dissociability, both as characterological defense and ego-dystonic state, are fundamental to the
psychopathic process.

The following is a brief postmortem psychological analysis
of a 32-year-old male psychopath who was shot to death by an
off-duty policeman who found him holding a female hostage in the

back seat of a car with a knife to her throat.[1] This incident occurred three months after his release from Vacaville Medical Facility, a maximum security prison hospital in California. This individual was also suspected of murdering his wife and her friend in 1983, but charges were never filed because of insufficient evidence:

> T. R. had an early history of sexual involvement and aberrant parenting by his principal caregivers. He claimed that his stepfather had been abusive and had raped him on many occasions. He further stated that he had been forced to engage in sexual activities with his sister.
>
> T. R.'s mother had been arrested for child endangerment stemming from charges that she misappropriated welfare funds to buy "witches' paraphernalia" rather than food for her children. It was alleged that the stepfather was also charged with sexually molesting the children. T. R. was first arrested for receiving stolen property at the age of 17 and became a ward of the court. Subsequent investigation uncovered a history of forced sexual activity by T. R. with his stepsister and another younger female, a neighbor, both age 12. T. R. had also reportedly held a knife to their throats during these assaults. He was placed in a boys' ranch until age 18, then released. He was arrested again in 1981, at age 27, for child molestation. A state hospital commitment was recommended, but instead, T. R. was held in jail, served five months of a six-month sentence, and was released on probation to attend psychiatric day treatment. He complied for a brief period of time, and then was terminated by the

[1]My thanks to Eugene Schiller, L.C.S.W., for this postmortem psychological vignette.

program for insufficient motivation. T. R. was subsequently arrested for forcible rape in 1983 and was detained for three months in the Psychiatric Security Unit, a maximum security inpatient treatment program, for suicidal ideation and intent. Clinical records indicate he was narcissistic, attention-seeking, and childlike. He reported to several staff members a history of work as a professional clown in a traveling circus. He was also quite adept at theatrical performances while on the unit. He was prescribed several medications, and finally discharged to the mainline portion of the jail on Sinequan 50 mg q.i.d. and Thorazine 50 mg t.i.d. While on the unit, it was clinically documented that T. R. spent much time drawing, and on one occasion the subject had been nude women. The psychiatrist wrote that T. R. had dreams of "cutting up women and eating them." He had stated to a nurse, "I'm not gonna get involved with a woman again when this is over because it's always got me in trouble." There were several instances of T. R. acting out while on the unit by pushing the panic alarm, somersaulting over chairs that resulted in facial abrasions, and fist-fighting with a male patient that resulted in seclusion and restraints. He was also noted to have been "flirtatious with staff." T. R. was discharged with a diagnosis of mixed substance abuse and borderline personality disorder with histrionic and dependent features.

T. R. showed an extensive history of violence toward women, more specifically, sexual sadism that involved elements of compulsiveness and psychopathy.

The overt behavioral displays throughout this young man's life that imply both histrionic and psychopathic processes, in the relative absence of any intrapsychic data, are compelling.

I have also found anecdotal evidence that histrionic-personality-disordered females are particularly attracted and vulnerable to psychopathic males. Although I have no empirical studies to support this hypothesis, the few case studies available of criminal psychopaths in relationship contain historical accounts of their intimate associations with hysterical females (Mailer 1979, Michaud and Aynesworth 1983, O'Brien 1985). I would suggest several psychodynamic reasons for such heterosexual liaisons between histrionic females and psychopathic males who may socially, or antisocially, behave quite differently, but object relationally share similar characteristics.

The hysterical-personality-disordered female is likely to be enamored of the psychopath. Organized at a borderline level of personality function, she can easily carry, as a projective container, his alternating idealizing and devaluing psychic material. She is able to assimilate his highly affectively charged and opposite-valenced object percepts of her since they are fully consonant with her own reality testing and self-percepts. Her inability to integrate good and bad self-concepts into more realistic, ambiguous, and modulated self-representations resonates with the psychopath's propensity to dichotomize reality into goodness and badness.

She is able, at the same time, to reciprocate in this projective-introjective cycle by predominately *idealizing* the psychopathic character. Her need for attachment and dependency complements his drive for detachment and autonomy; she perceives others as all-giving and benevolent, and he perceives others as all-taking and malevolent. But why would the psychopathic character foster such bonding by the hysterical female to him? It is precisely because her primary idealization of the psychopath accentuates his grandiose self-percepts and heightens his omnipotent control of her as a submissive object.

The hysterical female is cognitively vulnerable toward the psychopath for several reasons. First, the global and diffuse nature of hysterical thought (Shapiro 1965) makes her quite susceptible to believing the psychopath's rationalizations of his behavior and disinclined to study carefully, perhaps with some obsessive detail, the illogic of his thought. She would also be immune to developing a healthy suspicion when details and circumstances don't fit, or do not corroborate, the psychopath's oral version of his history. Second, the hysterical use of denial as a defense to ward off conscious experience of certain sectors of reality, perceived by others as evil, badness, pain, malevolence, or simply unpleasantness, allows her to judge the psychopath's most abhorrent behavior in a benign, optimistic, and pollyannaish manner.

The hysterical female is also affectively vulnerable to the psychopath. She will undoubtedly display affects with great frequency and ease and although they may be quite superficial, will nonetheless be arousing, perhaps even exciting, for the psychopathic character with a psychobiologically higher threshold for autonomic arousal. Her superficiality of affects may also be appealing because of his pseudoidentification with them as a model of adept role-playing, or imposturing, to accomplish certain social manipulations. He may learn to imitate or simulate her affective displays.

The hysterical personality-disordered female's sexual innocence, whether feigned or genuine, with its concurrent flirtatiousness, will complement the psychopath's sexual fantasies, pervaded with themes of dominance and submission. He may believe her innocence betrays her unconscious desire to submit to him. They may act this out in reality through sadomasochistic activities initiated by either partner.

Theodore Bundy received this letter from a woman named "Janet" while on Florida's Death Row in September 1979 after responding once to her many missives:

> I got the letter you sent me and read it again. I kissed
> it all over and held it to me. I don't mind telling you I

am crying. I just don't see how I can stand it anymore. I love you so very much, Ted . . . I adore you and I just can't stand not hearing from you. It's absolutely tearing me apart. You are so precious to me. I want you so much I can almost taste it. What I wouldn't give to have an hour alone with you. I would show you in every way how much I love you. There's nothing I wouldn't do. [Michaud and Aynesworth 1983, p. 278]

This letter is remarkable in its portrayal of the histrionic style of its author. We must be mindful that this woman had never met Theodore Bundy and only received one letter from him. His letter seems to carry the psychological import of a transitional object for her, as she holds it, kisses it, and cries. She conveys a masterful sense of the hyperbole in her exaggeration of love, adoration, finality, and distress. She facilely moves from romantic innocence to sexual provocativeness in an implicit scatological reference to boundless sadomasochism. It typifies the histrionic-psychopathic heterosexual dynamic.

The psychopathic character will also find a correlate of his own extroversion in the histrionic partner's propensity to be outgoing, social, and gregarious. Like him she will aggressively pursue object relatedness, but in a more overtly dependent and socially acceptable manner. Her affectional needs will highly arouse the psychopath's sexual and aggressive desires, particularly since she will allow him to exercise omnipotent control in their expression and use of her physical self.

R. W. was a 32-year-old Caucasian female who was diagnosed by me as a severe borderline personality disorder with histrionic traits. Initially in psychotherapy she was timid, seductive, and fearful. She had been married five times, and currently was living with a dominating and emotionally abusive male who barely tolerated her twice weekly visits with me.

During the course of my psychosocial history taking and psychodiagnostic interviews, she revealed that she had met her first husband in a laundromat. He had threatened her, dragged her into his car, and asked her to marry him. She consented, and they drove to Utah and exchanged vows. He then locked her in his remotely located mobile home for a week, and only gave her a small amount of food and water. She stated to me that after five days of this, she thought that maybe she had made a mistake and was in some trouble.

The hysterical female may also be quite unconsciously fascinated with the overt violence of the psychopathic character. This may be her way to vicariously express her own forbidden aggressive impulses through projective, almost adhesive (Bick 1968), identification with the psychopath.

Psychopathy and Multiple Personality Disorder

The psychological and psychiatric communities have recently begun to acknowledge the credibility and frequency of multiple personality disorder (Kluft 1985). Given the empirical and psychodynamic relationship between hysteria and psychopathy, it is only logical to hypothesize that psychopathy and multiple personality disorder may clinically coexist in the same individual, although I have yet to evaluate such a patient. Multiple personality disorder case histories, moreover, often identify a subpersonality with clear-cut antisocial behavior and its accompanying affect states (Schreiber 1973, Bliss 1980, Keyes 1981, Howe 1984).

Janet (1889) was the first to link dissociation to multiple personality disorder. Breuer and Freud (1893–1895) identified what they considered abnormal "hypnoid states" of consciousness that were associated with a splitting, or dissociation, of memories of early childhood trauma. Fliess (1953) characterized this phenomenon as a hypnotic evasion that protected against the work of remembering early trauma; and Loewald (1955) theorized that dissociation was unconsciously chosen as an alternative pathway, instead of abreaction or associative absorption, to cope with early trauma.

The weight of current knowledge indicates that multiple personality disorder has both biological and social learning determinants (Spiegel and Spiegel 1978, Bliss 1980, Braun 1984). Braun and Sachs (1985) emphasized two necessary criteria for the eventual clinical manifestation of multiple personality disorder. First, a natural-born capacity to dissociate must exist. And second, childhood exposure to severe and sadistic trauma is frequent, unpredictable, and inconsistent. Silber (1979) spelled out the psychodynamic relationship between childhood sexual abuse and hypnoid states in adult patients.

If psychopathic individuals are more vulnerable to multiple personality disorder as an extreme dissociative state, they are also more likely to consciously malinger such dissociative pathology to disavow responsibility for their actions. Their subjective sense of consciousness may seem quite discontinuous (Hilgard 1980), particularly given their imitation and simulation of others' behavior through projective identification. Their memory of self, both perceived and conceived (Meloy 1985), may be both sentimentalized and compartmentalized, owing to the idealizing and splitting processes of their psychology. Such heterogeneous representations of self, and their accompanying opposite-valenced affects, predispose the psychopathic character to feign more ego-dystonic dissociative states, from psychogenic amnesia to multiple personality disorder, in the search for exculpation in a forensic setting. In a sense, real dissociative traits may intentionally serve illusory dissociative states.

Bradford and Smith (1979) studied thirty persons who had committed murder and found that nearly two-thirds (60 percent) claimed amnesia for their alleged crime. Lynch and Bradford (1980) attempted to use polygraphy to determine which persons claiming amnesia for their offenses were telling the truth. They concluded that 30 percent of those without major psychiatric illness and 63 percent of those with personality disorders had used deception. Polygraph measures of such variables as malingering, however, have been criticized for their limited reliability and validity (Schacter 1986a). Nevertheless, claims of amnesia by persons accused of homicide range from 40 to 70 percent (Howe 1984) and may be due to organic, psychogenic, a combination of organic and psychogenic causes, or conscious malingering (Suarez and Pittluck 1975, Whitty and Zangwill 1977, Simon 1977).

The psychopathic character may also use the hypnotic interview to fake multiple personality disorder. Even a deeply hypnotized individual can retain the ability to lie (Orne 1961). If an individual is pretending to be hypnotized (Schacter 1986b) and faking multiple personality disorder, the likelihood that he will go undetected is considerable (Hilgard 1977, Orne 1977, Diamond 1980, Orne et al. 1984). The relationship between various forms of genuine and simulated amnesia is poorly understood (Schacter 1986c).

The most recently celebrated case of malingered multiple personality disorder occurred during the jailing of one of the "Hillside Strangler" suspects, Kenneth Bianchi, in 1979. Age 26 and 44 at the time they began killing women in Los Angeles, Kenneth Bianchi and Angelo Buono were cousins who raped, tortured, strangled, and murdered ten young women and girls between October 1977 and February 1979.

When Bianchi was apprehended in Bellingham, Washington, and charged with the murder of two Whatcom County girls, he claimed amnesia for the evening of the killings, January 11,

1979 (O'Brien 1985). Both his defense attorney and psychiatric social worker suspected a psychiatric problem, and they retained Donald Lunde, M.D., a forensic psychiatrist from Stanford University, to evaluate him. Bianchi had done considerable reading in psychology and psychiatry and was also fortunate enough to view the movie "Sybil," based upon the book of the same name that portrayed a multiple personality disorder (Schreiber 1973), broadcast on BCTV, March 9, 1979, two days prior to his interview with Lunde.

Lunde, however, did not evaluate the presence or absence of multiple personality disorder, but suggested that either hypnosis or sodium amytal be used to probe Bianchi's claimed amnesia. Schacter (1986c) called this form of forgetting "limited amnesia" and defined it as a pathological inability to remember a specific event, or small number of events, from the recent past.

Bianchi's attorney subsequently retained John Watkins, Ph.D., a psychologist from the University of Montana and reputed expert in the field of dissociative reactions. Watkins began his interview of Bianchi on March 21, 1979, stating, "Maybe I could be of some help to you. I don't know if I can or not but maybe if we talk a little bit together, I could be of some help" (O'Brien 1985, p. 233).

I find this particularly striking as an example of professional role confusion. The psychologist was attempting to establish a psychotherapeutic, "helping" context, whether feigned or real, and if the doctor wasn't confounded about his role as a psychotherapist, in contrast with the role of a forensic psychological investigator (Shapiro 1984), it surely established a questionable premise for any individual being examined for diagnostic, rather than treatment, reasons.

After exploring with Bianchi his childhood and attitudes toward hypnosis through the use of such leading statements as "John [Bianchi's social worker] was telling me a little bit about your life . . . I understand it's been kind of a rough one, it hasn't been all peaches and cream, your life, all together. . . ." (O'Brien 1985, p. 234), Watkins proceeded with his thirty-minute hypnotic induction of Bianchi, which suggested the emergence of a separate personality:

> . . . I've talked a bit to Ken, but I think that perhaps there might be *another part* of Ken that I haven't talked to, another part that maybe *feels somewhat differently* from the part that I've talked to. And I would like to communicate with the other part . . . *Part*, would you please come to communicate with me? And when you're here, lift that left hand off the chair to signal to me that you are here. Would you please come, Part, so I can talk to you. Another Part, *it is not just the same part of Ken* I've been talking to . . . Part, would you come and lift Ken's left hand to indicate to me that you are here? [italics added]. [O'Brien 1985, p. 236]

Bianchi's left hand rose from the chair. Watkins had provided ample opportunity for Bianchi to consciously imitate a multiple personality disorder and furthermore created a supportive environment in which Bianchi's unconscious simulative processes could begin to work. Watkins proceeded to establish a receptive atmosphere for Bianchi to exaggerate the opposite-valenced affects of splitting, or dissociative defenses, with which he was probably quite familiar:

> *Watkins*: Part, are you the same thing as Ken, or are you different in any way?
> *Bianchi*: I'm not him. . .
> *W*: You're not him. Who are you? Do you have a name?
> *B*: I'm not Ken.

W: You're not Ken. Okay. Who are you? Tell me about yourself.

B: I don't know.

W: Do you have a name I can call you by?

B: Steve.

W: Huh?

B: You can call me Steve.

W: . . . tell me about yourself, Steve. What do you do?

B: I hate him.

W: You what?

B: I hate him.

W: You hate him. You mean Ken.

B: I hate Ken.

W: You hate Ken. Why do you hate Ken?

B: He tries to be nice.

W: . . . how do you mean —

B: I hate a lot of people.

W: You hate a lot of people.

B: He tried to be friends.

W: He tried to be friends. Who do you hate?

B: I hate my mother.

[O'Brien 1985, pp. 237–238]

Bianchi then established a motive for "Steve" as a subpersonality unknown to Ken, to compel him to kill:

Bianchi: I made [Ken] think all these real morbid thoughts.

Watkins: Like what?

Bianchi: Ah, like there was nothing wrong with killing cause it was like getting back at his mother, and I made sure he didn't really know what was going on

. . . He thought it was his mother and he thought it was people he hated. [p. 239]

O'Brien (1985) noted that at this point Bianchi had erred in his deception, since Bianchi had already said that "Ken" did not hate anyone and was always kind and polite. Watkins, moreover, gave no indication in the transcript of noticing this slip. Moments later Bianchi repeated his mistake, "cause Ken hates women," but quickly interjected in the feigned role of Steve, "I mean, I hate women" (p. 239).

Bianchi appeared to draw on his cousin, Angelo Buono, for his characterization of "Steve." This suggests that quite conscious imitation, as well as the unconscious process of malignant pseudoidentification, existed throughout his apparent dependency on Buono during their sadistic killings in Los Angeles. Bianchi also fashioned "Steve" after one of the subpersonalities of Sybil, portrayed by Sally Field in the movie he had viewed for the second time on March 12, 1979.

During the psychiatric and psychological investigations of Bianchi's feigned multiple personality disorder, he implied therapeutic "progress" through his jail diary:

The name Steve that keeps popping into my head has been familiar. I think I know something now about myself—there is another stronger person inside of me. I think he calls himself Steve. He hates me—hates my mom—hates a lot. I feel this person wants to get me. I've had dreams of someone who is a twin but he was exactly opposite from me—for the past few days I feel like my insides were at war—for the past two nights just as I'm about to fall asleep bits and pieces have been forming—the name—the struggle, me against him—in my dreams it felt like the body of the twin was exactly mine but the attitude totally foreign. I feel stronger

but scared. I feel hate but I don't feel like reacting to
the feeling . . . Why does he hate me so much? Where
did he come from? [O'Brien 1985, pp. 249–250]

Bianchi also began writing poems on April 17, 1979, suggestive of
an anxious, somatizing patient struggling to integrate an unfa-
miliar and despicable part of his personality:

I'm scared
my stomach hurts
there's no place to run
now,
it was easy to run away
before.
I feel strong, in control
but still unsure
of someone I've come to know,
someone I don't understand
as well as I know myself now. . .
I'm so alone now, somewhat
I feel naked.
I'm knowing me.
I wish I were free of him.
I want help.
I don't care for him
and he doesn't like me.
I feared confinement but
I'm thankful for it now.
[pp. 250–251]

Ralph Allison, M.D., a psychiatrist without forensic experience
at the time, but an expert in multiple personality disorder, was
brought in by the defense to evaluate Bianchi on April 18, 1979.

Allison's leading, suggestive questions are reminiscent of Watkins, but now without hypnotic induction:

> *Allison*: Did you ever hide inside your own head?
> *Bianchi*: Sometimes, just to get away.
> *Allison*: What do you do in there?
> *Bianchi*: Talk.
> *Allison*: Anybody else in there to talk to?
> [p. 253]

Meanwhile Dr. Watkins ended his sessions with Bianchi as he had begun them, as a psychotherapist rather than an investigator: "You, Ken, are getting stronger every day, I don't know how everything's going to come out, but I suspect you'll be able to handle things better" (p. 259).

Bianchi had identified "Steve Walker" as his one and only subpersonality. Subsequent police investigation determined that Bianchi had sent a letter to the registrar at California State University, Northridge, asking for a diploma with the name not filled in, and had signed it "Thomas Steven Walker." Bianchi had enclosed a $90 money order, which the school accepted and then mailed the diploma. Bianchi also had California State University, Northridge transcripts with his name on them. The transcripts and social security number were determined to match those of an actual Thomas S. Walker. Walker was located in Van Nuys, California, and he told the police that he had responded to an ad in the *Los Angeles Times* for a psychological assistant, forwarding his transcripts to a "Dr. R. Johnson" who happened to reside at Bianchi's Verdugo Avenue address in Los Angeles. Bianchi had erred, victimized by his own grandiosity and arrogance, by identifying his one subpersonality with the actual name of an individual he had deceived to secure fraudulent transcripts and a college degree (O'Brien 1985).

The prosecution retained Martin Orne, M.D., Ph.D., a psychiatrist and psychologist from the University of Pennsylvania and an international authority on hypnosis, to investigate Bianchi's multiple personality disorder. Orne initially addressed the question of Bianchi's actual or feigned hypnotic state. Orne had developed procedures for uncovering malingered hypnosis that he called double hallucination, single hallucination, suggested anesthesia, and source amnesia (Orne 1961).

Orne invited Bianchi, in a claimed hypnotic trance, to visually hallucinate his defense attorney in an empty chair. Bianchi did so, and Orne pointed out the actual presence of his defense attorney in an adjacent room. Bianchi reacted to this by stating that the hallucinated man had disappeared, and wondering quite vociferously, *while still hypnotized,* how the same person could exist in two different places at the same time. Orne was cognizant of the evidence that a hypnotized subject will accept the reality of the suggested hallucination despite circumstances that violate Aristotelian logic, that is, the paralogic (Von Domarus 1944) that A can physically exist in two places at the same time (Meloy 1986b). Bianchi also shook hands with the visual hallucination without any hesitancy, suggesting the unprecedented spatial and temporal contiguity of a visual and somesthetic hallucination.

Orne's (1961) suggested anesthesia procedure also depended upon empirical evidence that hypnotized subjects rely on the paralogic of the hypnotized state, even if it violates Aristotelian logic. He drew an imaginary circle on the back of Bianchi's hand and told him he would feel pressure when touched outside the circle, but not when touched within it. Bianchi was instructed to say "yes" when touched outside the circle and "no" when touched within the circle. Bianchi had been placed in a double bind and a logical contradiction: how could he say "no" when he wasn't supposed to feel anything? He chose to say nothing when touched within the circle, yet was mistaken. The genuinely hypnotized subject would say "no" when touched within the circle, accepting the logical contradiction as the moment's reality as defined by the hypnotist, despite its illogic. Bianchi had fallen prey to the Aristotelian law of contradiction, that A cannot be both A and B at the same time (Von Domarus 1944).

The source amnesia test was inconclusive. Orne completed his investigation by testing the hypothesis that Bianchi's multiple personality disorder was genuine. He suggested to Bianchi, much as Watkins and Allison had done, but now using suggestion as a conscious investigatory tool, that usually more than two personalities existed in a multiple personality disorder. He did this without Bianchi being hypnotized, further hinting that there might be a problem with the diagnosis as a defense unless more than two personalities were present.

Following Orne's hypnotic induction several hours later, Bianchi produced a third personality, "Billy." Orne was now convinced that Bianchi had not only feigned hypnosis, but had consciously malingered these "multiple personalities."

Distressed by these untoward events in his attempts to build an insanity defense, Bianchi wrote a will while in jail, quite pathognomonic of his psychopathic process:

I, Kenneth A. Bianchi, being of sound mind and body, do hereby write this, my last will and testament. To my son Ryan I leave all my worldly goods, as little as that may be, it goes to him with my deepest love. It is profound to me that I have had to experience more confusion and mistrust and insincerity in society, if only the right people had been wise enough to follow through with their responsibilities, during the years of forming me into the mold of adulthood, I wouldn't be where I am now. There's a sadness in misunderstanding, an emptiness like a hollow egg. The egg which can produce life in two ways, one in creation and one in

sustenance and not realizing the potential of either.
[O'Brien 1985, p. 274]

Bianchi began plea bargaining with the Los Angeles County
District Attorney's Office, agreeing to testify fully and truthfully
against his cousin, Angelo Buono. He subsequently did neither.

Part III

VIOLENCE, PSYCHOSIS, AND RELATED STATES

6

Modes of Aggression

The *San Francisco Chronicle* published this article on Friday, November 21, 1986:

> Malcolm R. Schlette was absolutely convinced that he was the victim of a conspiracy in 1955 that kept him behind bars for 20 years for a $6 arson fire.
>
> "There can be no doubt that a conspiracy existed in this case in which criminal overt acts were committed from such a conspiracy by persons herein named," Schlette wrote at one point, naming four of the five men who ultimately ended up on his death list.
>
> The 72-year-old ex-convict exploded in a vengeful rage Tuesday and killed the man who prosecuted him 31 years ago. After gunning down the first man on his death list, former Marin County District Attorney William Weissich in San Rafael, Schlette swallowed poison and died.
>
> In April 1955, Schlette was convicted of arson for burning six wooden beer crates stacked against the Bleu Baie Tavern at Marshall, a bar run by his estranged wife.
>
> The damage done in that fire, which occurred in

September 1954, amounted to $6, according to the court records contained in two trunks sent to The Chronicle by Schlette.

A second charge in the same case that he subsequently burned the Seaside Tavern to the ground in February 1955, was dismissed after a jury could not arrive at a verdict.

Schlette (pronounced Shlettuh) was charged in the bar fires after being arrested and questioned as a suspect in a March 9, 1955, fatal motel fire that left eight dead. He insisted on his innocence in that case too, and a grand jury refused to indict him.

While in custody, Schlette confessed to the bar fires. He claimed that the confession was coerced during a nightlong interrogation in which authorities promised to free his brain-damaged 13-year-old son, who was being held in Juvenile Hall, in exchange for his confession.

In the reams of documents, a picture emerges of a disturbed man who believed he was unjustly prosecuted for crimes he did not commit. The voluminous records detail his long-festering allegation of a "monstrous wrong" inflicted on him by the courts.

Whether Schlette's conspiracy theory was a figment of his tormented mind or not, court records show that Weissich and the sentencing judge, Thomas Keating, feared him and wanted him put away for as long as possible.

On the day he received a two- to 20-year sentence for the beer crate fire, Schlette stood in open court and promised to kill Keating and prosecutor Weissich.

"I believe he is a dangerous psychopath," the late Judge Keating said in one document forwarded to state parole authorities in 1955.

In the same document, Weissich urged that Schlette

be held until prison psychiatrists could assure that "he no longer is a menace to society."

"Should this assurance not be forthcoming . . . then it is my opinion that he should be held in custody until the law compels his release," Weissich wrote in 1955.

During two decades in prison, Schlette repeatedly denied any wrongdoing in appeals to higher courts and letters to family members and friends. The documents in the trunks weigh 470 pounds.

His agonizing pleas for justice read like pages from "Les Miserables," the Victor Hugo classic about a man sentenced to a long prison term for stealing a loaf of bread.

In 1971, after being in prison for more than 16 years, Schlette said that he was being punished far more severely than others convicted of similar crimes.

"The average time for release in this type of conviction is about 2.5 years," he told the parole board. "Thus my present confinement exceeds the average by about 14 years, and this has been done without my having a criminal record prior to this conviction."

Schlette noted in one of his many appeals that all charges against him at one point were dismissed by both Keating and a municipal court judge.

The charges were reinstated only after Weissich obtained an indictment from the grand jury.

"The district attorney knowingly used perjury and subornation of perjury to obtain an indictment of the same two charges, circumventing the rulings of the municipal and superior court dismissals by having three witnesses lie to the grand jury," Schlette argued in a 1967 petition for freedom.

Schlette, who had a long history of mental illness, was paroled after 11 years in prison.

He failed to report to his parole officer and instead

traveled to Los Angeles, where he attempted to buy guns to kill the five men he believed had "framed" him in 1955.

He was captured after five days and sent back to prison to serve the remainder of his twenty-year term.

Seething with a fury nurtured during his long years in prison, Schlette was released in 1975 when authorities could no longer legally keep him behind bars.

Human beings are particularly adept at intraspecies killing. The tendency of *Homo sapiens* to mass murder one another has resulted in the death of over 59 million individuals from wars or other disputes between 1820 and 1945 (Richardson 1960). The total number of individuals killed during the past 35 years exceeds the total number of soldiers killed in both world wars in this century and is estimated to be an additional 25 million people (Cafiero 1979). In California the homicide rate (the intentional killing of another) is 10.6 per 100,000 individuals (California Department of Justice 1984), in contrast with the Interpol world homicide average, which is 1.7 per 100,000 individuals. The homicide rate in Los Angeles in 1985 (17.6 per 100,000) was very close to the homicide rate in Lebanon in 1982 (18.8 per 100,000). Individuals awaiting legally sanctioned execution in the United States, and residing on Death Row, attained a homicide rate of 73.3 per 100,000 during the 1977–1982 period (Lester 1986).

Despite the relative statistical rarity of homicide in particular, and violence in general, its continuous and variable expression among individuals has compelled numerous researchers to attempt to classify modes of aggression in both animals and humans from a variety of sociological, psychological, and biological perspectives (Valzelli 1981).

My intent in this chapter is to understand this seemingly diverse range of human aggressive and violent behaviors as broad categories of either *affective* or *predatory* aggression (Eichelman et al. 1981). This simplified classification system has primarily evolved from animal research with cats and their underlying neurochemical and neurophysiological mechanisms during aggressive behaviors (Flynn 1967, Flynn et al. 1970, Chi and Flynn 1971a, 1971b, Flynn and Bandler 1975). Affective and predatory aggression appear to have distinctive neuroanatomical pathways and to be under the control of different sets of neurotransmitters (see Chapter 2).

This system of classifying aggression as either affective or predatory has yet to be empirically applied to the study of human aggression and therefore should not be considered a reliable and valid measure of human aggression. It does, however, appear to have important conceptual relevance for the clinical study of human violence and to be a rich source of hypotheses that await further investigation.

I will also present the psychoanalytic hypothesis that *the psychopathic process predisposes, precipitates, and perpetuates the expression of predatory violence.* In other words, the psychopathic character is particularly suited to predatory violence for a variety of object relational and psychobiological reasons.

AGGRESSION AND VIOLENCE

The distinction between aggression and violence is critical to a clear understanding of both behavioral constellations. I am borrowing a definition of aggression (Valzelli 1981) that is psychobiologically grounded yet behaviorally measurable: "Aggressiveness is that component of normal behavior which, under different stimulus-bound and goal-directed forms, is released for satisfying vital needs and for removing or overcoming any threat to the physical and/or psychological integrity subserving the self- and species-preservation of a living organism, and never, except for predatory activity, *initiating* the destruction of the opponent" (p. 64). This definition includes two psychobiological principles common to most attempts to delineate aggression: maintenance of internal homeostasis and self or species preservation.

I will use a much narrower definition of violence (Megargee 1976) that makes no psychobiological or object relational assumptions yet clearly defines violence as a behavioral act with certain consequences: acts characterized by the application or overt threat of force that is likely to result in injury to people.

The reader should note that modes of aggression may include acts of violence, but not necessarily. On the other hand, aggression is a necessary component of all acts of violence. Neither definition addresses issues of intent, psychopathology, or morality, which are appropriately left to further scientific and philosophical investigation.

AFFECTIVE AGGRESSION

This first mode of aggression subserves aggressive displays that have traditionally been characterized as irritable, intermale, territorial, or maternal. It is the most common mode of aggressive vertebrate behavior and the mode of aggression that underlies most human violence. It begins with an intense and patterned sympathetic activation of the autonomic nervous system due to external or internal threatening stimuli. It is accompanied by threatening and defensive postures and increased vocalization. Often it is an end in itself and seldom correlates with feeding or predation in animals. It may, however, sequentially precede or follow predatory aggression in humans.

It appears that neuronal pathways mediating affective aggression are widely distributed in the central nervous system of vertebrates. Many of the pathways are closely related to the spinothalamic tract and periaquaductal gray, which may neuroanatomically explain the close association between affective aggression and pain responses (Eichelman et al. 1981).

As noted in Table 2–1 (p. 26) circulating levels of serotonin appear to negatively correlate with affective aggression, while relative neurotransmission levels of norepinephrine, dopamine, and acetylcholine appear to positively correlate with affective aggression.

Affective aggression, specifically affective violence in humans, has a number of discrete characteristics, which I will now elaborate on.

1. *Intense sympathetic arousal of the autonomic nervous system.* The sympathetic mobilization of the autonomic nervous system in preparation for an increase in voluntary muscular activity precipitates all affective violence. The release of epinephrine by the adrenal medulla and adrenocorticotropic hormone by the anterior pituitary breaks down protein and increases glucose levels in the blood. Breathing accelerates, increasing blood oxygen levels. Glucose and oxygen flow to the voluntary musculature is increased by elevated heart rate and arterial constriction (Schneider and Tarshis 1975). Physiologically the organism has entered an initial alarm state (Selye 1950) because its internal environment's cellular homeostasis is being threatened. The purpose of the sympathetic arousal is to return the organism to an optimal state of cellular activity as soon as possible.

The behavioral clues that signal autonomic arousal and that may foreshadow affective violence include increased and shallow breathing, skin flush, muscular rigidity, pupil dilation, increased perspiration, attacking or defending postures, and increased frequency and loudness of vocalizations.

2. *The subjective experience of conscious emotion.* Notwithstanding the historical controversies concerning the neural basis of emotion (James 1884, Lange 1885, Cannon 1927, Lashley 1938, Duffy 1941, Lindsley 1951, Schachter and Singer 1962, Wasman and Flynn 1962), an individual who has engaged in affective violence will usually retrospectively report intense emotional states, described as either anger or fear.

3. *Reactive and immediate violence, if present.* There is a

close temporal contiguity between affective aggression and violent behavior due to the reactive nature of the behavioral sequence. Violence will follow within seconds or minutes of sympathetic arousal if it is to be considered a product of affective aggression. Psychobiologically the human organism is not equipped to sustain a high level of sympathetic arousal. It is predisposed to return to a state of homeostasis as quickly as possible in the service of cellular efficiency. When forced to maintain intense levels of autonomic arousal, the organism will enter a state of resistance (Selye 1950), which has an immunosuppressant effect.

4. *An internally or externally perceived threat.* Affective violence is a reaction to a stimulus that threatens the homeostasis of the organism. The perceived threat may impinge the organism at a biological or psychological level, the former referring to states of self- or species preservation, the latter primarily referring to self-esteem, or affective, regulation.

The threat may originate in an actual object that is attended to through the sensory-perceptual apparatus, or it may be an intrapsychic representational object, usually an object percept, that is phenomenally experienced as "not-I." The most common clinical manifestation of internal threats are auditory, or verbal, hallucinations. Such formed ideational experiences, whether psychogenic or physiogenic in origin, have phenomenological, psychological, dynamic, emotional, logical, and interpersonal dimensions (Lothane 1982).

In a minority of cases, command hallucinations compel the paranoid schizophrenic to act (Ennis 1986). Most individuals with auditory hallucinations will resist those that command activity, but hallucinations of a persecutory nature may precipitate such autonomic arousal and be perceived as so imminently threatening that affective violence results.

F. S. had completed junior college, was married, and had no criminal history. At the age of 22 he began hearing "the voice of Satan" and sought the help of his wife and minister to eradicate this troublesome experience. For a brief two months he also visited a psychiatrist and was given medications, but his wife and their entire congregation, a Christian fundamentalist group, persuaded him that only prayer would be effective. He stopped the psychiatric care, and despite a worsening of psychotic symptoms, embarked on a futile journey to exorcise the "demons" through daily prayer meetings with his wife and church members. Two years after the onset of the acute paranoid schizophrenic symptoms he developed a delusional identification with the Devil. The command hallucinations intensified. One evening he heard the voice of "Satan" tell him to "kill the one you love the most." In a frightened and extremely agitated state, he ran into the bedroom. His wife screamed, "In the name of Jesus, Satan be gone!!!" He assaulted her and strangled her to death. He then sat down and called the police. F. S. was admitted to our forensic inpatient unit in an acutely psychotic and agitated state.

Delusional thought content may also be perceived as internal threatening stimuli in the absence of auditory, or other sensory-perceptual, hallucinations, precipitating autonomic arousal and subsequent affective violence.

D. T. was a 28-year-old Caucasian male who was found guilty of second-degree murder and willful cruelty to a child, and Not Guilty By Reason of Insanity in the death of his girlfriend, P., on September 20, 1986.

As the patient entered the house of his girlfriend, P., on Friday evening, September 19, he saw her 6-year-old son playing in the living room. The boy said to the patient, "Hey, there, hotshot, how are ya?" The boy then said to his mother, within earshot of the patient, "Mom, I want an Uzi machine gun, a real one." The patient stated that at this point he believed that the company he was working for in Los Angeles was tied to the Mafia, the Mafia was a functional arm of the devil on earth, and the boy had become a "beast" of the devil. During these early hours Friday evening, P. supposedly behaved toward the patient in a terse and very cold manner. They went to bed and had no sexual contact. The patient woke up in the middle of the night and reported a spontaneous thought, "I've got to kill the boy." He stated that while P. was sleeping, her left leg crossed his as he was lying there awake, and he thought, "I'm terrified, she knows what I'm thinking." He stated that he had planned to get a pitchfork and do away with the boy, but because of P.'s leg resting on his, he was stopped from doing this. He stated he then went back to sleep, believing that P. was controlling him and being very fearful of her son.

On Saturday morning, September 20, the patient found himself compelled to behave in a very docile and dependent manner toward P. and her son throughout the day. He delusionally believed that they were both possessed and he had no other recourse than to follow their orders. He recounted several events during that Saturday that indicate ideas of reference and the patient's propensity to delusionally believe that his thoughts were being controlled: He stated that he attempted to use a spray bottle to clean appliances, the spray did not work, and he knew this was a sign from the devil that he should not be cleaning those appliances; he took a shower, the water was pulsating, and he knew the devil was pulsating the water, and therefore he did not have P.'s permission to take a shower; he entered the laundry room, attempted to do the laundry, noted that the cycles of the machine were "rather odd," and knew that the devil was controlling the laundry machine. When P.'s son woke up, he wanted to roughhouse with the patient. He did this, but was quite passive, believing that the son was the beast of the devil and was in control of the patient's responses. They attended a soccer game during which one of the bystanders pointed toward a woman in a red dress. The patient believed this was a reference to the devil. He heard church bells ringing and knew that this was a sign from God to "break out of this tailspin." He then drove with the son to return home, and during this car trip, several other events confirmed his psychotic delusions concerning the son's identity. The son appeared to make an engine noise stop by moving his arm up and down; he made shadow animals with the sunlight coming into the car, and the patient thought this was a sign of "the jackal, the beast." The son wanted to look at an old scar on the patient's hand that had been caused by a drilling accident a year prior, and the patient knew at that moment that the son had caused the accident. He believed the son tried to control his thoughts by playing music on the car stereo tape deck over and over again. He knew the son made a car stop at a median pedestrian crosswalk when they stepped onto it. The patient and the son then went to a discount store with the intent of buying a Bible and to some degree fend off the demonic control he was feeling.

Later that evening, in a state of intense autonomic arousal, the patient got out of bed, picked up the son's pet tarantula, took it into the kitchen, and began cutting it in half with a spoon. P. awoke, came into the kitchen, and started screaming. She grabbed at him and pushed him away. He reported that "things began to speed up." He began to rapidly eat a peach from the refrigerator, hoping it would give him more energy. He remembered repeating the phrase, "The Father, the Son, and the Holy Ghost." He hoped that by saying this, he would "bathe in protective words." P. reportedly ran into the room with her son and attempted to hide. The patient broke down the door, grabbed her, and attempted to knock her out with a wooden box on the bookcase. He stated that if he could control her, he could take her the next day to a local church and have her exorcised. He took both P. and her son to the garage, choked P. into a semiconscious state, and bound both of them with Mylar tape. He described binding their legs, hands, waists, and mouths. P. regained consciousness and began to panic. He strangled her to death, and remembers thinking, "that boy made me kill his mother because I wouldn't be recruited into the devil's brigade." He stated that he was not consciously aware of any emotion during the actual strangling, but remembered being covered with sweat.

Koehler (1979) distinguished between pseudohallucinations as "an experience in the head" and true hallucinations as "an experience in external space . . . substantially in objective space." Although the localization of hallucinatory phenomena is primarily metaphorical, I think it has important phenomenological implications for the patient that may determine the correct diagnosis.

Borderline personality-disordered individuals may subjectively experience persecutory introjects as "voices" that are distinguished from the auditory hallucinations of the schizophrenic process by two characteristics: first, the "voices" are localized within the mind by the patient but are experienced as ego dystonic, or "not-I," object percepts rather than self-percepts; and second, despite the alien nature of the phenomena, such patients, if asked, attribute the origin of the "voices" to their own psychological processes. This, of course, is a paradox, and it is determined by the defensive, splitting processes that foster such contradictions in the verbalized cognitions of the borderline. In contrast, hallucinating schizophrenic patients will localize the "voices" within or outside their mind and will usually disavow the "voices" as a product of their psychological processes.

Borderline-personality-disordered individuals, including those identified as psychopathic, nevertheless may be autonomically aroused to affective violence through the internally threatening stimuli of persecutory introjects. Such threatening intrapsychic material, however, usually arises in the midst of an intensely negative transference reaction with an actual object, unlike the auditory hallucinations of the schizophrenic, which are not as dependent upon such actual transference arousal. The schizophrenic's hallucinations may, in fact, phenomenologically diminish once interpersonal dialogue begins.

5. *Goal is threat reduction.* The immediate objective of affective aggression, or affective violence, is to reduce or eliminate the perceived threat so that the organism can return to a state of biological efficiency and psychological homeostasis. This is usually done through behavioral repertoires involving fight or flight and is emotionally accompanied by anger or fear, respectively.

6. *Rapid displacement of the target of aggression.* High levels of autonomic arousal and its accompanying affect states seem to precipitate the rapid displacement of the perceived threat from one actual object to another. In other words, during states of sympathetic arousal immediately prior to affective violence, the intrusion of a third party into an escalating situation between two individuals may result in an assault against the third party. It is an accepted convention, supported by empirical data (Moorman 1986), that peace officers are at substantial risk of physical harm when intervening in domestic, or family, disturbances. It is ordinary police practice to immediately separate the individuals and remove them from each others' sensory-

perceptual sphere to facilitate a parasympathetic return to base-line.

The internalized representation of the threatening object as the intrapsychic vehicle for the actual displacement of the threat seems to lose sensory-perceptual clarity as autonomic and affective arousal increases. This would render the threatening representational object more vulnerable to displacement among actual objects as the "goodness of fit" becomes less perceptually rigorous. The loss of sensory-perceptual definition as an object representation would invite such displacement and projection on a variety of dissimilar actual objects:

> R. M. first began using cocaine in 1975-1976 in conjunction with his wife and other friends. It was also at this time that he began to exhibit signs of jealousy and suspicion toward his wife for having extramarital affairs. It is possible that these beliefs had some basis in reality.
>
> R. M. also became involved in the selling of cocaine. This activity reached its peak in 1980 when the patient was independently trafficking cocaine from Florida to Los Angeles and was also identified as a threat to established cocaine dealers in his neighborhood. He reports that he engaged in this activity because "it was easy to make a lot of money," and he did not consider any grave consequences that might occur. He reports that his marriage began to fall apart at this time, and they divorced when he was certain L., his wife, was having an affair. R. M. states that he was threatened and harassed by established cocaine dealers during this period, and there appears to be some basis for believing that this actually occurred. This is not to discount the fact, however, that the patient was also becoming increasingly paranoid and delusional. The recent history since 1982 clinically

supports the age-old maxim, "even paranoids have enemies."

The most recent focus of R. M.'s difficulties has been a neighbor named J. D. It appears that J. D. was an optimum target for the patient's paranoid fears since J. D. is described by many people as an explosive, aggressive, and unpredictable individual who was quick to respond to any aggressive behavior by the patient. For the past year they have engaged in mutual harassment of each other that has included the slashing of tires, throwing a brick and a fish through glass windows, J. D. chasing the patient down the street with a gun, and J. D. threatening the patient's 16-year-old son in court as he shoved the patient's attorney.

During the course of these actual neighborhood conflicts, the patient became increasingly paranoid. He believed that J. D. "and others" were putting Nair in his shampoo, injecting needles into his heel, harassing him with electronic signals in the air, and poisoning his food. On one occasion he visually hallucinated J. D. coming through his bedroom wall. In response to his increasing paranoid delusions and the actual conflict with J. D., the patient purchased a 9 millimeter semi-automatic pistol, a .45 Colt, a .32 caliber revolver, a shotgun, and two .22 caliber rifles.

The patient also acted out his psychosis in a quite obsessive-compulsive fashion: on one occasion he froze some of his fecal material to have it tested for semen, believing that he had been sodomized while he slept; on another occasion he found a piece of lint on his couch, thought it was a parasite, and took it to the Public Health Department to have it analyzed since he was sure it had been deliberately placed in his home. He was undaunted when Public Health told him he was overreacting.

This case illustrates the displacing of affective aggression onto a variety of targets over a period of time and implies the sensory-perceptual diffuseness of the threatening object representations, facilitating the displacement process, when under intense levels of arousal. It is also unusual because of the multiple perceived threats, both internal and external, actual and fantasied, that reactivated the aggression, and because of the use of a potent psychostimulant that would heighten the autonomic arousal. I diagnosed this individual as having a chronic paranoid disorder in addition to his episodic cocaine abuse. There was also some evidence that the patient had a paranoid personality disorder prior to any use of illicit drugs.

7. *A time-limited behavioral sequence.* Since affective violence is fueled by intense levels of sympathetic arousal, it is always circumscribed and can usually be measured as a discrete behavioral event lasting seconds or minutes. As I mentioned earlier in this chapter, the biological organism's capacity to sustain this "alarm" state is limited, and if the perceived threat continues, it will psychobiologically adapt through a "resistance" state with certain immunosuppressant effects (Selye 1950).

8. *Prefaced by public ritual.* I am defining public ritual as stereotyped attacking and defending postures characteristically displayed prior to the actual affective violence, the goal of which is to reduce or eliminate the perceived threat. The display is public because it is meant to be observed by the threatening object; otherwise, it would lose its utilitarian value.

The public ritual is usually a parody of fighting or fleeing. The attacking or defending postures display the organism as fiercer or more timid and helpless than it actually is. On an object relational level, the intent of the public ritual is to disrupt the threatening person's perceptual "goodness of fit" of the target, rendering the latter an unworthy object of attack.

Characteristic behaviors of individuals engaging in public ritual prior to affective violence include certain demeaning gestures, challenging and obscene language that is intended to intimidate or humiliate the threat, clenching of the fists, certain physical posturing intent on protecting the more vulnerable, ventral side of the body, expansion of the abdominal-thoracic region to visually appear larger than usual, and vocal displays that are louder, higher pitched, and harshly toned.

Behaviors that are publicly ritualized to parody flight or submission include fawning or officious language, exposure of the ventral portion of the physical body to symbolize surrender, hand gestures intent on establishing a submissive alliance with the threat, contraction of the abdominal-thoracic region, and vocalizations that are quieter, lower pitched, and gently toned.

9. *A primary affective dimension.* As the descriptive adjective implies, affective violence fundamentally correlates with affective arousal and display, whether consciously felt as emotion or unconsciously defended against.

Subjects who engage in affective violence and retrospectively report consciousness of emotion may describe themselves as being "carried away" or metaphorically transported by the intensity of the emotion into the violent behavior. Psychobiologically, the intensity of the affect may disinhibit impulse control to the degree that shock and disbelief by both the perpetrator and observers follow the violent event. It may be perceived as a completely "out of character" display as the characterological defenses against such impulses have been momentarily overrun.

Emotion that is present yet unconsciously defended against may only be inferred by the degree of violence that is observed. The borderline personality organization is particularly suited to the dissociation, or splitting off, of affect during episodes of violence. Higher-level neurotic personality organization supports the capacity of the individual to consciously experience emotion during affective violence, and, retrospectively, to both remember and process the emotional state.

The narcissistic defense against affects within borderline personality organization may also keep emotion out of awareness during episodes of affective violence. Modell (1975) has termed this a "massive affect block" (p. 275) that is common among narcissistic personalities in the initial phases of psychoanalysis. He differentiates it from isolation, which is a more focused intrapsychic defense against the overwhelming intensity of the affects. An "affect block" is motivated by a fear of closeness to the actual object.

Although the context in which I am applying the term *affect block* is different, it is useful in further explaining the absence of conscious emotion during affective violence in narcissistically disturbed, especially psychopathic, individuals. It deepens our understanding of the patient C. V. described earlier and his use of dissociation during the murder of the stranger female hitchhiker.

The narcissistic affect block is invariably supported by a fantasy of grandiose self-sufficiency. The degree of nonrelatedness to the actual object paradoxically correlates with the intensity of the object hunger. In an affectively violent situation, the insatiable, possessive hunger of the narcissist, heretofore defended against through detachment (Bromberg 1979), is acted out through the expression of hate that is sadistic, remote, and determined. The hate, above all else, *feels* real and preserves the grandiose self-structure by expressing the individual's "entitlement to survive" (Buie and Adler 1973). The narcissist's fear of his own devouring greed and the perceived retaliatory desires of the actual object are ironically managed through his affective violence, which once again establishes a detached control over the interpersonal sphere.

The dynamics of affective violence in the psychopathic process are virtually identical, but oftentimes are distinguished by the presence of predatory violence before or after the affective aggression. The psychopath may also express affective violence in a more sadistic manner than the narcissistic personality without psychopathic characteristics. This is correlated with the degree of childhood violence the psychopath experienced and the consequent intensity of annihilatory fear encapsulated in the grandiose self-structure. This fear may be expressed as rage in order to hurt and control (Glasser 1986), rather than destroy, the maternal introject, for a moment projected onto, and perceived within, the actual victimized object.

10. *Heightened and diffuse sensory awareness.* Affective violence is marked by the individual's hypervigilance to all stimuli in the external environment. A diffuse, exteroceptive attentional set, a scanning of the environment to ferret out all perceived threats, is characteristic of affective violence.

This diffuse awareness facilitates the displacement of the perceived threat onto other actual objects that may be quite noninvasive and benign. It is akin to the hypervigilance of the paranoid individual who must remain in a state of readiness against the perceived malevolence of any, and perhaps all, actual objects (Shapiro 1965, Meissner 1978). The paranoid individual's diffuse attentional set is distinguished, however, by its chronicity. The scanning hypervigilance of the affectively violent individual diminishes as autonomic arousal lessens.

11. *Self- and object percept dedifferentiation.* Intense levels of autonomic arousal and affective violence may be accompanied by an intrapsychic loss of distinction between self- and object percepts. Self-percepts are the "I" represented in dreams, daydreams, purposeful visualizing, sexual and aggressive fantasies, intentional or spontaneous visual images, or auditory sounds "heard" in the mind and embraced as a part of "I." They are phenomenally located as coming from within the self and are identified as belonging to the self. Object percepts encompass the "not-I" represented in dreams, daydreams, purposeful visualizing, sexual and aggressive fantasies, and intentional and spontaneous visual images or auditory sounds "heard" in the mind. Although phenomenally experienced as coming from within the self, they are identified as not belonging to the self, hence, an object (Meloy 1985).

This self- and object percept dedifferentiation can be psychobiologically understood as a limbic domination of the higher cortical primary and secondary associational areas. This momentary collapse and fusion of self- and object percepts is characteristic of acute personality regression to a psychotic level of functioning (Mahler 1960). The loss of intrapsychic boundary between self- and object percepts would affectively transport the individual vulnerable to psychosis, such as the borderline personality, to intensified levels of annihilatory fear and subsequent violence. There would be a momentary loss of the sensory-perceptual distinction between past and present time, self- and other image, and thus the safety of a bulwark against invasive psychic material.

The self- and object dedifferentiation may also chronically exist in the psychotic individual with schizophrenia, schizoaffective, or bipolar disorder that is refractory to treatment. Such patients have usually abandoned all actual relations with others in the service of dedifferentiated self- and object representations that have no sensory-perceptual fit with external reality. Actual relationships may exist only toward the nonhuman environment as perceived by the patient:

> ... Violent acts which are so typically latent among schizophrenic patients ... are in part referable to the patient's poor differentiation between the living and nonliving, human and nonhuman ingredients of the world in which he lives. Thus the violent act can be thought of as made possible by the patient's failure to distinguish, for example, between a living baby and an inanimate doll, and at the same time as expressing his effort to achieve such a differentiation, as part of his undying struggle to establish a more mature ego functioning and a better relationship to reality. [Searles 1979, p. 327]

Such affective violence usually has no pattern of victim selection and may be quite random, arbitrary, and therefore, extremely dangerous:

J. M. had a ten-year history of chronic paranoid schizophrenia. He was unpredictably assaultive and hurtful
of others. Neuroleptics and lithium carbonate resulted
in a tenuous stability of behavior, but no diminution of
his auditory hallucinations, persecutory and grandiose
delusions, and formal thought disorder. He could be
observed, when standing alone, becoming very angry,
listening intently, laughing hysterically, or arguing.
Victims of his affective violence were usually unlucky
individuals who happened to be physically close to him
at the moment of his motor aggression.

We found that the most frequent and severe histories of affective
violence in a sample of chronic schizophrenics were accompanied
by organic impairment when measured by standardized neuropsychological testing (Adams et al. 1987). Such impairments were
localized in areas of the cortex associated with social adaptation,
such as expressive speech, reading, and writing.

12. *Possible loss of reality testing.* As suggested by the
intrapsychic loss of self and object differentiation that may occur
during affective violence, the violent individual may be clinically
judged to have lost contact with reality and therefore be considered psychotic at the time of the affective violence.

Reality testing is the *sine qua non* of all psychoses, regardless of etiology (Frosch 1983a). It is the capacity to measure
intrapsychic experience against the actual and immediate interpersonal experience; and when this capacity is lost, a failure of
reality testing has occurred. Reality testing, however, is to be
carefully distinguished from reality sense, distortions of the
latter pathognomonic of dissociative states and sensory-
perceptual illusions (see Chapter 5; Frosch 1983a).

Individuals who can adequately test reality have the capacity to delineate between their internalized object world, regardless of how bizarre it is, and their actual relations with
others. There is no confusion concerning what affects, ideations,

or impulses are contained within the self, such as occurs at a borderline level of personality organization. There is also no confusion as to the boundaries of the self, such as occurs at an episodic moment or chronic level of psychotic personality organization.

I would like to introduce the concept of *psychotic envelopment* to metaphorically suggest the various degrees to which the psychotic portion of the personality impairs the ego's capacity to reality test, along which a point exists where reality testing is completely lost. The following case is illustrative of this phenomenon, which is critical to understanding the relationship between escalating levels of affective violence and loss of reality testing:

K. I. had chronic paranoid schizophrenia for twenty years. He knew well that the first sign of his psychosis returning was the "space commander's voice" telling him what to do. His history of affective violence, however, had usually been directed toward himself. During the past decade, when psychotic, K. I. had severed his ear lobe and his penis.

One year ago, while living alone in a studio apartment, he heard once again the space commander's voice telling him to burn down his room. Frightened by his familiar auditory hallucination, and recognizing it as a symptom of his impending psychosis, he called both the police and fire departments and told them he had a "compelling urge" to burn down his apartment and he needed help. The dispatcher recorded his conversation but did not respond to the call. Several hours later, as the psychosis, in the form of an auditory hallucination, and now the added delusion that the space commander's voice was real, enveloped K. I., he lost all capacity to test reality and resist his impulses. He set the fire, ran for help, and was subsequently arrested and charged with Felony Arson.

Although the prosecution had ample evidence through the recorded telephone calls that K. I. could distinguish right from wrong immediately prior to the crime, the case did not go to trial and K. I. was found Not Guilty By Reason of Insanity.

K. I. had initially been able to test reality despite the presence of a familiar auditory hallucination. Yet as the psychosis enveloped him, he lost the capacity to test reality, that is, to recognize that the hallucination was a symptom of his paranoid schizophrenia, and delusionally believed that it was real and its imperatives must be followed. This psychotic envelopment appeared to correlate with increasing levels of autonomic and affective arousal, contributing in K. I.'s case to conscious feelings of terror and help seeking. The affective violence occurred at the point where K. I.'s reality testing was lost. Prior to that point in time K. I. was able to contain the psychotic portion of his personality and recognize its symptomatic expression as a product of his schizophrenia.

The concept of psychotic envelopment has both temporal and spatial dimensions. The temporal dimension implies that psychotic symptoms, such as hallucinations and delusions, may be present yet the time has not been reached when the individual cannot distinguish actual, interpersonal reality from these symptoms. The approximate time at which reality testing is lost usually correlates with a loss of socially adaptive behavior. In the case of K. I., this resulted in affective violence directed toward his property.

The spatial dimension is metaphorical, but has conceptual importance and some empirical validity (Grotstein 1978, Meloy 1984, Ogden 1985, Stewart 1985, Szekacs 1985). It is implicit in several commonly used clinical descriptors, such as encapsulated, contained, and concealed psychotic symptoms.

Grotstein (1977, 1978) described psychic space as a "veritable workbench of thinking" (1978, p. 55). He conceptualized the psychotic as experiencing an actual closing of the space he is in because of a defect in his perceptual capacity to organize and represent internal space. This is caused by a regressive disorganization of both ego boundaries and reality-testing apparatus, as well as a dysfunction of the vestibular apparatus.

Grotstein's concept chiefly involves the ontogenesis of a sense of space from zero dimension to one dimension, to two, and three dimensions. In the zero dimension of psychosis the universe is mathematically that of a point and is experientially that of boundless, infinite space "where all phenomena relate to the self and all causation radiates from the self . . . the collapse of the walls of psychic space with consequent dysdimensionalization is . . . a true invariant of psychosis. . . . " (Grotstein 1977, p. 440). Psychosis can be conceptualized as mental content without a container.

In a small empirical study (Meloy 1984), I found that a sample of biological parents of schizophrenics showed significant negative correlations between variance of primary process material in their dreams, a measure of one-dimensional space, and a measure of formal thought disorder when awake. Such a constriction of variability in primary process content of manifest dreams could be a regressive marker that is clinically validated by the presence of an increase in formal thought disorder. As Grotstein (1977) wrote, "Thoughts, like armies, need space in which to manoeuvre. When psychic spatial collapse ensues, the manoeuvring of thoughts becomes handicapped and the thoughts 'freeze' as concretions" (p. 436).

This capacity to experience internal space appears to be a primary apparatus of ego autonomy (Hartmann 1939), and with psychotic envelopment and the ensuing collapse of internal space, self- and object representations are dedifferentiated and reality testing is lost.

The reverse of psychotic envelopment is the partially recompensated schizophrenic individual who is still experiencing psychotic symptoms but has regained the capacity to test reality.

In other words, such individuals recognize their symptoms as such and are able to measure them against actual interpersonal reality and distinguish between the two. This is, of course, prognostically quite favorable, especially when the fully recompensated schizophrenic individual has the evocative memory capacity to reflect on his or her psychotic experience and learn from it.

It is, however, potentially destructive when schizophrenic individuals are able to dissemble, or conceal, their psychotic symptoms because they have regained the ability to recognize what behaviors are socially acceptable. This is particularly malignant in forensic settings when restoration of sanity or competency issues are in the forefront and it is to the patient's advantage to appear fully recompensated. The individuals' thoughts may be pervaded by private delusions, yet they can choose to vocally express only those thoughts that will be perceived by others as logical and sensible. I have seen this phenomenon on several occasions when a paranoid schizophrenic is able to present himself in an affectively appropriate and cognitively organized manner until his actual object relationship to me precipitates a delusional upsurge of paranoid content that can be sudden, fantastic, and quite threatening. Such immediate psychotic envelopment is usually accompanied by autonomic arousal and the heightened probability of affective violence.

13. *Lowered self-esteem.* The perceived threat that always precedes affective violence is related to either the biological or psychological homeostasis of the organism. In the latter case, affective regulation, or self-esteem, is involved. Lowered self-esteem, the affective complex that correlates with the self-representations and bathes the subjective experience of self with certain negative valenced emotions, may be impinged upon during an affectively violent event in two characteristic ways: First, the individual's defensive operations that maintain the homeostasis of the self-affect are directly assaulted by the perceived threat and are phenomenally experienced as confusion,

fear, anger, or acute anxiety immediately prior to or during the affective violence; or second, the individual's affectively violent behavior results in profound feelings of guilt, remorse, and shame in the aftermath of the event, causing a more negatively valenced emotional state surrounding the subjective sense of self. This affective descent in self-regulation is clinically apparent in symptoms of depression and implies the presence of superego elements in the personality. It contraindicates any psychopathic object relational structure.

Affective violence in the psychopathic process may be followed by periods of acute dysphoria and narcissistic rage, particularly if the individual is involuntarily contained through commitment or custody (see Chapter 4). These affects, however, are closely associated with the grandiose self-structure and convey no sense of empathy toward the victim. Occasionally in the psychopathic process, one will observe the individual feigning remorse for the victim as an imitative, self-serving gesture. Interpretation and confrontation of this imposturing will usually surface the righteous indignation and profound contempt that has been consciously suppressed.

PREDATORY AGGRESSION

The second mode of aggression characteristically results in the destruction of prey. In animal models its primary purpose is to secure food. Unlike affective aggression, it involves minimal or no autonomic arousal, vocalization, or elaborate behavioral displays. It is not associated with increased irritability, and the animal may be so attentionally riveted to the prey that there is a selective suppression of other sensory input (Hernandez-Peon et al. 1956). Predatory aggression usually occurs between species, with humans being the exception. There are characteristic, species-specific killing patterns. For example, most land mammals stalk their prey and attack with lethal strikes to the dorsal side of the neck (Eichelman et al. 1981).

Neuroanatomical pathways of predatory aggression remain to be defined, but they appear to project from the hypothalamus into the ventral midbrain tegmentum. For example, frog killing by the rat is facilitated by intracerebral injections of cholinergic agents or electrical stimulation of specific sites within the lateral hypothalamus, thalamus, and ventral midbrain (Bandler and Moyer 1970).

As noted in Table 2–1 (p. 26), the neurotransmitters serotonin and the catecholamines appear to inhibit predatory aggression. Cholinergic agents, such as acetylcholine, appear to facilitate predatory aggression. The anatomy of the cholinergic pathways subserving predatory aggression may overlap the central cholinergic systems described by Shute and Lewis (1967).

Predatory aggression, specifically, predatory violence in humans, has certain characteristics that correlate with, yet are in contrast to, those I have used to define affective violence.

1. *Minimal or absent autonomic arousal.* There is a striking absence of sympathetic arousal of the autonomic nervous system prior to or during acts of predatory violence. A consequence of this lack of an "alarm state" (Selye 1950) is a dearth of behavioral indicators that precede, and therefore predict, predatory violence.

Predatory violence, however, may occur sequentially with affective violence, the latter's presence indicated by high levels of sympathetic arousal. Skin-boundary contact with the victim may correlate with a shift to affective violence that has been preceded by a period of predation. This is a common occurrence among sexual psychopaths who will be predatorily violent until they are in actual physical contact with the victim and then psychobiologically shift to a state of affective aggression and violence due to the sensory-perceptual triggers of the victim; in a sense, the victim may be perceived as invading the psychopath's visual, auditory, olfactory, gustatory, and somesthetic fields despite *his* aggression, leading to high levels of sympathetic arousal.

On the other hand, predatory violence may follow a period of affective violence. This most commonly occurs among psychopathic or narcissistic individuals who will find themselves in the midst of an explosive, affectively violent episode and as autonomic arousal subsides, the pattern of violence will shift to a predatory mode. The psychobiological and psychodynamic alteration in aggressive paradigms is precipitated for one of several reasons: The individual may want to gratify sadistic impulses by exploiting the already existent suffering of the victim through the infliction of additional emotional or physical pain, or the individual may intentionally carry out acts of predatory violence to deceive forensic investigators and conceal the true motives of the affective violence. This sequential shifting between modes of affective and predatory violence may be determined by a variety of interpersonal and intrapsychic factors.

2. *No conscious experience of emotion.* The predatorily violent individual will retrospectively report an absence of conscious emotion. If any emotion is experienced, it will usually be described as feelings of exhilaration, and it is most prevalent during time periods prior to the actual violence when the victim is being stalked. The conscious feeling is embedded in defensive processes of projective identification and omnipotent control, and this usually conveys a clinical sense of the magnitude of the grandiose self-structure. Conscious affect in predatory violence, however, appears to subserve, rather than dominate, the cognitive-conative complex of predatory violence (criterion number 9 below). As Theodore Bundy, the convicted sexual psychopath, stated, "The fantasy that accompanies and generates the anticipation that precedes the crime is always more stimulating than the immediate aftermath of the crime itself" (Michaud and Aynesworth 1983, p. 111). This is in contrast to the

affectively violent individual who will feel literally transported by the intensity of the emotion.

3. *Planned and purposeful violence, if present.* Predatory violence is intentional, consciously planned, and purposeful. It is a unilateral activity, rather than one that is precipitated by a perceived threat.

It is intentional in the sense that the predator chooses when the violence occurs, against whom, and to what degree. Conscious intent, however, may be eroded by other less conscious, instinctual, or defensive processes. Predatory aggression in subhuman species is usually intended as food-seeking behavior and is precipitated by interoceptive sensations of hunger; it is virtually always an interspecies behavior. Predatory violence among humans, notwithstanding the collective predation that is sanctioned as armed strategy between nation states, and despite its conscious intent, may have several unconscious or defensive purposes. It may be used to gratify certain vengeful or retributive fantasies. It may be subjectively experienced as a repetitive, necessary behavior that would be clinically assessed as compulsive.

This type of intentional erosion is most apparent in compulsive murderers (Revitch and Schlesinger 1981), who will usually commit homicide in a serial fashion, and it is oftentimes dynamically explained as displaced matricide. The intent, however, is still quite present, but the choice to kill is exercised against a background of intrapsychic "fueling" by the unconscious wish, or repetition-compulsion. Theodore Bundy provides a telling example of this blending of background compulsivity and foreground intentionality in his own words, but using the third person:

> In the wake of a particular crime . . . he was not in a state of remission. That is, he actively wanted to go out and seek a victim. But he knew that he could not afford

to do so without creating an intolerable amount of more public frenzy and panic, as well as police activity. . . .

Frequently after this individual . . . committed a murder he would lapse . . . into a period of sorrow, remorse, et cetera. And for a period of time he would do everything to overcome and otherwise repress the . . . overt behavior. Indeed, on one particular occasion he went to extraordinary lengths to do this following a crime, and he felt that he had succeeded, that the abnormal course of conduct had just sort of . . . extinguished itself.

But in this instance, the cracks in the facade, as it were, began to appear. He then would attempt to channel the desire within him into a different area, into something which was still . . . improper, immoral, illegal, but something that was less serious, less severe . . . and so he in sort of a compromise decided that rather than go out and inflict this mortal injury on someone he would search out a victim in such a way that there would be no possibility of detection and *he would not be forced into a position of having to kill.* In essence, he compromised into just going out and performing an act of rape, as it were.

So he . . . began to just go out driving around the suburbs . . . in this city . . . that he was living in, and one particular evening he's driving down a fairly dark street and saw a girl walking along the street. . . .

Because the area was dark and she was alone, he decided to select her as the victim for this intended act of sexual assault. He parked his car down the street and . . . then ran up behind the girl. Just as he came up on her they were at a place where there was an orchard, or a number of trees or something. As he came up behind her she heard him. She turned around and he brandished a knife . . . and grabbed her by the arm and told her to do what he wanted her to do . . . to follow him.

He pushed her off the sidewalk into this darkened wooded area and . . . told her to submit and do what he wanted her to do. She began to argue with him and he kept telling her to be quiet. She said she didn't believe he would do anything to her, anyway. . . .

Then he began to try to remove her clothes and she would . . . continue to struggle in a feeble manner. And also voice verbally her objections to what was going on. And then . . . the significance now is that *his intent with this victim was not to harm her.* He thought this was going to be a significant departure; perhaps, even a way of deconditioning himself, to climb down that ladder or, I can't think of a good word, de-, de-escalate this level of violence to the point where there would be no violence at all. Even no necessity for that kind of encounter at all. . . .

But he found himself with this girl who was struggling and screaming . . . not screaming, but let's say just basically arguing with him. There were houses in the vicinity, and he was concerned that somebody might hear. And so, in an attempt to stop her from talking or arguing, he placed his hand over her mouth. . . . She stopped and he attempted to remove her clothes and she began to object again. At this point, he was in a state of not just agitation, but something on the order of panic. He was fearing that she would arouse somebody in the vicinity. . . .

So, not thinking clearly, but still intending not to harm her, let's say he placed his hands around her throat . . . just to throttle her into unconsciousness so that she wouldn't scream anymore. She stopped struggling and it appeared she was unconscious. But not, in his opinion, to the point where he had killed her. . . .

> Then let's say he removed her clothes and raped her
> and put his own clothes back on. At about that point he
> began to notice that the girl wasn't moving. It ap-
> peared, although he wasn't certain, that *he'd done what
> he promised himself he wouldn't do, and he had done it
> really almost inadvertently* [italics added]. [Michaud
> and Aynesworth 1983, pp. 132–135]

This hypothetical analysis also illustrates the sequential shift
from predatory to affective violence, a psychobiologic and psychodynamic alteration seemingly triggered by physical contact
with the resistant victim.

Intent may also be fueled by a need to exercise omnipotent
control over the victim through compulsive manipulation and
deception (Bursten 1973a; see also Chapter 5). Omnipotent control may also need to be exercised for instrumental gain, rather
than just intrapsychic reasons. Such is the case in acts of predatory violence where the intent is monetary profit or expediency.
Levin and Fox (1985) noted that violence against prosecution
witnesses who intend to testify about illegal activities is a
common form of expedient violence. In a personal conversation,
Richard Rappaport, M.D., noted the political and monetary expediency of predatory violence committed by organized crime
members and mercenary operatives. Revitch and Schlesinger
(1981) would classify this form of violence as "socially and envi-
ronmentally stimulated homicides" and would view it as the most
exogenously motivated form of murder. Such typological characteristics are useful, but are one step removed from the intrapsychic structure that allows such predatory violence and the psychobiology that supports it.

4. *No or minimal perceived threat.* The immediacy of a
perceived threat, and the consequent reactivity of the violence, is
absent in the predatory mode. In predatory violence, the aggressor must initiate motor activity to be in close physical prox-

imity to the victim. The target of the violence is actively sought, rather than reactively attacked. The term *stalking* is oftentimes used to describe this quiet, unobtrusive predation.

5. *Multidetermined and variable goals.* Unlike affective violence where the singular goal is to reduce the perceived threat, predatory violence may be stimulated by a variety of conscious and unconscious objectives: the gratification of vengeful fantasies, relief from compulsive drives, the gratification of sadistic desires, the repetitive exercise of omnipotent control to evacuate persecutory introjects, relief from psychotic symptoms such as paranoid delusions or auditory hallucinations, the attenuation of jealous or envious emotion that is pathognomonic of narcissistic disturbance, the satisfaction of perversions, the consummation of command hallucinations, or the resolution of a chronic catathymic crisis (Wertham 1937, Revitch and Schlesinger 1981). The latter situation is particularly interesting, and refers to violence within the framework of an ego-threatening relationship. The chronic catathymic crisis occurs in three stages: incubation, violent act, and relief. The predation is apparent during the first stage when the idea that violence must be committed is compelling. The predation is marked by obsessive preoccupation with the victim, depression, and frequent formal thought disorder wherein suicidal ideation intermingles with homicidal plans. The incubation period may last several days to a year (Revitch and Schlesinger 1981):

C. C. was a 28-year-old Caucasian male charged with second-degree murder in the death of his 60-year-old mother. He was admitted to our forensic treatment unit due to suicidal ideation and intent following his arrest.

C. C. had been living alone with his mother for the past year following the dissolution of a marriage and difficulty holding jobs for any period of time. He was reportedly argumentative and suspicious with all employers and would accuse fellow employees of belittling and betraying him.

Approximately six months prior to the instant offense, C. C. became convinced that the only two choices he faced in his current situation were to kill his mother or himself. He found her degrading and provocative, as she would angrily accuse him of the failures in life that were becoming increasingly apparent to him. He was an only child; the father had left the family when C. C. was a small boy.

C. C. began increasing his daily usage of cocaine and became obsessively preoccupied with thoughts of suicide and homicide. One evening he decided to kill his mother, and following a brief conversation with her while she was in bed, he drew a .22 caliber revolver from a cabinet in the hallway, returned to her room, and shot her in the forehead. He cleaned up as best he could, pulled the covers up around her neck, and left her face up, reclining against her pillows.

C. C. stayed in the house with his mother for two months. He would leave the house to secure food and cocaine, but otherwise remained. As putrefaction began to occur, he stuffed towels around the bedroom door and attempted to seal off the room. He watched home movies in the adjacent living room, films of his dead mother, his abandoning father, and himself.

Neighbors involved the police, and C. C. was subsequently arrested at home and charged with his mother's murder.

Psychodiagnostic testing and interviews revealed a schizoid personality disordered individual who subjectively experienced relief following the shooting death of his mother but was otherwise quite detached from any conscious feeling states. He showed no guilt or remorse for his act and evidenced a heightened level of arrogance and narcissistic disturbance once he had adjusted to the maximum-security environment. His suicidal ideation rapidly remitted, and he was discharged from the forensic treatment unit a week after his admission.

His indifferent attitude toward his crime frightened members of the treatment staff, and he was jokingly characterized as a perfect understudy for Norman Bates in Alfred Hitchcock's "Psycho."

This case accentuates two structural personality characteristics that are invariably present in individuals who are violent as a result of a chronic catathymic crisis: a borderline personality organization that facilitates a limiting and polarized perception of reality, in this case a symbiotic envelope that allowed only the death of self or selfobject, and psychopathic processes within the borderline personality that facilitate the predatory planning and intent that accompanies the catathymic buildup of tension and distress.

The goals of predatory violence may also be primarily determined by environmental and situational factors. Ideological commitments, religious beliefs, cultural values, commercial media and television, organized criminal activities, youth gangs, terrorist groups, criminal subcultures, family systems that disinhibit aggression, and acute socioeconomic stressors may all be primary catalysts in the perpetuation of predatory violence.

Leyton (1986) approached the recent phenomenon of serial murder in the United States from a cultural-anthropological perspective in his study of six well-known cases. He hypothesized that the primary mission of the modern serial murderer was to wreak vengeance upon the established social order. His small sample appear, from a sociological perspective, to be among the very class conscious, obsessed with nuances of status and power.

> Yet both serial and mass murderers are overwhelmed
> with a profound sense of alienation and frustration
> stemming from their feelings that no matter how fierce
> their ambitions may be . . . no matter what they might
> do, they could not achieve the place in society to which
> they aspired. . . . They aim high, these multiple mur-
> derers: they have not, like Durkheim's contented man,
> accepted their station in life. . . . In such a milieu, a
> sense of personal mission begins to incubate. [Leyton
> 1986, p. 30]

Leyton's first case is illustrative of his hypothesis. Edmund
Kemper murdered his grandmother and grandfather when he
was 14. He was incarcerated until the age of 21, when he was
paroled to his mother against the advice of his treating psychiatrists. After two years of "rehearsal," that is, picking up pretty
female hitchhikers in the Santa Cruz, California, area, he began
an eleven-month murdering spree that left eight additional
women dead, all young, attractive coeds, except for his final two
victims, his mother and her best friend. Kemper mutilated,
decapitated, and sexually assaulted after death, most of his
victims. Leyton noted that he killed in perfect symmetry: first
two kin, then six beautiful young women, and then concluded
with a kinswoman, his mother, and quasi-kin, her intimate friend.
Kemper stopped his serial murdering, and was finally able to
convince the local law enforcement agency that he was the
perpetrator.

Leyton (1986) interpreted Kemper's murders as a task with
which he confronted the social order with the fact of his excommunication; he chose young women for victims because they
were "the front line . . . the flamboyant sexuality" of the class that
humiliated him through their acts of indifference. He completed
what Leyton referred to as a trilogy of communal, sexual, and
familial revenge, establishing his identity in the social order.

I find Leyton's work compelling, since predatory violence,

in this case serial murder, does occur in a sociocultural milieu that undoubtedly influences the nature and extent of the aggression itself. Leyton's work, however, is flawed for several reasons: First, it does not account for the false positives, that is, the multitude of individuals who have experienced virtually complete social and self-alienation yet do not resort to the task of extreme and predatory violence; and second, the *capacity* of an individual to carry out acts of predatory violence must always and fundamentally return to the personality structure of the individual, regardless of the sociocultural milieu that may predispose such behaviors. And, of course, this personality structure has dynamic processes that are both quite characterologically predictable by adulthood and are undergirded by certain psychobiological substrates. If the goal of predatory violence is primarily extrapsychic, which may be the case, the clinician must be careful to appreciate that personality structure *always* provides the vehicle for the violence itself, regardless of the motivational or instrumental context.

This confusion of personality structure with functional content is a common public misconception. When Richard Ramirez, the alleged "night stalker" responsible for fourteen serial murders in California in 1985, was apprehended, most of the public media focused upon his association with satanism and attributed his behavior to witchcraft, devil worship, and heavy metal rock music, sociocultural phenomena that could then be judged as "spreading signals of societal disintegration."[1] Again, the failure to explain the false positives, those adults or adolescents intensely involved in satanism and heavy metal rock music who do not become serial murderers, is obvious.

   6. *Minimal or absent displacement of the target of aggression.* The defensive operation of displacement does not appear to play a significant role in predatory violence. The actual target of the aggression fits a more rigorous sensory-perceptual object

---

[1]*Sunday Journal-Star*, Lincoln, Nebraska, September 22, 1985.

representation, or object percept; the latter being more impervious to vicissitudes of autonomic and affective arousal. The actual object of predation, irrespective of motivation, will be much more tenaciously pursued, and less quickly abandoned, than objects of affective violence.

Several variables account for this phenomenon: First, minimal or absent autonomic and affective arousal appears to support the enduring clarity of higher cortical representational constructs. Second, multidetermined goals of predatory violence are more object specific than the goal of affective violence. In other words, they require a more disciplined "goodness of fit" within the perceptual-motor apparatus to initiate predation. And third, the selective suppression of other sensory input (see criterion number 10 below) supports a focused, "tunnel" effect linking both object percepts and actual objects of predation.

7. *A time-unlimited behavioral sequence.* In the absence of intense levels of autonomic and affective arousal, the organism is not temporally limited in its behavioral sequence. The initiation and termination of predatory violence has no physiological restrictions other than the capacity of the aggressor to actually inflict the violence. Human predation may be momentary or it may last for years. The opening case study of this chapter is illustrative.

8. *Preceded or followed by private ritual.* The distinctions between public rituals during affective violence and private rituals associated with predatory violence are twofold. First, private ritual in predatory violence is intentionally hidden from the target of the aggression; and second, the private ritual, despite its stereotype, is more pervaded with quasi-magical and symbolic meaning than the public ritual of affective violence.

The goal of private ritual associated with predatory violence is not to reduce or eliminate a perceived threat, but is, in fact, to gratify certain pathognomonic narcissistic wishes that usually remain unconscious. In preparation for the predatory violence, the individual may select certain objects, such as clothing, figurines, jewelry, charms, unusual weapons, makeup, masks, religious symbols, nationalistic emblems, and so on, that enhance feelings of grandiosity. Unconscious fantasies of omniscience, omnipotence, infallibility, and immortality are revitalized through the use of private, ritualistic devices that defensively ward off residues of fear and anxiety. These objects may be anthropomorphized and imbued with quasi-magical powers, rendering them transitional objects (Winnicott 1953). Such predators, in a sense, create their world in which their ritualistic items are felt to be subjective objects completely under their control and pave the way for their targets of aggression to be experienced as selfobjects also under their control. Omnipotence becomes a matter of experience (Winnicott 1962).

Private ritual may also involve the ingestion of certain drugs, usually psychostimulants, which also enhance feelings of grandiosity and omnipotence. These psychostimulants, commonly cocaine or methamphetamine hydrochloride, are also quintessential transitional objects. The drug is physically held and controlled by the subject, it can be used or set aside whenever necessary, it carries the grandiose projections of the subject, it can be orally incorporated whenever wished, and once ingested, its real chemical properties create a subjective state of self-confidence, perceived omnipotence, and heightened cortical arousal.

> The symbolic magic . . . of the transitional object is extremely primitive. Belonging to the earliest period in life, it offers an illusory bridge — or bridges; it comforts and fortifies the young venturer in taking his first steps into the expanding realities of the outer world . . . It offers a cushion against distress of frustration before reality testing is at all secure, and provides dosages of omnipotence according to infant needs. [Greenacre 1969, p. 161]

The transitional object as a symbolic link prior to or during predatory violence has both a progressive and a regressive side

(Modell 1968). It facilitates both distancing, or disidentification, with reality and the imagined object of aggression, while at the same time ensuring that the imagined object is perceived as a further extension of the grandiose self-structure, a selfobject imbued with certain projective characteristics that heighten the predator's sense of omnipotent control. It becomes a Janus-faced symbol that both disavows and heightens differences.

The transitional object of the predator may also become a fetish that is linked with the delusion of a maternal phallus (Winnicott 1953, Greenacre 1969, 1970). Such "objects as fetish" may rekindle sexual fantasies that are then acted out during the predatory violence with the actual victim. This may be grotesquely apparent during sadistic rape when the victim may have certain phallic objects thrust into her vagina or anus, and, if death occurs, may be left with certain objects protruding from her vagina or anus, suggesting a sadistic mockery of, or delusional attempt to display, the maternal phallus.

Fintzy (1971) and Volkan (1973) theorized and clinically supported the presence of transitional fantasies in borderline, especially narcissistic, patients. In an autonomous and recurrent manner, a particular fantasy becomes a transitional object and is perceived as both separate and symbiotically linked to the individual's wishes.

The transitional fantasy in predatory violence maintains the illusion of omnipotent control and may function as a rehearsal fantasy for the predatory individual. This is most common in sexual psychopaths who will render their future victims one-dimensional, gratifying objects in their minds and glorify and idealize their own sexual abilities. This may occur months, if not years, before any actual predatory violence begins. David Berkowitz, the convicted sexual psychopath responsible for the shooting death of five young women and a man in New York City, recounted his transitional fantasies:

> Almost every waking moment . . . I find myself fantasizing. . . . But I'm greatly troubled by my fantasies.

They are almost all either sexual in nature or violent. I'm really quite perverted . . . I do believe, however, that others fantasize the same things as me. If I could be absolutely sure they do, I'd be greatly relieved. [p. 168]

. . . I do fantasize about women and my fantasies are not violent. That is, when I'm making love to them in these daydreams. I envision myself as a lover who is passionate, well endowed, and is able to please my mate by giving her a multitude of orgasms. I picture myself as one who has no qualms about performing oral sex with the female genitals. In fact, I know I would enjoy it very much. I would also be able to prolong (delay) my ejaculation for hours until my partner has numerous orgasms and is begging for mercy. . . . My violent fantasies are miles apart from my heterosexual fantasies. [p. 176]

Berkowitz's last female victim was Stacy Moskowitz on July 31, 1977:

I watched Stacy on the swing and then they stopped swinging. Her and her date then started to kiss passionately for several minutes. At this time, I too, was sexually aroused. I had an erection. Shortly after their deep kissing, they went back to the car . . . I had my gun out, aimed at the middle of Stacy's head and fired. One bullet struck her head and another nicked her. I didn't even know she was shot because she didn't say anything nor did she moan. Then I got in my car and drove off. [Abrahamsen 1985, pp. 176–177]

Private ritual that occurs during or after the predatory violence generally is motivated by two factors. First, the individual is attempting to act out sadistic fantasies that have been previously rehearsed with imagined victims. These sadistic fantasies defensively heighten the predator's grandiosity and sense of omnipotent control through humiliation and degradation of the victim. The acting out of such fantasies renders the actual object a more suitable receptacle for his projected, persecutory psychic material that he wishes to expulsively discharge, or ritualistic postmortem behavior indicates a reidealization of the victim. There is evidence that Theodore Bundy, the convicted serial murderer and sexual psychopath, on at least one occasion kept the body of one of his victims for several days, moving her between a closet and a bed as his sexual desires waxed and waned, and would redo her makeup and shampoo her hair (Michaud and Aynesworth 1983).

The second factor that motivates ritualistic behavior during or after predatory violence is a desire to taunt or mock the individuals, usually authority figures, that will find the victim. Albert DeSalvo, the so-called Boston Strangler, would decorate his female victims with a necktie and then position them with their genitals exposed in such a manner that the first individual entering the crime scene would be visually assaulted by the sight to the point of physical revulsion and nausea (Frank 1966).

The following case (Douglas et al. 1986) illustrates the commingling of these two motivational factors in ritualistic behavior during and following an act of predatory violence:

> A young woman's nude body was discovered at 3:00 P.M. on the roof landing of the apartment building where she lived. She had been badly beaten about the face and strangled with the strap of her purse. Her nipples had been cut off after death and placed on her chest. Scrawled in ink on the inside of her thigh was, "You can't stop me." The words "Fuck you" were scrawled on her abdomen. A pendant in the form of a Jewish sign (Chai), which she usually wore as a good luck piece around her neck, was missing and presumed taken by the murderer. Her underpants had been

pulled over her face; her nylons were removed and very loosely tied around her wrists and ankles near a railing. The murderer had placed symmetrically on either side of the victim's head the pierced earrings she had been wearing. An umbrella and inkpen had been forced into the vagina and a hair comb was placed in her pubic hair. The woman's jaw and nose had been broken and her molars loosened. She suffered multiple fractures caused by a blunt force. Cause of death was asphyxia by ligature strangulation. There were post-mortem bite marks on the victim's thighs, as well as contusions, hemorrhages, and lacerations to the body. The killer also defecated on the roof landing and covered it with the victim's clothing. . . . The investigative profilers noted that the body was positioned in the form of the woman's missing Jewish symbol. [pp. 415–418]

The murderer in this scenario both acted out sadistic ritual fantasies that resulted in his sexual gratification and also displayed and mutilated his victim in a manner that contemptuously mocked his persecutory objects, now actualized as law enforcement authorities.

The case I have referred to earlier (see Chapter 5) concerning the rape, electrocution, and suffocation of the adolescent hitchhiker also illustrates the expression of private ritualistic and sadistic fantasy, but in a manner that was not conscious and was not intended as an afterthought to mock authority. The perpetrator attached alligator clips to the victim's nipples while she was bound and alive and subsequently ran an electrical current through them. This heinous act is highly symbolic of condensed unconscious fantasy. The perpetrator's self-esteem was closely tied to his skill with electrical components and his employment in an auto service garage. This condensing of electrical-mechanical skills regressively telescoped back, in the midst of a highly aroused dissociative state, to a primitive and condensed fantasy of the breast as both a part-object of nurturance in infancy and sexual arousal in adulthood. The breast as part-object became the literal symbiotic attachment of his infantile sadism and could be devoured by the electrical current. At the same time, the victim, completely subjugated, would convulse in a parody of orgasm, gratifying his sexually sadistic fantasies as a genitally active adult.

As Shapiro (1981) noted, sadomasochistic sexuality is a highly ideational matter. The ideas and symbols of erotic sensuality are exciting, especially in their most concentrated, extreme, and detached forms. It is consistent with rigid character because it is a sexuality of purpose, of the will, where the idea of subjugation is so erotic because the actuality of sexual abandonment is inimical.

9. *A primary cognitive-conative dimension.* Predatory violence in humans appears to be highly dependent on vicissitudes of higher cortical functioning, such as purposeful ideation and fantasy, and intentional behavior, such as planned, goal-directed activity. Affective arousal, if present, clearly plays a secondary role in predation.

This delimitation to the cognitive-conative spheres, rather than the affective sphere, of mental activity underscores the planned, purposeful nature of the violence (the case of C. C. discussed earlier in Chapter 6), its multidetermined and variable goals, and the use of fantasy during private ritual.

10. *Heightened and focused sensory awareness.* The most easily observed naturalistic example of this criterion is the immutability of the stalking animal. This attentional fixation, and consequent absence of distractability, appears to have a physiological basis. It was characterized by Hernandez-Peon and colleagues (1956) as a selective suppression of other sensory input. This focused sensory-perceptual phenomenon partially accounts for the minimal or absent displacement of predatory violence onto another actual target (the case described by Douglas et al.

1986 above), a characteristic that is quite common during affective violence.

This object specificity during predation by humans appears to have certain psychodynamic correlates that Brenman (1985) conceptualized as a singular and cruel narrowmindedness of purpose. The obliteration of the whole object representation to a part object that the predator owns restricts both conscious love and guilt. The world is representationally reduced to a cruel and loveless place, and demands can be foisted upon the actual target, or object, to be idealized or vengefully pursued. There are usually elements of sadism in human predation, and the primacy of the paranoid-schizoid position in the developmental life of the predator succeeds in breaking up these whole object representations. Predatory violence is most difficult for those who have developmentally reached the depressive position because of the latter's toleration of whole objects and its affirmation of love while knowing hate (Bion 1963). Brenman (1985) noted that cruelty is maintained because omnipotence is felt to be superior to love, depression is defended against, and grievance and revenge are sanctified.

This heightened and focused sensory awareness is notable in a letter written by David Berkowitz:

> While shooting these people, I actually became transfixed with the event. The report of the gun, the screams, the shattering of glass and windshields, the blaring horn, it all just possessed my mind so that I'd take no notice of anything else. During the first incident, I had become so transfixed that I could not move until that car horn started blasting in the quiet night. That horn brought me back to reality in a way. I got back my senses and realized what I had done and just took off running to my car. I don't mean that I departed reality. I knew what I was doing. [Abrahamsen 1985, p. 179]

11. *Self- and object concept dedifferentiation.* During an act of predatory violence the target of the aggression is likely to become a conceptual extension of the inflated and expansive self. This is particularly true among narcissistic and psychopathic individuals wherein others are habitually regarded as conceptual extensions of the grandiose self-structure.

This dedifferentiation between self- and object concepts, however, does not necessarily mean a dedifferentiation of self- and object percepts. Therefore reality testing, if defined as a capacity to distinguish between internal and external sensory-perceptual experience, remains unimpaired (see Chapter 3).

Self- and object concepts refer to a modal "frame of reference" that have both form and value (Spiegel 1959). They may be associated with perceptual experience, but are usually more abstract and symbolic representations of self and other. Self- and object concept representations implicate meaning and value, rather than perception and sensation (Meloy 1985).

Again, the serial murderer provides a cogent example. He will usually select his victims for their "goodness of fit" to a particular physical stereotype, the latter an interpersonal expression of an internal object percept. This visual image in the mind could be a derivative of the biological mother or a flamboyant and sexually provocative representation of a certain, unattainable social class (Leyton 1986).

Along with the perceptual selection, in many cases quite predictable according to certain physical typologies, the actual target is conceptualized on a more abstract and symbolic level. Self- and object concept dedifferentiation transposes her into a ragefully devalued, or enviously idealized, object, despite the predator's lack of any emotional attachment to the victim. There may be a condensing of values, attitudes, and judgments from past experiences with women that form an aberrant, perhaps even delusional, concept of who she is distinct from the relatively accurate perception of how she appears. This is why a serial murderer's selection of his victims may be perceptually quite predictable, yet his violence against the person is so obviously psychotic in proportion.

This schism between conceptual fusion and perceptual distinctiveness is supported by another paradoxical process that is stimulated by private ritual: the use of transitional objects that both distance the predator from the object of violence while at the same time ensuring the actual object is conceived as a further extension of the grandiose self-structure. This concurrently progressive and regressive process may be phenomenally described by the predatory individual as both a compulsion to act and a dissociative state of mind during the act itself.

12. *Unimpaired reality testing.* The capacity of the individual to distinguish between interoceptive and exteroceptive sensory-perceptual stimuli remains intact during predatory violence. Indications of impaired reality testing strongly suggest the presence of a psychotic disorder that may catalyze predation, but usually introduces additional affective dimensions to the violence (see Chapter 7).

Adequate reality testing, however, should not preclude the search for the presence of self- and object concept dedifferentiation during the act of predation. This is highly probable in aggressively narcissistic and psychopathic characters since the grandiose self-structure predisposes such representational fusion at a conceptual level.

This narcissistic regression or fixation can be seen in the typical pattern of violent psychopathic behavior where motivation is evident, such as instrumental gain or vengeance, but the proportionality of violence is such that a reasonable person finds it abhorrent. Psychopaths do not conceptualize others as separate individuals deserving of empathic regard, but as psychodynamic extensions of their grandiose conceptual self-representations:

> Two youths robbed a woman of ten dollars near her apartment. She put up no resistance, and, almost as an

afterthought, one of the young men had her kneel down and shot her in the back of the head with his .22 caliber "Saturday night special." When arrested and questioned, he freely admitted his act, saying only that he "felt like it. It was no big deal."

Because of the preservation of perceptually accurate self- and object percepts, psychopathic individuals present a dilemma to the diagnostician when reality testing is addressed. Clinical investigation should focus on their conception of others. Is there sufficient evidence through reminiscences, evaluations, judgment, and affective responses that they conceptualize others as three-dimensional, whole, and separate individuals? Or do they reflect, at best, a narcissistic self-absorption, or at worst, a callous disregard for the thoughts and feelings of others? The interpersonal history is the most critical data source for understanding the psychopath's object relations, reality testing, and reality sense. I will address the use of the Rorschach in assessing these areas in Appendix III.

13. *Heightened self-esteem.* Predatory aggression in humans is usually accompanied by increased self-esteem. Private ritual involving transitional fantasies or actual totems, fantasied rehearsal of the violence, psychostimulant use, goal attainment, and predisposing narcissistic personality structure all contribute to a subjective sense of confidence and expansiveness during the entire sequence of predatory violence.

Predation appears to solidify the narcissistic defenses of projective identification, devaluation, and omnipotent control. It provides a behavioral channel for the affective experience of sadistic pleasure and contemptuous delight (see Chapter 4). It necessitates the conscious exercise of deception, simulation, and object control (see Chapter 5) to be purposeful and successful.

Table 6–1 summarizes and compares the thirteen criteria that define and differentiate affective and predatory violence.

Table 6-1

Criterion Comparison of Affective and Predatory Modes of Aggression and Violence

Affective	Predatory
1. Intense sympathetic arousal of the ANS.	Minimal or absent ANS arousal.
2. The subjective experience of conscious emotion.	No conscious experience of emotion.
3. Reactive and immediate violence, if present.	Planned or purposeful violence, if present.
4. An internally or externally perceived threat.	No or minimal perceived threat.
5. The goal is threat reduction.	Multidetermined and variable goals.
6. Rapid displacement of the target of aggression.	Minimal or absent displacement of the target of aggression.
7. A time-limited behavioral sequence.	A time-unlimited behavioral sequence.
8. Prefaced by public ritual.	Preceded or followed by private ritual.
9. A primary affective dimension.	A primary cognitive-conative dimension.
10. Heightened and diffuse sensory awareness.	Heightened and focused sensory awareness.
11. Self and object percept dedifferentiation.	Self and object concept dedifferentiation.
12. Possible loss of reality testing.	Unimpaired reality testing.
13. Lowered self-esteem.	Heightened self-esteem.

235

PSYCHOPATHY AND PREDATORY VIOLENCE

It should be apparent that the psychopathic process is particularly suited to predation. *It is my hypothesis that the psychopathic process predisposes, precipitates, and perpetuates predatory violence by virtue of its structural and dynamic characteristics.*

The absence or minimization of autonomic arousal during predatory violence is supported by the peripheral autonomic hyporeactivity of the psychopathic process. Psychopaths are psychobiologically well suited to the predatory task because their autonomic baseline and evoked responses do not interfere with, and, in fact, sustain, the hyporeactive sequence during predation. This should be contrasted with individuals who are not autonomically hyporeactive yet attempt to consummate an act of predatory violence; their autonomic reactivity may publicly betray, through behavioral cues (see the case of D. T. above), the predatory intent and thus minimize its effectiveness.

The varieties of dissociability that defensively organize the psychopathic process support the splitting, or warding off, of affect during predation. The psychopathic process sustains the absence of conscious emotion during predatory violence and may contribute to feelings of exhilaration and contemptuous delight during the stalking phase of the violence prior to any actual physical contact with the victim. These subjective feelings are products of projective identification and omnipotent control, further defensive operations that necessitate splitting, and imply the presence of a grandiose self-structure. Repressive operations in the neurotic personality organization (Kernberg 1984) during an act of predation will usually catalyze conscious feelings of anxiety and fear because of the instinctual threats from within and the environmental threats from without.

The perceived malevolence of actual others by the psychopath, implying sadistic introjects outside the grandiose self-structure, will oftentimes sustain the planned, purposeful, and goal-directed nature of predatory violence. Since there is no time limit to predation, in contrast to the "alarm state" of affective violence, an individual carrying out a predatory act is subject to many antecedents that may moderate, or even extinguish, the desire to engage in predation. Such diminution of intent to plan and carry out a violent act is less likely in the psychopathic process because of the sustained malevolence that is consistently perceived in others.

This hypervigilant suspicion, which may reach paranoid dimensions, can be developmentally traced to the fused selfobject concepts within the grandiose self-structure, in particular the stranger selfobject, the object of primary identification (see Chapter 3) for the psychopath. Predators are unconsciously fearful of being the victims of predation because of the projective-introjective cycling of their own aggressive and sadistic material. But this fear and its allied defenses, such as projective identification and omnipotent control, sustain the predatory planning and intent despite actual moderating variables from the environment; in other words, experiences that might soften the neurotic personality's desire to engage in predation, since ambiguous realities and the accompanying ambivalent emotions can be perceived, are consistently devalued by the psychopathic process.

The absence of an immediate threat in predatory violence begs the motivational question; but the psychopathic process answers it. The predatory violence of the psychopath, regardless of the precipitant, such as revenge or monetary gain, is always carried out against a background of intrapsychic threat that is projected onto others; potential warring factions that must be enveloped by the grandiose self-structure to be rendered impotent yet also remain sources of envy and greed.

The time-unlimited nature of predatory violence is also supported by the blending of intentional choice and compulsivity that may coexist in certain psychopathic individuals (see the case of C. C. described earlier in this chapter). This manipulative cycling (Bursten 1972) may be highly sexualized and compulsive, exemplified by the serial murderer, yet still subserve affective arousal to the degree that it can be postponed, altered, or stopped for periods of time. David Berkowitz provides a cogent example of this capacity for delay of gratification, despite the compulsive nature of his killing:

> I went out . . . to the Hamptons in the first week of August. I had instructions to kill many people in Southampton. In the afternoon I looked at a map to drive out there. I had the guns with me and came to Southampton . . . late in the afternoon. I drove to the beach, Asparagus Beach, Amagansett. I sat on the sand a couple of hours. I had to wait until nightfall. It started to rain and I had to go then. *The operation had to be postponed* to the following weekend. Disappointed. Ten o'clock. I was very tired when I came back to town and had something to eat and went to bed. [Abrahamsen 1985, p. 107]

My italicized portion of this quote is to note Berkowitz's subtle shift from the first-person active to the third-person passive when the act of murder is directly addressed. This indicates the intrapsychic tension between his intent and compulsion, and his disidentification and detachment from the act itself. This further suggests his remarkable dissociative and simulative defenses, and imitative abilities, which reached their highwater mark in his partially successful feigning of paranoid schizophrenia but eventual diagnosis as a psychopathic personality with paranoid and hysterical traits.

The lack of attachment, or affectional bonding, in the psychopathic process is particularly suited to predatory violence for several reasons. First, there is no empathic identification with the actual victim to interfere with the projective-introjective cycling and polarized idealizing and devaluing of the targeted object. These splitting processes must distort reality in order to work. The absence of empathy also disinhibits the pursuit of sadistic gratification through actual violence. Second, the coexisting processes of sadomasochistic attachment, or aggressive attempts to bond, and profound detachment from others' affective experiences (see the case of R. described in Chapter 2) behaviorally predict recurrent, aggressive, and cruel interactions with others where there is little affection and a large capacity for predation. And third, disidentification with the victim, or with anyone for that matter, magnifies the impact of transitional objects during the private ritual of predatory violence (see the case of C. V. described in Chapter 5). Malignant pseudoidentification (see the case of C. V. described in Chapter 5), however, may be quite apparent during predatory violence where the narcissistic characteristics of the victim are simulated and fuel fantasies of oral aggression and greed.

The grandiose self-structure of the psychopathic process contributes in many ways to the consummation of predatory violence. I have alluded to it earlier, but want to underscore several primary characteristics that directly relate to it as a corollary of predation. First, the conceptual fusion between the ideal self- and ideal object representations as a stranger selfobject sustain an understanding of self as alien, aggressive, and perhaps perverse, yet endowed with a multitude of grandiose characteristics. This sense of self as a stranger in a hostile land predisposes both a rationale for predatory violence and a safeguard against being the victim of predation.

Second, the grandiose self-structure is predisposed to the heightened expansiveness that can be artificially induced through the use of various transitional objects during the private ritual of predatory violence. The ingestion of psychostimulants prior to predatory violence is particularly common among psychopathic individuals and is a clinical reminder of the continual aggrandizement of the grandiose self-structure that is defensively necessary in the psychopathic process.

Third, the rehearsal fantasy that often precedes predatory violence, imbued with grandiose conceptions of self as omniscient and omnipotent, finds rich fertilization in the fused self- and object concepts of the grandiose self-structure (see Chapter 3). The object of predation is conceptualized as an extension of the grandiose self-structure and not as an object concept separate from the self-concept. At the same time, self- and object percepts remain distinctive and relatively accurate, so that the predation can proceed with adequate reality testing.

Fourth, the act of predation itself, particularly if it attracts media attention and catalyzes both public fear and fascination, will reinforce in actuality the psychopathic individual's defensive conception of self as larger than life.

The Ivan Boesky insider trading scandal on Wall Street in the fall of 1986 is one example of nonviolent predation that captured national media attention by virtue of its sheer enormity. The J. David Dominelli Ponzi scheme in La Jolla, California, 1982–1984, that bilked a thousand investors of $80 million, is another (Bauder 1985). These nonviolent acts of predation and the dynamic characteristics of the individual perpetrators, some of whom are clearly psychopaths, often have much in common with the more overtly violent acts of predation. The ideation and affect of the murderer, however, are a much greater public curiosity than the mind of the arbitrageur.

One does, at times, find convergence. The following article appeared in the *Los Angeles Times* on March 17, 1987:

> The Securities and Exchange Commission on Monday rejected the application of a killer who had hoped to run an investment counseling business from the Colorado penitentiary.
>
> The SEC refused to register Herbert David Marant,

who was convicted in 1981 of first-degree murder and conspiracy in the contract killing of his former wife.

"While not unmindful of Marant's desire to build a future for himself while still in prison . . . the major concern is whether the record reflects that Marant can be trusted to adhere to the high standards of conduct required of an investment advisor," said Warren E. Blair, the commission's chief administrative law judge.

Marant filed the application Dec. 22 under the name Michael David Marant, seeking permission to counsel investors as the Light Investment Co. Marant disclosed his murder conviction, the SEC said, but he did conceal a few pertinent facts. . . .

In a real sense, the popular media may mythologize predators to the degree that they do become a legend in their own minds. This verification in reality of that which heretofore had only been experienced in fantasy leads the psychopath to consider predation as the sole means to achieve notoriety.

7

Psychosis and Psychopathy

Psychologists and psychiatrists have historically resisted the diagnostic juxtaposition of psychosis and psychopathy. This was no more apparent than in the DSM-III (American Psychiatric Association 1980), which stated, "Severe mental retardation and schizophrenia preempt the diagnosis of antisocial personality disorder, because at the present time there is no way to determine when antisocial behavior that occurs in an individual with severe mental retardation or schizophrenia is due to these more severe disorders or to antisocial personality disorder" (p. 319).

This is particularly revealing and contradictory, given the American Psychiatric Association's historical support of the insanity defense and its cognitive, and sometimes volitional, prongs, which state that *a specific antisocial behavior* is the "result of a mental disease or defect" and can be so determined, through expert testimony, by the trier of fact.

Despite historical changes in the insanity defense since the M'Naghten Case (10 C. & F. 200, 8 Eng. Rep. 718 [H.L. 1843]), such as the Model Penal Code (Section 4.01 [1961] of the American Law Institute), every legal definition of insanity has implicitly assumed that a mental disorder, if one exists, can be diagnosed, and correlated with, a specific antisocial behavior that resulted in criminal prosecution.

Some of the reasons for the clinical unwillingness to link psychosis and psychopathy are found in the historical distinction between autoplastic and alloplastic adaptation. Ferenczi (1919, 1930) defined autoplastic adaptation as an alteration in the organism itself, whereas the environment is altered through flight or defense in alloplastic adaptation. Furthermore, neurosis was interpreted as an autoplastic alteration and symbolic distortion of psychic reality, whereas in character disorder external reality was used for direct instinctual gratification in an alloplastic manner (Frosch 1983a). This dichotomizing of adaptational modes, in my view, has resulted in an unfounded, but pervasive, clinical hesitancy to recognize the fundamentally *alloplastic* adaptation of both psychosis and character disorder and their interactive patterns. Frosch (1983a) noted the alloplastic nature of psychosis in its modification of both psychic and material reality and a consequent loss of reality testing, what he called an ego-syntonic and reality-dystonic adaptation. The alloplastic adaptation of the character disorder, however, was the denial and minimalization of reality, but it would not be replaced, as in psychosis, by autistic productions. The distinction between the psychotic and characterologic expressions of alloplasticity was reality testing.

Frosch (1983a) seemed to find, however, his own distinction between psychosis and character disorder adaptation somewhat ephemeral: ". . . patients with character disorders . . . will not *for any consistent period* replace [reality], as psychotics do . . ." (p. 415). "In the alloplasticity of some character disorders the capacity to test reality *may wear thin under certain circumstances*, but it is never really lost" (p. 415). "In the antisocial and impulse-ridden characters we may have an ego-syntonic yet reality-dystonic adaptation *not too unlike the psychotic*, but reality testing (*although at times minimal and somewhat impaired*) is not basically lost" (p. 416, italics added).

Frosch (1983a) also noted the confusion between alloplastic and autoplastic adaptation that is engendered by the lack of definition of external and internal environments. Is one talking about material reality, psychic reality, or both, when adaptational alterations are being proposed? If there is no expression of a patient's delusion and the patient makes no attempt to act out in material reality his or her delusional thoughts, and, in fact, is quite functional as a result of the encapsulation of the delusion, has an alloplastic adaptation occurred?

This lack of clarity between autoplastic and alloplastic adaptation and the close association of alloplastic adaptation within psychotic and characterologic traits are precisely the reasons why an attempt to understand the interactive relationship between psychosis and psychopathy is so critical.

Furthermore, the convention of ruling out antisocial personality disorder when a severe and chronic psychotic disorder is present appears to have little basis in clinical reality, despite the dearth of empirical literature addressing the differential diagnosis of psychosis, whether state or trait, and psychopathy in the same individual. In fact, there appears to be only one empirical report (Meloy 1986a) in the research literature that delineates this issue. In that paper a differential scheme was presented for the rapid classification of the functionally psychotic individual in custody, using two predictor and eight criterion variables. The Type II Mentally Disordered Offender was distinguished by the presence of an Axis I psychotic disorder and an Axis II personality disorder, usually antisocial, narcissistic, histrionic, or borderline.

I will pursue in this chapter the relationship between psychosis and psychopathy by exploring several quite pertinent questions. First, are there fundamental psychodynamics that link psychosis and psychopathy? Second, are there characteristic avenues of psychotic expression, such as paranoia and mania, in the psychopathic process? Third, what are the clinical manifestations of schizophrenia and affective disorder in the psychopathic character? Fourth, in what manner and under what circumstances will the psychopathic character dissemble or malinger psychosis? Fifth, what is the relationship between affective violence, predatory violence, psychosis, and psychopathy? Sixth, what is the clinical and theoretical relationship between organic psychotic states, perhaps caused by a known psychoactive substance, and psychopathy? And seventh, are there characteristic patterns of relationship between mental retardation and psychopathy?

CHARACTEROLOGICAL TRAITS AND PERSONALITY ORGANIZATION

Kernberg (1975, 1976, 1984) took the lead in proposing a two-dimensional, perhaps orthogonal, approach to the systematic understanding of character and personality organization. On one dimension are various characterological traits, such as hysteria, narcissism, dependency, masochism, infantilism, obsessionalism; and on the second dimension are three *levels* of personality organization: neurotic, borderline, and psychotic. Each predominate characterological trait could hypothetically be organized at any one of the three levels of personality, discriminated on the basis of identity integration, defensive organization, and reality testing (Kernberg 1984).

The relationship between psychosis and psychopathy puts Kernberg's two-dimensional, object relational approach to the test. Is it theoretically parsimonious, and clinically sound, to describe psychopathic character formation at a psychotic level of personality organization? I think that it is.

Several caveats are in order. Recall that Kernberg's (1975) hypothesis, and mine, is that psychopathic character formation is a more aggressive and deviant form of narcissistic character. I have outlined in Chapter 2 the criteria that differentiate this subtype from the more generic narcissistic character disorder. Furthermore, despite this chapter's focus on psychosis and psychopathy, I find it exceedingly difficult to propose a psychopathic

character at a neurotic level of personality organization, primarily because of the absence of superego formation and the presence of a grandiose self-structure. Implicit in neurotic personality organization are sharply delimited, whole object
representations and the capacity for object constancy; the operation of repression and other higher level defenses; and preserved reality testing with a capacity for insight. Any one of
these psychological processes would rule out the diagnosis of a
psychopathic character. Despite my reluctance, however, to
apply Kernberg's scheme to psychopathy and neurotic personality organization, the task being addressed is psychotic personality organization and the psychopathic process.

Identity Integration

At a psychotic level of personality organization self- and object
representations are poorly delimited and emptied of any polarized values. Fusions of self- and object representations at both a
conceptual and perceptual level (Meloy 1985) will occur. Because
of the absence of boundaries among internal representations of
self and others, actual experience of others and self may be
delusional. In the psychopathic character this is marked by
delusional identification with the aggressor:

> S. T. was a 28-year-old black male admitted in a chron-
> ically psychotic state to our forensic inpatient unit
> following a charge of possession of marijuana for sale.
> His chiefly articulated symptom was the hallucinated
> voice of his father which bothered and disturbed him.
>   The patient was nonresponsive to neuroleptic
> medication. Psychosocial investigation revealed an in-
> dividual who was raised in foster homes following the
> death of his mother when he was 5 years old. This
> traumatic event, subsequently corroborated by the

staff, involved the patient's father shooting his mother to death while she was holding him.

Psychological testing indicated an individual with a full-scale IQ of 84. He had a historical diagnosis of schizophrenia, chronic, undifferentiated type, and adult antisocial behavior. The Bender-Gestalt suggested additional signs of right parietal lobe organicity.

As the patient became more comfortable on the unit, he began to discuss his delusional belief that he *was* his father and his command hallucinations to kill his girlfriend. He reassured himself that this wouldn't happen, because whenever he purchased any weapons, his girlfriend would quickly take them away from him.

Gross identity disturbance is also sometimes seen in the confusion within memory of fantasy and reality. In the psychopathic and psychotic character, grandiose and aggressive fantasies that have repeatedly occurred will be remembered as actual events and adamantly defended as reality. One psychopathic patient, who was also quite delusional, recalled events when he was a 1-year-old involving malevolent treatment by his parents. He vociferously defended a striking visual fantasy as an actual reality that was perpetrated against him. Sometimes such striking commingling of reality and fantasy in memory in the psychopathic character organized at a psychotic level of personality are revealed in more abstruse ways:

R. T. was a 32-year-old Caucasian male seen by me in weekly outpatient individual psychotherapy for one year. He had served as a Marine Recon in Vietnam for two tours of duty, and his primary tasks involved the infiltration of enemy territory and the planned assassination of certain identified Viet Cong leaders.

During the initial clinical assessment, R. T. was diagnosed as schizophrenic, paranoid type, chronic. He was prescribed chlorpromazine, 200 mgs. h.s. prior to beginning psychotherapy with me. He gladly accepted the psychiatrist's medication and was initially quite compliant with treatment, although he preferred sessions at odd hours so he did not have to sit in the waiting room with other individuals. He usually attended sessions dressed in a black t-shirt, camouflage drawstring pants, and combat boots.

As the supportive psychotherapy continued, R. T. revealed a remarkable, although quite marginal, adaptation to his current reality. He lived with his two teenage sons on an avocado grove several miles from the nearest neighbor. He bought food for himself and his sons at a supermarket where the cashier would always open an additional checkout line so R. T. did not have to wait; this also happened regularly at the bank where he deposited his V.A. disability check.

R. T. was of short stature and very muscular. He clearly frightened nearly everyone he encountered. He was quite adept in the martial arts, which included the use of certain oriental weapons, and had an M-16 assault rifle and .45 caliber semiautomatic pistol at home for protection.

R. T. revealed to me that he also was taking 15 mgs. of diazepam daily. He secured this anxiolytic drug by periodically walking in to a local HMO outpatient setting where he had received his first prescription and demanding it.

R. T.'s favorite weapon was his crossbow. He would construct "targets" with bales of hay throughout the avocado grove, dress in his combat fatigues, and enter a state of "combat reverie" where his memories of Vietnam would blend into a quite psychotic and grandiose reality. At one point in the psychotherapy R. T. stated to me that when he was most angry at me he would imagine my face on one of the bales of hay. I was quite concerned by this psychotic condensation of hatred that was developing as a transference factor in the treatment.

Over a period of several months R. T. recalled with both intense pleasure and pain his combat experience. I was struck, however, by my familiarity with some of his memories, particularly since I had never been in combat nor in Indochina. Certain villages resonated with me, but I was not dumbfounded until he mentioned his association with Colonel Kirk.

Joseph Conrad's *Heart of Darkness.* The film "Apocalypse Now." "The horror, the horror, the horror." I was momentarily swept away by this patient's utterances and the psychotic, perhaps psychopathic, implications that he was revealing to me. I began to question his potential for malingering such a psychosis, as well as his capacity to continue to function as an outpatient with such pervasive delusional material.

Subsequent clinical questioning through weeks of psychotherapy gleaned little in the way of new information. R. T. denied any literary or cinematic source for his reminiscence and angrily denied the absence of a basis in actual reality for Colonel Kirk. His psychotherapy continued to be a blend of extremely grandiose, paranoid, and aggressive memories that were subjectively experienced and valued as actual events yet were clearly a confusion of intrapsychic psychosis and interpersonal trauma.

It has also been my clinical experience that a recompensated individual's capacity to recall his psychotic state and identify it as such is a favorable prognostic indicator. In the psychopathic character organized at a psychotic level of personality, this is an extremely rare event. When I have observed this in psychopathic individuals, it is usually an adaptation to the wishes of the treatment team and may be a "malignant pseudoidentification" on the part of the psychopath to secure certain advantages (see Chapter 5).

Defensive Organization

Borderline defenses predominate in the psychopathic character organized at a psychotic level of personality, but they serve different functions (Kernberg 1984). In the borderline personality organization, these defenses protect against intrapsychic conflict, but at the cost of weakened ego functioning. In the psychotic personality, these defenses protect the patient from further disintegration of boundaries between the self and object, both intrapsychic perceptual representations and actual interoceptive-exteroceptive discriminatory sensory-perceptual experience. Such defensive operations will manifest themselves as auditory hallucinations, grandiose and persecutory delusions, and formal thought disorder. Each of these symptom complexes dynamically shores up the grandiose self-structure with a consequent loss of reality testing.

Auditory hallucinations in the psychopathic character are usually identified with an aggressive object and further prompt the individual's identification with that aggressor. Characteristics of the hallucinating object will resemble the grandiose self-structure in a grossly exaggerated and fantastic form. The psychopathic individual will perceive the auditory stimulus as external to his physical and psychological self, or in cases of severe borderline pathology where a differential diagnosis of psychosis is difficult, the individual may complain of persecutory introjects heard within the mind as "voices" but experienced as "not-I," an alien object percept (Meloy 1985). Despite the subjective experience of the hallucination as foreign and outside the self experience, the psychopath will be quick to identify with the sensory-perceptual stimulus as its agent or provocateur, rather than as a victim of its commands.

This allegiance to the auditory hallucination may catalyze aggressive behavior and result in the perpetuation of predatory or affective violence during the psychosis. In other words, the psychopathic process disinhibits the behavioral expression of auditory, or command, hallucinations since there is a profound absence of superego constraint. Acts of danger, particularly toward others, can be exercised without moral or judgmental hesitation and with recurrent sadistic pleasure. This is in stark contrast to the vast majority of schizophrenic patients who successfully resist command hallucinations, if they occur, and show no greater frequency of assaultive behaviors despite their command hallucinations to do so (Hellerstein et al. 1987).

> N. G. was booked into custody for attempted rape following his attack against an inpatient nurse on the psychiatric ward to which he was committed. He had a history of chronic paranoid schizophrenia, but did not appear to be psychotic at the time of his arrest. I asked the patient if he was hearing voices at the time of the assault and attempted rape, and he responded, "Yes, they told me if I tore off her panties, I'd get a surprise." When asked if the voices told him anything else, he said, "Yes, they told me I did not know the difference between right and wrong."

This patient's rather creative and humorous use of one prong of the M'Naghten test of insanity (10 C. & F. 200, 8 Eng. Rep. 718 [H.L. 1843]) as the articulated content of his hallucinations was only matched by his grossly poor judgment in reporting it to me within hours of his offense. Such dramatic, aggressive, and, at times, humorous exaggerations of psychotic symptoms are typical of the psychotically disturbed psychopathic character.

The following excerpts are from a psychological evaluation[1] of a 39-year-old Caucasian male found Not Guilty By Reason of Insanity to a charge of Assault with a Deadly Weapon. The patient was diagnosed as both chronic paranoid schizophrenic and antisocial personality disorder:

> According to records provided to the examiners, on August 12, 1986, J. C. entered an eating establishment in San Diego and stabbed a woman who was seated at a nearby table. At the time, the defendant indicated that God had told him to stab this individual. J. C. was subsequently arrested and placed in San Diego County Jail.
>
> J. C. alleges that he does not remember details about the stabbing. However, later in the interview process, the defendant stated that he had hallucinated that the victim was a "snake." As he said this, the defendant laughed and it was noted that he had told another examiner previously that he had hallucinated that the woman was a "dragon."
>
> . . . J. C. alluded to experiencing aural hallucinations consisting of "noises and voices." The defendant also was questioned regarding other hallucinatory experiences and stated that he experiences olfactory hallucinations. The defendant experiences these smells as "garbagelike odors," or odors that smell like feces. The defendant also stated that he realizes that he becomes agitated, and that this has a negative effect on people with whom he comes in contact. In this regard, however, it must be noted that the defendant seemed to enjoy the idea that he could scare or intimidate others with his actions.

---

[1]Many thanks to Annette Lau, L.C.S.W., and Gregg Michel, Ph.D., for permission to use excerpts from their evaluation.

According to information contained in the report by Dr. J., J. C. has experienced a pattern of violent actions, which appear to be spontaneous, with little or no premeditation or planning. Since 1985 he has had four assaults–two in San Diego on unsuspecting women whom he had never met. He repeatedly fails to demonstrate even minimal judgment in terms of taking responsibilities for his own actions. He has in the past made statements such as "God told me to. . . ."

J. C. demonstrated inappropriate and somewhat grandiose ideas regarding future goals to the undersigned examiners. He stated that he believed he could get out of jail, and hoped to become a police officer in San Diego. In this regard, the defendant stated, "I think it would be real enjoyable if I could become a policeman in San Diego. It would set things right. . . ."

He is impulsive and acts out in violent acts of aggression. The undersigned examiners concur with Dr. J's observation that this patient "hides behind" his pathology; that is, his "craziness" gives the defendant, in his own mind, a license as well as an explanation for a lack of responsibility for his own actions. J. C. does not exhibit any remorse toward his victims, and further, emotionally is not, at the present time, capable of generating guilt. This makes him extremely unpredictable and very dangerous. . . .

While he does experience severe psychopathology, he amplifies this pathology in order to defend himself against it. For instance, when he becomes confused, or hears any auditory hallucinations, the patient will explain that by saying, "I enjoy hallucinating because I see God, Jesus, Angels, all the evil against them, too, you know?" The patient, in effect, romanticizes the more bizarre aspects of his symptomatology.

This case illustrates the fundamental psychodynamic and behavioral link between psychosis and psychopathy: *the psychotic state will be aggressively expressed and malevolently used to perpetuate the sadomasochism of the grandiose self-structure*, within which the stranger selfobject has malignantly grown to fantastic and delusional proportions. Aggression will persist until the psychosis disorganizes the personality to such a degree that conscious intent is severely impaired or the behavior becomes so outrageous that external social and legal sanctions bind the aggression.

The delusions of the psychopathic character who is also psychotic parallel the dynamic implications of the hallucinatory experiences. As a final defensive operation against massive psychological disorganization, the delusions are the confused self- and object concepts of the grandiose self-structure, expressed in a fantastic and unrealistic manner. The delusions also concretize the stranger selfobject, the primary identification of the psychopathic process.

Delusional thought content that suggests a psychopathic character organized at a psychotic level is distinguished by the lack of superego constraint apparent in its behavioral expression; the sadistic pleasure experienced during and following the acting out of the delusion; tenacious attempts to rationalize or deny the presence of the delusion in situations where such dissembling will yield impressive gains; suggestions within the delusion of projective identification with evil and its metaphors, such as demons, Satan, the devil, the fallen angel, the AntiChrist, or the forces of darkness; accompanying dysphoria during recompensation, usually because of involuntary treatment, since the delusional material is less accessible; and heightened self-esteem as a result of the grandiose content of the delusions.

The following description illustrates several of these characteristics. The patient was a 31-year-old black male found Not Guilty By Reason of Insanity to one count of Burglary. These are excerpts from a psychological evaluation[2] to determine whether the patient should return to the community following a three-year commitment to the state hospital. The patient was diagnosed as paranoid schizophrenic and antisocial personality disorder:

R. D.'s arrest history began when he was 12 years old. He was charged with Assault with a Deadly Weapon and committed to the California Youth Authority. In 1970 and 1972 he violated parole and was returned to the CYA on both occasions. In 1974 he was charged with Burglary. In 1976 he was arrested for Possession of a Deadly Weapon, Petty Theft, and Resisting an Officer. In 1977 he was found Incompetent to Stand Trial and was committed to Patton State Hospital. In 1978 he was charged with Robbery with a Gun, and in 1979 for being Under the Influence of Drugs and escape from Chino Prison . . .

On or about January 27, 1984, R. D. pried open the door of a house with a crowbar and went inside. He was found in the basement wearing a fatigue jacket belonging to one of the residents. When arrested he claimed he had millions of dollars, that the house belonged to him, and that he was a famous football player. . . . The most salient feature that emerges from a review of his records is his delusional system. He committed the instant offense actually believing that the owners were his aunt and uncle, and they had given the house to him. From time to time he believed himself to be King Tut and other mythical figures, as well as famous sports stars . . .

R. D. presents as a tall, muscular black man who

---

[2]My thanks to Judith Meyers, Psy. D., and Eugene Schiller, L.C.S.W., for permission to use portions of their evaluation.

appears slightly younger than his stated age. . . . He was oriented in all three spheres. There were, however, periods when he did evidence mild disorganization and confusion . . . When asked about the instant offense, he states: "I was suffering from a delusion about the people who lived in the house. I thought that they were my aunt and uncle. They were trying to sell it, and I wanted to buy it. I was not looking for anything. I had a delusion that I lived in the house before."

When asked why he committed the crime he stated that voices were telling him to do it. He stated the voices had given him the combination to the safe. . . . R. D. was questioned about the delusions that he was King Tut and famous baseball players. He smiled, denying he currently thought he was King Tut, "I do not have a logical explanation." He indicated that he just wanted to be great, but thought these identities were basically harmless.

R. D. was asked if he had any regrets or remorse about the crime. He stated that he did. "If I could turn back the hands of time, I'd rather be without the incident. I regret losing three years of my life for something that is not mine. I could have been on the street."

R. D. was asked about an incident in 1985 during a psychotherapy group while in custody. At that time he had expressed a desire to return to the house and kill the occupants. When confronted with this, he stated he was not serious and was "just trying to make people laugh. . . ."

R. D. denied any drug or alcohol abuse at any time in his life . . . as he relaxed, however, anxietal interferences to memory lessened. There were gaps and inconsistencies, however, in his reporting, probably due to his denial system . . . he reports a history of antisocial behavior which began at age 11 when he shot a girl in the eye with a BB gun for beating up his brother. "They locked me up for two years." R. D. reports being expelled from high school at age 16 for running a burning flag up the flagpole. He states he was celebrating the last day of school. He smiled slightly when he recounted the incident, but appeared to barely grasp the inappropriateness of the act. . . .

When asked why he would continue [treatment if released], he stated, "If I don't, I'll wind up dead somewhere."

R. D. was administered the Minnesota Multiphasic Personality Inventory and the Rorschach. Not surprisingly, he produced a two-point 49 profile on the MMPI ($T = 81$ [Scale 4]; $T = 74$ [Scale 9]). The Rorschach produced 13 responses, including 1 human response that was spoiled, 1 reflection response, 1 aggression response, and 1 morbid response. I interpreted the psychological test results as follows:

R. D. would have a high probability of interpreting reality differently and idiosyncratically from others around him. He also would be inclined to confuse external reality with his internal wishful images and perceptions. Although not overtly psychotic at present, the patient shows some signs of confusion of reality in recalling what he considers memories that in actuality are only fantasies that tend to reach quite grandiose proportions . . . R. D. has minimal interest in other people. He has little capacity to empathize with others, and to understand, appreciate, and respect other people's feelings and actions. He is distrustful of other people, yet also dependent upon them to gratify his momentary wants. This would tend to keep him internally in conflict, as he both seeks gratification and does not trust the source of the gratification.

He does not identify with conventional social values and rules. In fact, he is excited by antisocial behavior and derives satisfaction in doing things against the law. There is a marked absence of conscience, but he is able to verbalize conventional rules of conduct if he senses it would please the interviewer or derive gain for him.

The patient evidences chronic anger which he attempts to control and deny within himself. He is moderately impulsive, and will tend to rationalize, blame, and project responsibility onto others for his behaviors, and in circumstances he finds himself.

He has a generally narcissistic attitude toward others in the world, which is exhibited through a sense of entitlement and indignation. He has learned, however, to control this to some degree since he recognizes it will work against his release from custody. His aggressive impulses, and derivative emotions, tend to be unmodulated and intense. He will be inclined to generalize these feelings, and the emotions themselves will perceptually "flood" him and distort his understanding of reality. He does show an ability to think logically and perceptually organize his environment when not emotionally aroused.

R. D. recognizes fully the behaviors that should be manifest to increase his chances of being released from custody. He is quite skilled at dissembling, or concealing, any thoughts or feelings that he considers indicative of pathology and that might work against him.

Three days prior to the evidentiary hearing to determine whether he should be released to the community, and several months after these evaluations, R. D. stated in a psychotherapy group that he owned a Lear Jet, had twenty children, and used to play professional football when he was 12 years old.

Formal thought disorder in the psychopathic character is also pathognomonic of psychotic personality organization. The most striking and revealing example of formal thought disorder expressed to me by a psychopathic personality was the patient who blurted, "I have skeptophrenia." Here a neologism unconsciously betrayed the individual's intent to malinger and exaggerate certain symptoms for behavioral gain; and, in a prescient manner, foreshadowed my own doubt as to his credibility.

The multiple variations of formal thought disorder are the phenotypic expressions of the primary process mechanisms of condensation and displacement (Meloy 1986b):

> The shift toward formal thought disorder through the mechanisms of primary process can be conceptualized on two dimensions. First, the primary process of condensation is a horizontal condensing of abstract, functional, and concrete representations that violates conceptual boundaries of Aristotelian logic and compels identification and equivalence of only similar representations. Second, the primary process of displacement is a vertical shift from abstractions (connotations) to objects and functions (denotations) to phonemes (verbalizations). [p. 54]

The use of the term *formal thought disorder* also implies the maladaptive use of such paleologic thinking. Thought organization is embedded in a social, or object relations, context, and can only be judged disordered when it sabotages the reality-adaptive tasks of the individual (Johnston and Holzman 1979).

Formal thought disorder appears to have significant trait characteristics, especially in the schizophrenias (Holzman 1986). When treated with neuroleptics, thought disorder in chronic schizophrenia does not reduce to normal levels, but the most severe levels are affected (Spohn et al. 1986). And, most germane to the psychopathic process, formal thought disorder appears to be qualitatively, rather than quantitatively, distinctive when comparing manic and schizophrenic psychoses (Andreasen and Grove 1986, Holzman et al. 1986).

I have not seen any clinical expression of formal thought disorder in the psychopathic process that distinguishes it from thought disorder in the absence of psychopathy. Its differential expression in mania and schizophrenia, particularly paranoid schizophrenia, however, does facilitate the oftentimes difficult diagnosis of type of psychosis when seen in the context of a psychopathic character. It is especially relevant to a hypothesis that I will elaborate later in this chapter; namely, that the *characteristic avenues of expression of psychosis in the psychopathic process are mania or paranoia.*

Andreasen and Grove (1986) examined the frequency of thought disorder in 100 psychiatric patients, including two samples of twenty-five manic disordered patients and twenty-five paranoid schizophrenic disordered patients, using their Scale for the Assessment of Thought, Language, and Communication (Andreasen 1978). Considering the eighteen types of thought abnormalities, the manic sample most frequently displayed the following types (in descending order): pressure of speech, derailment, loss of goal, perseveration, circumstantiality, illogicality, incoherence, and distractible speech. The paranoid schizophrenic sample most frequently displayed the following types (in descending order): derailment, poverty of speech, loss of goal, incoherence, perseveration, circumstantiality, tangentiality, and pressure of speech. They concluded that patients with mania tend to be more fluent and disorganized, with a more prominent "positive" thought disorder, whereas patients with schizophrenia tend to be more empty and disorganized, with a more prominent "negative" or impoverished thought disorder. Among the schizophrenias the degree of disorganization may differentiate subtypes; on the other hand, across the entire range of functional psychoses, fluency and productivity may differentiate between affective and schizophrenic disorders.

Holzman and colleagues (1986) reached similar conclusions to those of Andreasen and Grove (1986) in their study of manic, schizophrenic, and schizoaffective patients using the Thought Disorder Index (Johnston and Holzman 1979). The TDI was based on the work of Rapaport and colleagues (1946) and Watkins and Stauffacher (1952) using verbal protocols from the Rorschach. In its most current revised form, it identifies twenty-three categories of thinking disturbance at four levels of severity. Previous work indicated the TDI was highly elevated in all psychotic populations (Johnston and Holzman 1979). Nonpsychotic hospitalized patients, such as personality disorders, had the lowest levels. Gender, ethnicity, social class, and intellectual level did not account for differences between groups (Haimo and Holzman 1979).

The Holzman and colleagues (1986) study identified five factors that embraced fourteen of the TDI categories and best discriminated the schizophrenic and manic patients. In Table 7-1, I and II indicate the manic factors; III, IV, and V indicate the schizophrenic factors. They wrote,

> Manic thought disorder manifests itself as loosely tied together ideas that are excessively and immoderately combined and elaborated. Often, there is a playful, mirthful, and breezy quality to their productions. Intrusions of incongruous ideas into social discourse is one consequence of this propensity.
>
> Schizophrenic thought disorder . . . shows . . . fluid thinking, interpenetrations of one idea by another, unstable verbal referents, and overly concise and contracted communications [giving] the impression of inner turmoil and confusion.
>
> There is, moreover, a set of thinking disorders that appears to be nonspecific . . . vagueness, loss of set, and inappropriate distance. [p. 369]

Table 7-1
Factors Discriminating Manic and Schizophrenic Patients

	TDI Categories
I. Irrelevant intrusion	2. Flippant
	13. Looseness
II. Combinatory thinking	8. Incongruous combinations
	14. Fabulized combination
	15. Playful confabulation
III. Fluid thinking	9. Relationship verbalization
	17. Fluidity
	21. Contamination
IV. Confusion	5. Word finding difficulty
	12. Confusion
	18. Absurd responses
	22. Incoherence
	23. Neologism
V. Idiosyncratic verbalization	4. Peculiar verbalization

Both of these studies suggest qualitative differences between formal thought disorder in manic and schizophrenic psychosis. Andreasen and Grove (1986) noted the particular difference between mania and paranoid schizophrenia, while Holzman and colleagues (1986) were able to discriminate between manic and schizophrenic thought disorder using several factor analytic approaches. Viewed against a background of psychopathic character formation, the nature of the formal thought disorder becomes a clinical marker for determining whether the manic or paranoid mode of psychosis is evident.

Reality Testing

The relative presence or absence of reality testing is the third psychogenic structure noted by Kernberg (1984) to distinguish between borderline and psychotic personality organization. Exner (1986b) compared eighty schizophrenic and eighty-four borderline subjects and found that the X-%, his Rorschach measure of perceptual inaccuracy, was significantly different ($p < .01$) between the two groups. The mean X-% for nonpatients is 6 percent; in the borderline sample it was 13 percent, and in the schizophrenic sample it was 34 percent. Usually, an X-% that exceeds 15 percent indicates problems in perceptual accuracy significant enough to interfere with psychosocial functioning. One-fourth of the borderline subjects (27 percent) exceeded this percentage, perhaps accounting for the presence of transient psychotic states in borderline patients (Kwawer et al. 1980), whereas 90 percent of the schizophrenic patients exceeded this percentage.

I have referred to reality testing in the psychopathic process in several different contexts earlier in this book. For the sake of brevity, I will summarize my earlier points, with appropriate references, concerning the distinctive characteristics of impaired reality testing in the psychopathic process.

First, reality testing is the *sine qua non* of all psychoses, regardless of etiology (Frosch 1983a). When this capacity to measure intrapsychic experience against the actual and immediate interpersonal experience is lost, the psychopathic character is considered psychotic. Reality testing must be carefully distinguished from reality *sense*, distortions of the sensory-perceptual experience, which is pathognomonic of dissociative states in psychopathy (see Chapter 5). Alterations in reality sense, such as depersonalization and derealization, are quite common during acts of both predatory and affective violence in the psychopathic character and must not be misconstrued as a loss of reality testing, hence a psychotic state.

Second, a loss of reality testing in psychopathy implies boundary loss among intrapsychic *conceptual* and *perceptual* representations. The psychopathic process developmentally implicates the conceptual fusion of self- and object representations within the grandiose self-structure (see Chapter 3), but psychotic personality organization brings with it the additional dedifferentiation, or confusion, of self- and object percepts both intrapsy-chically and interpersonally.

Third, the primitive defenses within the psychopathic pro-cess, such as denial, projective identification, simulation, and splitting, and their parallel conscious processes of deception, control, and imitation call for the continuous and massive incor-poration and evacuation of psychic material (see Chapter 5). These processes, however, never imply a loss of sensory-perceptual boundary in and of themselves. What is exchanged is that which is contained, not the container itself (Bion 1977a). The loss of the container, that is, self- and object percept dedifferen-tiation, heralds psychosis, since the distinction between intero-ceptive and exteroceptive stimuli is also lost.

Fourth, *psychotic envelopment* (see Chapter 6) in the psy-chopathic process suggests a gradual loss and recovery of reality testing. Appendix II graphically illustrates the ways in which psychosis can recurrently envelop a psychopathic individual and, at the same time, be used by that individual to perpetuate the sadomasochism of his grandiose self-structure.

This factor is particularly difficult to assess in a forensic context since conscious intent and unconscious psychotic defense may be inextricably bound. It is most relevant to the legal question of insanity and oftentimes goes to the heart of the cognitive prong of the insanity defense: could this individual understand and appreciate the criminality of his act or know that what he was doing was wrong? As noted earlier (see Chapter 6), psychotic envelopment has both temporal and spatial dimension, the former most important to the determination of sanity: De-spite the presence of psychotic symptoms, at what point in time did the individual lose the capacity to distinguish between these symptoms and actual, interpersonal reality? As noted in Ap-pendix II, there is usually much to be gained for the psychopathic character with a psychotic personality organization to both ma-linger and dissemble his psychosis. The malingering usually precedes the finding of insanity; the dissembling precedes the finding of restoration of sanity. It is all the more baffling since psychotic envelopment may be only partial, and a semblance of ego control allows such individuals to use their genuinely psychotic disorders for personal gain. Oftentimes a careful sequential analysis of the violent offense itself, focusing on both the subjective experience of the perpetrator and independent evidence gathered by the criminal investigation, will reveal patterns of affective and/or predatory violence that unravel these issues.

PARANOID ANNIHILATION AND MANIC TRIUMPH

The characteristic avenues of psychotic expression in the psychopathic process are paranoia or mania. From a descriptive psychiatric perspective (American Psychiatric Association 1980, 1987) the most common diagnoses involving both psychosis and psychopathy are schizophrenia, paranoid type, and antisocial personality disorder, or atypical bipolar disorder and antisocial personality disorder. Note, however, that the first Axis I-II diagnosis, although commonly seen in forensic settings, is technically not allowed according to standards established by the DSM-III (American Psychiatric Association 1980), but it is allowed in DSM-III-R (American Psychiatric Association 1987).

The atypical bipolar disorder Axis I diagnosis, for lack of a better fit, is used to describe the manic or hypomanic psychotic personality seen in forensic settings. This individual shows no complete bipolar cycle and oftentimes appears to remain in a rather stable manic or hypomanic state with no history of depressive cycling.

Paranoid Annihilation

The psychosis envelops the psychopathic process with paranoid delusions that naturally, although deviantly, exploit the predatory fear of the grandiose self-structure. The early childhood identification with the aggressor in psychopathy, and its internalization within the grandiose self as the stranger selfobject, leaves a projective residue that continually haunts the psychopath; that is, this individual perversely and aggressively does to others as a predator what may, at any time, be done to him.

This sense of being abandoned by the love object, or invaded by the hate object, has its ontogenetic link in the knowledge of being outside the family or group as a stranger, alienated and subject to predation. This proliferation of predatory anxiety is striking in the hallucinations and delusions of the paranoid schizophrenic (Grotstein 1986); and when linked to the psychopathic process, predatory behavior becomes a vehicle to end such annihilatory fears.

The grandiosity and omnipotence of the defensively organized grandiose self-structure also supports the paranoid delusional material of the psychosis. The grandiosity implicit in paranoid ideation when reality testing is lost is only an enhancement of the legendary self-concepts that already inhabit the grandiose self-structure as fusions of ideal self- and object representations (Kernberg 1975).

In a real sense, the psychotic grandiose self-structure becomes a caricature of aggression and malevolence that has lost contact with reality and is "creepy crawling"[3] in a world of predatory shadows, once persecutory introjects in the individual's mind, now projected onto and into others. (I am grateful to

---

[3]This expression was used by followers of Charles Manson to describe a series of activities that were, in retrospect, rehearsals for the killings of seven individuals known as the Tate-LaBianca murders in Los Angeles, August 1969. Members of the "Family" would surreptitiously enter a home while the occupants were sleeping, and silently "creepy crawl" throughout the home, rearranging as much furniture and belongings as possible without waking the inhabitants. Then they would leave. It markedly increased the Family members' sense of omnipotence, grandiosity, and predatory skill (Bugliosi and Gentry 1974).

Paul Lerner, Ph.D., [personal communication] for this important
distinction between projection [onto] and projective identification [into] through the use of different prepositions [see also
Klein 1946]. It captures the countertransference difference between projection and projective identification: When feelings
and percepts are projected *onto* another, there is little countertransference reaction. When feelings and percepts are projectively identified *into* another, there is a tormenting and uncomfortable sense of being controlled, of now being burdened with
certain internal states that one has no choice but to contain for
the moment, and a desire to evacuate the alien state as soon as
possible. During interactions with the psychotically paranoid
psychopath, the operation of projective identification is quite
apparent. One suddenly knows that he or she is the target of
predation and explicitly feels a sense of weakness, vulnerability,
and foreboding.)

Many of the structural and functional relationships between
paranoid psychosis and psychopathy are apparent in the case of a
31-year-old Caucasian male who was found Not Guilty By Reason
of Insanity for the murder of his father and stepmother. I have
had four years of contact with this individual, immediately following the killings in 1983 until his most recent attempt to seek
release from his state hospital commitment.

P. S. has been descriptively diagnosed as schizophrenic,
paranoid type, chronic, and mixed personality disorder with
narcissistic and schizoid features. He has both an individual and
familial history of antisocial behavior.

> P. S.'s criminal record goes back to age 25 when he was
> charged with Possession of Controlled Substances. He
> was also charged with Disorderly Conduct and Prosti-
> tution. At age 27 he was charged with Possession of
> Controlled Substances and drunk driving. At age 28 he
> was charged with Forgery of credit cards as an accom-

plice to a woman he was going with at the time. At age 30 he was charged with public nudity. . . .

It is stated that P. S.'s brother had also been in jail and his uncle, a half-brother of his father, was convicted of the murder of his own wife. The grandmother was said to be obsessed with voodoo and kept voodoo dolls about with one rolled up in a rug, impaled with a pin.

The patient had a history of sympathomimetic drug abuse, namely methamphetamine and cocaine. He also had experimented with LSD and heroin, but the psychostimulants were his preferred drug. This is highly unusual in just paranoid schizophrenia and is usually pathognomonic of an additional personality disorder with both antisocial and narcissistic features (Meloy 1986a).

The patient's psychotic disorder appeared to begin following the death of his mother of cirrhosis of the liver when he was 26 years old. At this time the patient was obese, and during the next year, he lost 100 pounds. He reports, and psychiatric records corroborate, that he was hounded by anxieties, phobias, and incipient beliefs that people were making fun of him. Records indicate brief and multiple contacts with various providers of psychiatric services.

He lived away from home with various women and acquaintances during the next several years, holding jobs for brief periods of time, but generally finding himself unemployed. He moved back home in February 1982, at the age of 30, reportedly feeling depressed and isolated. His father had remarried a woman named Helena, but was also suffering from severe back problems.

In May 1982, P. S. was taken by his father to the

psychiatric hospital, reporting that he had "lost his temper." The patient admitted hearing voices, telling him he was "lazy, a fag, a queen, and fat." The father reported he needed back surgery, but was afraid to leave P. S. alone in the house with his stepmother. He was prescribed antipsychotic medications, but did not voluntarily continue them.

P. S. "house sat" during 1982 and worked at a local xerox shop. His father entered the hospital in January 1983, and the patient reported being frightened. He perceived his father as "losing all the goals in his life" and his stepmother being partially responsible for this. When his father returned home in March 1983, he appeared "weak, slow moving." P. S. began to hallucinate again.

He first heard the voices of his stepmother and father, "We want you to leave but we're not going to let you go." He began to feel rectal sensations, most noticeably at night. These sensations he later described as a "ball being thrown at your rectum," and delusionally believed that his stepmother was promoting them. He called this sensation, "rectal esophagus."

He continued to be tormented by auditory hallucinations throughout the day, "We want you to be a homo . . . we want you to kill us . . . we will kill you by giving you a heart attack." He confronted his father with his molestation by his stepmother, and the father adamantly denied it.

In early May 1983, P. S. purchased a 12-gauge shotgun and began target shooting. He reportedly had never owned a gun before. On Wednesday night, May 27, 1983, he loaded the gun and heard voices in the middle bedroom. He became frightened, returned to his own room, and unloaded the gun. His stepmother's daughter visited the family the following day, and P. S.

believed she was also afflicting him. On May 29, he was hired as a park aide by the state of California. He drank a six-pack of beer throughout the day, but couldn't sleep that evening. The voices were telling him, "Kill us if you can, kill Helena, kill J. J." He was angry and agitated.

At 0230 on Saturday morning, May 30, 1983, P. S. entered his father and stepmother's bedroom. He shot-gunned his father to death while he lay on his back; he vividly remembers then seeing *his stepmother smile with her eyes closed* before he fired upon her. He then shot his father one more time and called the police.

When P. S. was admitted to our forensic inpatient unit he was acutely psychotic. He did not respond to neuroleptic medications, however, and his hallucin-atory-delusional symptom complex changed dramati-cally. He believed that his muscles were being stripped from his bones, and he could actually feel the tearing as a somasthetic hallucination. This may have been a psychotic embellishment of actual dystonic reaction to the neuroleptics. P. S. now reports that once he left the forensic treatment unit and was committed to the state hospital, these sensations disappeared and have never returned.

The state hospital report concerning his response to treat-ment, written three years after his commitment in February 1987, reads,

His progress in therapy has been slowed by several factors. He is schizoid and has difficulty relating to others. Thus in groups he is reluctant to reveal his own problems and does not "connect" emotionally with oth-ers, and therefore does not benefit much when they talk. He reacts to feedback from both the therapist and peers as criticism and becomes argumentative. He is quite rigid and very reluctant to change. He minimizes his problems. . . . He has difficulty relating to others. He socializes very little and has no close friends. He spends most of his free time alone or sleeping. When he does interact it is to get his own needs met. . . . When he talks about his crime he does so in a very matter of fact way. He expresses little grief or emotion, and seems more concerned about the fact he is locked up. He is just beginning to understand intellectually why he did it, but does not understand his feelings. For a long time he said it was "opportunistic" in that his father and stepmother just happened to be there. He is now beginning to realize that he resented his father remarrying and the fact that he could not talk to his stepmother since she spoke little English . . . and . . . he identified with his father's helplessness. He needs to work more on understanding his sexual delusions at the time of the crime. . . . He feels that his problem will be worked out by getting married, yet he has great difficulty even talking to women, but denies this.

The psychopathic process was not as apparent in P. S. prior to the murder of his father and stepmother. Yet, in retrospect, much of his behavior emerges as an interaction of both his paranoid psychosis and his psychopathic process. Although virtually nothing is known about P. S.'s early environment, four factors stand out that suggest psychopathy in addition to the insidious psychotic disorder: first, a familial antisocial pattern involving first-degree blood relatives of his father; second, an individual antisocial pattern; third, the use of a variety of illicit drugs, but a strong preference for psychostimulants, or more specifically, sympathomimetics such as cocaine and methamphetamine; and fourth, a polymorphous and perverse sexual history. This last factor is based on the cumulative experiences of seven years of homosexual activity, a prostitution arrest, a public nudity arrest, and multiple transient and sequential heterosexual arrangements prior to the murders. The sexuality of P. S. plays a prominent role in the psychosis and predatory violence that ensues and even takes on a perverse negation: P. S. states that he has had no sexual contact with anyone since the murders and adamantly denies that he masturbates. He reports a complete absence of sexual feeling toward males or females and believes that when he marries it will then be time to be sexual again. Clinical records over the past several years support P. S.'s asexual existence. This pattern of perverse sexuality, from polymorphous expression to schizoid abstinence, is typical of the psychopathic process because of the incapacity to form an empathic, caring bond to the eroticized object. This absence of attachment behavior leads to sexual expression as sensory-perceptual novelty without intimacy: the continual pursuit of eroticized skin contact without whole object relatedness.

The psychosis and predatory violence were highly sexualized. The homosexual object choice of P. S., which he had alloplastically expressed years earlier, was transformed into conscious hate and was the basis for his paranoid psychosis (Freud 1911). The articulation of the somesthetic hallucination as "rectal esophagus" suggests a condensation of anal and oral libidinal areas, a regression to a point of maximal sadism for the development of paranoia (Abraham 1954, Klein 1964). "Rectal esophagus" conjures up images of forced incorporation and evacuation of feces-penis-food: a psychotic condensation of both objects and aims.

The paranoid psychotic behavior of P. S. also mirrors an aspect of evolutionary aggression Neuman (1987) called the "paternal male–male power root." The origins of this strong male (the so-called *alpha* bull) and the weaker, effeminized male (the so-called *beta* bull) relationship are found in the higher mammalian task of defining the hunting territory and protecting the group, and thus a pecking order of strength must be established.

An aspect of this competitive male–male interaction, with strong undercurrents of homosexual dominance and submission, is the rage of the *beta* male, effeminized by forced rectal intercourse. Neuman (1987) noted the phylogenetic roots of this rage and the ways in which it was both sublimated and perverted in Greek, Roman, Nordic, and Christian cultures.

In a real sense, the psychotic regression of P. S. recapitulated this alpha–beta bull root form of aggression in his paranoid rage against the father for attempting to anally invade him and transform him into an effeminized, homosexual male.

His rage toward the father was also toward the father's weakness. P. S.'s anger toward the insufficient mother who had died was now displaced to the weak father who could no longer protect him from predation outside the family or provide protection from the devouring, incorporating (step)mother within the family.

The oedipal dimensions of this paranoid psychosis are striking. P. S. kills his father and perceives the stepmother to smile at him. The maternal introject of the biological mother was projectively identified into the stepmother at that moment, resulting in the perceived smile. The pleasure of the maternal introject, communicated to P. S. through a projective identification during the act of patricide, becomes a talismanic expression of the sadism inherent in the oedipal wish.

This acting out of the oedipal wish in the most violent fashion is empirically supportive of the persistence of oedipal conflict in preoedipal, in this case psychotic, regression. Perhaps more cogently, it suggests a rooted oedipal myth existent at a symbiotic level of dyadic relationship to the mother (Mahler et al. 1975). This "oedipal myth preconception" (Grinberg 1981) is a precursor of ego functioning that discovers psychic reality and leads to investigation of the relationship with the parental couple. This "private Oedipus myth" (Bion 1963) within P. S. suffers destructive attacks due to the envy, greed, and sadism of the psychotic personality organization and results in both intrapsychic and interpersonal catastrophe.

P. S. is initially tormented by the stranger selfobject, phenomenally experienced by him as auditory and somesthetic hallucinations: the taunting command to become homosexual and later to kill his stepmother and father. The transformation that occurs because of the psychopathic process is the gradual identification with the auditory hallucination, or stranger selfobject, and its reintegration into the grandiose self-structure as conceptually fused with the ideal self. The auditory hallucination remains as a sensory-percept coming from outside the self, yet the self becomes an agent provocateur of the command hallucination and identifies with its purpose. The intrapsychic transformation is the conceptual fusion of real self + ideal self + ideal object (stranger selfobject) = grandiose self-structure at a psychotic level of expression where perceptual distinctiveness has also been lost among self- and object representations. This contrasts with only the loss of *conceptual* self- and object differentiation in the narcissistic personality's grandiose self-structure (Meloy 1985).

In the interpersonal sphere, reality testing is gone and violence is acted out in a most primitive fashion through a restitutional attempt to symbiotically penetrate and join, through hatred (H), both the stepmother and the father. P. S. shoots his father in the *back* and his mother in the *front*.

But is there empirical support for these intrapsychic transformations that set them apart from a paranoid decompensation without the presence of psychopathy? There are several. First, P. S. *was* an active homosexual prior to the torment of the auditory hallucinations and had alloplastically expressed himself in several polymorphously perverse ways before he became psychotic. Second, unlike the vast majority of schizophrenic individuals (Hellerstein et al. 1987), he did not resist his command hallucinations, but instead became their agent of action. Third, he engaged in purposeful activity, whether conscious or not, to secure both the weaponry and skill necessary to carry out the command hallucinations. Fourth, he showed indications of predation (see Chapter 6) during the two weeks prior to the murders. Fifth, he describes the killings as "opportunistic" and when questioned as to his meaning, states only that his stepmother and father happened to be in the house and that is why they were killed. And sixth, P. S. is very resistant to developing any insight into the nature of his psychotic personality organization. He is continually argumentative and defensive when approached psychotherapeutically and perceives others as psychologically attacking him.

In a rather unusual psychopathic maneuver, P. S. developed a pattern of reporting to subsequent psychiatric investigators that the prior investigator "misinterpreted" what he said. More specifically, he contended that his *memories* of psychotic symptoms were misinterpreted as present psychotic symptoms by each psychologist or psychiatrist that talked to him. He did acknowledge that such psychotic phenomena may have occurred once, but had not occurred since the killings, despite ample documentation of the latter. This rationalization of psychosis as only a memory of psychosis is pathognomonic of the dissociative defenses and states that are rampant in the psychopathic process (see Chapter 5). In such states of mind, actuality may be only a memory, and a memory may have only been a dream. It grossly attenuates a sense of responsibility for experience, yet facilitates the grandiose elaboration of the self as agent in a fantasy-laden, and projectively identified, world (Grotstein 1981, Cahill 1986).

The most recent MMPI profile of P. S. yielded a two-point 94 code type ($T = 70$), with a MacAndrew score of 27 and a moderately "fake good" validity scale configuration. Such a profile suggests an individual who is moderately prone to alcohol and drug addiction and is a poor candidate for psychotherapy because of both conscious defensiveness and unconscious denial of psychological problems. Such individuals with this configuration are not symptomatically psychotic, but are impulsive, energetic, extroverted, and aggressive. They are unconventional and may behave in antisocial ways. They are not depressed, anxious, or ruminative and are quite content with their own sense of self. They are alienated from their family and show a marked degree of social imperturbability.

Manic Triumph

The alternative avenue of psychotic expression in the psychopathic character is mania. It is usually diagnosed as an atypical bipolar disorder (American Psychiatric Association 1980) since there may be a lack of significant depressive cycling. Affective cycling in the manic psychopath oftentimes is quite subtle, and clinicians will find hypomanic character disorders with no apparent cycling (Eckblad and Chapman 1986).

The mania of the psychopath is the expression of predatory triumph. It is the elation following the killing of the predator. Mania provides the affective vehicle, which may reach psychotic proportions, that defensively triumphs over the persecutory and sadistic introjects that lie in the shadows outside the grandiose self-structure.

The manic psychopath is fearless. Identification with the stranger selfobject within the grandiose self-structure reaches such grandiose proportions that persecutory introjects pale in comparison. Such individuals truly fear no evil because they have become the grandiose, malignant force once perceived in others. The fear of annihilation is disavowed through conceptual and perceptual fusion with the annihilator, a psychotic caricature of the stranger selfobject.

The biological predisposition to manic-affective states fuels the grandiosity inherent in the psychodynamic construction of the self in the psychopath. Mania is consciously welcomed because of the autonomic hyporeactivity and consequent sensation seeking of the psychopath (see Chapter 2). It is oftentimes artificially sought through the ingestion of psychostimulants such as methamphetamine hydrochloride. The manic psychopath is notoriously noncompliant with prescribed medications, such as lithium carbonate, intended to stabilize and dampen an affective disorder.

The cruelty and sadism of the psychopath will also be exaggerated in states of manic excitement. The desire to control and degrade the actual object, which may be projectively identified as the container of persecutory introjects, may be fueled by the mania, which, in turn, may be fueled by the sadistic pleasure inherent in the behavior. This interactive effect of the manic state and sadistic arousal, spiraling upward in a vicious pattern of behavior, will oftentimes be assessed by the individual, in retrospect, in a quite flippant manner:

> M. P. was charged with kidnapping. He was diagnosed as an atypical bipolar disorder and antisocial personality disorder. When I asked him what he had done, he stated that he had handcuffed his girlfriend to the stickshift of his sportscar and drove, despite her protestations, to Las Vegas from California. When I asked him why he did this, he said, "It was my Italian way of saying, 'I love you.'"

The loss of reality testing in manic psychosis is usually signaled by delusional identification with a warlike force, a predator of mythological proportions. In the case I will analyze below, B. L., in states of manic psychosis while in custody, would dress himself as an Indian warrior using his feces as warpaint. Similar to the paranoid avenue in psychopathy, the loss of reality testing in manic psychosis is the perceptual fusion of real self, ideal self, and ideal object (the stranger selfobject) within the grandiose self-structure, in addition to the already fused conceptual self- and object representations, a correlate of narcissistic personality disorder. The manic psychopath is not similar to, but identifies with, the myth of the warrior. The primary process of condensation violates conceptual boundaries of Aristotelian logic and compels psychotic equivalence of only similar representations (Meloy 1986a). The manic psychopath is truly a Dionysian figure.

The manic avenue of psychotic expression in the psychopath is vividly illustrated by a 26-year-old Caucasian male whom I have clinically known for the past three years. He has historically been diagnosed as bipolar disorder, mixed type, and antisocial personality disorder. Despite his superior intelligence, education, and family background (his father is a urologist), B. L. has a history of medication noncompliance and violent behavior toward authority figures since age seventeen.

For the past two years, B. L. has nurtured in fantasy a highly erotic and aggressive relationship toward an attractive, female Superior Court judge with whom he initially had brief criminal dispositional contact. The situation escalated to the point where his conditions of probation explicitly forbade him to send any correspondence to the specific judge or to enter any courthouse in the state of California without his attorney, probation officer, or conservator present.

Despite these conditions, B. L. continued to send written correspondence and several audiotape recordings to the judge, which resulted in his probation violation in 1987 and commitment. His psychodynamics that blend both mania and psychopathy are quite apparent in samples of correspondence that he sent the judge:

> Red blood out and black blood in, my Nannie says I'm a child of sin. How did I choose me my witchcraft kin? Know I as soon as dark's dreams begin. Shared is my heart in a nightmare's gin. Never from terror I but may win.

This poem reflects the patient's identification with evil, intrapsychically represented by the fusion of ideal self and the stranger selfobject within the grandiose self-structure. It is a defensive refuge against a paranoid condition that he is unable to master (Klein 1935).

On March 17, 1987, he sent her the following messages:

As I sit in sunny Poway, California, I jerk off just thinking about you.

a Zen Koan

I love you because you've got the balls to wear black.

Ten days later his sexually distasteful, but clever, notes became more grandiose and aggressive, expressing the sense of omnipotence that foremost characterizes mania:

For America, for this righteous nation, Let's show the world we're not licked and then I'll fuck you so hard and so strong you won't walk for a week (God willing).

Two days later he had decompensated to the point of forsaking all eroticism and wanting only to aggressively master and control his internalized objects, projectively identified with the female judge. He denied the importance of his good object representations, while at the same time betraying the menacing qualities he felt from his persecutory introjects (Klein 1935).

The question was, how does a man become so dashing, so strong, so smooth, so debonnaire, so suave, so cool and collected under pressure, so loving, so giving, so altruistic, so sensitive, and yet remain so humble?

Well, very simply, it's none of your fucking business, and if you don't get that pud out of my face I'm going to put your ass through a wall.

love, B. L.

Klein (1935) also noted that the manic masters his internal objects to not only prevent them from injuring him, but also from damaging each other during dangerous sexual intercourse. This could result in the death of both good and bad object representations, both within and outside the grandiose self-structure. The manic psychopath's hunger for objects, what Freud (1921) called the feast of mania, finds this prospect intolerable. He is both contemptuous of his internalized objects, yet also hungers for them. This intrapsychic phenomenon is curiously illustrated in another letter written by B. L.:

> Judge _____, your objection is overruled. The fact that you are already married is irrelevant. What you are going to do is tell the old man that you love him deeply and always will *and* that you would like to have an open arrangement for awhile. Teach me, _____, teach me.

The threatening letters and tapes that the judge communicated to me presented an obligatory clinical situation in which I felt it necessary to evaluate the patient to determine whether or not he represented a substantial threat of serious physical harm to her. Below are excerpts from that report that further illustrate the dynamic relationship between the psychopathic process and manic psychosis:

> It is my professional opinion that B. L. does pose an imminent and serious personal threat to you at the present time. I have based my opinion on the following facts and opinions.
>
>   First, B. L. has a criminal history dating to November 8, 1978, that includes four different episodes of violence and two dangerous weapons charges. At least two of these episodes involve violence toward authority figures, and on at least one occasion a peace

officer was injured. I have also personally observed B. L. threaten and physically intimidate psychiatric staff, security staff, and other inmates while in custody on several occasions since 1983.

Second, B. L. has a documented history of carrying weapons, especially knives, and also has received training in the martial arts. His actual skill as a martial artist, however, is unknown to me.

Third, B. L. has a history of affective disorder since age 17, generally of the manic type. When he is in a manic and psychotic state, he is grandiose, threatening, impulsive, and is inclined to be violent toward others. I have personally observed this behavior when he has been in custody.

Fourth, despite B. L.'s intelligence, which is estimated to be in the superior range; the support of his family of whom his father is a physician; his six-year license as a Psychiatric Technician in the state of California; and his comprehensive knowledge of his affective disorder and appropriate treatment for it, he is regularly noncompliant with his medication. In other words, he chooses to stop taking his medications as prescribed, usually lithium carbonate, and then decompensates within a two- to four-week period into a psychotic state.

Fifth, in addition to his affective disorder, B. L. also has a personality disorder which can best be described as narcissistic and antisocial. This increases his risk of violence because he has little genuine empathy for others, he tends to disparage acceptable social conduct, and he has a very self-centered orientation to others and the world. His personality disorder is such that he is able to consciously use his psychotic disorder for his own pleasure, and to frighten and intimidate others, until he becomes so disorganized that he can no longer function. I have personally observed him malinger and exaggerate certain psychiatric symptoms to frighten others and to gain certain gratifications. He has refined this ability quite well, and it substantially increases his violence risk.

Sixth, B. L. appears to have a capacity for both predation and sadism. In other words, he appears to derive pleasure from both inflicting emotional distress on others, as well as planning certain aggressive behaviors. I have observed this when he is in custody, and his aggressiveness and sadism are clearly apparent in his letters and tape recordings to you.

Seventh, he has fixated upon you as a hated, yet erotic, sexual object in his mind. This fixation, at present, has a two-year duration, including escalation in March 1987 to direct threats of violence toward you ("I'm going to put your ass through a wall") and explicit sexual obscenities ("You're so prim and proper I'll bet you have lilacs for pubic hairs, you whore.") The recent escalation is also supported by his risking sending you audiotapes that indicate his extreme and sudden emotional lability when he believes he is communicating directly to you. He has taken the step of communicating to you on a more intimate and direct level. He clearly feels rebuffed and rejected by you as a once idealized, and now ragefully devalued, female object.

Eighth, B. L. is willing to exercise deception to secure what he wants. One example is his deception of his probation officer to seek her permission to send further correspondence to you.

Ninth, he refused to follow a request by the court not to write to you, showing some disdain for the authority of the court, as well as a willingness to taunt it with sexual references ("I love you because you've got the balls to wear black").

Tenth, B. L. refused to cooperate with me when I attempted to interview him on April 20, 1987. He remained intentionally mute, but did nod when I asked him if he was choosing to be mute and refusing to talk. I did not inform him of the purpose of my interview and made no statements concerning his threats toward you. At present he continues to take his medication voluntarily, his lithium blood levels were in therapeutic range as of April 16, and he currently shows no signs of psychosis. It must be remembered, however, that the medication does not treat his personality disorder, other than to allow him to organize and better control his behavior.

Eleventh, B. L. prides himself, partially because of his martial arts training, in having a "warrior mentality." This is ominous. It means that he probably derives pleasure from adversity, especially when faced with threats from authorities he perceives as quite powerful, such as judges; and he will strive to have little conscious regard for his own personal safety, holding forth for some higher ideal instead. I have no idea what this "ideal" might be, or how it would change when he becomes psychotic.

The alternative avenues of psychotic expression in psychopathy, in my clinical experience, rarely overlap. This may be due to the independent biological loading for the schizophrenias and affective disorders that has some empirical support (Andreason et al. 1987).

In summarizing the distinctions between paranoid and manic psychosis in psychopathy, I find several pertinent characteristics: first, both exaggerate certain functional, but different, patterns of the grandiose self-structure. The paranoid psychosis exaggerates the fear of annihilation from persecutory introjects outside the grandiose self, whereas the manic psychosis exaggerates the grandiosity and omnipotence within the grandiose self.

Second, manic psychosis serves a defensive function against paranoid decompensation. It could be viewed as a developmentally higher level of psychotic expression since there is an object hunger, although expressed in a cannibalistic, incorporative fashion (Klein 1935).

Third, both paranoid and manic psychoses involve identification with the stranger selfobject, the ideal object within the grandiose self-structure. This identification, however, takes on psychotic proportions since there is a loss of both conceptual and perceptual boundaries among object representations. The purpose of such psychotic identification in manic psychosis is to *master and control*; in paranoid psychosis the purpose is to *destroy*.

And fourth, the psychopathic process intensifies and facilitates the alloplastic expression of these intrapsychic maneuvers. In other words, actual reality provides a stage upon which these primitive object relational conflicts can be acted out, sometimes in a most violent and heinous manner. Paranoid psychopaths, however, will express their psychopathology in a most virulent and angry way; manic psychopaths will be more teasing, arrogant, and sadistically playful.

MALINGERING AND DISSEMBLING

A very important clinical question is the degree to which the psychopathic character can dissemble or malinger functional psychosis. As noted above, the concealment of a psychosis has particularly important ramifications when forensic issues of disposition are being considered. Malingering issues usually arise in forensic settings during periods of preconviction or presentencing. Several authors have recently addressed these issues from a clinical perspective (Shapiro 1984, Cavanaugh and Rogers 1984, Rogers 1986). I wish instead to focus on a more subtle, and inferential, question: Given the presence of a functional psychosis, and given the presence of a psychopathic character structure, can the clinician reasonably expect malingering or dissembling? And if so, why?

Malingering

I have already explored the psychopathic inclination, and defensive predisposition, to malinger various psychopathological states such as amnesia and multiple personality disorder (see Chapter 5). I have found clinically that psychopathic individuals are usually dismal failures when they attempt to malinger a psychotic disorder when, in fact, no such disorder exists. Here I am concerned with the psychopathic individual who actually does have a functional psychotic disorder at times, but will use knowledge of this disorder to feign or exaggerate symptoms for the purpose of avoiding behavioral responsibility.

Such an individual, diagnosed as paranoid schizophrenic and antisocial personality disorder, is the focus of my evaluation in Appendix II, and this report should be reviewed before proceeding further.

In cases such as this, especially in a forensic setting, the clinician should reasonably expect malingering, or at least exaggeration, of psychotic symptoms. In fact the forensic clinician, during the pretrial period of time, should rigorously attempt to *disprove* the psychotic hypothesis through all clinical and investigatory means available to him or her. One should assume malingering unless there is clear and convincing evidence that the psychosis genuinely exists at the time of the evaluation.

In evaluation situations where a retrospective analysis of the patient's mental state is in order, such as a Not Guilty By Reason of Insanity plea, it is critical that the clinician *not* make the following assumptions without strong clinical support: that the crime (or behavioral event) occurred during a psychotic state because the person has a history of psychosis; that the crime was a direct result of the psychosis because the person was evidencing psychotic symptoms at the time of the crime; that reality testing was lost, and the person was completely enveloped by his psychosis, because he evidenced psychotic symptoms at the time. Each of these assumptions, in a pretrial forensic context, must be carefully tested as hypothesis and fail to be disproved before it can be accepted as clinical fact.

For instance, an individual who reports command hallucinations as the reason for his criminal behavior, in the absence of other psychotic symptoms such as formal thought disorder or delusional thought content, puts himself in a very small normative group and should be viewed with much suspicion: Most functionally psychotic individuals do not experience command hallucinations, and of those who do, they generally successfully resist them (Hellerstein et al. 1987). Furthermore, hallucinations are usually accompanied by other psychotic symptoms (American Psychiatric Association 1980, 1987).

The intentional exaggeration or malingering of a psychotic state in the psychopathic character with a history of psychosis serves several intrapsychic functions: It facilitates the manipulative cycle (Bursten 1972) and through the deceptive act leads to conscious affective states of exhilaration and contempt; it allows for the denial of whole sectors of reality as a fundamental defense in the psychopathic process; it provides an opportunity to imitate and simulate (see Chapter 5) psychotic behavior, whether it has been learned from the psychotic portion of the self or from other psychotic patients that the psychopath may be exposed to on acute psychiatric inpatient wards; it allows for the further disavowal of responsibility by transforming memories into psychotic experiences and perhaps psychosis into dream; it allows the psychopathic character to identify with the stranger selfobject during periods of psychosis and thus seek such pseudoidentification at other times as a defensive operation against persecution from without or within; and the psychosis may simply provide a rationalization for behavior in a situation where one is demanded.

Dissembling

The concealment of psychosis by the psychopathic character is most commonly seen in forensic commitment settings where issues of restoration of competency or insanity are being considered. The positive reinforcement for such behavior is usually the prospect of transfer to a less restrictive environment.

As with malingering, the clinician should assume dissembling in a psychopathic character with a history of psychosis, especially in postconviction, commitment settings. Rigorous clinical attempts should be made to disprove the hypothesis that the patient is no longer psychotic. The following assumptions should *not* be made without strong clinical support: The patient is symptom-free because he no longer verbalizes hallucinations or delusional thought content; the patient's reality testing is adequate because he verbalizes an understanding of his psychotic disorder; the absence of reported hallucinations means the accompanying delusions have remitted; the patient would tell the clinician if he was still experiencing psychotic symptoms; the patient does not have the ego control to intentionally conceal his psychotic symptoms; the psychosis either exists or it doesn't — there is no such thing as psychotic envelopment or partial remission.

The case of R. D. described earlier illustrates the capacity of the psychopathic character to dissemble psychotic symptoms. His dissembling was revealed by careful perusal of his hospital records, conversations with several hospital staff members over a period of time, and administration of the Rorschach and MMPI as complementary projective and objective personality measures.

The case of P. S. also illustrates dissembling in a psycho-pathic character with a history of paranoid schizophrenia. I noted the unusual clinical manner by which P. S. would attempt to convince subsequent evaluators that reports of his psychotic symptoms were only misinterpretations of his reported *memories* of psychotic symptoms.

The uncovering of concealed psychosis usually requires, as in these cases, the use of both psychological testing and a 24-hour behavioral database. I have found the Rorschach most useful in assessing the reality testing of the individual since it is done by measuring sensory-perceptual convergence with a normative group that is independent of the patient's efforts to conceal thought content. The Rorschach can be "beaten," however, by giving so few responses that the test is invalid (Exner 1986a). Such behavior should alert the clinician to a patient who does not want his psychological operations explored, which would increase the probability of dissembling. The MMPI is an excellent, complementary self-report measure of personality variables and psychiatric symptomatology. Its usefulness in issues of dissembling is twofold: to confirm or disconfirm Rorschach hypotheses and to yield validity scales, such as "fake good" and "subtle-obvious" configurations, that may support a dissembling hypothesis.

Dissembling serves several intrapsychic functions: to carry out the manipulative cycle (Bursten 1972) through deception, leading to affective states of exhilaration and contempt; to deny whole sectors of reality, in this case the psychotic portion of the personality; to heighten a sense of control (Doren 1987) over the environment and the perceived sense of self; to imitate or simulate the psychological health the patient perceives in those he envies and devalues; to protect the grandiose self-structure from annihilation, especially in states of partially remitted paranoid psychosis; and to support the dissociative or splitting aspects of the psychopathic character by encapsulating or containing psychotic experience.

PSYCHOTIC MODES OF AGGRESSION

The two modes of aggression detailed in Chapter 6, affective and predatory, are both available to the psychopathic character organized at a psychotic level of personality. An analysis of each discrete violent event to determine whether it is predominately affective or predatory should be done independently of the psychodiagnostic configuration.

A microanalysis of the violent event may also yield a pattern of sequential change between modes of aggression. For example, a psychopathic individual may repeatedly engage in acts of predatory violence that are motivated by an encapsulated delusion that contains a number of fantasied persecutors. At the moment of actual physical contact with a victim, however, the predatory mode of aggression gives way to an affective mode, and the paranoid psychopathic individual is intensely autonomically aroused, reactive, and threatened; in other words, most of the criteria for affective violence listed in Table 6–1 (p. 235) will be met. In both modes of aggression, however, the psychopathic character continues to be psychotic and delusional, but psychopathy has facilitated the use of predatory violence.

The sequence may be reversed. A psychopathic individual who is psychotic may engage in a sudden, unplanned, and reactive episode of affective violence; in the aftermath of the physical violence, he may quickly shift to a predatory mode of aggression. This could result in planned, purposeful, and sadistic abuse or mutilation of the victim or in carefully planned maneuvers to disguise the affective violence or establish evidence that some other individual perpetrated the act. Throughout the sequential shift, however, the individual could still remain quite psychotic.

The use of predatory violence by a paranoid and psychopathic individual is illustrated by the case in Appendix II. The pattern in this case of an individual who engages in repeated acts of predatory violence, motivated by paranoid delusions, and then is able to use his paranoid schizophrenia to be found Not Guilty By Reason of Insanity, is classic.

The case of P. S. illustrates a slightly different pattern of aggression. Here the predominant mode of aggression is affective, but the psychopathic character of the patient supports the planned and purposeful nature of the predatory behavior that eventually leads to the murder of his stepmother and father. In the case of B. L., the manic psychopath, on the other hand, the patient is predominately predatory toward the female judge despite his enveloping manic psychosis.

All of these cases underscore the fundamental independence but interactional relationship between modes of aggression and levels of personality organization. Affective and predatory represent the poles of the aggressive dimension, borderline and psychotic represent the poles of the personality dimension. I have said earlier, however, and it bears repeating, that predatory violence is not independent of the psychopathic process, and, in fact, appears to be quite dependent upon psychopathy as a characterological template for its expression. Affective violence may also be supported by the psychopathic need for compensatory autonomic stimulation.

Returning to the Kernberg (1984) distinction between character type and level of personality organization, modes of aggression appear to correlate with the former and function independently, although they interact, with the latter. This apparent distinction is critical for accurate psychological evaluations, particularly in forensic settings involving criminal responsibility.

DRUG-INDUCED PSYCHOSIS AND PSYCHOPATHY

As I have noted throughout this book, the psychopathic process supports the use of psychostimulants. I have found this hypothesis clinically valid through my own experience, and it gains

construct validity through its close relationship to the psychopath's peripheral autonomic hyporeactivity, sensation-seeking,
and use of such drugs as transitional objects. Antisocial behavior
in individuals who abuse central nervous system depressants
such as barbiturates and opiates is usually not caused by a
psychopathic process, but is secondary to an economic need to
support a drug habit.

The illicit drugs of choice for the psychopathic character
appear to be cocaine hydrochloride and various forms of amphet-
amine and methamphetamine. All of these chemical substances
share psychostimulant, or sympathomimetic, properties, and all
may induce states of psychosis in the abusing individual.

The psychodynamic impact of these substances on the psychopathic process is essentially identical to the functional psychoses. When enough of these substances are introduced into the
central nervous system a loss of reality testing occurs and the
individual is clinically psychotic. The alternative manic and paranoid functional avenues of psychotic expression in the psychopathic process may, however, comingle when artificially induced
by a chemical substance. Acute intoxication with methamphetamine will clinically mimic paranoid schizophrenia, but the accompanying autonomic arousal will also mimic manic or hypomanic
symptomatology. Chronic abuse of methamphetamine appears to
induce paranoid delusions or, at least, a hypervigilant, suspicious
attitude toward the environment that will sometimes persist for
three to six months following the last ingestion of the drug. This
last finding is suggested by anecdotal clinical experience and has
not, to my knowledge, been clinically researched in any systematic fashion. One colleague of mine, Ben Bensoul, M.D., has
hypothesized that trace elements of the metamphetamine metabolites may remain in the cerebral spinal fluid and cause such
residual personality alterations.

Acute and chronic use of cocaine hydrochloride also inter-
acts with the paranoid and manic avenues of psychosis in the
psychopathic character. Acute intoxication may precipitate para-

noid rage reactions with concomitant affective violence. Chronic abuse of cocaine will usually signal the development of a paranoid state, symptomatically expressed in irritability, labile moods, hypervigilance, suspiciousness, ideas of reference, and persecutory delusions. The violence that may ensue during chronic use of cocaine will oftentimes be predatory in nature, but is motivated by delusional thought content that usually centers upon the illegal possession and sale of the substance.

The clinical properties of both methamphetamine and cocaine exaggerate the characteristics of the grandiose self-structure: An already conscious sense of self as being larger than life is further inflated; windows of ego vulnerability are temporarily closed; a sense of omniscience and omnipotence is heightened; and actual others can be regarded, without the intrusion of reality, as conceptual extensions of the self. On the other hand, the psychodynamic relationship between the grandiose self-structure and persecutory introjects outside the grandiose self is intensified to a paranoid degree: The evacuation of these persecutory introjects into the environment is more easily accomplished because their projective fit is no longer constrained by reality testing; actual objects assume psychotic identities as conspirators and persecutors of the psychopath; autonomic reactivity is heightened, therefore affective violence is more likely; and the inclination to engage in predatory violence may find its rationale in paranoid delusions.

The following excerpts from a forensic case are illustrative. This individual was diagnosed with a cocaine delusional disorder and mixed personality disorder with antisocial and paranoid traits. This precommitment report was done following a finding of Not Guilty By Reason of Insanity to charges of Attempted Murder, Assault with a Deadly Weapon, Use of a Gun, and Ex-Felon in Possession of a Gun.[4]

---

[4]Many thanks to Judith Meyers, Psy.D., and Edward Calix, Ph.D., for these excerpts from their report.

According to police records, B. W. broke several windows in an apartment where he was living at the time, and began to throw furniture toward the outside. He was yelling for others to call the police, as he believed someone was trying to kill him. When uniformed police officers came to the door, the defendant refused to let them in. When they heard three gunshots inside the apartment, they left the area and called the SWAT team. When the SWAT team arrived, they tried to contact the defendant, with no results. Eventually they entered the apartment after they threw tear gas and found B. W. barricaded in the bathroom. At that time gunfire was exchanged and B. W. was shot seven times by the officers.

B. W. spent the entire night before the instant offense "coking." He was staying with his girlfriend, Mathilda, and their daughter. At 0600 he asked them to leave. He believed he saw two men lurking outside and was protecting his family, as well as himself.

Once his family left, B. W. believed that he saw the windowshades moving, and the closet door sliding in the bedroom. He was sure that men were going to kill him and were hiding in the closet. Within 10 or 15 minutes, he believed that the gas had been turned on outside of his apartment, and was becoming dizzy from the smell. Not knowing what to do, he began to break out the windows with a chair. It was then that he believed he saw the outside door begin to move. He felt an attack was imminent. He indicated that in a state of terror he began to scream for his life, pace back and forth and break windows to get the attention of others. He was sure that he heard voices saying, "There is no way out, motherfucker. Why don't you make a run for it." In the process of breaking windows, he cut himself and was bleeding profusely.

B. W. eventually barricaded himself in the bathroom. He was growing weaker. When the SWAT team arrived, he did not believe they were really the police. He recalled shots being fired back and forth and that he fired three shots "straight up in the air" in an attempt to get help from "the real police." During this time, B. W. believed that the real men hiding in the closet made a getaway and escaped the detection of the SWAT team.

Evaluations that were done following the offense all came to the same conclusion–that B. W. was suffering from cocaine delusional disorder at the time of the offense. Dr. A. stated, "The paranoid psychotic state, with delusions, ideas of reference, false perceptions, and misinterpretations of reality" characterized B. W. at the time of the offense. "Although from the SWAT team point of view it looked like he was attacking them, he was in his delusional reality defending himself against being murdered by a gang of drug dealers."

Dr. K. stated, "B. W. is an intelligent young man with both antisocial and paranoid personality traits. The latter made him vulnerable to the long-term effects of cocaine, and he developed a psychotic, paranoid, delusional state, which went beyond the acute intoxication effects of cocaine in both quality and duration."

Dr. F. stated, "Typical of cocaine psychosis, B. W. developed ideas of reference in an organized, persecutory delusional system, that came to encompass more and more of what went on around him in the environment. He became increasingly sensitive to environmental events that fit in with his initial premise and ignored those that did not."

B. W. is a 34-year-old Hispanic male. His initial

presentation was somewhat arrogant and defensive, but he became less so as our interview progressed.

He was asked to recount the instant offense. He stated, "I got shot by the SWAT team. There was a contract out on my life. I wasn't dealing drugs, though."

B. W. went on to say that he felt people were out to kill him due to their thinking he had informed on them. Leading up to the day of the shooting, he had gone to the bank and withdrawn money to send to his wife in Los Angeles. He also had a gun. That same day he was sure that he saw drug dealers from San Ysidro on his block. He became increasingly frightened, and by 0600 the following morning, he had his girlfriend and daughter leave.

He described his pacing around the room, checking the house, and believing others were there. He heard someone state, "Go ahead and try to make a run for it, you motherfucker." He tried to fire his gun, but it jammed. He felt this was further evidence that he was being framed.

He went on to describe how he broke the windows as a way of getting attention. "I got excited and tried to jump out a window. I cut myself bad. I tied a tourniquet on my arm and went into the bathroom. I laid on the floor. I felt that was the only way I could defend myself. The cops came with tear gas. They knocked the door in. I didn't know they were cops, so I shot. The door was still closed when I shot." B. W. was then asked why he pled insanity. He admitted he did no feel that he was psychotic, "just hysterical." He felt that he had been using too much cocaine, and had a "breakdown."

B. W. was asked whether he felt he overreacted. He stated that he did not think that he overreacted. At the time of the interview he still believed that drug dealers thought him an informant, and that he was just trying to defend himself. He also believed that the police were partly at fault for what happened. He felt they should have announced themselves. He felt it was a ridiculous situation that he wound up shooting the police. "I was the guy calling the cops."

B. W. went on to state that he had believed for a long time that he was vulnerable. He stated that he had written a letter naming men who would be out to kill him. He stated that he gave this letter to his girlfriend in case he got killed. This letter is in his police file . . . .

B. W. was oriented in all three spheres. He presented as intelligent and cogent. His thoughts were logical and goal-oriented. He did not appear to be delusional at this time, but he has little insight into his crimes. He believes that he was justified in his actions, and that the conspiracy on his life did, in fact, exist.

B. W. does not understand the effects that drugs have on his behavior. He stated that he could benefit from a drug rehabilitation program, but only to remove him from a drug life-style, not necessarily the effects of the drugs. "Yes, coke started the whole thing, but not the effects of the drug. It was the people." When further questioned about the emotional side effects of taking cocaine, he stated, "It makes you docile. I'm not going anywhere on cocaine."

MENTAL RETARDATION AND PSYCHOPATHY

Psychosis and mental retardation do not necessarily correlate in any clinical population, but they have both been woefully neglected as areas of research adjunctive to psychopathy.

The mentally retarded psychopath does not fit the clinical or popular stereotype of the psychopathic character; such individuals are not socially facile, charming, or highly intelligent. More-over, they will usually present as socially inept, transparent in their manipulation, and predisposed to impulsive violence when frustrated.

The research concerning the mentally retarded psychopath is quite limited. Heilbrun (1979, 1982) hypothesized that the unsocialized qualities and lower intelligence of the psychopath correlated with violent and impulsive crime, and he outlined several models in which cognitive and psychopathic factors com-bine to precipitate several types of violence. Heilbrun based his selection of psychopaths, however, on self-report measures that have been shown to be quite unreliable in determining psycho-pathy (Hare 1985a).

Hare and McPherson (1984) used a twenty-two item check-list (Hare 1980) to differentiate ninety-eight inmates into psycho-pathic, nonpsychopathic, and mixed groups. They further differ-entiated them into high (>102) IQ and low (<102) IQ groups based upon the Weschler Adult Intelligence Scale and the Re-vised Beta Examination. They found that the relationship be-tween violence and psychopathy was unaffected by intelligence, except for frequency of weapon use. The high IQ psychopathic group used a weapon significantly more often ($p<.01$) than the low IQ psychopathic group. These results, however, were oppo-site to those that would be predicted from Heilbrun's (1979, 1982) findings.

Bailey (1987) argued that intelligence is a major mediator in his theory of phylogenetic regression–progression: "High intelli-gence . . . provides the potential for progressing beyond animal needs into the world of ideas and reflection. Low intelligence, on the other hand, limits the possibilities for phylogenetic progres-sion" (p. 52). MacAndrew and Edgerton (1964) associated ex-tremely low intelligence with an impaired capacity for encultu-ralization. Other researchers have argued that the mentally retarded individual has a greater reliance on subcortical mecha-nisms such as territoriality and dominance (Paluck and Esser

1971, Hereford et al. 1973) and a heightened sensitivity to phylogenetically conditioned releasing stimuli such as the predatory
stare (Bailey et al. 1977). The male with lower than average
intelligence has been noted to be at higher risk for regressive
acting out in the form of juvenile delinquency (Sagarin 1980),
physical violence or murder (Holland et al. 1981, Holcomb and
Adams 1982), and sex offenses such as rape (Rada 1978).

In my own anecdotal clinical experience, I have found that
mentally retarded individuals brought into custody are invariably charged with one of two felony offenses: child molestation or
arson. The former may be due to a developmental "felt twinship"
between the offenders and their chronologically younger victims,
expressed through their biologically mature sexual impulse; the
latter offense, arson, may be attributable to anger that is passive-
aggressively expressed through this particularly dangerous "set
and run" behavior.[5]

Research concerning the prevalence of the mentally retarded offender is also quite limited. Brown and Courtless (1971)
found the prevalence rate of mentally retarded inmates across
state institutions to range from 2.6 percent to 24.3 percent, with
a national mean of 9.5 percent. Denkowski and Denkowski (1985),
however, found in a more recent and carefully designed study
that the national rate of mental retardation in state prisons, as
derived through a Weschler Adult Intelligence Scale-Revised
diagnosis using an IQ cutoff of < 70, did not exceed the 3 percent
level that characterizes society in general. This rate (2 percent
prevalence average among twenty state prison systems) was
one-third the magnitude of those prisons using group IQ testing
to identify retarded inmates (6.2 percent prevalence average
among ten state prison systems).

Although several research efforts have been made to diag-
nose psychopathology among mentally retarded adults (Sovner

---

[5]I would like to thank Richard Rappaport, M.D., and Park Dietz, M.D., for
this adept description of some arsonists.

and Hurley 1983, Senatore et al. 1975), diagnosis of coexistent psychopathology is complicated by "overshadowing," in which clinicians predominantly focus on the patient's intellectual deficiencies rather than signs of emotional disturbance (Reiss et al. 1982).

Studies that investigate any psychological, biological, or social aspects of the mentally retarded psychopath using empirically derived measures to define the population, such as Hare's (1980) psychopathy scale and the Weschler Adult Intelligence Scale-Revised, have yet to be done. But I would like to offer some clinical observations and psychodynamic formulations concerning the relationship between psychopathy and mental retardation.

There does not appear to be any correlation between psychopathy and intelligence, but interactive effects clearly exist. Mentally retarded psychopaths are not socially facile and interpersonally charming. They will clinically present as fundamentally instinctual individuals whose behavioral repertoire is primarily sexual or aggressive in nature. There will be no refinement of emotionality; in other words, in addition to an absence of empathy, there is little capacity for the internal experience of various gradations of emotion. Furthermore, the motivation or capacity to cognitively process such emotional vicissitudes, if they existed, is virtually absent.

A lack of immediate gratification will often result in impulsive, antisocial behavior that is usually channeled through sexual or physical violence. This behavior, however, is quite transparent and is consequently much more predictable than in the intelligent psychopath who has learned to use deception as a social instrument. Although the mentally retarded psychopath is more predisposed to predatory violence than the mentally retarded nonpsychopath, the planning, preparation, and rumination are usually more obvious. Such individuals will also be more prone to affective violence than the intelligent psychopath as a result of reduced capacity to cognitively inhibit their impulses.

The internalized object relations of the mentally retarded psychopath parallel those of psychopathy in general but will not have the same conceptual refinement. Immediate self- and object percepts will play a more predominant intrapsychic role, with concomitantly less capacity to abstract and remember conceptualizations of self and others. The grandiose self-structure will consequently be more vulnerable to interpersonal and intrapsychic attack, which lowers the threshold for perceived persecution by others and retaliatory violence. Both grandiosity and paranoia will be clinically displayed by the mentally retarded psychopath in a transparent and gross manner.

The defensive operations of the mentally retarded psychopath are virtually identical to the psychopathic process. Such individuals are organized at a borderline level of personality and will verbalize their defensive operations in a very direct and concrete manner. They will not, however, use the conscious corollaries of their unconscious defenses in such an adept fashion as the more intelligent psychopath. In other words, deception, imitation, and object control will be attempted but often ineptly presented (see Chapter 5).

Most important and basic, the mentally retarded psychopath is a clinical fact, rather than a psychopathological fiction. Such individuals are most distressing because they stir a countertransference reaction that is both largely sympathetic of their cognitive deficits and very suspicious of their predatory behavior.

Part IV

TREATMENT

8

Psychotherapeutic Issues

The psychopathic process is not immune to psychotherapy, but it does present major countertransference and resistance issues to the mental health professional. The response of most clinicians to the psychopathic patient is to question the possibility of psychotherapeutic change, which may be either a countertransference reaction to psychopathic devaluation or a realistic decision based upon sound clinical judgment.

My purpose in this chapter is to identify and discuss issues pertaining to the psychotherapeutic treatment of psychopathically disturbed individuals, regardless of treatment orientation or technique. Although my own practice is psychoanalytic psychotherapy, and it is my opinion that long-term, intensive psychodynamic psychotherapy is the treatment of choice for preoedipal disturbances, I am not going to propose a new model for treating the psychopath. Extensive reviews are available concerning the nature and efficacy of treatment approaches to antisocial behavior (Reid 1978, Reid et al. 1986).

FUNDAMENTAL PREMISES

For those clinicians that have both the heart and soul to attempt psychotherapeutic treatment of psychopathically disturbed individuals, there are fundamental premises that should be understood. These premises define the parameters of treatment with these individuals and also predict areas of conflict and adversity that will undoubtedly occur.

Treatment versus Evaluation

The premise of treatment is to heal. It incorporates an attitude of caring, empathy, and optimism for the eventual well-being of the patient. This is fundamentally different from the premise of evaluation, particularly forensic evaluation, wherein the purpose is to gather valid and reliable information to address certain psycholegal questions. I have found this to be an area of confusion, especially for beginning professionals who are defining their roles as clinicians and do not, as yet, have the experience to shift smoothly from one attitude to another. It also may be apparent in seasoned clinicians, as I have discussed in the case of Kenneth Bianchi (see Chapter 5). Clarifying roles is necessary, if not crucial, to the treatment of psychopathically disturbed individuals because of the inclination of these patients to deceive others.

Mental health professionals, whether they be psychologists, psychiatrists, or social workers, are implicitly taught throughout their training to believe what patients tell them. This is supportive of the role of healing, but it is very unrealistic in a forensic context where deception may be characterologically expectable or institutionally reinforced. Psychologists or psychiatrists functioning as forensic investigators know this and will make allowances for deception through careful corroboration of their data. In fact, my assumption in doing forensic work is that the individual being evaluated *will* deceive me and therefore I must disprove my hypothesis to arrive at the truth. This is a safe and reasonable way to approach forensic psychological investigations, but it is sometimes antithetical to psychotherapy.

Psychopathically disturbed individuals being considered for

psychotherapy consequently present a dilemma: They should be believed, yet the prediction is that they will deceive. There is no simple answer to this conundrum, and the psychotherapist who has made the conscious decision to treat, rather than evaluate, the psychopathically disturbed patient must recognize both his or her commitment to healing and honesty and the nature of the character disturbance to be treated. The conscious tolerance of these ambiguities will innoculate the clinician against the countertransference impulse to polarize, split off, and devalue the psychopathically disturbed patient as untreatable, a practice that Lion (1978) called therapeutic nihilism.

Psychopathy as Process

Throughout this book I have emphasized that psychopathy is a deviant developmental process that is manifest as a disturbance of personality function. From a treatment perspective it is most usefully conceptualized on a hypothetical continuum, ranging from mild to severe. This premise is particularly important for avoiding the already-noted countertransference reaction to psychopathy: The patient is a psychopath, therefore he is untreatable. Here the clinician has fallen prey to his own disidentifying and dehumanizing impulse, a predictable, and common, reaction to psychopathy.

The clinical perspective of human behavior as continuous, rather than dichotomous, is more amenable to psychotherapeutic formulations. I think it is also more representative of actual reality, and it is important in refining our understanding of psychopathic disturbance.

Severity of Psychopathic Disturbance

The more severe the psychopathic disturbance, the more likely psychotherapy will fail. The severity of psychopathic disturbance also dictates the necessary restrictiveness of the treatment approach; for example, mild psychopathically disturbed patients may benefit from weekly individual psychotherapy, in contrast to severe psychopathically disturbed patients who will need a highly structured inpatient milieu to derive any treatment benefits.

Treatability of psychopathically disturbed individuals correlates with their capacity to form attachments and their degree of superego pathology. Both characteristics should be assessed to determine the least restrictive environment within which treatment will be attempted.

The capacity to form attachments is related to the degree to which the patient can form a genuine emotional relationship to the psychotherapist, regardless of the transference distortion within that relationship. Since psychopathy signals severe deficits of internalization, the nature and extent of object representations, and their respective introjected or identified characteristics, need to be scrutinized. Patients, for example, who evidence a strong identification with the stranger selfobject within their grandiose self-structure, manifest in continuous cruel and aggressive behavior with no attempt to justify their activities or paranoia concerning their consequences, would be exceedingly poor candidates for psychotherapy. On the other hand, patients who evidenced intermittent grandiosity and aggressiveness, but at other times expressed dependent and masochistic features, such as suicide attempts in the face of perceived rejection by their psychotherapist, would suggest a more conflictual internal object world with both grandiose identifications and introjected, persecutory objects. Such an internal representational world would predict a capacity to attach, albeit in a self-effacing and masochistic manner, and would suggest a more ambivalent relationship to the internal stranger selfobject. These patients would be better candidates for psychotherapy.

The patient's degree of superego pathology is also a prognostic indicator of psychotherapeutic success. Psychopathically disturbed individuals evidence a range of superego pathology, which should be evaluated on the basis of their internal relationship to the social environment, rather than according to legal definitions of social conduct (Kernberg 1984).

Jacobson (1964) outlined three layers of normal superego development that focused on internalization processes and integration of structure: The first layer is composed of sadistic superego precursors that are essentially projected aspects of the infant's own persecutory objects, cast out in an effort to deny its own aggression in the midst of parental frustration; the second layer is composed of the fusion of ideal self- and ideal object representations, heretofore called the ego ideal; the third layer is composed of the realistic, demanding, and prohibitive characteristics of the actual parents that signal a dampening of the previous two layers and mark the superego as integrated structure during the oedipal period.

Kernberg (1984) used Jacobson's (1964) layers of superego development and formulated six levels of superego pathology, or failure. These levels provide important benchmarks for the assessment of superego functioning along the continuum of psychopathic disturbance.

The first level is the antisocial personality proper, what I would designate as the severely psychopathic individual. These individuals are only identified with the grandiose self-structure, the stranger selfobject, and their primary mode of relatedness is aggression, usually experienced by them as sadistic pleasure. Kernberg (1984) posited a continuum between the passive, exploitative, parasitic psychopath and the frankly sadistic criminal. He warned that enactment of an overtly sadistic triumph through extreme depreciation of the psychotherapist may render this patient extremely dangerous.

These individuals will verbalize full knowledge of the moral requirements of society, but do not understand what it means to internalize such standards. Fusions within the grandiose self-structure are complete, and identification with the stranger selfobject is primary. Kernberg (1984) wrote, "It is as if the patient identified himself with a primitive, ruthless, totally immoral power that can obtain satisfaction only through the expression of unmitigated aggression and requires no rationalization for its behavior" (p. 281). The only hint of sadistic superego precursors is the necessity of sadism to achieve pleasure. Such individuals are not amenable to psychotherapy and, if treated, should be seen only in a highly structured and secure inpatient setting.

The second level is the narcissistic personality with antisocial features. These individuals are differentiated from the first level by their paranoid features in the transference, the enraged quality of their antisocial behavior, and subtle dependencies in psychotherapy. They will also conjure up readily available moral justifications for their sadistic and exploitive behavior. The latter suggest the intrapsychic presence of a primitive ideal, although omnipotent and cruel, and mark a slight evolution from the sadistic precursors of the first level. These patients convey through psychotherapy an identification with a cruel and aggressive primary parental object that was internalized out of fear of annihilation. It is probable that this second level of superego pathology is more sociogenic than the first level and therefore more treatable. The severe psychopathic disturbance of the first level appears to be more biogenic in etiology.

The third level is represented by the borderline patient who is dishonest in treatment but shows no overt antisocial behavior. Kernberg (1984) noted the largely protective nature of these sins of commission and omission and their shame avoidance, unconscious denial, and conscious deception motivations. The origins of such behavior may be quite complex, but the behavior also reveals both a capacity for attachment, perhaps out of retaliatory fear, and an awareness of punitive consequences.

The fourth level is represented by the narcissistic personality without antisocial behavior. It is clinically characterized by the denial of moral responsibility for one's actions. These patients maintain what Kernberg (1984) called an "affective discontinuity"

(p. 284), an aspect of splitting that protects them from both anxiety and guilt. This moral abdication is quite ego-syntonic and may disarm the psychotherapist in the absence of overtly illegal behavior. There is an arrogant "participant–observer" quality to these patients' lives, and a consequent absence of any object relations in depth. Their relationships are emotionally vacuous, but they seem emotionally content. Moral responsibility is a moot question because they have ceased comparing good and bad objects, the intrapsychic genesis of superego development and morality. Kernberg (1984) argued that these patients have not internalized Jacobson's (1964) third level of superego formation, the realistic parental prohibitions and demands. Sadistic and idealized superego precursors have been minimally integrated, so that conventional morality may be imitated, but actual communication may be "false, cynical, and hypocritical . . . fragmenting all intense emotional involvements with significant others" (Kernberg 1984, p. 286).

The fifth level is represented by the majority of borderline personality organized patients without antisocial or narcissistic features. They are aware of strong and contradictory impulses that are uncontrollable and are able to articulate their unacceptable nature. The psychopathic disturbance at this level is found in the role that splitting and dissociation play in the expression of unacceptable behavior that would not be tolerated in another ego state. These patients show a capacity for concern for themselves and others and will express remorse following aggression toward actual objects. They will clinically present in a more chaotic, dependent, and affectively charged manner than preceding levels, but this may convey a capacity for object relations and an internalization of more realistic parental representations. Psychotherapeutic management of these patients may be difficult, but the prognosis is much more positive than earlier levels of superego pathology.

The sixth and final level of superego pathology is represented by the neurotic personality with an excessively severe and sadistic superego. Freud (1916) referred to these patients who commit antisocial acts as "criminals from a sense of guilt," and, unfortunately, they appear to be rather rare in criminal populations. Kernberg (1984) saw these patients as suffering from an unconscious dominance of infantile morality coupled with an oedipal fixation on parental prohibitions and demands. Because of the existence of a superego structure and the absence of borderline defensive operations, these patients would not technically be considered psychopathically disturbed. Unlike others with more severe levels of superego pathology, they are treatable with psychotherapy.

The preceding six levels of superego pathology provide markers for the location of particular patients along a continuum of psychopathic disturbance.

Assessment of Severity

The severity of psychopathic disturbance can be assessed both quantitatively and qualitatively. This is necessary during the initial contacts with the prospective patient to determine the usefulness of psychotherapy, if any, and the least restrictive alternative for treatment.

The quantitative assessment of psychopathic disturbance can be accomplished through the use of Hare's (1985b) psychopathy checklist, a twenty-item objective instrument derived from extensive research to empirically refine Cleckley's (1941) original sixteen criteria of psychopathy (Hare 1980, 1981, 1985a, Hare and Jutai 1983, Hare and McPherson 1984). This checklist has high internal consistency and interrater reliability when used as a research instrument with criminal populations (Hare 1985a); and there is a growing body of research concerning its validity (Hare 1985a, Gacono 1988, Heaven 1988).

The checklist items (Hare 1985a) are scored on a 3-point ordinal scale (0,1,2) and are listed as follows:

1. Glibness/superficial charm
2. Grandiose sense of self-worth
3. Need for stimulation/proneness to boredom
4. Pathological lying
5. Conning/manipulative
6. Lack of remorse or guilt
7. Shallow affect
8. Callous/lack of empathy
9. Parasitic lifestyle
10. Poor behavioral controls
11. Promiscuous sexual behavior
12. Early behavior problems
13. Lack of realistic, long-term goals
14. Impulsivity
15. Irresponsibility
16. Failure to accept responsibility for own actions
17. Many short-term marital relationships
18. Juvenile delinquency
19. Revocation of conditional release
20. Criminal versatility

Items that do not apply are scored 0; items that apply to a certain extent or for which a fit is uncertain are scored 1; items that apply and are a reasonably good match are scored 2. Hare (1985b) noted that it is very important that both a structured interview and corroborative data be used when scoring this instrument; this will attenuate the patient's potential deception and manipulation.

Hare (1985a) stated that a cutting score of 30 should be used to differentiate nonpsychopathic from psychopathic individuals. The maximum attainable score is, of course, 40. In keeping with a continuous, rather than a dichotomous, theory of psychopathic disturbance, I would propose the clinical grouping of individuals according to severity of psychopathic disturbance:

Mild psychopathic disturbance 10–19
Moderate psychopathic disturbance 20–29
Severe psychopathic disturbance 30–40

These three groupings can be used by the clinician to quantitatively measure the severity of psychopathic disturbance. Although Hare (1985a) has limited his use of the psychopathy
checklist to research with criminal populations, I am proposing
its use as a clinical instrument for both treatment and evaluation
purposes. The clinician should be forewarned, however, that
there is no validity, as yet, for this instrument outside of criminal
populations. Its predictive validity in relation to treatment has
yet to be demonstrated. Definitions and scoring criteria for each
of the twenty items are available in the scoring manual (Hare
1985b).

The severity of psychopathic disturbance can also be quantitatively assessed using the Rorschach technique and scoring
according to the Exner Comprehensive System (1986a). The
criteria that I have derived in Appendix III can be used to
establish a percentage of agreement with the predicted psychopathic indices.

The qualitative assessment of psychopathic disturbance and
treatment implications centers around the clinical interview with
the patient. I have found Kernberg's (1984) structural interview
most helpful in gathering information relevant to the diagnostic
and treatment decisions concerning the patient.

Kernberg wrote,

The structural diagnostic interview, then, combines a
psychoanalytic focus on the patient–interviewer interaction with a psychoanalytic technique for interpreting
conflictual issues and defensive operations in this interaction in order to highlight simultaneously the classical
anchoring symptoms of descriptive psychopathology
and the underlying personality structure. [1984, p. 30]

Rather than beginning with a decision-tree model of interviewing, the structural interview is cyclical in nature, exploring anchoring symptoms of psychopathology that allow for a return to those symptoms in a different context and from a different perspective. For example, the patient described in Appendix I illustrates my cyclical focus upon the patient's pathological lying as a characterological trait. I returned to the event in question, the suicide *or* homicide attempt, on several different occasions to test the veracity of the patient's statements and his capacity to hold accurately in memory his confabulated story. This cycling was premised on my early hypothesis in the interview that pathological lying was a core psychopathic trait of this individual, which subsequently was proven to be accurate.

In addition to a structured approach that allows for recycling of material, Kernberg (1984) also posited a linear framework to the interview which consisted of three phases. The first phase involves questions that are close-ended in nature and allows for the assessment of more obvious descriptive and behavioral pathology. Within this first phase a mental status exam or psychosocial history taking might be quite appropriate. The evaluation of the psychopathically disturbed patient during this phase is usually uneventful, unless severe psychopathy is present and questions concerning descriptive symptomatology, such as the presence or absence of hallucinations, evoke an intense and primitive defensive operation. The psychopathic individual will usually produce normative findings during this phase of interviewing unless the psychopathy is accompanied by another mental disorder, such as an organic or functional psychosis. Psychosocial and psychiatric history taking, however, may reveal contradictions or omissions that the interviewer will want to return to in subsequent phases of the interview.

The second phase of the structured interview is more open-ended and focuses upon pathological character traits: difficulties in interpersonal relations, adjustments to the environment, and internally perceived needs (Kernberg 1984). This immediately moves the interview to a deeper personality level and usually begins with a question such as "Now I'd like to know more about you as a person. Can you tell me about yourself?" In psychopathic disturbance such a question will signal the mobilization of narcissistic and borderline defenses, and depending upon the severity of the disturbance, certain reactions may be evoked. Some patients may respond in an aggressive and paranoid manner; others may see this as an opportunity to further "put something over" (Bursten 1973a) on the interviewer and may simulate certain descriptions in a deceptive fashion.

This is the point in the structural interview when clinicians should pay close attention to their own affective reaction to the patient. This is critical to understanding the object relationship that has been activated in the patient and it is fundamental to constructing the transference dispositions and countertransference dispositions between the patient and clinician. The affective dispositions of the patient create concordant or complementary affective dispositions in the clinician (Racker 1968).

While attending to their own affective reactions, clinicians are beginning in the second phase to explore the patients' inner representational world through their questions. They will also be forming mental representations of how patients perceive themselves, and, as questions move toward patients describing significant others in their lives, a mental representation of how patients perceive others will also be forming.

Psychopathically disturbed individuals, unless they are quite adept at imitating normative interpersonal attitudes, will usually reveal elements of their grandiose self-structure and aggressive impulses toward their representations of others. The more severely psychopathically disturbed the individual, the greater difficulty the individual will have in containing this activated self-object constellation, and the more likely it will be acted out in the clinical interview. This will be countertransferentially felt by the clinician as either anger or fear. If carefully explored by the clinician, the anger will probably have sadistic elements to it. The fear will be atavistic in nature and may be felt quite primitively as a sense of predation. One severely psychopathic patient whom I evaluated for treatment while in custody, and who was ostensibly quite revealing, told me at the end of the interview that I now "knew too much" about him, and such knowledge had gotten other people killed. For a moment I was frozen because I could not evacuate the knowledge he had given me about himself, and it had suddenly become a malignant threat to my well-being rather than a benign source of clinical information. This experience of projective identification, where a portion of his mental content, in this case self-knowledge, was placed *in* me, I could not expel it, and he could use it to control me, was quite disconcerting.

Attempts to evoke representational images of others that are affectional will usually be unsuccessful. Since the object concepts of the psychopath are so vacuous, if the clinician persists the descriptions of others become descriptions of the self. When one psychopathically disturbed patient was asked to describe his wife, he said, "she's head-over-heels in love with me."[1]

As the clinician proceeds through the second phase of the structural interview, transference and countertransference predictions for treatment should be more apparent. As primitive defenses are mobilized during this probing of character pathology, the clinician may feel a loss of a sense of freedom in interacting with the patient (Kernberg 1984). With psychopathically disturbed patients, this may be experienced as a sense of being "under his thumb." The clinician may also feel an inner sense of devaluation, affectively experienced as a diminution of self-esteem, without being able to pinpoint any behavioral trigger by the patient. A sensitivity to spontaneous and fleeting sadomasochistic visual images in the mind of the clinician may also be diagnostic of the transference–countertransference paradigm that will be intensified during treatment.

---

[1] My thanks to Linda Helinski, Ph.D., for this patient's comment.

The third phase of the structural interview begins with the question, "What do you think I should have asked you and have not yet asked?" (Kernberg 1984). This question gives patients an opportunity to reveal information they think is important or that the clinician should know. It is also critical to further understanding of the psychopathic disturbance. Until this phase of the interview, the clinician with the psychopathic patient may have been forced to engage in a power and control struggle to determine who will direct the interview. This is quite pathognomonic of psychopathy since the disturbance is manifest in relationships premised on gradients of power rather than affection.

The third phase of the structural interview allows the clinician to intentionally abdicate control of the interview and *see how the patient responds*. A multitude of responses is possible, ranging from intensified aggression and sadism toward the clinician to a sudden loss of interest on the part of the patient because the narcissistic pursuit, the struggle for control, has been accomplished.

This third phase also allows clinicians to experience themselves and the patient and think about the interview. The time to think is often woefully inadequate in clinical and custody settings.

At the conclusion of the structural interview, the clinician should be ready to formulate a treatment plan, if one is possible, and determine the least-restrictive alternative for such treatment. Reasonable predictions should also be possible concerning the transference and countertransference problems that will arise once treatment has begun.

The Decision Not to Treat

There are individuals who are so psychopathically disturbed that, in my opinion, no attempts should be made to treat them. The decision not to treat should be as carefully made as the decision to offer treatment, but oftentimes the sources of data are much more limited.

Two questions that are central to this decision focus upon the individual's amenability to treatment and the danger the individual poses to the treating professional. It is, simply put, a risk–benefit ratio.

Generally, those psychopathically disturbed individuals who score ≥ 30 on the Hare Psychopathy Checklist (Hare 1985b) are not candidates for any form of individual psychotherapy on an outpatient basis. If treatment is attempted with such an individual, a more restrictive alternative should be selected, such as an inpatient, milieu, or custody setting.

Interpersonal and intrapsychic features of the patient that contraindicate *any* form of treatment include the following:

1. *Sadistic* aggressive behavior in the patient's history that resulted in serious injury, maiming, or death to the victim.
2. A *complete* absence of any remorse, justification, or rationalization for such behavior.
3. Intelligence greater than or less than two standard deviations from the mean. This would place the individual in the very superior or mildly mentally retarded range of general intelligence.
4. A historical absence of any capacity, or inclination, to form a bond or an emotional attachment to another person.
5. An atavistic fear of predation felt by experienced clinicians when in the patient's presence without any overt behavior precipitating such a countertransference reaction.

COUNTERTRANSFERENCE

Although there are many understandings of countertransference in the literature, I will begin with the definition proposed by Reich (1951) and Greenson (1974), namely, the psychotherapist's countertransference reaction is his or her distorted and inappropriate responses to the patient derived from his or her unresolved, unconscious past conflicts. I believe this is an *endogenous* dimension of countertransference, and it underscores the necessity of intensive psychotherapy or psychoanalysis during the training of any psychotherapist.

There is, however, a *reactive* dimension to countertransference, which is the therapist's experiential response to the patient's preverbal mode of communication, which oftentimes reenacts the patient's relationships to early parental objects. These responses may be concordant (Racker 1968), and thus identical in nature to the patient's own internal experience of affect and defense, or they may be complementary (Racker 1968), and thus different or opposite in nature from the patient's internal world. Oftentimes the complementary, reactive countertransference recapitulates an early parental reaction to the patient.

Countertransference, however, does not encompass the totality of reactions to the patient. That would negate the importance of the *real* relationship to the patient (Greenson 1974). Such a broad definition of countertransference, for instance, would make it difficult to discriminate the working therapeutic alliance from concordant identifications (Racker 1968) with the patient. The discrimination of this real relationship, the therapeutic alliance, however, is problematic in the treatment of psychopathically disturbed individuals *for it is precisely this real relationship that may be absent with the psychopathic individual.* A state of nonrelatedness may exist outside the boundaries of the transference–countertransference paradigm.

Endogenous countertransference reactions, whether persistent or transitory, are more clearly distinguished if assigned to one of several types (Reich 1951): a simple impulse derivative, such as identification with the patient's behavior; a defense against an impulse, such as intense anger and a wish to punish the patient who acts sadistically; general character problems of the therapist, such as pathological therapeutic ambition (Greenson

1974); and narcissistic gratification, such as highly sexualized curiosity toward the patient. Racker (1968) also noted the fundamental importance of the "law of talion" in countertransference: that is, for every positive or negative transference reaction on the part of the patient, there is also a positive or negative countertransference reaction on the part of the psychotherapist.

Reactive countertransference to the psychopathic individual was the focus of several authors (Frosch 1983b, Strasburger 1986), and I would like to elaborate further upon their work.

Therapeutic Nihilism

Lion (1978) noted this most common countertransference reaction to psychopathically disturbed individuals. It is the stereotypical judgment that all psychopathically disturbed individuals, or antisocial personality disorders, *as a class*, are untreatable by virtue of their diagnosis. Such a judgment ignores both individual differences and the continuous nature of severity of psychopathy. I have most commonly observed this reaction in public mental health clinicians who are assigned patients on referral from probation, parole, or the court; and assume, because of the coercive nature of the treatment referral, that the patients must be psychopathic and any psychotherapeutic gain is impossible.

Such reactions are often the product of attitudes that have been internalized as an "oral tradition" during training from senior, teaching clinicians. They are rarely the product of direct, individual experience. It is, in a sense, a mass retaliatory attitude where moral judgment impinges on professional assessment. The behavioral pathology of the psychopath, to devalue and dehumanize others, becomes the concordant identification of the clinician doing to the psychopath what the clinician perceives the psychopath doing to others.

However, judgments of untreatability based upon individual assessments do commonly occur, and are absolutely essential at times, when evaluating psychopathically disturbed patients. Therapeutic nihilism is only suspect when a diagnostic *class* of individuals is systematically excluded from treatment opportunities without an individual structured interview.

Illusory Treatment Alliance

The opposite countertransference reaction to therapeutic nihilism is the clinician's illusion that a treatment alliance exists when, in actuality, there is no such realistic bond between the patient and psychotherapist. The therapeutic alliance is the reality-based cement that bonds the psychotherapist and, at least, a portion of the patient's personality to the task of maturation, development, and healing.

This reaction is particularly insidious in treatment of the psychopathically disturbed patient because the patient is predisposed to deception, compulsive manipulation, and malignant pseudoidentification (see Chapter 5). The latter defense, an aspect of projective identification, is the patient's gratification of the therapist's narcissistic wishes by simulating or imitating desired thoughts, affects, and behaviors. The psychotherapist is consequently enamored by the apparent progress of the psychopathically disturbed individual, believing that a treatment alliance has been formed. In actuality, however, the clinician is only witnessing the chameleonlike quality of the patient to mirror the narcissistic wishes of the primary parental object. The psychotherapist who readily *desires* change in the psychopathic patient is most vulnerable to this countertransference reaction.

Fear of Assault or Harm

Strasburger (1986) noted the important distinction between real and countertransference fear in work with psychopathic patients. Reality-based fear must not be discounted and can be distinguished by a careful assessment of the demographic characteristics of the patient and his or her intrapsychic reality at the time of the perceived risk (Meloy 1987). The clinician should also be familiar with the distinction between predatory and affective violence (see Chapter 6) and the psychopathic individual's propensity to engage in the former. A history of predatory violence supports the reality-testing of the clinician's fear and a highly secure treatment environment would be needed to attenuate this risk. Any act of predatory violence in a history of affective violence is also quite ominous and should convey to the therapist the patient's capacity to suspend all empathic regard for his victim.

Countertransference fear of the psychopathic individual is an atavistic response to the predatory nature of the grandiose self-structure. It is the sense of being prey to the stranger within the patient. It is also the fear of being controlled by the sadism of the patient, which is the manner in which the patient controls his persecutory introjects. These fears, which are oftentimes felt in a quite visceral and autonomic way, are diagnostic of the preverbal, skin-boundary developmental experience of the patient (see Chapter 3). Fear is usually a complementary, rather than concordant, identification (Racker 1968) in the countertransference field of the psychopath. The recognition of this countertransference reaction, however, should not rule out the possibility of *real danger*. Both may, and probably do, coexist. The clinician must be careful, in the midst of the regressive pull of the psychopath's splitting defenses, to not treat countertransference fear and real fear as mutually exclusive, polarized experiences.

Denial and Deception

I have elaborated upon these corollary unconscious and conscious defenses in Chapter 5, but they can also surface as countertransference reactions in treatment.

Denial is most commonly seen in counterphobic responses to danger when treating psychopathic individuals. Vulnerability to predation, after all, is the ultimate narcissistic insult, and this may trigger a reaction formation that one is physically invincible (Maltsberger and Buie 1974). Lion and Leaff (1973) wrote that denial is the most common defense against anxiety generated by violent patients. Denial of danger when working with psychopathic individuals may reflect the therapist's concordant identification with the grandiose self-structure of the patient. Psychotherapists may find themselves enamored with the stories, perhaps exploits, that they hear from patients during treatment. Instead of empathy for the victims of the psychopath's exploits, they may find themselves identifying with the exhilaration and contemptuous delight of patients as they recount their fantastic, perhaps fantasized, history. These concordant identifications may deny the interpersonal position that the psychotherapists are unconsciously assuming the role of the prey.

Denial may also be apparent in psychotherapists' unwillingness to participate in the prosecution of patients who have committed felonious acts and have clearly endangered the lives of treating professionals. This reluctance to acknowledge the real dangerousness of certain patients is rationalized as antithetical to therapy or damaging to the therapeutic relationship. Several authors (Hoge and Gutheil 1987, Miller and Maier 1987) recently researched the positive value to both patients and clinicians of using the criminal justice system in response to felonies committed by patients toward staff. In their judgment, aversive conditioning, reality-testing and limit-setting for the patient, and the reinforcement of the value of the staff and their safety, were a few of the positive outcomes of such action.

Deception of the patient by the psychotherapist should also be noted. This is usually quite subtle in work with psychopathic patients, but it is often used to manage anxiety engendered by the patient's confrontation and devaluation of the therapist. False reasons for altering the parameters of treatment, vague and misleading interpretations, and the withholding of certain interventions because of their potentially explosive consequences may all lead to a chronic pattern of deception of the patient. Such behavior may indicate superego pathology in the psychotherapist, the gratification of sadistic impulses, the avoidance of signal anxiety, the management of fear, passive-aggressive rejection of the patient, or concordant identification with the psychopathic individual's deceptive skills.

The psychotherapist must be *fiercely honest* with the psychopathic patient. Psychopathic patients will regressively surface the psychopathic predispositions in their therapists if at all possible. This is a product, once again, of the malignant twinship (Kohut 1971) identifications that can unconsciously occur between patient and therapist. In the case of the psychopath these identifications are fundamentally narcissistic and self-serving.

Honesty, however, does not mean self-disclosure. And self-disclosure with the psychopathic patient should rarely be used. Rigorous honesty may mean silence in the midst of an impulse to rationalize, confrontation when mollification would be safer, limit-setting when "flexibility" would be easier, empathy expressed when felt, and adherence to one's *frame* of doing psychotherapy (Grotstein et al. 1987).

Helplessness and Guilt

The novice psychotherapist may feel helpless in the face of massive resistance by the psychopathically disturbed patient and subsequently may feel guilty that genuine change has not occurred (Strasburger 1986). This may be an endogenous countertransference reaction, what Reich (1951) called the "Midas touch" syndrome: the irrational belief that every patient the psychotherapist sees will show dramatic improvement. Or it may be a reactive countertransference caused by the internalization of devalued selfobjects projected by the patient into the clinician.

Strasburger (1986) argued that such a reaction may be transformed into rage toward the patient that is passively expressed as withdrawal or through a reaction formation that "smothers" the patient with attention. Psychopathic patients will actively solicit anticipatory guilt from the withholding and ungratifying clinician:

> H. approached me in the courthouse as I was leaving for lunch. He was well known to me as a difficult, psychopathic individual with a manic affective disorder. He greeted me kindly and told me that he had just been released from the county jail across the street and needed some money.
>
> I told H. that I didn't give money to anyone. He began talking more rapidly, but softly, telling me that brother and mother were exploiting him, and he just needed twenty dollars for the weekend. When I refused him again, his affect suddenly became angry, and he said, "Listen, Meloy, I'll go out and rob somebody, or a bank, if you don't give it to me right now!!" I told him he could do that, but it probably wasn't very wise since he had just been released from jail, and seemed to be enjoying his newfound freedom. He walked away from me in a disgusted and contemptuous manner.

I had a momentary feeling of dread and responsibility when he threatened a crime in the face of my refusal to gratify him, because I knew he was quite capable of such an act. Such countertransference reactions are magnified by the real fear of being held responsible for injury to third parties by recent statutory and case law (Appelbaum and Meisel 1986).

Devaluation and Loss of Professional Identity

If clinicians measure their competency only through the perceived change in the patient, psychopathically disturbed individuals may be a source of continuous narcissistic wounding. Inexperienced therapists are especially vulnerable to feeling devalued (Strasburger 1986) and may respond to such emotions with an attitude of therapeutic nihilism. Psychotherapy may begin with idealization of the clinician, but it will quickly shift to devaluation because patients must aggressively purge themselves of persecutory introjects to maintain their narcissistic equilibrium. Despite the most adept therapeutic management of a patient's contempt, it is difficult to not *feel* despicable because of the primitive and preverbal nature of this purging cycle (Bursten 1972). The psychotherapist's responses to devaluation may be retaliation, indifference, rage, masochistic submission, or heroic attempts to "fix" the patient.

Hatred and the Wish to Destroy

Few other patients will compel psychotherapists to face their own antipathy and destructive impulses (Galdston 1987). Psychopathically disturbed patients may hate goodness itself and through their envy and oral rage destroy all that the clinician offers. The experience of pleasure is not reciprocal for the psychopath (Strasburger 1986), and, in the most severe cases, it is available only through sadistic channels of power and control (see Chapter 4).

The psychotherapist may concordantly identify with the patient's hatred, and in a talionic manner, respond in kind. Hatred, however, is an affect (Giovacchini 1972) and may be the only source of therapeutic work if the psychotherapist can recognize his or her hatred as diagnostic of the preoedipal experience of the patient (Searles 1965, 1979, 1986). Hatred may ironically become the basis for a therapeutic alliance. It is usually acted out by the therapist only if it remains unconscious.

The Assumption of Psychological Complexity

The most subtle countertransference reaction to the psychopathically disturbed patient is the assumption of psychological complexity. It is the projective assumption by the clinician that the patient has the psychological structure and function of the clinician, which only has to be realized or discovered in psychotherapy. This is particularly common among novice clinicians working with intelligent, but preoedipally disturbed, individuals when there is no overt symptomatology and the patient may initially present in a very logical and coherent manner.

The assumption that a relationship exists between intelligence and ego functioning, moreover, has received little research attention since Hartmann (1939). Allen and colleagues (1986), in one of a few recent studies, found in a sample of inpatient psychiatric subjects that Bellak and colleagues' (1973) ego functions scale did have a significant global relationship to intelligence as measured by the WAIS-R (Weschler 1981). The subscales of autonomous functions and thought processes had the strongest relationship to intelligence ($p < .001$), followed by object relations, mastery-competence ($p < .01$). and reality testing ($p < .05$). Intelligence, however, did not significantly correlate with object constancy, superegoguilt, superego–ego ideal, judgment, or drive regulation. These latter findings are especially relevant to the psychopathically disturbed individual since attachment and superego deficits are central to the psychopathic process. In other words, intelligence does not necessarily convey a personality structure organized at a neurotic level (Kernberg 1984), and it may, instead, mask a borderline level personality organization that is vertically, rather than horizontally, structured (see Chapters 3 and 5). There is no tripartite personality structure composed of id, ego, and superego processes; but instead, the personality is composed only of dyadic relations between self- and object representations both within and without the grandiose self-structure that are polarized, dissociated, and split off given certain psychobiological, psychodynamic, and psychosocial contingencies.

The psychotherapeutic realization of this absence of structure is further confounded by the malignant pseudoidentification of psychopathic individuals. They will strive to imitate and simulate such structuralization for a variety of reasons, including malingering, dissembling, and the initial establishment of a twinship transference with the therapist. Evidence of neurotic personality structure (tripartite characteristics such as third-level superego development and repression of unacceptable impulses) should not be assumed in psychopathic patients unless corroborated by behavior outside the psychotherapy hour.

PREDICTABLE RESISTANCES DURING PSYCHOTHERAPY

The psychotherapist treating the psychopathically disturbed patient should be cognizant of certain expectable resistances during the course of psychotherapy. These resistances, expressed in transference behavior, reflect core elements of the psychopathic process which have been extensively reviewed elsewhere in this book. They must be therapeutically managed if treatment is to remain viable.

Manipulative Cycling

The patient will engage in a compulsive pattern of manipulation of the clinician as set forth by Bursten (1972). This pattern consists of a goal conflict, an intent to deceive, the carrying out of the deceptive act, and contemptuous delight once the act has been completed. It is a cognitive-behavioral sequence that produces an affective state that is highly rewarding to the psychopathic patient. Unconsciously it is the purging and evacuation of devalued introjects that are projectively identified into the clinician and thus maintain the safety and homeostasis of the grandiose self-structure. This process also wards off envy and oral rage, which are affectively quite threatening when the object is initially idealized. The devaluation inherent in the manipulative cycle supports the destruction of the goodness of the actual object and renders it a bad object that can be controlled.

Manipulative cycling is most common in forms of psychotherapy that plan or direct the course of treatment and assume the goal definition of treatment for the patient. It is less problematic in expressive psychoanalytic psychotherapy wherein the work is defined by the material presented by the patient during the hour. The manipulative cycle shadows the other resistances noted below and can be pondered by asking the question: What opportunities am I presenting for this patient to engage in a manipulative cycle with me?

Deceptive Practice

Deception as a conscious and intentional behavior is central to psychopathy. It is important that the clinician attempt to distinguish between deception as a chosen behavior and denial as an unconscious defense, although this may not always be possible. Both deception and denial are linked (see Chapter 5) by their alloplastic expression through words and acts.

Deception is an integral part of the manipulative cycle and consciously devalues the psychotherapist by rendering him ignorant of the truth. Deception is unconsciously used to ward off persecutory anxiety and to shore up the grandiose self-structure.

The management of deception during psychotherapy is exceedingly difficult since it is hard to recognize and may trigger intensely negative countertransference reactions. Like the manipulative cycle, however, it should be assumed to exist, like any other resistance, with certain genetic, transferential, and interpretative meanings. Oftentimes the acknowledgment of this general suspiciousness toward the patient, and placing the burden of proof upon the patient to convince the clinician he is being honest, is quite useful. This can be the first step in the patient's analysis of his deception rather than its exploitation as a resistance to treatment.

Malignant Pseudoidentification

The conscious imitation and unconscious simulation (see Chapter 5) of the psychopathic individual contribute to the process of malignant pseudoidentification during psychotherapy. This resistance is recognized by the internalization and reflection of the clinician's narcissistic vulnerabilities for purposes of control.

The dearth of internalizations within the psychopathic process prompts a hunger for such identifications, but this psychological appetite is tainted by three characteristics: The identifications will invariably be superficial and short-lived; they resonate most easily with the nefarious and narcissistic characteristics of others; and they are used for hurting and controlling the object of identification, in this case, the psychotherapist.

In a sense, however, these malignant pseudoidentifications are pathways toward the core identification of the psychopath, the stranger selfobject (Grotstein 1982). This is oftentimes the most deeply internalized selfobject representation, and it usually has its roots in identification with a cruel and aggressive primary parental object. The malignant pseudoidentifications can direct the clinician to this core element of the grandiose self-structure through interpretation and confrontation of their meaninglessness for the psychopathic individual.

The imitation and simulation of various affective states is also pathognomonic of malignant pseudoidentification. Patients will either consciously imitate the expression of certain affects, usually through words to imply a certain feeling, or they will unconsciously simulate certain feeling states, usually through nonverbal channels, such as posturing or facial expressions.

The conscious imitation of affect begins with the patient intentionally choosing certain feelings that he believes are socially appropriate and desirable. The patient then will talk about these feelings "as if" they are genuinely felt. Usually a clinical question such as "Tell me more about your feeling" or more directly "How do you know you're feeling _____? Can you describe to me what it's like for you to feel _____?" will elicit material that will differentiate the genuinely felt emotional state from the imitated one.

The unconscious simulation of affect is more difficult to discriminate. It is the psychopathic propensity to identify, in a chameleonlike manner, with socially desirable emotional states without having any understanding of the empathic or meaningful dimensions of such emotion. The clinician's countertransference reaction to such simulated affect is most diagnostic, but this assumes training and education that allows the clinician to differentiate between his own endogenous and reactive countertransference states.

Simulated affect on the part of the psychopathically disturbed patient may leave the clinician feeling skeptical and distant, rather than empathically resonant. The patient will not gradually recompensate from the affective expression but will *end* it as if the performance is over. Treatment of the psychopathically disturbed patient, however, must embrace the possibility of genuine affective expression, or therapeutic gain will be impossible. Again, the sources of genuine affect are inextricably bound to the stranger selfobject and are clinically characterized by persecutory fear, hatred, envy, rage, sadistic pleasure, contemptuous delight, and boredom. Without accessing these affective complexes the treatment must remain at a superficial, pseudoidentification level.

Sadistic Control

Kernberg (1984) described a phenomenon he called "malignant narcissism" in the treatment of narcissistic personalities who are undergoing resolution of the grandiose self-structure. The clinical picture of malignant narcissism is characterized by a pathological condensation of grandiose, sadistic, and aggressive strivings.

He elaborated upon four characteristics of malignant narcissism, all of which may occur in the treatment of the psychopathically disturbed individual: paranoid regression in the transference, chronic self-destructiveness as a triumph over the therapist, dishonesty in the transference, and overt sadistic triumph over the therapist (Kernberg 1984). Each of these resistances is a behavioral expression of the grandiose self-structure attempting to regain control of the treatment situation in the face of a perceived annihilatory threat, and two are most relevant to sadistic control.

Chronic self-destructiveness as triumph over the therapist is most clinically apparent in manipulative suicidal attempts or self-mutilating gestures by the psychopathic individual. I referred in Chapter 4 to the patient who eventually committed suicide but also prior to that engaged in continual self-mutilating gestures, including burning his arm with a cigarette in front of me during group psychotherapy. Such behaviors are clearly masochistic, but the sadism derives from the pleasure inherent in the act, which punishes the therapist who would threaten the primitive identifications of the patient. Kernberg (1984) referred to this fourth level of masochism as the most severe form, since it represents an identification with a primitive, sadistic parental image: what I would refer to as a stranger selfobject (Grotstein 1982) that is within the grandiose self-structure, that is a condensation of both ideal self- and ideal object concepts, and is cruel and aggressive. Any threat to the omnipotent control of this grandiose self-structure must be preemptively destroyed: consequently the fantasized, or actual, attempts to destroy the good object, the psychotherapist. Suicide attempts, in this case, are understandable as a primitive, condensed, and grandiose fantasy that if one destroys oneself, one destroys the goodness of the

world. It is an omnipotent fantasy that may unconsciously motivate individuals who commit mass murder and are compelled to
act out such a homicidal-suicidal dynamic. Postmortem psychological analyses of such individuals often suggest a history of
paranoid personality disorder.

Overt sadistic triumph over the psychotherapist was also
termed "malignant grandiosity" (Kernberg 1984, p. 295). Such
displays are ego syntonic and may range from verbal devaluation
of the therapist to more overt forms of psychological and physical
aggression. The syntonic nature of this sadism toward the psychotherapist is a key to treatment prognosis: In cases wherein
the sadism is not conflictual and no dependency is evident in the
transference, expressive or supportive psychotherapy should
not be continued. Such individuals, usually seen in probation or
parole settings, are not treatable, but may respond to strict
conditions of release where intensive supervision of overt behavior is the only mode of interaction between the individual and
the identified "professional." Heroic attempts at psychotherapy
will usually result in a profound dehumanization of the treatment
process and may place the clinician in actual danger because of
the perceived threat of the clinician's "goodness." Intolerable
envy of the good object will be warded off by devaluation or
destruction.

Sadistic control is also an element of perversion and is
pathognomonic of psychopathic disturbance that is usually untreatable by psychotherapy:

> J. S. was evaluated at Atascadero State Hospital fol-
> lowing his confinement for attempted murder and dis-
> position as a mentally disordered sex offender. J. S.
> had a history of strangling women which began at age
> 10 when he attempted to choke a 9-year-old neighbor.
> J. S. is currently 35 and almost killed his most recent
> victim.
>
> He adamantly denied any sexual arousal during

his strangling of his victims and attributes the activity
to a retaliatory impulse for being "put down" by the
woman. He denied any sexual activity other than masturbation at the hospital. His psychologist, however,
reported that he was bisexual and currently in an
active homosexual relationship.

It is clinically inconceivable, given the compulsive nature of this
activity, the antisocial history, the lack of remorse, and its
talionic motivation ("I just wanted them to feel the pain that I
felt, I didn't want to kill anybody"), that both aggressive and
sexual drives were *not* interwoven and consciously felt, despite
the patient's protestations.

Kernberg (1984) proposed that malignant narcissism illustrates a deep level of superego pathology. I would agree, but
would reformulate his considerations as evidence of psychopathic
disturbance. In other words, the malignancy of the narcissism
signals the severity of psychopathic disturbance, with its concomitant superego deficits, internalization difficulties, attachment deficits, and condensed sexual and aggressive drive derivatives that are dedifferentiated and confused (Meltzer 1973,
Chasseguet-Smirgel 1978).

CONCLUSIONS

Ogden (1983) wrote that the analysis of transference derives
from the willingness of psychotherapists to expose themselves to
the insults of projective identification. This adage is no more
apparent, nor dramatically confirmed, than in the treatment of
the psychopathically disturbed individual.

Yet, if psychopathic disturbance is conceived as a deviant
developmental process, and therefore varies in severity and
degree, some individuals may be amenable to various forms of
treatment. Psychopathic disturbance may also be a secondary

problem for the patient and not the primary focus of clinical concern. In such cases, an understanding of psychopathy as a clinical problem, but not necessarily the overriding clinical concern, is important to its containment and the resolution of other symptomatic or more treatable conditions.

In this chapter I have focused on the fundamental premises when considering treatment of psychopathic individuals, expectable countertransference reactions during such treatment, and predictable resistances to treatment. These premises and predictions, despite their psychoanalytic grounding, are applicable to all modes of treatment of psychopathy regardless of the particular technique that is being applied. If one is a mental health professional, the interpersonal encounter with the patient fundamentally defines the humanity, or lack of humanity, of the treatment: a task that is most rigorously tested when the psychopathic patient is commonly perceived, at least in part, as inhuman.

Appendix I

Jonathan Guard – Deception and Denial in Psychopathy

Honorable Robert J. Donovan
San Diego County Superior Court
Department 46

RE: GUARD, JONATHAN
CR 56843 DA B96754
GENDER: male DOB: May 7, 1948

Dear Judge Donovan:

Pursuant to your order dated August 15, 1986, I am submitting the following evaluation per Sections 1603 and 1604 of the California Penal Code. The intent of this evaluation is to determine whether Mr. Guard would be a danger to the health and safety of others, including himself, if under supervision and treatment in the community.

I interviewed the patient on September 8, 1986, for approximately two hours in the Psychiatric Security Unit of the San Diego County Central Detention Facility. I also consulted with the following individuals: Michael B., L.C.S.W., Constance W., L.C.S.W., Cliff W., United States Secret Service, Donald T. Ph.D., Program Manager for the Psychiatric Security Unit, and

Ben B., M.D., Staff Psychiatrist in the Psychiatric Security Unit. I reviewed the following records:

1. The Patton State Hospital clinical records.
2. Letter by Constance W., L.C.S.W., dated July 30, 1986.
3. Letter written by Michael B., L.C.S.W., dated May 16, 1986.
4. Psychiatric evaluation by Donald S., M.D., dated February 4, 1986.
5. Psychological evaluation by Katherine D., Ph.D., dated December 19, 1985.
6. The Atascadero State Hospital assessment, dated October 1, 1985.
7. Psychiatric evaluation by Carl L., M.D., William V., M.D., and Bernard H., M.D., dated February 24, 1977.
8. Psychiatric evaluation by Donald D., M.D., dated January 4, 1977.
9. Psychiatric evaluation by Dean A., M.D., dated December 15, 1976.
10. The patient's United States Secret Service Records.

The following psychometric instruments were used in this assessment: Minnesota Multiphasic Personality Inventory, the Rorschach Projective Test, Forensic Adaptation of the Brief Psychiatric Rating Scale, and the Hare Psychopathy Checklist.

It is my understanding that Mr. Guard has one year and ten months remaining of possible custody.

Mr. Guard was originally committed to Patton State Hospital by the Superior Court of San Diego County on March 10, 1977, under Penal Code Section 1026, having been found Not Guilty By Reason of Insanity for violation of Penal Code Section 211, Robbery. Two previous offenses of robbery were committed while he was heavily involved in abuse of drugs, specifically phencyclidine. He has a history of escaping from jails and also Patton State Hospital. Over the past eleven years he has been confined in a number of penal institutions in Texas and California.

In September 1985 the patient was returned to Patton under his P.C. 1026 commitment from San Diego County. On September 18, 1985, he was transferred to Atascadero State Hospital for security reasons, where he remained until his return to San Diego County for proceedings consonant with his application for a sanity hearing under P.C. 1026.2. On March 26, 1986, the patient was found "not a danger to the health and safety of himself, other persons, or their property," by a jury of the Superior Court.

Mr. Guard was admitted to the Conditional Release Program of Los Angeles County, and resided at Hillcrest Mental Health Center, as ordered by the Court due to a lack of an appropriate treatment facility in San Diego County. His release began May 8, 1986, and Ms. Constance W., L.C.S.W., director of Hillcrest, reported that his adjustment to the program was "highly satisfactory" up until July 24, 1986.

On that date Ms. W. reported that a telephone call was received from the patient's brother-in-law, Dewey, indicating that the patient had telephoned him stating he was depressed and felt like killing himself. The brother-in-law further stated that he believed the patient was delusional, suicidal, and possibly should be hospitalized. He reported the patient fantasizing about his niece, Andrea, and that he loved her and wanted to marry her. It was learned at that time that the patient's 15-year-old niece had accompanied him in his truck during his working hours.

When the patient returned to Hillcrest, he was questioned about the telephone discussion with his brother-in-law. The patient denied that he was depressed or suicidal, stated he loved his niece, but denied any romantic fantasies about her. His version of the telephone call to his brother-in-law was that he became upset after hearing a tape about suicide that his niece had played for him, and he felt she was disturbed and needed help. He described the whole conversation as a misunderstanding which had been resolved, and this could be verified by telephoning his brother-in-law. At this time Ms. W. reported that the patient was calm, oriented, speech was coherent, and there were no symptoms of depression or suicidal ideation. Neither the brother-in-law nor the sister, Julie, supported the patient's explanation of the situation, and continued to state emphatically that he needed psychiatric treatment. They refused to disclose specifically the statements the patient had made about returning to their home, saying only, "It was personal," and they could not discuss it. At this time they also stated that the patient could not return to their home, nor should he attempt to contact them by telephone. The sister felt Mr. Guard would be welcome at his brother Joseph's home, and agreed to request that Joseph remove the patient's clothing and personal possessions from their home. The patient appeared surprised when informed of his sister and brother-in-law's responses, and that their home was no longer available to him. In the interim his brother Joseph called to confirm that he had been contacted to remove the patient's clothing, and that the patient could visit Joseph at his home.

Although Mr. Guard was requested not to report to his job on Friday, July 26, 1986, in order to be available for further evaluation and discussion of his family difficulties, he left Hillcrest, leaving a note that he was needed at his job and would return immediately after work. When the patient did not return to Hillcrest by curfew, and there was no communication from him, a Missing Persons report was filed with the Police Department, and he was reported AWOL to the Secret Service on Saturday, July 26. Ms. W. reported that a Secret Service agent contacted her on Monday, July 28, 1986, and stated that a man named Mr. Guard had stabbed himself during a rock concert on a previous weekend. The identity of the patient was confirmed through the Inglewood Police Department, and later in contact with members of the treatment staff at UCLA Medical Center, where he was medically stabilized. He was subsequently returned to Patton State Hospital for approximately one week after being brought into custody on July 27, 1986. He was transported and admitted to the Psychiatric Security Unit in the San Diego Central Detention Facility on August 8, 1986, where he remains today.

The patient's version of these events is quite different from those reported by Ms. W. During our clinical interview, he reported to me that he had never had sexual or romantic contact with his niece, Andrea. The patient also denied threatening suicide, and stated that he had never attempted suicide and has never had any suicidal thoughts. The patient did confirm that his brother had agreed to let him stay at the brother's home following his exclusion from his sister and brother-in-law's residence. He states he did return to Hillcrest Residential Center, in contrast to the report of Ms. W., on July 25, 1986. He stated to me that he returned to the Center, signed out, and a staff member told him that he should not go anywhere. He further stated that he felt it was not important enough for him to stay there. Mr. Guard told me that he spent Friday evening, Saturday and Sunday, July 25 through 27, at his brother's house. He stated that he went to "the beach, to Hollywood, I spent some of Saturday night at my brother's." When I asked him if his brother could confirm this, he told me that his brother was with his girlfriend, Nicole, and would not be able to do so. He then stated that he had his own key to his brother's residence.

Regarding what Ms. W. called a "suicide attempt," there is also extensive contradictory data. The patient states to me in the clinical interview that he did not attempt suicide. Instead he was involved in a "knife fight" at the Forum in Los Angeles. When I asked him about the specific event, he stated to me that he had gone to a rock concert, to which he had purchased a ticket. When he arrived at his seat, he found that a couple was occupying the place, and when he asked the male partner to show him his ticket, the man refused to do so. He states he then attempted to secure an usher to settle the issue. Mr. Guard states to me that this male then left, came back in approximately fifteen minutes, and continued to talk to his girlfriend. Mr. Guard then states that his male individual left again, and came back, wherein he knelt in front of his girlfriend, who at this time was sitting in the seat to the left of Mr. Guard. The patient then tells me that at one point during the concert, he stood up and began clapping for the band, and this unidentified male lunged upward from a crouched position in front of his girlfriend, and with his right hand thrust a five-inch knife into Mr. Guard's abdomen. The patient states he grabbed the perpetrator's hand and the knife and attempted to hold onto the knife so that he could not be stabbed again. He states, "I was trying to hold my stomach, I couldn't feel anything." He then tells me he fell forward onto the floor, and was there for approximately ten minutes. He also adamantly states that he received only one stab wound from this assault.

Later in the interview I asked Mr. Guard to once again detail for me this "assault" at the Forum. The patient essentially reported the same details, but added that he had attempted to force this unidentified individual out of his seat, and the individual had said, "don't threaten me." The patient denied any loss of consciousness during this entire event. He stated that he told the authorities it was not a knife fight because he is currently on prison parole, and this would be used against him. He denies any prior knife fights, and reports this is the first time he has ever been stabbed.

In my search to confirm whether the patient was assaulted or whether these were self-inflicted wounds, I pursued several avenues. I was unable to establish telephone contact with the Inglewood Police Department or the UCLA physician that treated Mr. Guard following the stabbing. I was, however, able to speak with Ms. W. by telephone. She reported to me that she also had not seen the police arrest report or the medical examiner's report. She reported that much of their information was gathered from newspaper reports concerning this particular event, and she read to me statements from the *Daily News*, a San Fernando Valley newspaper dated July 29, 1986: "Guard stabbed himself nine times as teenagers cheered him at a rock concert Sunday night, police said . . . he stood on a chair and drove a hunting knife into his bare tattooed chest. As the crowd cheered louder, he said he gained more energy, allowing him to shove the knife blade deeper and deeper, Inglewood Police Department Sergeant Norman B. said." I was unable to reach Sgt. B. at the Inglewood Police Department (tel. 213-421-5210).

Michael B., L.C.S.W., reported to me in a telephone conversation on September 10, 1986, that he was the social worker who originally approved Mr. Guard's conditional release. He also reported to me that he interviewed Mr. Guard on August 20, 1986, at Patton State Hospital, and the patient did describe stabbing himself at the Forum. He stated to Mr. B. that he had grabbed the knife from other people at the concert, and had gotten carried away with the music and the crowd. Mr. B. also reported to me that he had viewed a urine drug screen of the patient two days after the concert, and it was negative for illicit drugs.

I met with Cliff W., special agent for the United States Secret Service, on September 8, 1986. He allowed me to review the Secret Service records concerning this patient. Those records indicate that the patient was interviewed by the Secret Service on July 29, and Mr. Guard stated to the interviewing agent that he had stabbed himself because he loved Andrea. He also stated to the agent that he wanted the world to know of his love for Andrea by stabbing himself. He recalled that he stood on the floor area near the stage, and the crowd cheered as he stabbed himself, allowing him more energy to stab more deeply. The agent indicated that the patient had nine stab wounds to his chest and abdomen.

When the patient was confronted by me during the interview with his contradictory information, he stated that he did not want to report a knife fight because of the possibility his parole would be violated. He consented to show me the scars on his chest and abdomen, and I brought in Ben B., M.D., to also examine Mr. Guard's chest to see what scars were present. That examination indicated that Mr. Guard had five scars on his abdomen and thorax, all between 1 and 4 cm in length. The patient acknowledged during this exam the presence of two scars, and stated that one was for the abdominal surgery and one was the original wound. When confronted by Dr. B. concerning the other three scars in his thorax area, the patient attempted to squeeze one of the scars, telling us, "it's a pimple." When faced with our skepticism of his statement, he sat back in his chair, pulled down his t-shirt, and said, "Oh, forget it."

In the absence of a police arrest report and the direct testimony of the examining emergency room physician from UCLA, it is not possible to determine beyond a reasonable doubt whether Mr. Guard's wounds were self-inflicted or not. But the preponderance of the evidence is that they were.

CURRENT INPATIENT TREATMENT

Mr. Guard was admitted to the Psychiatric Security Unit on August 8, 1986. Review of those inpatient records indicates the following entries:

August 8, 1986, "hostile and demanding"; August 12, 1986, "hostile, angry, defensive"; August 15, 1986, "hostile, arrogant"; August 22, 1986, "denies escape threats"; August 27, 1986, "placed in seclusion for being unable to follow directions and being verbally abusive"; August 28, 1986, "attitude continues to be one of superiority towards peer and staff"; August 29, 1986, "nursing staff reports witnessing what appears to be this patient intimidating or threatening another patient"; September 2, 1986, "patient sat laughing most of the time throughout group."

The patient's DSM-III psychodiagnosis is:

Axis I: Mixed substance abuse
Axis II: Antisocial personality disorder

Borderline personality disorder
Axis III: No diagnosis
Axis IV: 4
Axis V: 4

The patient is currently receiving no regular medications except for a sedative-hypnotic on an "as needed" basis for sleep.

There is no indication from the Psychiatric Security Unit inpatient records that he has been physically assaultive or psychotic while in custody. In other words, the patient has been able to maintain both contact and some semblance of control during his stay in a maximum security inpatient unit. This is generally characteristic of his history in other hospital and inpatient settings.

I would like to quote from a progress note written by Mica E., R.N., the patient's primary therapist, written on September 8, 1986: "This patient keeps a low profile on the unit, but has made his presence well known. His views on psychiatry are known to all patients and have contributed significantly to hostility and lack of cooperation from his peers. He is quite open and verbal about his opinions. He feels psychiatric patients are treated as if they are less than human, and that they have no rights. He goes on to elaborate that psychiatric care givers are only interested in persecuting their patients and dictating their own moral values. He much prefers jail because he feels he is treated with respect and has control of his life there. He gives the reason for this as, 'the guards don't hassle you because they know what will happen to them if they do.' He felt he was allowed to do pretty much as he pleased in prison. He told me of his respect for Charles Manson, that 'he'll be locked up forever, but he's really got it made. People all over the world write him and send him things – they feel he is a political prisoner.' The patient feels he is the victim of a political system intent on persecuting him for reasons he cannot comprehend. He has convinced several of his peers that they are also the undeserving victims of the mental health system. He urges them to rebel against the system by not cooperating whenever possible, and fighting for their rights as he feels he is doing. He has no insight into his own responsibility for his current situation."

MENTAL STATUS EXAM

The patient is a 38-year-old Caucasian male of medium height and build. He is oriented to person, place, and time. He is alert. His affect is somewhat blunted, but appropriate to his thought content. His mood remains mildly defensive and guarded throughout the interview. The patient shows no indication of formal thought disorder. There is no evidence of hallucinations or delusions. The patient shows no impairment of remote, long-term, short-term memory, or immediate recall. Concentration and attention are in the normal range. The patient's intelligence is estimated to be in the superior range (IQ 120–129). He shows no indication of homicidal or suicidal ideation or intent while in custody. His attitude toward the interviewer is one of begrudging cooperativeness, colored by a sense of arrogance and superiority. From statements the patient makes it is clear that he wants to present himself in a very rational and positive light, and goes to great length to explain, excuse, and rationalize his behavior. His predominant psychological defenses are projection, rationalization, and denial. It also appears that this individual has great facility in being able to lie and intentionally deceive this examiner. When the patient is asked about his behavior while in the Psychiatric Security Unit, he tells me that he had had a personality conflict with the social worker, "She doesn't like what I've said. I've consistently said that I don't need medication." The patient also begins the interview by asking me if I will provide for him a fair and impartial examination. He then goes on to talk about his "so-called disruptive behavior." He adamantly denies that he had made any verbal threats to escape, despite this information being documented by staff on the unit. He states, "That's ludicrous, why would I tell someone if I had a .38 and a box of shells? That wouldn't be sophisticated." He goes on to further state, "I've been kindly and generous . . . nothing but a father figure to these patients . . . I would never hurt them for anything in the world." He reports this despite documentation of his threatening another patient, and having to be placed in seclusion on August 27, 1986.

He states to me that in his opinion, "I am not a danger to anyone." He states that he was "working steadily and abiding by the Hillcrest rules." When the patient is asked about his consistent diagnosis of antisocial personality disorder throughout all the evaluations and records that I reviewed, he states that, "I think I was a sociopath, but it means nothing more than being lazy. I spent eleven years in the pen in California and Texas . . . as a child I used to shoplift, way down deep I think there is an area in me that thinks it's kind of slick to be a criminal. But I've seen for eleven years the pain that criminals cause, and I don't want to do that."

The patient showed no residual effects of his extensive history of drug abuse, which has been characterized by a preference for psychostimulants. The patient denies any drug use during 1986. He reports that he prefers psychostimulants, and also phencyclidine, because he can talk very well and feels euphoric when ingesting them. His experience with drugs would be characterized as one of grandiosity and psychomotor acceleration, typical of the psychostimulants such as methamphetamine. When I asked him about what he had learned from this event at the rock concert, he states, "I'm not going to any more rock concerts. I wish I hadn't gone."

PERSONALITY PROFILE

Mr. Guard experiences minimal conscious anxiety or depression, and is quite comfortable within himself. He also shows little conscious need for affection from others. He may oftentimes be openly hostile in social situations; and is generally suspicious and distrustful of others. There are also indications of persecutory thoughts which may have no basis in reality.

The patient has difficulty expressing emotion in a modulated fashion, and will oftentimes use projection (attributing to others one's own thoughts and feelings) to keep people at an emotional distance. This individual would often be described by others as tense and irritable, but he would deny these feelings if confronted. He is likely to overreact to environmental stimuli, and will often exhibit poor behavioral control and a heightened general activity level. He may have a reduced ability to concentrate and organize his thinking in a logical, sequential, and goal-directed manner. Explosive outbursts of aggression are a distinct possibility.

There are strong indications of paranoia, grandiosity, and self-aggrandizement. He is very facile in developing superficial, casual relationships that have no emotional depth or substantial meaning for him. Mr. Guard, however, will appear very comfortable in most social situations. He tends to have his own internalized system of behavioral rules that would most likely be judged by others as amoral.

He shows a moderate level of addiction-proneness to both drugs and alcohol.

What is particularly disturbing is a lack of capacity to form emotional attachments to others. He shows a pronounced tendency to view other people as objects, and to have little empathy concerning other people's feelings. There is also a strong indication that this individual will unconsciously deny aggressive impulses, and has great difficulty, therefore, expressing them in any kind of modulated fashion when they surface. Mr. Guard would be characterized as having a psychopathic personality disorder wherein others are viewed as extensions of his own grandiose self. This pathologically narcissistic attitude toward others in the world, coupled with impulsivity, hyperactivity, and paranoid ideation, are chiefly characteristic of this individual's current personality function.

Although no formal testing of his intelligence was attempted, past psychological records indicate that this individual has a superior IQ. This would contribute to his facility in deceiving others by presenting rationalizations to those who would choose to naively believe that he is not responsible for his actions. Such manipulation would historically leave people feeling quite angry, disappointed, and generally exploited by this individual.

ASSESSMENT OF DANGEROUSNESS

Based upon my evaluation of Mr. Guard, it is my opinion that he does constitute a danger to the health and safety of others if under supervision and treatment in the community. I have arrived at this opinion for the following reasons:

1. The patient is a male psychopath. This fact alone, without considering any other individual characteristics, demographically places him in a group which is at higher risk for violence than nonpsychopathic criminals.

2. The events of July 27, 1986, indicate that this individual was in a life-threatening encounter involving a weapon in a public place. Regardless of whether the patient's wounds were self-inflicted or other inflicted, such a documented event impresses upon me this individual's poor social judgment, impulsivity, and proneness to engage in situations in his very recent past that clearly create an imminent danger to self and others.

3. The patient shows virtually no insight into his psychopathic (antisocial) personality disorder. Specifically, an inability to form emotional attachments, a lack of empathic capacity toward other individuals, and a tendency to be deceptive and manipulative of others, are not easy psychological areas for this individual to reflect upon.

4. In addition to this individual's well-documented antisocial

personality traits is the heightened risk of danger due to his current guarded, angry, and suspicious state. There is also a distinct possibility that he harbors completely false persecutory beliefs, that is, delusions, that he is intelligent enough to conceal from this examiner at this time.

5. This individual's behavior in his most current inpatient psychiatric setting has continued to support my conclusion that he is rebellious against authority, blames other individuals for situations of which he has at least a shared responsibility, and will intentionally lie and deceive those people who are obligated to provide him with mental health care.

6. Despite his lack of overt violence while in the Psychiatric Security Unit, his disruptive behavior managed to land him in seclusion on one occasion. This is remarkable, given the fact that he is not psychotic, and is intelligent enough to recognize that his clinical behavior has been carefully documented by the inpatient staff and will be considered in this evaluation. It leads me to conclude that, despite the fact that he is in a maximum security inpatient setting, the most controlled treatment milieu in the county, he still shows difficulties with his impulse control.

7. The patient has an extensive and versatile history of criminal behavior, and does not appear to have any sense of the impact on his victims of his acts, particularly the two robberies. He shows no empathic understanding of the "force and fear" that he was convicted of inflicting upon them.

8. Mr. Guard's violent behavior was done in a public place when he was surrounded by strangers. The fact that he would seek out such an arena, and the fact that he would engage strangers in this behavior, either as perpetrators or as an audience, renders his potential victim pool, including himself, extremely large: much more extensive than the individual whose potential dangerousness is limited to family members or friends. We have here an individual who is quite inclined to act out publicly during times of emotional stress, which increases the probability of his violence potential and dangerousness.

9. The patient denies access to or ownership of any weapons;

yet there was a weapon involved in this July 27 incident. The Secret Service reports also indicate that the patient, at one time, had two Cobra .38 caliber revolvers at his wife's residence. The patient denies this. Again, we have here an individual who denies attraction to and use of weapons, yet has a history of criminal offenses that supports his access to and possession of weapons. His potential for violence is increased because of his propensity to secure weapons and his deliberate lying that he has never done so.

10. The patient is considered a threat to the President of the United States by the Secret Service. Their records indicate that these threats are not short-lived, but date back to December 1978 when Mr. Guard first threatened President Jimmy Carter. Their records also document a history of involvement with Satanic cults, a hatred of minorities, and generally a racist attitude, all suggestive of paranoid ideation.

11. Despite his denial of any current alcohol or drug use, both his history and psychological testing indicate a moderate addiction-proneness to either alcohol or drugs. These facts, and his personal preference for psychostimulants such as methamphetamine, correlate with dangerous behavior.

12. Mr. Guard is physically quite capable of inflicting violence on himself and others, particularly given his propensity to secure or be in the possession of lethal weapons.

13. This individual has shown to this interviewer, as well as to those involved in his case, a propensity to consciously deceive and lie to others. I cannot overestimate this individual's extremely facile capacity for conscious deception. In order to impress this upon the court, I would like to give a brief example. I will quote a paragraph from a psychiatric evaluation that was done February 24, 1977, concerning this patient's precommitment evaluation which found him Not Guilty By Reason of Insanity:

> The patient was then asked what is happening to him at
> the present time, if he still had the same experiences he

had before. The patient went on to say that he is in contact with Satan, and hears Satan's voice sometimes. He states he sees faces of people. He claimed he saw these faces "every day." He went on to say, "they materialize." He claims the last time he had this experience of seeing the faces was when he was on the "rack" in his cell in a meditation pose. He denies that he sees just faces. He says he sees complete beings, and they were touching him. Either these were two enemies or two friends of his, he couldn't say. The patient was asked about the last time he heard anything like voices, and he remarked, "Only once since I was in San Diego." The patient was asked if he felt the influence of "Baphlomint," and he responded, "Yes, that's my angel."

Nine years later this patient reported to a Secret Service agent on January 1, 1986, that his Satanic cult fixation, hallucinations, and delusions were methods of manipulating the system in order to get his insanity judgment, and it had worked. It is my opinion that this individual's skillful lying, although not directly tied to a prediction of violence, heightens the probability of his not being able to be successfully supervised in a conditional release outpatient program.

RECOMMENDATION

I would recommend that Mr. Guard be recommitted to Patton State Hospital and outpatient conditional release be revoked at this time.

If you have any further questions, please do not hesitate to telephone me at 544-2435.

J. Reid Meloy, Ph.D.
Community Program Director
Chief, Forensic Mental Health Services
San Diego County

CROSS-EXAMINATION OF JONATHAN GUARD

District Attorney: Mr. J. G., you are a habitual liar, are you not?

J. Guard: In your opinion, that's for sure.

D.A.: You haven't done a lot of lying recently?

J.G.: I have done a lot of eluding the truth recently.

D.A.: Is that a lie? Is eluding the truth a lie?

J.G.: It depends on the context.

D.A.: Well, let's talk about a couple of contexts. You told the Secret Service agent in January of 1986 that you had previously used a satanic cult fixation to manipulate the system, correct?

J.G.: Yes, I think I did tell him that.

D.A.: Which meant that sometime long ago you lied to psychiatrists, correct?

J.G.: I've talked to so many psychiatrists, I'm sure that I haven't told them all the absolute truth a hundred percent of the time, but that doesn't mean that I was purposely out to lie to them or to try to deceive them.

D.A.: You told Agent P. of the Secret Service that you were in love with your niece and you wanted to show the world your love for your niece so you stabbed yourself?

J.G.: I do not have any recollection of that. When the Agent came to see me, I was in intensive care, heavily medicated. I don't hardly remember him coming, much less what I talked to him about.

D.A.: So those words came rolling off, your lies?

J.G.: I don't remember what I said to him.

D.A.: You told Mr. B. of L.A. County Mental Health that you stabbed yourself, didn't you?

J.G.: That's true.

D.A.: And then you told Dr. Meloy that that was a lie, that you really hadn't stabbed yourself, that somebody else had stabbed you?

J.G.: Yes, I told Dr. B. that.

D.A.: Which one of those statements was a lie?

J.G.: When Dr. B—is that his name?

D.A.: Yes.

J.G.: When he came to see me, we talked about what he was going to do. He said he wasn't going to come and testify here.

D.A.: Listen carefully to my question.

J.G.: Okay. Wait. Listen to my answer. And therefore I felt that it would be to my best interests if I did not admit to Dr. Meloy that I had tried to commit suicide, because it's almost certain that I'm going to end up in Atascadero behind that action.

D.A.: Did you lie to Dr. Meloy?

J.G.: Yes, I did.

D.A.: You've been apparently telling other patients that they should fight the system. Is that correct?

J.G.: I read the report.

D.A.: Well, is that correct or not?

J.G.: No, it's not correct. What I told them was that they didn't have to take their medication if they weren't acting in a violent or abrasive, abusive manner towards the staff or other patients.

D.A.: Why did you feel you had the authority to tell them that?

J.G.: They asked me that.

D.A.: You were their lawyer?

J.G.: In a sense.

Defendant's counsel: I'll object, that's an argumentative question.

Court: Sustained.

D.A.: Did you perceive yourself as being in a position to give legal advice to other patients?

J.G.: No, I do not.

Defendant's counsel: I'll object. The same objection.

Court: Overruled.

D.A.: I'd like just to read one statement and have you tell me whether you agree with it or not. This is from page 11 of Dr. Meloy's report, the top, paragraph 13: "This individual has shown to this interviewer, as well as those involved in his case, a propensity to consciously deceive and lie to others. I cannot overestimate this individual's extremely facile capacity for conscious deception."

J.G.: I don't know what he's saying.

Court: He says you lie a lot.

J.G.: Again, your honor, I have—I have twisted the truth towards—and manipulated the facts of events to my gain a number of times in front of psychiatrists, but I only did it out of self-preservation. That was my motive, not because I'm a fucking habitual liar.

D.A.: No further questions . . .

DECISION OF THE COURT

Court: Well, I tell you, the world is full of productive sociopaths. Some of them hold high public office. Some of them are lawyers. It could be that a couple of them are judges, and sociopathy by itself is not necessarily a dangerous condition. It can be productive. I think it was Clarence Darrow who commented on that . . .

There was no real way that that jury could know how Mr. J. G. would do until he had a chance to do it. And there was no real way to know whether he would be one of those manageable sociopaths or a more unpredictable, volatile, dangerous one until he was confronted with the realities of the outside world after having been confined for as long as he was.

I think Dr. T. R. got conned. I felt that as I heard the trial. I think Dr. T. R. felt he got conned but also had a reasonable position to say that, "Even if I was, I still think that the man is in a position to go outside based upon what we know today, not what we knew nine years ago."

What we've now seen is something a bit more than a bad weekend. I mean, I don't think anybody ever suspected—I certainly didn't—that Mr. J. G. would go out in the streets and

immediately turn into some kind of a raving lunatic. He has an
incredible capacity for controlling himself up to a point; and then
certain stressors, because of his personality structure, cause him
to lose his control. And what happens is those stressors arose. It
might have been predicted. Everybody was hoping it wouldn't
happen. Some people have better impulse control than others.
He certainly doesn't.

Look what he did. Here's a man, spent all this time in the
hospital or whatever you want to call it, for a series of rather
bizarre crimes, under bizarre circumstances, at least, who probably, in my judgment—who perhaps not in the jury's—conned his
way into an insanity situation at a time when we probably
weren't as enlightened on such subjects as we are now ten years
later; but in any event, who has a history of some bizarre
behavior, unpredictable, explosive, bizarre behavior, who man-
ages for a brief period of time and then all of a sudden what do we
have? His whole life is riding on it. He's got two years in prison
riding on it, the kind of things that would motivate most of us in
the room to do the right things and tow the line.

And I was making a list . . .

First, there's this general demonstration of anger and dissatisfaction with the program. That's probably understandable.
He was anxious to be out. You could forgive that and not call it
anything important.

Then he goes AWOL from the program which is his umbilical cord to the civilized world. I mean, without that program he's
back in prison. One would think you'd be cautious about that, but
he goes AWOL, for whatever stimulus. He confronted the authorities at the program. He finds himself involved—or at least in
his mind involved romantically with a 14-year-old relative of the
very people who are harboring him, who are helping him, who are
again part of his umbilical cord, if you will. Is that an act which is
calculated to get yourself cut off? I hope to tell you.

You see, I'm convinced that he set himself up to go back. I
think he couldn't do it any better than to go to a rock concert and

try and stab himself in front of 20 or 30,000 people. Was it a suicide attempt? Of course it wasn't. It was a gesture. If it was an attempt, he would have killed himself. It was easy. He had a big knife. It's not that hard to do. And he gets up there and pokes himself for a while. He got his attention. It got him on the radio, in the papers, got everything done. It was terrific . . .

He then proceeds to lie serially to a group of psychiatrists, with full knowledge after ten years in this system they don't throw reports away . . . He lies to doctors that he knows are in the specific program that's treating him, that I daresay he knows are going to write a report to the court. He tells another story to the next doctor.

Is that a man who's in control of his environment, a man as intelligent as he is, as bright, articulate, and aware of those things? He's got all the talents. He doesn't have the ability to put it into a constructive use. That's why he can't make it on the outside. That's why he can't be managed on the outside, because they don't know what he's going to do next; he doesn't know what he's going to do next, and he admits it.

All somebody had to do is try to take that knife away from him in the wrong way at that concert, and God knows where we'd be today; or if he had decided to act out this delusion with this 14-year-old and he had gone off to Las Vegas with her, God knows where he'd be today.

His time on the street was one giant flirtation with disaster, and he finally succumbed to it and just decided it was enough and went back. I think he decided it was beyond him and had to go back, I think, for his own protection and the protection of the community.

I was as willing as anybody to give him a try, not because I thought he was not a danger, because I know enough about his personality sorts to understand that he was; but you get to a point after that number of years where you got to—I suppose you owe him a shot. He's had a shot, but I don't think he's used it very well. I don't think anyone in the room does . . .

He's clearly a danger to himself. He's demonstrated that. And I think he's a danger to others, because I don't know what he'll do next when the proper stressors are put on. Maybe the stressors of being out there are enough to make him a danger; and I don't think he intends to be a danger to anybody, but he gets upset with the world when things don't go his way, which is what the doctors have described, and he can do things that are not under his control . . .

I will make the findings indicated and order that he be recommitted to the state hospital as the law prescribes.

Anything further gentlemen? We're in recess.

Appendix II

Louis Cypher – Paranoid Schizophrenia and Psychopathy

Honorable Richard D. Jenkins
San Diego County Superior Court
Department 54

RE: CYPHER, LOUIS
CR 567812 DA 59867
GENDER: male DOB: October 7, 1949

Dear Judge Jenkins:

Pursuant to Judge David G.'s order for my evaluation of Louis Cypher, I am submitting the following report concerning appropriate treatment at the present time for this individual per Penal Code Section 1600 et. seq.

I reviewed the following clinical information in addition to evaluating Mr. Cypher on August 8, 1986, in the Forensic Department of the San Diego County Courthouse: County Mental Health records; Psychiatric Security Unit discharge summaries; the district attorney case file; psychiatric evaluations by the following doctors: Thomas R., M.D., David B., M.D., Donald D., M.D., David B., M.D., Dean A., M.D., Bernard H., M.D., and William V., M.D.; the United States Dept. of Justice FBI record

Number 678901; telephone conversations with Douglas E., M.D., on August 11, 1986, the patient's current treating psychiatrist.

Mr. Cypher is a 37-year-old Caucasian male with an extensive psychiatric and criminal history. A brief summary of his psychiatric history indicates that the patient was first hospitalized at age 17 following polydrug abuse of both LSD and methamphetamines. It is highly likely that these substances precipitated his first acute schizophrenic episode. Since that time, the patient has been hospitalized on several occasions at various state and local hospitals: The United States Public Health Hospital in San Francisco; Lima State Hospital in Ohio; Oregon State Hospital in Salem, Oregon; Fulton State Hospital in Missouri; Atascadero State Hospital and Patton State Hospital in California; San Diego County Mental Health; and the Psychiatric Security Unit in the San Diego Central Jail.

California State hospital records indicate that the patient was first admitted to Patton State Hospital from January 9 to February 7, 1969. His second admission was March 14, 1969, to May 20, 1970. His third admission was September 13, 1972, and due to multiple escape attempts, was transferred to the maximum security Atascadero State Hospital on April 13, 1973. He was confined there until April 16, 1975, but during that time escaped from December 23 to December 27, 1974. The patient was rehospitalized at Patton October 3, 1975, to December 12, 1975, August 26, 1977, to November 18, 1977, and April 16, 1982, to February 17, 1983. The patient has not returned to the state regional hospitals since that time. All of his hospital commitments were due to findings of Not Guilty By Reason of Insanity on various criminal charges which will be elaborated below. Local psychiatric history indicates that the patient was first treated on April 2, 1972. Twelve hospitalizations followed between 1972 and 1982, which included six AWOLs from that hospital. In 1983 the patient was seen twice at CMH Screening and referred to extended care. In 1984 the patient was hospitalized twice in the Psychiatric Security Unit in the Central Jail, once between February 22 and April 24, 1984, and a second time between July 17, 1984, and February 27, 1985.

The patient was most recently hospitalized in the Psychiatric Security Unit June 13 to July 11, 1986, when he was released by Judge Jones to hospital parole with the conditions that he would contact CMH within ten days, a conservatorship evaluation would be done, he would be tested for illicit drug use, and he would take all prescribed drugs. The patient did visit CMH Screening on July 21, 1986, exactly ten days after his release from custody. At that time the patient was clinically judged to not need further medication, and was referred to his private psychiatrist. No recent conservatorship referral has been made on this patient.

The adult criminal history of Mr. Cypher began at age 19 when he was charged with Malicious Mischief and Possession of Marijuana. Multiple arrests have occurred since then with no period longer than two years between criminal charges. Charges have ranged from multiple drug offenses, including Possession and Use, to Robbery and Battery of an Officer (1972), Assault with a Deadly Weapon (1973), Forgery and Burglary (1975), Burglary (1976), Burglary, Assault and Battery, Trespassing and Reckless Driving (1977), Robbery (1978), a Murder charge in Oregon (1979), which was dismissed, and Burglary (1981). The instant offense to which he was found Not Guilty By Reason of Insanity on July 13, 1984, was P.C. 597(a), Malicious Maiming, Wounding, and Killing of a Living Animal, and P.C. 487(f), Stealing a Dog.

It is my impression that charges have either been dismissed or reduced primarily because of the patient's history of chronic, paranoid schizophrenia. As noted earlier, the patient has been found insane on several occasions following the commission of felony offenses, and has subsequently been committed to various hospitals. In addition to the patient's extensive psychiatric and criminal history, there also is a pronounced history of drug and alcohol abuse. The various records note that the patient has reported multiple use of LSD in his late adolescence, addiction to heroin in 1974, use of phencyclidine on one occasion, and recent use of methamphetamine and cocaine. The patient, since I have known him, has also used marijuana and alcohol on a regular basis.

CURRENT SOCIAL SYSTEM

The patient is living at 1396 F Street, in an apartment complex with a roommate named George whom the patient reports is on probation. He does not know his last name. Mr. Cypher also has a pet dog named "Dog" that was left in the apartment building by another psychiatric patient that he had befriended. He lives in a one-room studio apartment with his roommate, and until one week ago, had a number of people living with him who had promised to pay him $200 a piece if he provided them with food. He did so, they refused to pay, and he "kicked them out." He reports that girls visit him from the local board and care home, and that he enjoys their company and does not have any feelings of loneliness. He reports that his contact with his parents, who live in Coronado, is "pretty good." I was unable to reach them by telephone. The patient reports that he enjoys visiting his parents because they are "the best friends I've got." He also has one brother and sister in San Diego, but has no social contact with them. When discussing contact with his parents, he reports that multiple arrests have occurred on Coronado Island by the local police department and states, "If I get a slick lawyer, I'll blast them out of the universe." He shows anger congruent with his thought content as he discusses how the local police do not want him visiting the island, and that he has been transported by police across the Coronado bridge on many occasions. The most recent event reportedly occurred on August 5 or 6, when he was securing money from his bank account at California First in Coronado and the police approached him and told him to leave.

He is quite angry at the police and attributes to them quite malevolent intentions. At one point he states, "A Coronado cop named Martinez threatened to cut my throat and cut my heart out and shoot me. I want to sue the shit out of him." He states that someone stole his kitchen knives and believes that someone has a key to his apartment and is continuing to steal things from him.

The patient states that his only major social problem is needing a social worker to help him manage his money. He has not been able to handle his money, so when he stocks food at the beginning of the month after he receives his Social Security check, he hopes to be able to provide for himself until the end of the month. When I interviewed him on August 8, he had no money left from his August 1 check. He currently receives $355 from Social Security Disability and $200 from Supplemental Security Income, totaling $555 per month. Rent is presently $375 per month, leaving him with $180 per month for food and incidental expenses.

When I asked Mr Cypher how he is spending his time, he responds that he is "reading the Bible and a love book by Buscaglia, playing with my dog, watching television, and listening to music." He reported that he plans to attend San Diego City College in the fall and resume classes on September 2. He hopes to take fourteen hours of coursework toward his associate arts degree in cabinet making. He reportedly has two years of school to his credit, but when asked what he would like to do if he were able to, he reports that he would like to join the Merchant Marines.

CURRENT PSYCHIATRIC TREATMENT

The patient is currently being treated by Douglas E., M.D. He is taking Navane 15 mgs. t.i.d., Benadryl 25 mgs. t.i.d., and receives an intramuscular injection of Prolixin Decanoate, 1.00 cc., the last one on August 5. As the patient talks about his relationship to the doctor, it is apparent he is quite angry and mistrustful of him. He states he requested both Ritalin and Triavil from the doctor. The former is methylphenidate hydrochloride, a mild central nervous system stimulant. The latter drug, Triavil, is a combination of antidepressant and antipsychotic. The patient states, "The fusion (of Triavil) makes the beauty of the pill." He admits to me that he doesn't trust Dr. E. and would prefer to be treated by Ernest G., M.D., a psychiatrist that he first met when admitted to the Psychiatric Security Unit in 1984. The patient is especially angry at Dr. E. for not injecting him with a "golden yellow" Prolixin that Mr. Cypher had brought to his appointment; and instead, the doctor injected him with some of his own "crystal clear" Prolixin.

I have had two telephone conversations with Dr. E. and he generally concurs with my assessment of this patient. He has been treating Mr. Cypher for several years, and feels much less comfortable with him than he used to. He feels Mr. Cypher is much more guarded and hostile in recent months. I advised Dr. E. of the patient's anger toward him, and he agreed to telephone me following the subsequent appointment by the patient. It is clear that Dr. E. no longer wants to treat this patient.

MENTAL STATUS EXAMINATION

Mr. Cypher arrived on time for his interview on August 8, 1986, at 1500. He was dressed in shorts, sneakers, and black socks, a T-shirt, and a cap. He was wearing sunglasses and listening to a portable tape recorder. He was friendly toward me, but guarded. The patient is a 37-year-old large Caucasian male. During the course of the interview the patient remained oriented to person, place, and time. He denied any difficulty concentrating, and remained alert and attentive throughout the interview. His IQ is estimated to be in the bright–normal range (110–119). The patient, when tested for concept formation, initially showed no impairment; but when asked, in what way is a fly and a tree alike, he responded, "If tree's a fruitfly, a fly will go to the fruit." This is a difficult abstraction, but shows some indication of formal thought disorder when he was asked to perform this task. When asked to explain several proverbs, he abruptly responded that they are not proverbs because they are not in the Bible, but then was able to elaborate the meaning of several of them. The patient denied any sleep difficulty. He reported that he is generally not hungry but that his appetite is as normal as usual. He reported that he occasionally becomes depressed, but is not currently feeling that way. He denied any current paranoid delusions with a shake of his head, but he kept his sunglasses on throughout the entire interview, implying a desire to keep some distance between himself and me. Mr. Cypher denied any thoughts of hurting himself or others. He denied thought insertion, withdrawal, and broadcasting, but did report that all those symptoms occurred when he was quite psychotic, most recently in June 1986. He denied any current use of illicit drugs, but did report that he was drinking beer daily. He stated he consumed a six-pack of beer on August 7. He attends Alcoholics Anonymous and Narcotics Anonymous occasionally, but stated, "They're all doing drugs anyways." When asked why he is not using illicit drugs, given his extensive history of use, he stated that during his last psychotic episode, he was told that the Americans would not help him and the Nazis would come over and get him if he used drugs anymore. This hallucination has reportedly sufficed to keep the patient away from street drugs. He does show some indication of somatic delusion. When asked to elaborate on this, he stated, "Instead of scraping the brain, we'd have a liquid to drink so that the tentacles of the tumor could be pulled out." When asked if he had any other bodily pain, he stated that he had some chest pain several days ago, but that he, "Held the baby to my chest and it made the pain melt away." The incident was reportedly in an apartment next to his own room.

When asked about the instant offense, Mr. Cypher stated that he was psychotic at the time of the killing of the dog, but that, "The damned dog had a code word to go for someone's throat. I had visions of him grabbing me by the throat (patient suddenly grabs his own throat) so I chopped his head off. I was psychotic but I stalked him, I stalked him." The patient went on to give me a rather bizarre and elaborate recapitulation of the way in which he dissected the dog and the manner in which he disbursed the various internal organs of the dog throughout his neighbor's home; "I was going to put the dog's intestines on a plate, like a plate of spaghetti, with the American flag in the center of them."

His father had smelled some of the remains of the dog in the basement of their Coronado home where the patient was staying, and subsequently called the police.

I want to note that in this elaboration by the patient, although he verbalized that he was no longer psychotic, were many primitive, and highly affectively charged, thoughts; the presentation was somewhat tangential and disorganized; and the patient showed no remorse or embarrassment concerning the instant offense. It became apparent to me at this point in the interview that Mr. Cypher was in only marginal contact with reality, and with any clinical probing would express some rather aggressive and primitive material.

The patient reported that he was experiencing feelings of fear concerning his psychiatric status and had requested the injection of Prolixin, "waiting for it to kick in." He had received the injection three days prior to my evaluation of him, and therefore was receiving some benefit from it at the time of my interview.

PSYCHODIAGNOSIS

Axis I: Schizophrenia, paranoid type, chronic.
Opioid dependence, in remission.

Hallucinogen and phencyclidine abuse, in remission.

Mixed substance abuse, including amphetamines and cannabis.

Alcohol abuse, episodic.

Axis II: Antisocial Personality Disorder.

Axis III: No diagnosis.

Axis IV: 3.

Axis V: 5.

ASSESSMENT OF DANGEROUSNESS

It is my clinical opinion that Mr. Cypher currently presents a danger to the health and safety of others in his current outpatient setting. I have arrived at this opinion for the following reasons:

1. The patient has an extensive criminal history over the past twenty years that includes both violent and nonviolent offenses. The patient's Axis II diagnosis of antisocial personality disorder is justified, in addition to his more obvious clinical diagnosis of paranoid schizophrenia. I have known this patient since 1983 and have been impressed by the way in which he uses his functional psychotic diagnosis to rationalize and diminish the severity of his antisocial acts. I think this is a case where the more flagrant, bizarre, and dramatic delusional material has overridden the fact that the patient also has a propensity to engage in dangerous and antisocial behavior in a predatory fashion. In other words, the antisocial behavior is planned, intentional, goal-directed, and unpredictable. This diagnosis has been missed in most of his prior psychiatric evaluations. A rather clear example of the patient's inclination to blend his antisocial behavior with his paranoid schizophrenia was in the interview on August 8 when I asked him if he felt he had a psychiatric disorder, and he responded that he believed he had paranoid schizophrenia. But when I asked him if his paranoid schizophrenia had caused him to commit the instant offense, he stated

that yes, he was quite delusional, but that he had intentionally stalked the dog and had deliberately planned to kill the animal. In my review of the patient's local records, I came across an MMPI evaluation that had been completed when the patient was 24 years old on October 16, 1973. At that time Dr. John C. diagnosed Mr. Cypher as a sociopathic (psychopathic) personality. He wrote, "There is no present evidence of a psychotic thought disorder. Personality integration indicates an adequate lifestyle."

2. When the patient does decompensate, he develops very clearcut paranoid delusions which he finds difficult to resist. These delusions, although he does not express any at present, make him a high risk for quite dangerous and predatory behavior.

3. The patient is a large Caucasian male with a physical stature capable of inflicting harm on others, and a demonstrated history of doing so.

4. The patient has an extensive history of multiple drug abuse, including recent use of two drugs that I have seen precipitate violence in paranoid schizophrenics, namely cocaine and methamphetamine. This is an ominous sign.

5. The patient has a history of being superficially quite compliant, and ostensibly quite good natured, with mental health professionals; yet, at various times he has successfully deceived them to get what he wants. I cite two examples: first, in a report dated June 8, 1984, by David B., M.D., the patient did not inform his psychologist-psychotherapist that he had been charged with the offense of animal mutilation. In the same report Dr. B. wrote, "He did not tell this therapist that he had committed a crime or that he was going to stop taking his prescribed antipsychotic medication." Second, the patient was also observed by me on several occasions during his stay in the Psychiatric Security Unit to engage in teasing behavior toward the more psychotic patients, and would also circumvent unit rules and regulations

whenever possible. When confronted, he would deny the behavior and diminish its importance.

6. Most paranoid schizophrenics are not violent and are able to resist command hallucinations. Mr. Cypher, however, represents a small proportion of individuals with schizophrenia who have a history of being quite violent when not on medication, do not resist command hallucinations, and recompensate very quickly when given appropriate medications (note the brief and multiple hospital stays). He also tends to be noncompliant with treatment unless required by an external authority. In other words, despite the patient's verbal statement that he has a mental disorder and needs treatment, these are quite superficially compliant words that have little internal motivation other than the desire to avoid further incarceration.

7. The patient is currently engaged in a rather hostile, dependent relationship toward his current psychiatrist. There appears to be no trust or sense of safety in his relationship to this particular doctor.

8. The patient has no reliable social support system and continues to pursue a relationship with parents who are quite ambivalent about seeing him at their home; and furthermore, they live in an area where the police are openly hostile to his presence.

RECOMMENDATIONS

It is my recommendation that Mr. Cypher should be committed to Patton State Hospital immediately under P.C. 1026, wherein he will be treated and evaluated by the inpatient staff.

J. Reid Meloy, Ph.D.
Community Program Director
Chief, Forensic Mental Health Services
San Diego County

Addendum

I received the following letter from Mr. Cypher four months after he was committed to the state hospital:

Dear Dr. Meloy,

I have hesitated in writing this letter because I was so mad at you. I felt we had something more than a doctor-patient relationship. That is why I would write you letters when I was not locked up.

I have been in hospitals for over twenty years and had a lot of doctors say I was insane but I was never angry at them.

You abused our friendship that is why my feelings were hurt.

But I almost had a heart attack smoking cocaine. You saved my life inadvertently.

I firmly believe I can stay off the drugs. I want to smoke marijuana but I am taking urine tests and will not turn in a dirty test. They say in NA that drug addiction is life long and you have to take it one day at a time. That is what I am doing.

After being in jail fighting your lies I could have kissed your feet when I got to Patton.

There were groups like Relapse Prevention, Thought Disorder, Anger Management, Friendship Group, Supportive Rap, and others I cannot remember. I was on the COT unit but now I am not.

The reason for my letter was because you got a phone call saying I threatened your life.

I was just joking. I mean a nurse came around asking what's the date, who's the President, do you want to commit suicide, do you want to hurt anyone.

I was sitting around with the guys bullshitting and this nurse started asking the questions. I was just being facetious. I said I was the President, the date was 1896 and I was going to hire a hit man she said who do you want hurt and just off the top of my head I said your name. I mean if she hadn't asked me it would not have come out. I don't even know anyone in the Mafia and even if I did I would wish you no harm.

You have a big responsibility and you are trying to show that your program works. I am just a victim of yours and your program.

I love you.

your ex-patient, L.C.

Appendix III

The Rorschach Psychodiagnosis of Psychopathy

I have selected four methods of analyzing and interpreting the Rorschach response process that illuminate various structural and dynamic properties of psychopathy.

First, the Comprehensive System as developed by Exner (1986a) is an atheoretical, empirically derived integration of the most valid and reliable Rorschach indices. Since its beginnings (Exner 1974) its evolution has been guided by an expanding body of research.

Second, a developmental analysis of the concept of the object (Blatt 1976) applies the developmental principles of differentiation, articulation, and integration (Werner 1948, Werner and Kaplan 1963) to human and quasi-human responses on the Rorschach. This integration of psychoanalytic and developmental principles scores the type of figure perceived (differentiation), the number and types of attributes ascribed to the figure (articulation), and the internality and interaction of the figure (integration). The system by Blatt and colleagues (1976) has demonstrated both reliability and validity as a measure of object relations on the Rorschach (Blatt et al. 1976, Blatt et al. 1980, Ritzler et al. 1980, Blatt and Lerner 1983, Lerner 1986).

Third, an assessment of primitive defenses in borderline personality structure (Lerner and Lerner 1980) is comprised of various operationally defined measures of splitting, devaluation, idealization, projective identification, and denial. This method of analysis emphasizes the structural concept of defense and is based upon the theoretical formulations of Kernberg (1975) and the clinical testing of Mayman (1967), Pruitt and Spilka (1964), Holt (1970), Athey (1974), and Peebles (1975). The basic unit scored is an entire human figure. This approach to the assessment of primitive defenses appears to be both reliable and valid (Lerner and Lerner 1980, Lerner et al. 1981). The test indices of projective identification have most accurately discriminated borderline-personality-disordered patients from both neurotic and psychotic-personality-disordered patients (Lerner 1986).

Fourth, Kwawer (1979, 1980) focused on primitive interpersonal modes of relating and the Rorschach. He regarded Rorschach content as a "profound, symbolic statement of personal mythology reflecting early interpersonal experience" (1980, p. 90). Extending the work of both Laing (1976) and Bion (1977a), he expanded the concept of symbiotic merging to include intrauterine modes of relatedness. The Rorschach content imagery symbolically depicts transitions toward selfhood from intrauterine life through the separation–individuation phase of childhood (Mahler et al. 1975). Kwawer's (1980) approach includes eight primitive modes of relatedness: engulfment, symbiotic merging, violent symbiosis, malignant internal processes, birth and rebirth, metamorphosis and transformation, narcissistic mirroring, and separation–division. Boundary disturbance and womb imagery responses are also noted as two adjunctive content areas. Kwawer's work (1980) is descriptive and exploratory, and does not lend itself, in its present form, to measures of reliability and validity.

I have selected these four approaches to understanding psychopathy for a variety of reasons, not the least of which is the depth and richness they bring to Rorschach interpretation. They also cover the psychological landscape – from a purely empirical standpoint to a highly inferential and primitive object relational approach that dares to assume an intrauterine template for self- and other representations.

RORSCHACH PROTOCOL I

The following Rorschach response protocol was produced by the patient in Appendix I. To refresh the reader's memory, this patient was diagnosed using the DSM-III criteria (American Psychiatric Association 1980) with an Axis I mixed substance abuse disorder and an Axis II antisocial personality disorder and borderline personality disorder. J.G. was also assessed using the Hare Psychopathy Checklist (1980) and received a quantitative score of 34 out of a maximum of 40 points. This places him above the 30-point cutoff for psychopathy (Hare 1986), and in my clinical opinion would qualify him as severely psychopathically disturbed. His two-point MMPI profile was 94, also supporting his psychopathic diagnosis (Graham 1987).

I have selected this Rorschach protocol since it has substantial external validity as a raw psychological product of a psychopathic personality disorder. I will present his associative and inquired responses without commentary or scoring, and then analyze and interpret it within the context of the four approaches noted above.

I. 1. Absolutely symmetrical, looks like it could be a caterpillar on a mirror. (Inquiry response: that's the reflection in the mirror.)
    2. Or a butterfly coming out of a cocoon. (Inquiry response: looks like the cocoon around our house in the high desert. (?) It just looks like that.)
II. 3. They're all symmetrical, two elephants kissing each other. (Inquiry response: standing on three legs, touching, not necessarily kissing, because the trunks are touching, their ears here.)
III. 4. It looks like a cricket or an insect because of the eyes

and antenna sticking out. (Inquiry response: eyes, fur, feelers, and the way their body is shaped. (?) yea, fur.)

IV. 5. Looks like a bat hanging upside down in a cave, hanging off the wall with his feet. I've seen bats in caves. (Inquiry response: the feet here, wings, paws to catch insects with.)

V. 6. Looks like a large moth, gypsy moths. It looks like that way both ways. (Inquiry response: he's flying along, in flight. His wings extended, motion, antennas, projections here.)

VI. I don't see anything in there.

7. This way it looks like clouds above a lake. (Inquiry response: I first saw it, clouds, but then . . .)

8. The bank of a riverbed, some plants and trees reflecting off the water. (Inquiry response: more examination – dark spots above the stems, a wet area, flower blossoms, very dark, scrub, chapparal, rocks.)

VII. I can't even guess what this is.

9. Iron slag. That's what it looks like. When you're welding. (Inquiry response: a jumble of images, pieces of iron melt and fall off, the bad part, it falls off in weird shapes like that.)

VIII. Very pretty colors.

10. Looks like a pine tree with two squirrels climbing up the branches. (Inquiry response: at the top, squirrels, out of proportion to the tree, holding on and climbing up, paws here and here.)

11. Also looks like a flower. (Inquiry response: a flower, orchid looks, the color and symmetrical arrangement of the petals.)

IX. 12. An ear of corn very ripe – needs to be picked off the bush, plant. (Inquiry response: very dim, stem and feathers. When corn is ripe this leaf sluffs off, here and here, the shape.)

X. 13. Looks like something under a microscope. Little pieces of algae, protoplasm floating around on a microscopic slide. (Inquiry response: bacterias here, algae, I took a course in biology in prison and studied them. It's all different colors, that's what it looks like.)

EXNER COMPREHENSIVE SYSTEM

Erdberg (in press) proposed a five-step procedure for interpreting the structural summary of a Rorschach protocol when scored according to the Exner Comprehensive System (Exner 1986a). These five steps include test-taking approach, internal operations, external operations, syndromes, and treatment planning. His procedure is a quite effective model for organizing the complex data produced by the Rorschach, and I will apply his first three steps to the systematic development of hypotheses concerning psychopathy and the Rorschach.

Test-Taking Approach

The psychopathic character's approach to the Rorschach is assessed by interpreting number of responses (R), Lambda (L), whole responses (W), synthesis responses, blends, space responses (S), and personalized responses (PER).

   1. *Number of responses* (R) is predicted to be low due to a restricted and defensive attitude toward the test. If Lambda exceeds .85 in a record of 10–12 responses, guardedness may be indicated. A record of less than 10 responses should always be considered invalid. Intellectual deficits and neurological impairments will also limit R.

   2. *Lambda* (L) represents the proportion of pure F responses in the protocol, which are the most simple and affect-free associations. It is predicted to be higher than normal (mean = .59 in normative sample, 1.51 in character disordered sample [Exner 1986a]) in the psychopathic protocol due to his uninvolved, constricted, and defensive attitude. Pure F responses ignore the complexities of the stimulus field and may represent situational

avoidance of the task or a more basic, simplistic coping style (Exner 1986a) that is quite characterological.

3. *Whole responses* (W) can be interpreted as an indicator of motivation to deal with the entire stimulus field, and are harder to produce than detail responses (D) on all cards except for I and V. The psychopathic character's need for control of the environment (Doren 1987), and thus his production of more W responses, however, would be attenuated by his lack of involvement with the test itself. It is predicted that W responses would not correlate with psychopathic disturbance.

4. *Synthesis responses* (DQ) are related to the willingness and capacity of the individual to internalize the stimulus field in a meaningful way (Exner 1986a). Again, intelligence and psychopathic disturbance may attenuate this indicator since the former may provide the capacity but the latter may not provide the willingness. It is predicted that DQ will not necessarily correlate with psychopathic disturbance, but Exner (1986a) noted that the presence of two or more DQv/+ scores may suggest that attempts to use a sophisticated cognitive level are aborted by a reluctance to commit to form. Heaven (1988) pointed out that this may correlate with the psychopath's glibness and superficial charm wherein a facade of cognitive sophistication is not borne out by substantive knowledge. Exner's (1986a) character problem sample produced an average of 0.91 DQv/+ responses (5 percent) while the nonpatient adult sample produced 0.33 DQv/+ responses (1.5 percent).

5. *Blends* indicate that more than one determinant has been used to formulate a response. Blends appear to be somewhat related to intelligence, and may be a useful indicator of the complexity of psychological processes. Absence of blends indicates psychological constriction and less sensitivity to oneself and the environment (Exner 1986a). In the context of test-taking attitude, it is the opposite of the pure F response, and demands both analytic and synthetic work on the part of the examinee. IQ does not appear to correlate with blends (Mason and Exner 1984), and 25 percent of the character problem sample produced no

blend responses. All the nonpatient adults in Exner's (1986a) sample produced at least one blend. It is predicted that the psychopathic character will produce blends less frequently due to his lack of commitment to the test-taking task.

6. *Space responses* (S) have been postulated to represent a form of oppositionalism or negativism (Rorschach 1921). As S responses increase in frequency beyond the mean (2), it indicates a more stable, characterological trait that can predict hostility or anger when autonomy is threatened (Exner 1986a). Although test-retest reliability for S responses is low, DdS responses have much higher temporal reliability, and such patients are reported by others to be sullen, angry, brooding, alienated, and distant (Erdberg, in press). It is predicted that S responses, especially DdS responses, will positively correlate with psychopathic disturbance.

7. *Personalized responses* (PER) suggest a need to be overly precise in defending one's self-image (Exner 1986a). Three or more personalized responses in the adult record may mean a brittle defensiveness, a compensatory shoring up of the grandiose self-structure in the face of a perceived threat. The mean and standard deviation for personalized responses in normal samples is one. Although less than half of the character-problem sample gave one PER response, 40 percent of these individuals gave at least three PER responses (Exner 1986a). It is predicted that psychopathy will positively correlate with personalized responses.

To summarize the test-taking approach hypotheses of the psychopathic individual:

1. Low R (13–17 responses)
2. Elevated Lambda ($>.85$)
3. W responses do not correlate
4. DQ response configurations do not correlate
5. Blends infrequent (<3)
6. Space responses elevated (>2) with DdS likely
7. Personalized responses frequent (>2)

Internal Operations

Erdberg (in press) formulated five areas of inquiry to address the question of internal operations: the preferred problem-solving style, the adaptive success of the style, the intrusiveness of internal operations, the complexity of psychological operations, and the balance and quality of time spent in self-focus.

1. The preferred problem-solving style is measured by *Erlebnistypus* (EB), the ratio between the human movement responses and the sum of the weighted chromatic color responses (M: .5FC + 1CF + 1.5C + 1.5Cn). This is a characterological trait by age 16 and is very stable over time in adulthood. Extratensives are defined as M < SumC by two or more points; introversives are defined as M > SumC by two or more points. Ambitents are within this two-point window.

The extratensive is inclined to use his interactions with actual objects to gratify basic needs, while the introversive habitually uses his internal processes for gratification. Given the habitually aggressive and sadomasochistic engagement of the psychopathic character with his actual objects, one would postulate a predominately extratensive problem-solving style.

The ambitent style, however, confounds the postulate. Between 40–60 percent of psychiatric population samples are ambitent, a style which is less flexible, adaptive, efficient, and consistent than either introversives or extratensives (Exner 1986a). Fifty-six percent of the character problem sample were ambitents (Exner 1986a). It appears that this coping style, in contrast to Rorschach's (1921) predictions, is more psychopathological.

It is therefore hypothesized that the psychopathic process, due to the severity of object relations disturbance and the predominance of borderline defensive operations, will be ambitent, with a tendency toward an extratensive style.

Erdberg (in press) noted that Lambda may also represent a basic personality style. He suggested that individuals with Lambda > 1.0 may be characterized by an inability to engage emotional complexity, either within themselves or perceived in others. Lambda may represent a simplistic, item-by-item response to life's demands wherein consequence, deliberation, and the perception of ambiguity are not considered. Such a characterological index in the Rorschach would support both behavioral (Hare 1986) and neuropsychological (Yeudall 1977, Yeudall et al. 1984) constructs concerning the psychopath. Forty-one and a half percent of Exner's (1986a) character problem sample had Lambdas > 1.5, while only 1.3 percent of the normal sample had Lambdas > 1.5.

2. The adaptive success of the style is measured by D, the content of es, Ma:Mp, and FC:CF + C.

D is the ratio of organized to unorganized internal resources. As a scaled difference score derived by subtracting es (totality of disorganized ideation and affect, internal "noise") from EA (totality of coping resources, ego strength), it appears to have no direct relationship to psychopathy. Exner (1986a) wrote, however, that if the personality traits that lead to sturdy controls, as indicated by an elevated D score, were organized at a developmentally premature level, such a resulting form of rigidity might produce an excessive distancing and insensitivity to the environment. This would contraindicate any psychotherapeutic change and is apparent in the behavior of the autonomous, arrogant, and aggressive character-disordered patient. It also may provide some data concerning the current effectiveness of the psychopathic process.

The content of es (sum of eb ratio) are the impinging, nonvolitional aspects of internal operations. Representing both unorganized ideation (FM + m) and unorganized affect (T + V + Y + C'), as an aggregate they appear to have no direct relationship to the psychopathic process. But several of these variables, when taken in isolation, inductively support a psychopathic character disturbance. The variable m indicates need-state ideation projectively experienced, a sense of "being under fire" (Erdberg, in press). It is an unstable variable that appears to be induced by situational stress (Exner 1986a). In contrast to FM, which indicates an internally perceived physiological need state, m may relate to the psychopathic propensity to feel persecuted, the target of predation, and when coupled with a psychotic state, delusionally paranoid. Both variables, however, are quite situational, although FM is more temporally stable than m (Exner 1986a).

The T (texture) variable indicates interpersonal neediness. It is the hope that others will understand and respond (Erdberg, in press). In Chapter 3 I noted the relationship between the T variable, dependency needs, and the absence of affectional skin contact in psychopathy. It appears that T represents the affective experience of emotional or dependency needs, and the absence of T is a characterological sign of interpersonal guardedness or distance (Exner 1986a).

Although the frequency and variability of T is quite small (mean = 1.16, S.D. = 0.80 in normal adults), a T response is found in 90 percent of adult records. In the character problem sample, however, a T response occurred in only 35 percent of the subjects. It is hypothesized that a psychopathic disturbance will typically produce a T-less protocol. In fact, the presence of one T response probably contraindicates a psychopathic disturbance.

The V (Vista) response is expected to be absent in any record except for those individuals who are clinically depressed. It appeared in only 17 percent of the character problem sample, but 80 percent of the depressed inpatient sample (Exner 1986a). Vista is an important variable in the prediction of suicide and infers a negative, anhedonic experience generated by introspection. It is the Rorschach index most closely associated with the experience of guilt (Erdberg, in press).

Given the dearth of motivation to introspect in the psychopathic process, and the hedonic defensive function of the grandiose self-structure, one Vista response would probably contraindicate a psychopathic disturbance. The one exception to this postulate might be the psychopathic character who is experiencing acute dysphoria, or the "zero state" (Yochelson and Same-now 1977), usually following some external sanction. It would be an exceptional gift, however, to secure a valid Rorschach protocol from a psychopathic individual at this moment.

The Y (diffuse shading) variable, like m, is not temporally reliable, and represents a state, rather than trait, of the individual. Contrary to early hypotheses concerning the relationship of Y to anxiety, it appears to correlate more closely with a sense of helplessness or immobilization in relation to the environment (Exner 1986a). Forty-seven percent of normal adults produce at least one Y, while 63 percent of a character problem sample produce Y (Exner 1986a). Given its state-dependent nature, the presence or absence of Y should not be considered pathognomonic of any character disturbance, but well-functioning psychopaths would be disinclined to experience a sense of helplessness, and therefore, would probably not produce any Y responses unless in custody.

The C' (achromatic color) response correlates with affective constraint. It may represent an intentional and defensive hesitancy to exchange affect with external objects, a metaphorical "biting of one's tongue" (Exner 1986a). C' is more likely to appear in "caught" psychopaths who are attempting to put their best foot forward (Exner and Leura 1977, Erdberg, in press). It is predicted that at least one C' will appear in the protocol of the psychopathic individual who is facing a criminal or civil suit. Although characterologically stable, it may fluctuate under some state determinants. Its mean and standard deviation are approximately one.

Ma:Mp (active human movement to passive human movement) when Ma < Mp suggests either flight into passive forms of fantasy as a defensive maneuver or engagement of others to solve one's problems, what Exner (1986a) called a "Snow White" phenomenon. In the extratensive, arrogant psychopathic character, such a ratio would be highly unusual, but it would be quite ominous in the more schizoid, introversive psychopath. In the latter case, Ma < Mp could be pathognomonic of rehearsal fantasy, and the concomitant use of internal representations as transitional objects. The sexual psychopath, for instance, attending to his own sadomasochistic fantasies, may spend months, or even years, refining coercive sexual encounters in his mind while gratifying sexual arousal through masturbation. Such subterranean fantasy will eventually be acted out against a victim in a profound act of dependency with intrapsychic corollaries of projective identification and object control (see Chapter 4). Ma < Mp could signal the *structure* of such intrapsychic phenomena, while the actual content might remain successfully hidden from the clinician.

FC:CF + C, the extent to which emotional discharges are modulated, is quite temporally stable. Equal or higher values of CF + C in relation to FC do not necessarily mean a lack of control, but do suggest an unwillingness or inability to modulate affective displays. Expressed emotion will be intense, and perhaps impulsive. Higher frequency of CF + C appears to correlate with both impulsive and aggressive behaviors (Exner 1986a).

CF or C responses, when isolated, do not tend to be temporally stable. The presence of more than one C response, however, should be viewed carefully as suggestive of ongoing difficulty with impulse control, and may be symptomatic of affective lability or intentional abandonment of control.

The FC < CF + C is hypothesized in psychopathic character disorder. Forty-three percent of the character problem sample produced at least one C; only 9 percent of the adult normals produced at least one C (Exner 1986a). Among psychopathic characters the FC < CF + C ratio must be carefully interpreted to avoid the mistake of attributing an *unwillingness* to modulate affect to an *inability* to control affect, particularly if the D score is adequate. The propensity of the psychopathic character to use affect as a means of object control (through intimidation or fear) or social manipulation (through "malignant pseudoidentification"; see Chapter 4) should be noted.

3. The intrusiveness of internal operations is measured by Lambda (L), Morbid Content (MOR), and Aggressive Movement (Ag) responses.

Lambda (L), a variable used to evaluate the test-taking approach, is also used to determine the individual's ability to operate in an affect-free environment within the self. When $L < .40$ (mean $= .59$ in nonpatient adult sample), the patient is driven by his own affective operations and has a markedly diminished ability to deal with problems in an affect-free manner (Erdberg, in press). It is closely allied to Rapaport and colleagues' (1946) concept of the absence of a conflict-free sphere of ego functioning. A low Lambda can also be produced by striving in the test situation to gain a sense of accomplishment, or to avoid error or failure (Exner 1986a).

Given the nature of the psychopathic defensive structure, particularly the narcissistic defenses that split off and dissociate intensive affect, a conflict-free ego sphere, and therefore an elevated Lambda, is hypothesized. The grandiose striving of the superior intelligence psychopath, however, could lower Lambda, with concomitant elevation of Zf, W, and DQ+ answers.

Morbid content (MOR) infers self and object concepts that are devalued, damaged, and negative. It conveys an anhedonic, pessimistic attitude toward the self and the future. It appears more frequently in the records of depressed children and adults (Exner 1986a). Morbid content, if it appears in the psychopathic protocol, is likely to have two characteristics: It will be combined with an aggressive movement (Ag) response; and the subject will identify with the aggressor rather than the victim within the morbid response.

Aggressive movement (Ag) responses indicate an increased likelihood of aggression, both verbal and nonverbal, and chronically negative or hostile attitudes toward others (Exner 1986a). Ag appeared in 78 percent of the character problem sample, (mean $= 1.06$, S.D. $= 1.07$), and 50 percent of the nonpatient sample.

The psychopathic character's predominant mode of relatedness is aggression with sadomasochistic features (see Chapter 1).
It is hypothesized that at least one Ag response will be found in
the psychopathic protocol, but a caveat is in order: Given the
obvious face validity, and transparency, of the Ag response, the
above average intelligence psychopath may choose to disregard,
and not verbalize, his Ag associations to the Rorschach.

Dr. Carl Gacono and I are currently researching a *Sadomasochistic* (SM) special score on the Rorschach. It is defined as the
expression of pleasurable affect by the subject (smiling, laughter,
etc.) during the articulation of devalued, aggressive, or morbid
content. We think this special score has particular relevance to
subjects evaluated in criminal forensic settings.

4. The complexity of psychological operations is measured
by M (Human movement), DQ (synthesis or developmental quality), and blends.

The M (Human movement) response itself is quite complex.
It is difficult to hypothesize the meaning of M in isolation, since it
is inextricably tied to the number and content of the figures, the
nature of the action, and its location. Exner's (1986a) summary of
the extensive research concerning M concluded: It always involves some form of projection; its relationship to creativity is
equivocal; it is related to fantasy; the form quality of M correlates
with psychopathology; it involves elements of reasoning, imagi-
nation, and abstraction; it implies a form of delay during which
deliberate ideation occurs; and aggressive M responses correlate
with verbal and nonverbal aggressive behaviors.

The potential for M responses in psychopathic disturbance
is attenuated by the relative absence of human content responses, regardless of the subject's psychological complexity, or
his capacity for deliberate, abstract thought. Although 99.5 percent of the adult nonpatients produced at least one M
(mean = 4.19), only 87.5 percent of the character problem sample
produced one M (mean = 2.33) (Exner 1986a). It is hypothesized
that psychopathic individuals will produce fewer M responses,

but one should be careful to not misinterpret this finding as an absence of psychological complexity. The absence of bonding in the emotional life of the psychopath limits the human content that can function as a projective vehicle to elicit M responses to the Rorschach.

DQ (developmental quality) and blends, and their relationship to psychopathy, have been detailed above. In an unstructured test setting, such as the Rorschach, the psychological complexity of the psychopathic character will usually be masked by his object relational configuration: The fearful, yet predatory, grandiose self-structure will disallow strivings for achievement and exhibitionism with an examiner who is probably viewed as an adversary or aggressor. Other projective techniques, such as the Thematic Apperception Test, and structured measures of intelligence, such as the Wechsler Adult Intelligence Scale-Revised, do not evoke such an aggressive and vigilant transference reaction, and therefore are more apt to capture the psychopathic character's psychological complexity.

5. The balance and quality of time spent in self-focus is measured by the Egocentricity Index $(3r+(2) / R)$, Morbid content (MOR), Reflection responses (Fr, rF), Vista responses (V), and Form dimension responses (FD).

The Egocentricity Index $(3r+(2) /R)$ is a measure of the proportion of reflection and pair responses in the protocol. It is a measure of self-focusing or self-concern (Exner 1986a) that may be either positively or negatively affectively toned. The presence of one reflection response in the Index infers a narcissistic tendency to overestimate self-worth (Exner 1986a).

Cut-off points of .31 to .42 appear to establish a normative range (Exner 1986a). An Index $>.45$ strongly suggests a pathologically narcissistic disturbance; $<.30$ suggests negative self-esteem and a proneness to depression (Erdberg, in press).

From an object relations perspective, the Index is the most direct measure of the grandiose self structure (Kernberg 1975). Given the narcissistic personality structure of the psychopathic individual, it is a compelling measure of the degree to which the self is grandiosely conceived. I would hypothesize that the Egocentricity Index in psychopathic disturbance would be > .45 and should be quite temporally reliable.

I have already addressed Morbid content (MOR) as a variable in the determination of the intrusiveness of one's own psychological operations. As a variable to measure the quality of self-focus, it suggests a negative or devalued attitude toward the self-percepts and concepts; it further implicates a tendency toward anger or depression. Morbid content in a psychopathic protocol, if the subject identifies with its victim, would suggest a failure of defensive functioning. It communicates a sense of being violated by another, and may correlate with a perceived external locus of control (Erdberg, in press).

The Reflection response (Fr, rF) suggests an intensely self-focused, narcissistically disordered individual. One reflection response in a normal protocol is highly unusual, but 32 percent of the character problem sample (Exner 1986a) produced at least one reflection response. It implies a sense of grandiosity and entitlement that are the hallmarks of the psychopathic character. I would predict that psychopathically disturbed individuals would produce at least one reflection response (mean = 0.41, S.D. = 0.54 in character problem sample).

The Vista (V) response as a measure of anhedonia during introspection infers a negative affective tone associated with the self-representations. It appears to be the affective correlate of Morbid content, and would contraindicate a psychopathic disturbance unless severe external stressors, such as sudden incarceration, disrupted the narcissistic defenses and precipitated an acutely dysphoric reaction.

Form dimension (FD) suggests a process of internal reflection that is more objective and balanced than the Vista (V) response (Erdberg, in press). It may be primarily a measure of psychological-mindedness, and its absence may indicate a lack of psychological insight. Although one FD response appeared in 75 percent of the adult nonpatient sample, only 37 percent of the character problem sample produced one FD (Exner 1986a). I would hypothesize that a psychopathically disturbed individual would not produce an FD response because of his primitive defensive structure, which is replete with various denial and splitting operations (see Chapter 4): dynamic maneuvers that obviate the need for introspection.

To summarize the internal operations hypotheses of the psychopathic process:

1. Preferred problem-solving style
   EB = ambitent
2. Adaptive success of the style
   $T = 0$
   $V = 0$
   $C' > 0$
   $FC < CF + C$
   $C > 1$
3. Intrusiveness of internal operations
   Elevated Lambda > 0.85
   $MOR = 0$
   $Ag > 0$
4. Complexity of psychological operations
   $M < 3$
5. Balance and quality of time spent in self-focus
   Egocentricity Index > 0.45
   $MOR = 0$
   rF or $Fr > 1$
   $V = 0$
   $FD = 0$

As the reader will note, I have listed only the more definitive hypotheses from the text. What is most striking is the *absence* of certain variables that define the internal operations of the psychopathic process. To paraphrase an adage, there is less there than meets the eye.

External Operations

Erdberg (in press) identified nine areas of inquiry to address the question of external operations: the efficiency of perceiving and processing data; the frequency of attempts to organize external reality; the efficiency of each organizational attempt; the degree of need to identify with external reality; the degree of need to achieve; the likelihood of affect to be processed; the productivity of affect when it is processed; interpersonal issues; and the self as actor or acted upon.

1. The efficiency of perceiving and processing data is measured by X + percent, X − percent, Dd, and special scores. These variables, as an aggregate, measure the individual's reality testing, convergence, and cognitive accuracy.

The X + percent is a measure of perceptual accuracy of the entire record. It is a measure of convergent form, a normative statement. Although perceptual accuracy is a component of it, it is probably more a measure of conventionality. The mean X + percent for nonpatients, both children and adults, tends to be 80 percent; for the character problem sample, the mean was 70 percent (Exner 1986a). It is the most temporally reliable variable when measured across the developmental spectrum.

Perceptual unconventionality may have many causes, including psychotic disturbances, failures of affective modulation, and a striving for individuality. A psychopathic character disturbance presupposes a degree of disidentification with conventional reality. I hypothesize that X + percent in the psychopathic process will usually be less than 70 percent.

X − percent, on the other hand, is a more specific indicator of perceptual distortion, a violation of the reality constraints of the percept. One FQ − response is found in most records, but when

X – percent exceeds 15 percent, there is some impairment in the accurate perception of exteroceptive stimuli. The character problem sample had an X – percent mean of 15 percent (S.D. = 9 percent).

A typical psychopathic protocol would be likely to display a low X + percent (< 70) and a low X – percent (< 15). Since perceptual impairment is only tangentially related to character disturbance, an X – percent > 20 in a psychopathic protocol would suggest a concomitant Axis I mental disorder with possible psychotic or organic features.

The Dd score is common in frequencies of one to three in average length records. When it occurs in greater frequency, it may represent an atypical, obsessional approach to reality (Exner 1986a). Only 8 percent of the nonpatient adult Rorschach responses involved a Dd location (mean = 1.73), while 14 percent of the character problem Rorschach responses involved a Dd location response (mean = 2.59) (Exner 1986a). Any Dd responses > 3 in a psychopathic protocol should be studied carefully for projective content, especially movement, and should be assessed for indications of perceptual-associative impairment. Dd and X – percent, however, are not necessarily pathognomonic of a psychopathic disturbance.

The six critical Special Scores, from least to most cognitive dysfunction, are deviant verbalization (DV), incongruous combination (INCOM), deviant response (DR), fabulized combination (FABCOM), inappropriate logic (ALOG), and contamination (CONTAM). As a group these scores represent problems in internal processing or cognitive slippage. From a psychoanalytic perspective, they are measures of formal thought disorder.

Although not pathognomonic of psychopathic character disturbance, elevations in the special scores is expected due to the borderline personality organization of the psychopathic individual, and subsequent distortions of formal thought secondary to his more primitive defensive operations. In fact, the weighted sum of these scores (WSUM6) averaged 6.52 in the character problem sample, compared to 3.96 in the adult nonpatient sample (Exner 1986a). At least one fabulized combination appeared in 37 percent of the character problem protocols, compared to 12 percent of the nonpatient protocols.

I would hypothesize a WSUM6 >6.0 in the psychopathic protocol, while a score appreciably higher than this would suggest that cognitive slippage is a problem in its own right.

2. The frequency of attempts to organize external reality is measured by the economy index (W:D) and organizational frequency (Zf).

The W:D ratio, the economy index, is expected to be 1:2 in a normative sample and concerns the economy of approach to the Rorschach (Exner 1986a). It must always be considered in relation to R, and in most psychopathic protocols, with an $R < 17$, $W = D$. In this context, by itself, it has little interpretative value.

The Zf score measures the frequency of organizing activity and is scored whenever there is a W or two synthesized D responses. A low Zf may indicate intellectual limitations or a hesitancy to engage the stimulus field. A high Zf may indicate striving, obsessional behavior, or hypervigilance (>50 percent).

The psychopathic process could influence Zf in either direction: a reluctance to be involved in the test-taking task because of perceived malevolence or general apathy would lower Zf; grandiose striving or paranoid hypervigilance would raise Zf. This may be one factor in the greater variance among Zf in the character problem sample (S.D. $=4.15$) when compared to Zf in the nonpatient adult sample (S.D. $=2.96$) (Exner 1986a).

3. The efficiency of each organizational attempt is measured by Zd. Zd scores >3.0 indicate a process of overincorporation, an overly cautious and thorough approach to external stimuli. It is apparent in obsessive and perfectionistic individuals. Zd scores < -3.0 indicate a process of underincorporation, an impulsive and arbitrary approach to external stimuli. Both stimuli processing styles appear with greater frequency in psychiatric sam-

ples, but do not necessarily indicate a specific psychodiagnosis (Exner 1986a). Seventy-five percent of adult nonpatients were in the normal range ($< +3 > -3$) while only 62 percent of the character problem sample were in the normal range.

The psychopathic process could support either overincorporation or underincorporation, but given the primitive defensive operations which could deny whole sectors of reality, the proneness to boredom due to autonomic hyporeactivity, and the narcissistic self-absorption of the grandiose self-structure, underincorporation is predicted, even if attenuated by perfectionist strivings.

4. The degree of need to identify with external reality is measured by extended form (X + percent), space (S), and popular (P) responses.

Both X + percent and S have been addressed in earlier sections. My prediction of X + percent < 70 in psychopathic character disturbance also suggests, in this area of inquiry, a disidentification with external reality or conventionality. The prediction of elevated space responses (S) hypothesizes oppositionalism and negativism toward the established order by the psychopathic individual.

Popular responses (P) range from five to eight in adult samples. Lower frequencies of P responses indicate an inability or unwillingness of the individual to give the most conventional and obvious answer (Exner 1986a). P does not measure reality testing, and does not significantly correlate with X + percent.

Psychopathic disturbance, in a truly *antisocial* manner, will tend to lower the proportion of P in a record, although lower P is not necessarily pathognomonic of psychopathy. I would predict P < 5 in the psychopathic protocol.

5. The degree of need to achieve is measured by the aspirational ratio (W:M).

The W:M ratio is a crude measure of achievement behavior in relation to psychological resources. The ratio is expected to be

2:1 in the majority of adults sampled, whether patient or nonpatient, and when it exceeds 3:1, a grandiose, unrealistic striving for achievement is probable (Exner 1986a).

Psychopathic individuals will generally score >3:1, given their unrealistic appraisal of their own internal resources. The character problem sample, on the average, also exceeded this ratio (Exner 1986a).

6. The likelihood of affect being processed is measured by the affective ratio (Afr).

Afr is the ratio of number of responses to the completely chromatic cards (VIII, IX, X) to the other cards (I–VII). The average range is .50 to .80, with patients tending to fall at the upper and lower extremes (Exner 1986a). The mean in nonpatient adults was .66 (S.D. = .19) and in the character problem sample was .51 (S.D. = .18).

The affective ratio is an indication of receptivity to emotionally provoking *external* stimuli. Individuals with ratios > .80 will be caught up easily by emotional stimuli, while those scoring < .40 will avoid an emotional response to stimuli. It tells nothing about emotional control, nor the reasons for receptivity or lack of receptivity to emotion.

Seventy-five percent of the character problem sample had an Afr < .55, suggesting a tendency to avoid emotionally toned stimuli. The psychopathic process would infer a seeking of emotional stimuli, but this may be dampened by a more hypervigilant, controlled, and wary response to the examiner and the test situation, lowering the Afr. I am not aware of any research that has externally validated the Afr outside the Rorschach response process.

I would predict that the Afr would distribute to the extremes in psychopathy, with the greater likelihood of avoidance of emotionally provoking stimuli in the test situation (< .55).

7. The modulation of response after affect is processed is measured by D, M, FC:CF + C, FM, and C'. All of these variables and summary scores have been discussed above, but in this

context they are used to address the nature and extent of modulation of affect.

D, when negative, suggests an affective overload situation with a predominance of disorganized psychological operations. M is a measure of capacity to delay affective response, a premeditation and deliberation variable. FC:CF + C is the metaphorical swimmer mastering the waves (FC) or being swept away by the current (CF + C). FM is a measure of ideational processes provoked by unmet need or stress-related states. Although reasonably stable over time, it has been shown to increase during diminished states of consciousness, such as those induced by alcohol (Exner 1986a). As FM increases, the potential for acting out increases; and FM > M may be one variable in the prediction of affective violence (Erdberg, in press). C′ measures the ability to contain affect, to deliberately delay emotional expression.

The psychopathic process would predict, as noted in the above sections, M < 3, FC < CF + C, and at least one C′. I would also hypothesize that FM > M due to the psychopathic propensity for both affective and predatory violence. The psychopathic character may desire to avoid affective stimuli for a variety of situational reasons, but his capacity to modulate and productively process such affect, once triggered, is noticeably impaired.

This impairment is probably due to the reservoirs of envy and rage in this narcissistically disordered character that may remain split off and dissociated for substantial periods of time; but once cathected are difficult to moderate due to their intensity and the primitive manner in which they have been warded off (see Chapters 3–4).

8. Interpersonal issues are measured by M, H + A:Hd + Ad, H, T, Fd, Isolate:R, Ag, and S.

Human movement (M) has already been discussed in several other contexts. It is most relevant to interpersonal behavior as a measure of empathy or identification with others. In this sense, however, the nature and quality of the M response, rather than the number of responses, is most important.

Mayman (1962) distinguished between the empathic M response in which an experience is shared, and the identifying M response in which unconscious projective identification is predominant. Responses based on empathic M were characterized by a wide range of images and characterizations of others; the seeing and describing of the percept with objectivity and realness; and an expressed warmth, interest, and pleasure in the activity of the percept, but in a way that makes clear the percept is not the subject.

Responses based on identifying M were characterized by extreme vividness and conviction; fabulized action that was quite arbitrary and had poor form quality; and an intense absorption in the movement of the percept, vicariously feeling the experience of the projection.

The identification M would characterize the human movement response within the psychopathic protocol. It is an empirical measure of the malignant pseudoidentification of the psychopath, his capacity to exploitatively use the narcissistic vulnerabilities of others. The content of the M response in the psychopathic protocol would also be likely to contain sexual or aggressive action, the latter indicative of subjects who view interpersonal relationships as being aggressive (Exner 1986a). The form quality of the M response would likely be u (unusual) or − (minus) in the Comprehensive System (Exner 1986a).

H + A:Hd + Ad is the ratio of whole human and animal content to human and animal detail. In normal samples, the ratio should be at least 4:1. As the proportion of human and animal detail responses increases, it suggests a more constricted, guarded, and suspicious view of the interpersonal environment (Exner 1986a). It is virtually identical to the meaning of H:Hd, but is more useful since many individuals, such as character disorders, will give very few H responses. By adding the A:Ad ratio to the equation, such a paranoid feature is less likely to be missed. Exner and Hillman (1984) found that 78 percent of paranoid subjects had a ratio of 2:1 or less.

The pure H (human content) response is expected to represent from one-fourth to two-thirds of all human content responses in adult subjects. While human content responses generically measure the extent to which the subject identifies with the environment and shows an interest in other people, pure H seems to indicate that relational attitudes are reality-based, rather than fantasy-laden.

In adult nonpatients, the mean for all human contents was 5.12, and the pure H mean was 3.07. In the character problem sample, the human content mean was 3.72 and pure H was 1.71 (Exner 1986).

The complete absence of human content is unusual, but would be pathognomonic of a psychopathic process. Lower frequencies of human content (<4) and pure H (<2), are to be expected in a psychopathic protocol due to the narcissistic detachment and absence of affectional bonding that is common in the psychopath. The nature and quality of human content, although more relevant to the other interpretative systems below, tells us much about the internalization process of the psychopath and his self and object representations.

The texture response (T) in an interpersonal context is a measure of emotional relatedness. I think it has quite primitive sensory-perceptual skin boundary correlates, and is an important measure of affectional needs to be gratified by others. One T response, as noted earlier, contraindicates a psychopathic process.

The food response (Fd) is quite rare in adult protocols, and appears to be associated with oral neediness (Schafer 1954). The mean for Fd in nonpatient adults is 0, and would be expected to be absent in a psychopathic protocol.

The Isolation Index (Isolate:R) is the ratio of Botany, Clouds, Geography, Landscape, and Nature content categories to total Rorschach responses. When Isolate $>.25R$, a strong tendency toward social isolation exists; when Isolate $>.33R$, poor interpersonal connectedness is suggested (Erdberg, in press).

The psychopathic individual is expected to attach more

readily to the nonhuman environment, either in fantasy or in material reality. I would therefore predict that Isolate:R would exceed 33 percent in the psychopathic protocol. This ratio does not necessarily infer interpersonal conflict or affective distress associated with the isolation.

The Aggressive content (Ag) and Space response (S) have also been elaborated above. Ag correlates with verbal or physical aggression in interpersonal relations, but may be withheld during testing due to its obvious face validity. S indicates a character-ologically hostile and angry person when >2. In the psychopathic process, both Ag and S would be expected to be elevated.

9. The self as actor or acted upon is measured by a:p and Ma:Mp.

The active-passive ratio of all movement responses (a:p) appears to measure ideational flexibility. The more discrepancy between the numbers, the more fixed and unalterable are the ideational sets (Exner 1986a). Although a high frequency of active responses does *not* necessarily equate with active or aggressive behaviors, when passive responses exceed active responses by more than one, there does exist a tendency toward passive and dependent behavior (Exner 1986a). It would be expected that $a>p$ in the psychopathic protocol, as it is in most adult protocols.

The active-passive ratio of human movement responses (Ma:Mp) was reviewed earlier in the context of internal operations. $Ma>Mp$ is expected as a behavioral correlate of the extratensive psychopath, but $Ma<Mp$ should not be disregarded in the introversive psychopath who engages in rehearsal fantasy prior to the acting out of predatory violence.

To summarize the external operations hypotheses of the psychopathic process:

1. Efficiency of perceiving and processing data
   $X+$ percent <70 percent
   $X-$ percent <15 percent
   WSUM6 >6

2. Frequency of attempts to organize external reality
   No hypotheses
3. Efficiency of each organizational attempt
   $Zd < -3.0$ (underincorporation)
4. Degree of need to identify with external reality
   $X + percent < 70$ percent
   $S > 2$
   $P < 5$
5. Degree of need to achieve
   $W:M > 3:1$
6. Likelihood of affect to be processed
   $Afr < .55$
7. Modulation of affect when processed
   $M < 3$
   $FC < CF + C$
   $FM > M$
   $C' > 0$
8. Interpersonal issues
   Identifying M
      Sexual or Aggressive content
      Unusual or minus form
   Human content < 4
   Pure $H < 2$
   $T = 0$
   $Fd = 0$
   $Isolate:R > 33$ percent
   $Ag > 0$
   $S > 2$
9. Self as actor or acted upon
   $a > p$
   $Ma > Mp$

The reader is referred to Protocol I to review its content in light of these hypotheses. The Comprehensive System scoring of this protocol was as follows:

Card	Location	Determinants	Contents	Pop	Z	Special
I.	1. Wo	rF −	A		1.0	
	2. Dd+	FMa−	A		4.0	PERS
II.	3. D+	Ma o	(2) A	P	3.0	FABCOM
III.	4. Ddo	F −	A			INCOM
IV.	5. Wo	FMp o	A		2.0	PERS, INCOM
V.	6. Wo	FMa o	A	P	1.0	
VI.	7. Dv	F o	Cl, Ls			
	8. Dd+	Fr. C′F−	Ls, Bt		1.0	
VII.	9. Wv	Fu	iron slag			
VIII.	10. D+	FMa u	(2) A, Bt	P	3.0	
	11. Do	CF o	Bt			
IX.	12. Do	F −	Bt			INCOM
X.	13. Wv	CF.FMp u	Sc, Bt			PERS

The structural summary of this protocol was computed, and the variables, indices, and ratios were compared to the psychopathic hypotheses to yield a goodness of fit (the indices that were repeated within the hypothesis sections above are not repeated below, producing 32 separate hypotheses):

Psychopathic hypotheses	Protocol I	Goodness of fit
R = 13 to 17	13	yes
Lambda > .85	.44	no
Blends < 3	2	yes
Space > 2	0	no
Personalized > 2	3	yes
EB = ambitent	ambitent	yes
T = 0	0	yes
V = 0	0	yes
C′ > 0	1	yes
FC < CF + C	0:2	yes
C > 1	0	no

Psychopathic hypotheses	Protocol I	Goodness of fit
Morbid = 0	0	yes
Aggressive > 0	0	no
M < 3	1	yes
Egocentricity > 0.45	0.62	yes
rF or Fr > 0	1	yes
FD = 0	0	yes
X + % < 70	38%	yes
X − % < 15	38%	no
WSUM6 > 6	10	yes
Zd < −3.0	−5.5	yes
P < 5	3	yes
W:M > 3:1	5:1	yes
Afr < .55	.44	yes
FM > M	4:1	yes
Identifying M (Ag or Sx)	0	no
H content < 4	0	yes
Pure H < 2	0	yes
Fd = 0	0	yes
Isolate:R > 33%	62%	yes
a > p	4:2	yes
Ma > Mp	1:0	yes

This single case study yields a goodness of fit of 81 percent when compared to the psychopathic hypotheses that I have deductively proposed from the Comprehensive System. Further nomothetic research could determine whether some of these hypotheses form a psychopathic constellation useful to the clinician.

In a preliminary study, Heaven (1988) found that a sample of 34 antisocial personality disordered (American Psychiatric Association 1987) inmates had a similar goodness of fit.

THE CONCEPT OF THE OBJECT

Blatt and colleagues (1976) developed a scoring system of the concept of the object based upon their research that "in normal

development, there was a significant increase in well differentiated . . . and integrated human figures (on the Rorschach) seen in
constructive and reciprocal relationships" (p. 364).

Blatt and Lerner (1983) noted that self- and object representations have both structure and content, and are the complex
mental schemata of significant objects encountered in reality.
Blatt (1974) wrote that earlier forms of representation are based
on action sequences associated with gratifying needs, interme-
diate forms are based on specific perceptual features, and higher
forms are more symbolic and conceptual. He emphasized a constant and reciprocal interaction between past and present interpersonal relations and the development of self- and object representations; the latter, in turn, providing a revised schemata for
experiencing new and more complex dimensions of interpersonal
reality.

Blatt and Lerner (1983) argued that the Rorschach is ideal
for assessing an individual's representational world because any
human images attributable to this essentially ambiguous stimulus must be shaped by the organization of the internalized self
and object representations. The scoring system developed by
Blatt and colleagues (1976) focuses upon human and quasi-human
responses to the Rorschach and judges them according to seven
characteristics. The first of these characteristics, accuracy, is
essentially a measure of reality-testing, and appears to be a
perceptual function that may be independent of the developmental maturity of the internal representations (Ritzler et
al. 1980). The other six characteristics are judged according to a
continuum based upon developmental levels, as noted in Table
III-1 below, elaborating upon Werner's (1948) developmental
principles of differentiation, articulation, and integration.

The most developmentally mature response in each category is the one noted last. For instance, the most mature human
representation would be Human (H), Appropriate (+), Perceptually and Functionally fully elaborated, engaged in Intentional
Action (Int), Congruent (Con), Benevolent (Ben), and Active-

Table III-1
Developmental Analysis of Object Representations
(Adapted from Blatt and Lerner 1983)

1. Accuracy:
   F−, F+
2. Differentiation:
   Quasi-human detail: (Hd)
   Human detail: Hd
   Quasi-human: (H)
   Human: H
3. Articulation:
   Inappropriate (−) or appropriate (+)
   Perceptual: Size (Sz), Posture (Po), Hair Style (Hsy), Clothing (Cl), Physical Structure (PSt).
   Functional: Sex (Sex), Age (Age), Role (Ro), Specific Identity (SpId).
4. Motivation for Action:
   No action (NoAct)
   Unmotivated action (Unmot)
   Reactive action (React)
   Intentional action (Int)
5. Integration of Object and Action:
   Fused (Fused)
   Incongruent (Incon)
   Non-specific (NonSp)
   Congruent (Con)
6. Content of Action:
   Malevolent (Mal)
   Benevolent (Ben)
7. Nature of Interaction:
   Active-Passive (A-P)
   Active-Reactive (A-R)
   Active-Active (A-A)

Active (A-A). Rorschach administration to score this procedure must follow the guidelines of Rapaport, Gill, and Schafer (1946). Inquiry follows each card, and the card is removed from the subject's sight so that elaboration of the response is done from recollection of the card, fostering more dependency on the subject's internal representations.

The fundamental problem with this scoring system to assess the nature of object relations is its dependency upon human content responses to the Rorschach. This issue becomes even more problematic when considering applications of this scoring system to the assessment of psychopathy and the predictable absence, or low frequency, of human responses to the Rorschach by the psychopathic individual.

If one attempts to apply the system of Blatt and colleagues (1976) to Protocol I, a single quasi-human response is found to Card II:

> They're all symmetrical, two elephants kissing each other. (Response to inquiry: standing on three legs, touching, not necessarily kissing, because the trunks are touching, their ears here.)

This response would be scored quasi-human (H) only because the animal is explicitly given qualities that only a human could possess. Blatt and colleagues (1976) noted the exceptional nature of this scoring, and that it is not meant to include all animal movement responses (FM). The response would be further scored as accurate (F +), Appropriate (+), Perceptual Articulation of Posture ("standing . . . touching"), Reactive action ("because the trunks are touching"), Incongruent integration of object and action, Benevolent content of action, and Active-active interaction. Unfortunately this one quasi-human response tells us virtually nothing about the internal representational world of this individual, and is useless as an example of this system's value in understanding the psychopathic character.

When psychopathic subjects do produce protocols with a series of human and quasi-human responses, however, the Blatt and colleagues (1976) system becomes quite compelling as an interpretative measure of object representations. I would like to illustrate this by applying the system to two protocols of psychopathic individuals who generated human responses.

The first partial protocol (human responses only) was produced by a 35-year-old Caucasian male who had a lengthy history of antisocial behavior. He was eventually convicted of two felony murders, and subsequently executed by the state.

RORSCHACH PROTOCOL II
(HUMAN RESPONSES ONLY)

III. 1. It's two people pulling a crab apart. (Response to inquiry: Here's one person and here's another person and here's their hands, and it looks like they're pulling something apart. I said it's a crab because that's what I said last time.)

2. Someone tumbling [D2]. (Response to inquiry: Yea, here's his head and here's his body.)

VII. 3. Two Cupids facing each other. (Response to inquiry: Yea, they have wings [Dd21]. This is their hair and their faces. They look like they're on a stand.)

4. It's a girl looking at herself in the mirror. (Response to inquiry: Here's her head, here's her arm, and then this part's her body.)

IX. 5. This is a space man, like the cover on a science fiction [W]. (Response to inquiry: He's got a big head [D8], the orange is the aura going out from him [D3], the green could be hands, and the red the rest of his body. He has an ominous look. He's an unfriendly bastard. I just noticed this, he's giving you the finger [Dd31]. I didn't see that at first.)

Table III-2 illustrates how the five human responses would be scored (Blatt et al. 1976).

Table III-2
Concept of the Object Scoring, Protocol II

Differentiation Accuracy±	Articulation		Motivation of Action	Integration of Object-Action	Content	Nature
	Perceptual	Functional				
III. 1. H (popular)	–	–	Unmot.	Nonsp.	Mal	A-A
2. H+	–	–	Unmot.	Fused	Ben	–
VII. 3. (H)+	PSt	Sex, Ro, SpID	Unmot.	Nonsp.	Ben	A-A
4. H+	–	Sex	Unmot.	Nonsp.	Ben	–
IX. 5. (H)–	Sz, PSt, Po	Sex, Ro	Unmot.	Nonsp.	Mal	A-P

The perceived object representations are mostly intact and accurately perceived human and quasi-human responses, beginning with a popular. On the last response, however, there is a sudden deterioration to a quasi-human figure that is inaccurately perceived and elaborated in a grandiose, threatening, and aggressive manner. In a striking way the *stranger selfobject* in a fully projected form is manifest as the last object representational content in this protocol, suggesting the primary identification of this individual.

The articulation of perceptual and functional characteristics, when it occurs in accurate object representations, is primarily feminine, with a concern for appearance, presentation, and form. There is an idealizing, narcissistic quality to this individual's internal representation of the female.

The action of the object representations, however, is always unmotivated, lacking in meaning, purpose, and intent. This suggests an individual who lacks inner direction and motivation, pathognomonic of impairments in underlying structure and organization. The nonspecific integration of object and action, however, suggests that interpersonal activity will, at least superficially, be socially appropriate and directable.

This is supported by the content and nature of the object representational action. Although initially malevolent and aggressive, the activity is shared and mutual, perhaps predicting this individual's expectation of first engagement with others: a distrustful, but shared, aggressive encounter. The nature of content then sustains, for a period of time, a mutual and benevolent interaction, epitomized by the idealization of the reciprocal, loving relationship in the myth of Cupid on Card VII.

The internalized relational world, however, predicts an end to this loving twinship with the emergence of a grandiose, malevolent, and aggressive figure: a representation that is quasi-human, but imbued with an ominous, fictional quality. The aggression, however, is not confabulated in a distant manner, but

dramatically loses distance and becomes an expression of disdain
and contempt toward the Rorschach examiner himself.

The second partial protocol was produced by a 21-year-old
Caucasian male who was convicted of the torture-murder of an
older homosexual male whom he had gone to visit with several
friends. This individual also had a lengthy history of antisocial
behavior beginning in early adolescence:

RORSCHACH PROTOCOL III
(HUMAN RESPONSES ONLY)

I.   1. Looks like the devil, see the ears, eyes, and horns on the
        head, that's what it's supposed to be, isn't it? (Response
        to inquiry: the ears, horn, mouth, teeth, chin here.)
II. 2. Two cartoon characters, clowns slapping their wrists
        together like this (gestures). (Response to inquiry: the
        hands and faces are red on each side, you could make the
        body look like that.)
III. 3. Two ladies, fighting over some grocery bags, the red
        stuff is the mess they're making, trying to rip the shop-
        ping cart bag in half, here's the stuff coming out of it.
        (Response to inquiry: legs, hips, boobs, neck, they're
        chickenpeople (?) yea, no mouths, just beaks. Marks here
        are rips. The stuff (?) like I don't know, broken mayon-
        naise jars, but mayo isn't red, strawberry jelly.)
VII. 4. A lady dancing and her hair's on fire [Dd22v] Buttocks,
        pointy shoes, one hand and one arm up through here, she
        got her head blown off (laughs), she's dancing. (Response
        to inquiry: the hair, arm here, head blown up.)
     5. Two Mexicans, you know with that on their head? [D1]
        They're snobby and looking over their shoulder. (Re-
        sponse to inquiry: like when you stick your tongue out,
        stuck up.)
IX. 6. The head and body of a baby [D6]. They didn't tie the

umbilical cord and the guts are shooting out. Can that really happen? Can it bleed to death? (Response to inquiry: the nose, the color, more of a flesh tone. He's red when he comes out, this is green and orange guts coming out.)

X.   7. Some guy's handing another guy something. [D6] (Response to inquiry: the blue here, on a cliff.)

8. Looks like a bug here [D7]. Someone used a drill press on him [D15], blood here [D13], drilling through one leg, the handle and power unit here [D15]. (Response to inquiry: cockroaches, two antenna and feet, and a wishbone here, the yellow handle.)

9. A man here, pulled along by two seahorses [D10]. Like with Shamu, guy gets on his back, you ever been there? (Response to inquiry: the hair, feet, and seahorses; a shotgun here.)

Table III-3 illustrates how the nine human responses of Protocol III would be scored (Blatt et al. 1976).

This individual presents a much more primitive and unstable representational world than Protocol II. Although he generally provides accurate and whole human responses, he begins in a very tentative fashion with a quasi-human detail that archetypically foreshadows, despite its inactivity, the malevolent, destructive, and evil nature of his self and object concepts.

His representational differentiation progresses in the second response to a whole and benevolent quasi-human relationship, although somewhat exhibitionistic; but then is spoiled as soon as it reaches a whole human response ("chickenpeople," response 3) and completely loses its accuracy as a whole human response that is filled with sadistic aggression (response 4). The patient is able to rebound to accurate, whole human responses throughout the rest of the protocol. The intrapsychic differentiation of this individual's object representations are generally adequate, but subject to sudden and brief fragmentation and a consequent loss of reality testing.

Table III-3
Concept of the Object Scoring, Protocol III

	Differentiation Accuracy±	Articulation Perceptual	Articulation Functional	Motivation of Action	Integration of Object-Action	Content	Nature
I. 1.	(Hd)+	–	Ro, SpId	–	–	–	–
II. 2.	(H)+	PSt	Ro	Unmot.	Nonsp.	Ben	A-A
III. 3.	H+ → (H)+	–	Sex	Unmot.	Nonsp.	Mal	A-A
VII. 4.	H–	PSt, Hsy	Sex	Unmot.	Incon.	Mal	A-P
5.	H+	Cl,Po	–	Unmot.	Nonsp.	Mal	A-A
IX. 6	H+	PSt	Age	React.	Con.	Mal	A-P
X. 7.	H+	–	Sex	Unmot.	Fused	Ben	A-P
8.	H+	–	–	Unmot.	Fused	Mal	A-P
9.	H+	Po	Sex	Int.	Nonsp.	Ben	A-P

This individual's degree of articulation is limited, averaging 1.6 features per response. It is also typical of a psychopathic individual, in that items are concerned with appearances, roles, and sexual identity: features of most interest to a pathologically narcissistic individual. There is an exhibitionistic, almost histrionic, quality to the articulation of these features. His identification of gender is also quite revealing, since both female responses (3, 4) are involved in malevolent activity, and both male responses (7, 9) are involved in benevolent activity. This suggests the conceptual representation of female objects as aggressive and distrustful, and probably reflects this patient's early primary object experience with the mother. It also suggests intense sexual orientation conflict and the probability of bisexual, or at least homosexual, acting out as an expression of this individual's rage toward the feminine, particularly his own maternal introjects.

A motivation for action is generally lacking, inferring an absence of meaning, purpose, and internality in this patient's interpersonal behavior. Surprisingly it becomes intentional on the last response, which may be prognostically significant.

This individual's capacity to integrate intrapsychic objects and action is quite variable. A *capacity* for developmentally mature congruency is evident (6), but it can only be reached in a dreadfully sadistic and aggressive manner. The attainment of this level is also quite tenuous, and subject to sudden regressive turns (7, 8) to developmentally primitive fusions of object and action.

This individual's object representational world is quintessentially frightening. It is populated by demonic and malevolent figures engaged in sadistic and aggressive behavior towards nonreactive, passive, and generally helpless objects. Of his human responses 63 percent of those involving two or more figures are engaged in destructive or aggressive activity, and 60 percent of these responses are toward an entirely passive figure. One would hypothesize interpersonal behavior that was generally sadistic, and escalated in sadism when the victim was perceived as, or actually rendered, helpless. This was tragically the case in the instant offense, since the victim was bound and gagged during his torture and murder.

Yet the irony of this patient, perhaps intrapsychically predictable if one looks carefully at his shift from an unmotivated, fused, and malevolent response (8) to an intentional, nonspecific, and benevolent last response (9), was his behavior immediately following the killing:

> A 10-year-old boy witnessed the torture and murder of the elderly victim from an adjacent room. When the perpetrator told the boy not to say anything to anybody, the boy, in a state of abject terror, agreed. The murderer left the apartment without harming the boy.

Psychodiagnostically this individual was viewed as a severe borderline personality with antisocial and histrionic features. He represents another point on the psychopathic continuum, particularly in contrast to the much less primitive, more stable, and more fully integrated, self- and object representations of Protocol II.

PRIMITIVE DEFENSE ANALYSIS

A third approach to an understanding of psychopathy in the Rorschach is offered by the work of Lerner and Lerner (1980) and their assessment of primitive defenses. Their system is based upon the theoretical formulations of Kernberg (1975) and the psychodiagnostic testing research of Mayman (1967), Pruitt and Spilka (1964), Holt (1970), and Peebles (1975).

In brief, their scoring system appears to have substantial reliability and validity (Lerner and Lerner 1980, Lerner et al. 1981, Lerner 1986, Gacono 1988). Their studies have consistently found significant differences in defensive operations, both type and developmental level, among schizophrenic, borderline, and neurotic groups (Lerner and Lerner 1980, Lerner et al. 1981). More specifically, individuals organized at a borderline level (Kernberg 1984) were the only group found to use projective identification as a defense, and were significantly more prone to use splitting and primitive levels of devaluation, idealization, and denial than either the schizophrenic or neurotic samples (Lerner and Lerner 1980, Lerner et al. 1981).

Lerner and Lerner (1980) have also been quite interested in the integration of their structural concept of defense with developmental object relations (Blatt et al. 1976). To this end they have also found that the postulated three levels of personality organization (neurotic, borderline, and psychotic) also produce significantly different human and quasi-human responses, with the latter group producing the fewest human-oriented responses (Lerner et al. 1981). Their work has lent substantial concurrent and construct validity to the research of Blatt and colleagues (1976).

The Lerner and Lerner (1980) scoring system consists of five defenses: splitting, devaluation, idealization, projective identification, and denial. Devaluation, idealization, and denial also require a ranking of the defense from most primitive to most advanced. The five-point continuum for devaluation and idealization is based upon the humanness of the figure, the temporal-spatial perspective of the figure, and the affective valuation of the figure. Denial is ranked on a three-point continuum based upon the degree of reality distortion involved in the response.

The basic unit to be scored is a whole human or quasi-human response, H or (H). Human detail responses are not scored, except for one of the categories of projective identification which involves a human detail response, a Dr location, an F(C) determinant, and aggressive content. All responses need to be scored for form level using the system devised by Mayman (1962), an elaboration of form level as delineated by Rapaport and colleagues (1946). Any response may receive more than one score.

Like the Blatt and colleagues (1976) system, the Lerner and

Lerner (1980) system's major liability is its dependency upon human responses to the Rorschach. It is even more selective because of its dependency on *whole* human responses; and this, of course, limits its usefulness in addressing psychopathy in the Rorschach. The Lerner and Lerner (1980) primitive defense system is inapplicable to Protocol I due to an absence of human and quasi-human responses.

Primitive defense analysis can be used to interpret Protocol II. The five human and quasi-human responses would be scored as follows:

1. Devaluation (highest level-1); Splitting
2. No defense score
3. Denial (highest level-1)
4. No defense score
5. Devaluation (lowest level-5); Projective Identification; Denial (lowest level-3)

This analysis yields significant interpretative data concerning this psychopathic protocol. Internal object representations are organized by splitting defenses; and, although depreciated, may be intrapsychically represented in interpersonally acceptable ways (1). This individual also has a capacity for higher level forms of denial, in this particular case involving the use of negation (3) to disavow certain aggressive impulses. This patient's structural defenses, however, also involve the use of projective identification in an aggressive and controlling manner (5). The utilization of this defense involves the projection *into* the object of aggressive impulses that are experienced as ego syntonic, leading to a loss of conceptual distinctiveness between self and object for the purpose of actual control of the object's characteristics. This regressive shift is accompanied by primitive forms of both devaluation and denial in which the humaneness of the actual object is lost and reality testing may be momentarily, but severely, compromised.

All of these defensive characteristics confirm the psychopathic process within this individual from a structural defense perspective, particularly the use of devaluation and projective identification: the latter defense pathognomonic of a borderline personality organization (Lerner and Lerner 1980).

Protocol III would be scored as follows:

1. No score (Hd) response
2. Denial (highest level-1)
3. Splitting; Devaluation (lowest level-5); Denial (lowest level-3)
4. Devaluation (level-2); Projective Identification
5. Devaluation (highest level-1)
6. Splitting; Devaluation (level-2); Projective Identification
7. No score
8. Projective Identification
9. Splitting; Denial (highest level-1)

Splitting was scored on response 9 because it immediately followed response 8 and represented an opposite affective valence.

Like the concept of the object scoring of this protocol, one sees an obvious and primitive borderline defensive structure. A capacity for socially acceptable uses of denial accompanies the first internal human representation (2), but then is followed by a regressive shift toward splitting and its phenotypic expression through lowest level forms of devaluation and denial (3). A compensatory gesture to regain intrapsychic control is found in response 4 through the aggressive use of projective identification, but with a consequent loss of reality testing. Response 5 signals a progressive shift, but then is followed by a devalued and split-object representation (6) that is also projectively controlled through a quite striking and primitive embellishment: a human content ("the head and body of a baby") that focuses aggression during the immediate postnatal moment ("they didn't tie the umbilical cord and the guts are shooting out").

Projective identification is used once again in response 8 in a confabulated response that is both sadistic and vague as to the nature of the human representation. The final response (9) infers a progressive return to higher level defensive operations with both acceptable form quality and the use of negation to deny the previous aggressive impulse.

This partial protocol also contributes to an understanding of psychopathy. The distinctive use of projective identification locates this individual at the borderline level of personality organization. The use of devaluation in the absence of any idealization other than the grandiose self-structure is typical of the internal representational world of the psychopath. And finally, the aggressive and sadistic content that the defensive structure supports is pathognomonic of the psychopathic process. I must note, however, that it is highly unusual for a psychopathic individual to be this revealing of his internal representational world.

PRIMITIVE INTERPERSONAL MODES

Kwawer (1979, 1980) developed a Rorschach model of borderline psychopathology that regarded "content as a profound, symbolic statement of personal mythology reflecting early interpersonal experience" (1980, p. 90). In the 1979 study he found that the borderline sample (N = 16) differed significantly from the control sample in that each Rorschach contained at least one response, and often more than one, that symbolized separation and differentiation problems with the primary object.

The 1980 paper hypothesized that symbiotic merging includes intrauterine modes of experience, and proposed a developmental schema to explore very early disturbances in interpersonal relations, ranging from intrauterine life through the separation–individuation phase of infancy.

Kwawer (1980) was careful to note that his eight modes of relatedness are not presented in a sequential or developmental hierarchy. They include engulfment; symbiotic merging; violent symbiosis, separation, and reunion; malignant internal processes, including primitive incorporation; birth and rebirth; metamorphosis and transformation; narcissistic mirroring; and separation–division. He also noted two adjunctive response varieties: boundary disturbance and womb imagery.

The strength of Kwawer's model of primitive interpersonal modes is its application to all, not just human or quasi-human, responses. This is particularly evident in applying his analysis to Protocol I, a psychopathic protocol that must be disregarded by both the Blatt and colleagues (1976) and the Lerner and Lerner (1980) systems due to the absence of human responses.

Protocol I yields six responses that symbolize this individual's early interpersonal experience (I have only repeated the initial response here, but in one case [9] the inquiry response was critical to scoring):

I.   1. Narcissistic mirroring. (absolutely symmetrical, looks like it could be a caterpillar on a mirror)
     2. Metamorphosis and transformation. (or a butterfly coming out of a cocoon)
VI. 8. Narcissistic mirroring. (the bank of a riverbed, some plants and trees reflecting off the water)
VII. 9. Separation–division. (iron slag. That's what it looks like. When you're welding)
IX. 12. Separation–division. (an ear of corn very ripe. Needs to be picked off the bush, plant)
X.   13. Metamorphosis and transformation. (looks like something under a microscope. Little pieces of algae, protoplasm floating around on a microscopic slide)

These responses vividly convey the underlying borderline personality organization of the psychopathic individual. In a constricted protocol of only thirteen responses, 46 percent of the percepts symbolically represent early interpersonal disturbance.

The narcissistic mirroring responses (1, 8) convey a self-absorption and self-involvement such that the primary object exists only as a conceptual extension, a mirror, of the grandiose self. The metamorphosis and transformation responses (2, 13) infer the enmeshment of the self *in* the biology of the primary object as it seeks developmental relatedness *to* the psychology of the primary object. And the separation–division responses (9, 12) infer the unconscious conflict and ambivalence concerning separation and reunion with the primary object.

Other responses from Protocols II and III that are devoid of human or quasi-human content also illustrate the usefulness of Kwawer's (1980) model when probing psychopathic disturbance:

> *Violent symbiosis, separation, and reunion*
> A horse being eaten by a bear. (Here, the horse head and hoof trying to get away.) [Card V, D4]
> *Violent separation combined with malignant internal processes*
> Bits and pieces of a pig, his head, they tore his stomach off, leg, head here. He's been chopped into little pieces, ya know? [Card VII, Dd22]
> *Malignant internal processes*
> A bug, eyeballs, skeleton, armor, feet, claws, his tail. [Card IX, W v]
> *Metamorphosis and transformation*
> It looks like a bunch of parts, maybe germs, like through a microscope. [Card X, W]
> *Narcissistic mirroring combined with malignant internal processes*
> A piece of liver reflected. [Card II, D2]

In summary, I have used four Rorschach interpretative models to expand and deepen our clinical understanding of the psychopathic process. These models include an empirically based, atheoretical system (Exner 1986a); a developmental analysis of the concept of the object (Blatt et al. 1976); a structural analysis of primitive defenses (Lerner and Lerner 1980); and a configurational grouping of primitive interpersonal modes of relating (Kwawer 1980). These approaches complement, rather than detract from, each other. They allow us to thoroughly, and more profoundly, understand the structure and function of psychopathy.

References

Abraham, K. (1954). *Selected Papers of Karl Abraham*. New York: Basic Books.

Abrahamsen, D. (1985). *Confessions of Son of Sam*. New York: Columbia University Press.

Adams, J., Meloy, R., and Moritz, S. (1987). Neuropsychological deficits and violent behavior in schizophrenia. Unpublished manuscript.

Aichhorn, A. (1925). *Wayward Youth*. New York: Viking.

Aleksandrowicz, M. K., and Aleksandrowicz, D. R. (1976). Precursors of ego in neonates: factor analysis of Brazelton Scale data. *Journal of the American Academy of Child Psychiatry* 15:257-268.

Alexander, F. (1923). *Psychoanalysis of the Total Personality*. English translation. New York: Nervous and Mental Disease Publications, 1930.

——— (1930). The neurotic character. *International Journal of Psycho-Analysis* 11:292-313.

——— (1935). *Roots of Crime*. New York: Knopf.

Allen, J., Coyne, L., and David, E. (1986). Relation of intelligence to ego functioning in an adult psychiatric population. *Journal of Personality Assessment* 50:212-221.

American Psychiatric Association (1980). *Diagnostic and Statistical Manual of Mental Disorders III*. Washington, DC: American Psychiatric Association

——— (1987). *Diagnostic and Statistical Manual of Mental Disor-*

ders III-Revised. Washington, DC: American Psychiatric Association.

Andreasen, N.C. (1978). *The Scale for the Assessment of Thought, Language, and Communication (TLC).* Iowa City: University of Iowa.

Andreasen, N.C., and Grove, W. M. (1986). Thought, language, and communication in schizophrenia: diagnosis and prognosis. *Schizophrenia Bulletin* 12:348–359.

Andreasen, N.C., Rice, J., Endicott, J., Coryell, W., Grove, W., and Reich, T. (1987). Familial rates of affective disorder. *Archives of General Psychiatry* 44:461–469.

Andrew, J. (1980). Are left handers less violent? *Journal of Youth and Adolescence* 9:1.

Appelbaum, P., and Meisel, A. (1986). Therapists' obligations to report their patients' criminal acts. *Bulletin of the American Academy of Psychiatry and Law* 14:221–230.

Archer, J. (1974). Sex differences in the emotional behavior of three strains in a laboratory rat. *Animal Learning Behavior* 2:43–48.

Arkonac, O., and Guze, S. B. (1963). A family study of hysteria. *New England Journal of Medicine* 266:239–242.

Athey, G. (1974). Schizophrenic thought organization, object relations and the Rorschach test. *Bulletin of the Menninger Clinic* 38:406–429.

Bach-y-Rita, G., Lion, J., Climent, C., and Ervin, F. (1971). Episodic dyscontrol: a study of 130 violent patients. *American Journal of Psychiatry* 127:1473–1478.

Bailey, K. (1987). Human paleopsychology: roots of pathological aggression. In *Origins of Human Aggression*, ed. G. Neuman, pp. 50–63. New York: Human Sciences.

Bailey, K., Tipton, R. M., and Taylor, P. F. (1977). The threatening stare: differential response latencies in mild and profoundly retarded adults. *American Journal of Mental Deficiency* 31:599–602.

Bandler, R. J., Jr., and Moyer, K. E. (1970). Animals spontaneously attacked by rats. *Communications in Behavioral Biology* 5:177–182.

Bandura, A., and Walters, R. H. (1958). Dependency conflicts in aggressive delinquents. *Journal of Social Issues* 14:52–65.

Bardwick, J. (1971). *Psychology of Women*. New York: Harper & Row.

Bauder, D. (1985). *Captain Money and the Golden Girl*. San Diego: Harcourt Brace Jovanovich.

Beaber, R., Marston, A., Michelli, J., and Mills, M. (1985). A brief test for measuring malingering in schizophrenic individuals. *American Journal of Psychiatry* 142:1478–1481.

Bellak, L., Hurvich, M., and Gediman, H. (1973). *Ego Functions in Schizophrenics, Neurotics and Normals*. New York: Wiley.

Bibring, E. (1953). The mechanism of depression. In *Affective Disorders: Psychoanalytic Contributions to Their Studies*, ed. P. Greenacre, pp. 13–48, 137–156. New York: International Universities Press.

Bick, E. (1968). The experience of the skin in early object relations. *International Journal of Psycho-Analysis* 49:484–486.

Bion, W. (1955). Language and the schizophrenic. In *New Directions in Psychoanalysis*, ed. M. Klein et al. London: Tavistock.

————— (1963). *Elements of Psychoanalysis*. London: Heinemann.

————— (1977a). *Seven Servants*. New York: Jason Aronson.

————— (1977b). On a quotation from Freud. In *Borderline Personality Disorders: The Concept, the Syndrome, the Patient*, ed. P. Hartocollis, pp. 511–517. New York: International Universities Press.

————— (1984). *Second Thoughts*. New York: Jason Aronson.

Birnbaum, K. (1914). *Die Psychopathischen Verbrecher*. 2nd Ed. Leipzig: Thieme.

Blatt, S. (1974). Levels of object representation in anaclitic and introjective depression. *The Psychoanalytic Study of the Child* 29:107–157.

Blatt, S., Brenneis, C. B., Schimek, J. G., and Glick, M. (1976). *A Developmental Analysis of the Concept of the Object on the Rorschach*. Unpublished scoring manual.

Blatt, S., and Lerner, H. (1983). The psychological assessment of object representation. *Journal of Personality Assessment* 47:7–27.

Blatt, S., and Schichman, S. (1981). Antisocial behavior and personality organization. In *Object and Self: A Developmental Approach*, ed. C. Kaye and M. Zimmerman, pp. 325–368. New York: International Universities Press.

Blatt, S., Schimek, J. G., and Brenneis, C. B. (1980). The nature of the psychotic experience and its implications for the therapeutic process. In *The Psychotherapy of Schizophrenia*, ed. J. Strauss et al. New York: Plenum.

Bliss, E. L. (1980). Multiple personalities: a report of 14 cases with implications for schizophrenia and hysteria. *Archives of General Psychiatry* 37:1388–1397.

Blondaux, C., Juge, A., Sordet, F., Chouvet, G., Jouvet, M., and Pujol, J.-F. (1973). Modification du metabolisme de la serotonine (5HT) cerebrale induite chez le rat par administration de 6-hydroxydopamine. *Brain Research* 50: 101–114.

Blumer, D., Williams, H., and Mark, V. (1974). The study and treatment on a neurological ward of abnormally aggressive patients with focal brain disease. *Confinia Neurologica* 36:125–176.

Boesky, D. (1983). The problem of mental representation in self and object theory. *Psychoanalytic Quarterly* 52:564–583.

Bonnie, R., and Slobogin, C. (1980). The role of the mental health professional in the criminal process: the case for informed speculation. *66 Virginia Law Review 427.*

Bowlby, J. (1969). *Attachment and Loss. Vol. 1. Attachment.* New York: Basic Books.

———— (1973). *Attachment and Loss. Vol. 2. Separation: Anxiety and Anger.* New York: Basic Books.

———— (1980). *Attachment and Loss. Vol. 3. Loss: Sadness and Depression.* New York: Basic Books.

Bradford, J. M. W., and Smith, S. M. (1979). Amnesia and homicide: the Padola Case and a study of thirty cases. *Bulletin of the American Academy of Psychiatry and Law* 7:219–231.

Brandt, J., Rubinsky, E., and Lassen, G. (1985). Uncovering malingered amnesia. *Annals of the New York Academy of Sciences* 44:502–503.

Braun, B. G. (1984). Towards a theory of multiple personality and other dissociative phenomena. *Psychiatric Clinics of North America* 7:171–193.

Braun, B. G., and Sachs, R. G. (1985). The development of multiple personality disorder: predisposing, precipitating, and perpetuating factors. In *Childhood Antecedents of Multiple Personality*, ed. R. P. Kluft, pp. 38–64. Washington, DC: American Psychiatric Press.

Bremer, J. (1959). *Asexualization.* New York: Macmillan.

Brenman, E. (1985). Cruelty and narrowmindedness. *International Journal of Psycho-Analysis* 66:273–281.

Breuer, J., and Freud, S. (1893–1895). *Studies on Hysteria*. New York: Basic Books, 1957.

Broadhurst, P. (1957). Determinants of emotionality in the rat. 1. Situational factors. *British Journal of Psychology* 48:1–12.

Broca, P. (1878). Anatomie comparee des circomvolutions cerebrales. Le Grand lobe limbique et la scissure limbique dans la serie des mammiferes. *Revue Anthropologique* 1:385–498.

Brodal, A. (1981). *Neurological Anatomy.* 3rd ed. New York: Oxford University Press.

Bromberg, P. (1979). The use of detachment in narcissistic and borderline conditions. *Journal of the American Academy of Psychoanalysis* 7:593–600.

Brown, B. S., and Courtless, T. F. (1971). *Mentally Retarded Offender*. Washington, DC: National Institute of Mental Health, Center for Studies of Crime and Delinquency.

Brown, G., Ballanger, J., Minichiello, M., and Goodwin, F. (1979). Human aggression and its relationship to cerebrospinal fluid, 5-hydroxyindoleacetic acid, 3-methoxy-4-hydroxy-phenylglycol, and homovanillic acid. In *Psychopharmacology of Aggression*, ed. M. Sandler, pp. 131–148. New York: Raven Press.

Bugliosi, V., and Gentry, C. (1974). *Helter Skelter*. New York: Norton.

Buie, D. H., Jr., and Adler, G. (1973). The uses of confrontation in the psychotherapy of borderline cases. In *Confrontation in Psychotherapy*, ed. G. Adler and P. Myerson. New York: Science House.

Bursten, B. (1972). The manipulative personality. *Archives of General Psychiatry* 26:318–321.

———— (1973a). *The Manipulator*. New Haven: Yale University Press.

———— (1973b). Some narcissistic personality types. *International Journal of Psychoanalysis* 54:287–300.

Butcher, S., Butcher, L., and Cho, A. (1976). Modulation of neostriatal acetylcholine in the rat by dopamine and 5-hydroxy-tryptamine afferents. *Life Science* 18:733–744.

Cadoret, R. J. (1978). Psychopathology in the adopted-away offspring of biological parents with antisocial behavior. *Archives of General Psychiatry* 35:176–184.

Cafiero, G. (1979). Prontuario dei conflitti: ed ecco le possibili guerre. *Il Settimanale* 6:20–22.

Cahill, T. (1986). *Buried Dreams*. New York: Bantam Books.

California Department of Justice (1984). *Homicide in California, 1984*. Sacramento: Bureau of Criminal Statistics and Special Services.

Campbell, H. (1967). The violent sex offender: a consideration of emasculation in treatment. *Rocky Mountain Medical Journal* 64:40–43.

Cannon, W. (1927). The James-Lange theory of emotions: a critical examination and an alternative. *American Journal of Physiology* 39:106–124.

Carroll, B., and Steiner, M. (1978). The psychobiology of premenstrual dysphorie: the role of prolactin. *Psychoneuroendocrinology* 3:171–180.

Cavanaugh, J., and Rogers, R. (1984). Malingering and deception. *Behavioral Sciences and the Law* 2:5–118.

Chassegeut-Smirgel, J. (1978). Reflexions on the connexions between perversion and sadism. *International Journal of Psycho-Analysis* 59:27–35.

Chatz, T. (1972). Management of male adolescent sex offenders. *International Journal of Offender Therapy* 2:109.

Chi, C., and Flynn, J. (1971a). Neural pathways associated with hypothalamically elicited attack behavior in cats. *Science* 171:703–706.

——— (1971b). Neuroanatomic projections related to biting attack elicited from hypothalamus in cats. *Brain Research* 35:49–66.

Chodoff, P. (1982). Hysteria and women. *American Journal of Psychiatry* 1399:545–551.

Christiansen, K. (1977a). A review of studies of criminality among twins. In *Biosocial Bases of Criminal Behavior*, ed. S. A. Mednick and K. O. Christiansen. New York: Wiley.

——— (1977b). A preliminary study of criminality among twins. In *Biosocial Bases of Criminal Behavior*, ed. S. A. Mednick and K. O Christiansen. New York: Wiley.

Claridge, G. (1967). *Personality and Arousal*. London: Pergamon.

Cleckley, H. (1941, 1976). *Mask of Sanity*. St. Louis: C. V. Mosby.

Cloninger, C. R., and Guze, S. B. (1970). Psychiatric illness and female criminality: the role of sociopathy and hysteria in the antisocial woman. *American Journal of Psychiatry* 127:303–311.

Cloninger, C. R., and Guze, S. B. (1975). Hysteria and parental psychiatric illness. *Psychological Medicine* 5:27–31.

Cloninger, C. R., Reich, T., and Guze, S. B. (1975). The multifactorial model of disease transmission, III: familial relationship between sociopathy and hysteria (Briquet's syndrome). *British Journal of Psychiatry* 127:23–32.

Cloninger, C. R., Sigvardsson, S., von Knorring, A-L, et al. (1984). An adoption study of somatoform disorders, II: identification of two discrete somatoform disorders. *Archives of General Psychiatry* 41:863–871.

Cockrum, E., and McCauley, W. (1965). *Zoology*. Philadelphia: W. B. Saunders.

Cooper, H. H. A. (1978). Psychopath as terrorist: a psychological perspective. *Legal Medical Quarterly* 2:253–262.

Coriat, R. C. (1927). Discussion of "the constitutional psychopathic inferior." *American Journal of Psychiatry* 6:686–689.

Dahlstrom, W., and Welsh, G. (1960). *An MMPI Handbook*. Minneapolis: University of Minnesota Press.

Dalton, K. (1961). Menstruation and crime. *British Medical Journal* 3:1752–1753.

Damasio, A., and Van Hoesen, G. (1983). Emotional disturbances associated with focal lesions of the limbic frontal lobe. In *Neuropsychology of Human Emotion*, ed. K. Heilman and P. Satz, pp. 85–110. New York: Guilford.

Denkowski, G. C., and Denkowski, K. M. (1985). The mentally retarded offender in the state prison system. *Criminal Justice and Behavior* 12:55–70.

Deutsch, H. (1942). Some forms of emotional disturbance and their relationship to schizophrenia. *Psychoanalytic Quarterly* 11:301–321.

Diamond, B. (1980). Inherent problems in the use of pre-trial hypnosis on a prospective witness. *68 California Law Review 313*.

Doren, D. (1987). *Understanding and Treating the Psychopath*. New York: Wiley.

Dorpat, T. (1983). Review of *Splitting and Projective Identification* by James Grotstein. *International Journal of Psycho-Analysis* 64:116–119.

Douglas, J. E., Ressler, C. K., Burgess, A. W., and Hartman, C. R. (1986). Criminal profiling from crime scene analysis. *Behavioral Sciences and the Law* 4:401–421.

Duffy, E. (1941). An explanation of "emotional" phenomenon without the use of the concept "emotion." *Journal of General Psychiatry* 25:283–289.

Eagle, M. (1984). *Recent Developments in Psychoanalysis*. New York: McGraw-Hill.

Eckblad, M., and Chapman, L. (1986). Development and validation of a scale for hypomanic personality. *Journal of Abnormal Psychology* 95:214–222.

Ehrenkranz, J., Bliss, E., and Sheard, M. (1974). Plasma testosterone: correlation with aggressive behavior and social dominance in man. *Psychosomatic Medicine* 36:469–475.

Eichelman, B., Elliott, G., and Barchas, J. (1981). Biochemical, pharmacological, and genetic aspects of aggression. In *Biobehavioral Aspects of Aggression*, ed. D. A. Hamburg and M. B. Trudeau. New York: Liss.

Eissler, K. R., ed. (1949). *Searchlights on Delinquency*. New York: International Universities Press.

Elworthy, F. (1895). *The Evil Eye*. London: Murray.

Ennis, B. (1986). Brief *amicus curiae* American Psychological Association in support of petitioner (Colorado vs. Connelly, no. 85-660). Washington, DC: Wilson-Epes.

Erdberg, P. (in press). The Rorschach. In *Handbook of Psychological Assessment*, ed. M. Hersen. Elmsford, NY: Pergamon Press.

Erikson, E. (1950). *Childhood and Society*. New York: Norton.

Exner, J. (1974). *The Rorschach: A Comprehensive System*. Vol. 1. New York: Wiley.

——— (1986a). *The Rorschach: A Comprehensive System. Vol. I: Foundations*, 2nd ed. New York: Wiley.

——— (1986b). Some Rorschach data comparing schizophrenics with borderline and schizotypal personality disorders. *Journal of Personality Assessment* 50:455–471.

Exner, J., and Chu, A. (1981). Reports of transitional objects among nonpatient adults as related to the presence or absence of T in the Rorschach. Workshops Study No. 277 (unpublished). Rorschach Workshops.

Exner, J., and Hillman, L. (1984). A comparison of content distributions for the records of 76 paranoid schizophrenics and 76 nonparanoid schizophrenics. Workshops Study No. 293 (unpublished). Rorschach Workshops.

Exner, J., and Leura, A. V. (1977). Rorschach performances of volunteer and nonvolunteer adolescents. Workshops Study No. 238 (unpublished). Rorschach Workshops.

Exner, J., Levantrosser, C., and Mason, B. (1980). Reports of transitional objects among first admission depressives as related to the presence or absence of T in the Rorschach. Workshops Study No. 266 (unpublished). Rorschach Workshops.

Eysenck, H. (1947). *Dimensions of Personality*. London: Routledge & Kegan Paul.

———— (1957). *Dynamics of Anxiety and Hysteria*. New York: Praeger.

———— (1962). Conditioning and personality. *British Journal of Psychology* 53:299–305.

———— (1967). *The Biological Basis of Personality*. Springfield, IL: Charles C Thomas.

Eysenck, H., and Eysenck, S. (1963). On the dual nature of extraversion. *British Journal of Social and Clinical Psychology* 2:46–55.

———— (1968). *Manual for the Eysenck Personality Inventory*. San Diego: Educational and Industrial Testing Service.

Farley, F., and Farley, S. (1967). Extroversion and stimulus-seeking motivation. *Journal of Consulting Psychology* 31:215–216.

Fast, I. (1974). Multiple identities and borderline personality organization. *British Journal of Medical Psychology* 47:291–300.

Fedora, O., and Fedora, S. (1982). Some neuropsychological and psychophysiological aspects of psychopathic and nonpsychopathic criminals. *Research Bulletin 62*, Edmonton: Alberta Hospital Edmonton Psychiatric Treatment Centre.

Feltous, A. R., and Kellert, S. R. (1986). Violence against animals and people: is aggression against living creatures generalized? *Bulletin of the American Academy of Psychiatry and the Law* 14:55–69.

Fenichel, O. (1935). The scoptophilic instinct and identification. *International Journal of Psycho-Analysis* 21:561–583.

———— (1945). *The Psychoanalytic Theory of Neurosis*. New York: Norton.

———— (1953). On the psychology of boredom. In *The Collected Papers of Otto Fenichel, First Series*, pp. 292–302. New York: Norton.

Ferenczi, S. (1913). Stages in the development of the sense of reality. In *Sex in Psychoanalysis*, pp. 213–239. Boston: Badger.

_____ (1919). The phenomena of hysterical materialization. In *Further Contributions to the Theory and Technique of Psychoanalysis*, pp. 89–104. New York: Boni and Liveright.

_____ (1930). Autoplastic and alloplastic. In *Final Contributions to the Problems and Methods of Psychoanalysis*, p. 221. New York: Basic Books.

Field, M. (1940). Maternal attitudes found in 25 cases of children with primary behavior disorders. *American Journal of Orthopsychiatry* 10:293–311.

Finell, J. (1986). The merits and problems with the concept of projective identification. *Psychoanalytic Review* 73:103–120.

Fintzy, P. T. (1971). Vicissitudes of the transitional object in a borderline child. *International Journal of Psycho-Analysis* 52:107–114.

Fitzhugh, K. (1973). Some neuropsychological features of delinquent subjects. *Perceptual Motor Skills* 36:474.

Fliess, R. (1953). The hypnotic evasion: a clinical observation. *Psychoanalytic Quarterly* 22:497–511.

Flor-Henry, P. (1974). Psychosis, neurosis, and epilepsy: developmental and gender-related effects and their aetiological contribution. *British Journal of Psychiatry* 124:144–150.

_____ (1979). Laterality, shifts of cerebral dominance, sinistrality and psychosis. In *Hemisphere Asymmetries of Function in Psychopathology*, ed. J. Gruzelier and P. Flor-Henry. Amsterdam: Elsevier.

Flynn, J. P. (1967). The neural basis of aggression in cats. In *Neurophysiology and Emotion*, ed. D. Glass, pp. 40–59. New York: Rockefeller University.

Flynn, J. P., and Bandler, R. (1975). Patterned reflexes during centrally elicited attack behavior. In *Neural Basis of Violence and Aggression*, ed. W. Fields and W. Sweet, pp. 41–53. St. Louis: W. H. Green.

Flynn, J.P., Vanegas, H., Foote, W., and Edwards, S. (1970). Neural mechanisms involved in a cat's attack on a rat. In *Neural Control of Behavior*, ed. R. Whalen, R. Thompson, M. Verzeano, and N. Weinberger, pp. 135–173. New York: Academic Press.

Frank, G. (1966). *The Boston Strangler*. New York: New American Library.

Franks, C., and Trouton, D. (1958). Effects of amobarbitol sodium and dexamphetamine sulphate on the conditioning of the eyelid response. *Journal of Comparative Physiological Psychology* 51:220–222.

Freud, A. (1936). *The Ego and the Mechanisms of Defense. Rev. Ed.* New York: International Universities Press, 1966.

———— (1949). The analytic treatment of major criminals: therapeutic results and technical problems. In *Searchlights on Delinquency*, ed. K. Eissler, pp. 174–189. New York: International Universities Press.

Freud, S. (1894). The neuro-psychoses of defense. *Standard Edition* 3:45–61. London: Hogarth Press, 1962.

———— (1900). The interpretation of dreams. *Standard Edition* 4, 5. London: Hogarth Press, 1953.

———— (1909). Family romances. *Standard Edition* 9:235. London: Hogarth Press, 1959.

———— (1911). Psychoanalytic notes on an autobiographical account of a case of paranoia (dementia paranoides). *Standard Edition* 12:3–82. London: Hogarth Press, 1958.

———— (1916). Some character types met with in psychoanalytic work. *Standard Edition* 14:309–333. London: Hogarth Press, 1957.

———— (1919). A child is being beaten. *Standard Edition* 17:175–204. London: Hogarth Press, 1955.

———— (1921). A differentiating grade in the ego. *Standard Edition* 18:129–133. London: Hogarth Press, 1955.

———— (1924a). The loss of reality in neurosis and psychosis. *Standard Edition* 19:183–187. London: Hogarth Press.

———— (1924b). Neurosis and psychosis. *Standard Edition* 19:149–158. London: Hogarth Press, 1961.

———— (1925). Negation. *Standard Edition* 19:235–239. London: Hogarth Press, 1961.

———— (1938). Splitting of the ego in the process of defense. *Standard Edition* 23:271–278. London: Hogarth Press, 1964.

Frosch, J. (1983a). *The Psychotic Process.* New York: International Universities Press.

———— (1983b). The treatment of antisocial and borderline personality disorders. *Hospital and Community Psychiatry* 34:243–248.

Gacono, C. (1988). A Rorschach analysis of object relations and defensive structure and their relationship to level of narcissism and psychopathy in a group of antisocial offenders. Unpublished doctoral dissertation. United States International University, San Diego.

Gaddini, E. (1969). On imitation. *International Journal of Psycho-Analysis* 50:475–484.

Galdston, R. (1987). The longest pleasure: a psychoanalytic study of hatred. *International Journal of Psycho-Analysis* 68:371–378.

Ganzer, V., and Sarason, I. (1973). Variables associated with recidivism among juvenile delinquents. *Journal of Consulting and Clinical Psychology* 40:1–5.

Gardner, J. (1986, March 1). The relationship between conscious and unconscious processes and individual creativity. Invited address, California State Psychological Association Convention, San Francisco.

Gellhorn, E., and Loofbourrow, G. (1963). *Emotions and Emotional Disorders*. New York: Harper.

Gill, M. (1967). The primary process. In *Psychoanalytic Essays in Honor of David Rapaport*, ed. R. Holt, pp. 260–298. New York: International Universities Press.

Giovacchini, P. (1972). Technical difficulties in treating some characterological disorders: countertransference problems. *International Journal of Psychoanalytic Psychotherapy* 1:112–127.

Glasser, M. (1986). Identification and its vicissitudes as observed in the perversions. *International Journal of Psycho-Analysis* 67:9–17.

Gouster, M. (1878). Moral insanity. *Review of Scientific Medicine* 38:115–131.

Graham, J. (1987). *The MMPI: A Practical Guide*. Rev. ed. New York: Oxford University Press.

Gray, J. (1972). The psychophysiological nature of introversion-extroversion: a modification of Eysenck's theory. In *Biological Bases of Individual Behavior*, ed. V. Nebylitsyn and J. Gray, pp. 182–205. London: Academic Press.

Greenacre, P. (1958). The imposter. *Psychoanalytic Quarterly* 27:359–382.

———— (1969). The fetish and the transitional object. *Psychoanalytic Study of the Child* 24:144–164.

———— (1970). The transitional object and the fetish with special reference to the role of illusion. *International Journal of Psycho-Analysis* 51:447–456.

Greenberg, A., and Coleman, M. (1976). Depressed 5-hydroxyindole levels associated with hyperactive and aggressive behavior. *Archives of General Psychiatry* 33:331–336.

Greenberg, J., and Mitchell, S. (1983). *Object Relations in Psychoanalytic Theory*. Cambridge: Harvard University Press.

Greenson, R. (1954). The struggle against identification. *Journal of the American Psychoanalytic Association* 2:200–217.

———— (1974). Loving, hating, and indifference toward the patient. *International Review of Psycho-Analysis* 1:259–266.

Grinberg, L. (1981). The "Oedipus" as a resistance against the "Oedipus" in the psychoanalytic practice. In *Do I Dare Disturb the Universe?* ed. J. Grotstein, pp. 341–355. Beverly Hills: Caesura Press.

Grinker, R., Werble, B., and Drye, R. (1968). *The Borderline Syndrome*. New York: Basic Books.

Groth, A. N. (1979). *Men Who Rape: The Psychology of the Offender*. New York: Plenum Press.

Grotstein, J. (1977). The psychoanalytic concept of schizophrenia II: reconciliation. *International Journal of Psycho-Analysis* 58:427–452.

———— (1978). Inner space: its dimensions and its coordinates. *International Journal of Psycho-Analysis* 59:55–61.

———— (1980a). *Splitting and Projective Identification*. New York: Jason Aronson.

———— (1980b). A proposed revision of the psychoanalytic concept of primitive mental states. *Contemporary Psychoanalysis* 16:479–546.

———— (1981). Who is the dreamer who dreams the dream and who is the dreamer who understands it? In *Do I Dare Disturb the Universe?* ed. J. Grotstein, pp. 358–416. Beverly Hills: Caesura Press.

———— (1982). Newer perspectives in object relations theory. *Contemporary Psychoanalysis* 18:43–91.

———— (1986). Schizophrenic personality disorder: ". . . and if I should die before I wake." In *Towards a Comprehensive Model for Schizophrenic Disorders*, ed. D. Feinsilver, pp. 29–71. Hillsdale, NJ: The Analytic Press.

Grotstein, J., Lang, J., and Solomon, M. (1987). *The Borderline Patient: Emerging Concepts in Diagnosis, Psychodynamics, and Treatment*. Vol. 2. Hillsdale, NJ: The Analytic Press.

Gunderson, J., and Kolb, J. (1978). Discriminating features of borderline patients. *American Journal of Psychiatry* 135:792-796.

Gupta, B. (1970). The effect of extroversion and stimulant and depressant drugs on verbal conditioning. *Acta Psychologica* 34.

Guze, S. B. (1964). Conversion symptoms in criminals. *American Journal of Psychiatry* 121:580-583.

Guze, S. B., Woodruff, R. A., Jr., and Clayton, P. J. (1971a). A study of conversion symptoms in psychiatric outpatients. *American Journal of Psychiatry* 128:643-646.

_____ (1971b). Hysteria and antisocial behavior: further evidence of an association. *American Journal of Psychiatry* 127:957-960.

Haimo, S. and Holzman, P. (1979). Thought disorder in schizophrenics and normal controls: social class and race differences. *Journal of Consulting and Clinical Psychology* 47:963-967.

Hall, C. (1941). Temperament: a survey of animal studies. *Psychological Bulletin* 38:909-943.

Hamburg, D., Moos, R., and Yalom, I. (1968). Studies of distress in the menstrual cycle and the postpartum period. In *Endocrinology and Human Behavior*, ed. R. P. Michael. London: Oxford University Press.

Hare, R. (1970). *Psychopathy: Theory and Research*. New York: Wiley.

_____ (1972). Psychopathy and physiological responses to adrenalin. *Journal of Abnormal Psychology* 79:138-147.

_____ (1975). Psychophysiological studies of psychopathy. In *Clinical Applications of Psychophysiology*, ed. D.C. Fowles. New York: Columbia University Press.

_____ (1978a). Electrodermal and cardiovascular correlates of psychopathy. In *Psychopathic Behavior: Approaches to Research*, ed. R. Hare and D. Schalling. London: Wiley.

_____ (1978b). Psychopathy and crime. In *Colloquium on the Correlates of Crime and the Determinants of Criminal Behavior*, ed. L. Otten. Rosslyn, VA: Mitre Corp.

_____ (1980). A research scale for the assessment of psychopathy in criminal populations. *Personality and Individual Differences* 1:111-119.

_____ (1981). Psychopathy and violence. In *Violence and the Violent*

Individual, ed. J. Hays, T. Roberts, and K. Solway. New York: Jamaica.

———— (1985a). Comparison of procedures for the assessment of psychopathy. *Journal of Consulting and Clinical Psychology* 53:7–16.

———— (1985b). *The Psychopathy Checklist*. Vancouver, Canada: University of British Columbia.

———— (1986). 20 years of experience with the Cleckley psychopath. In *Unmasking the Psychopath*, ed. W. Reid, D. Dorr, J. Walker, and J. Bonner, pp. 3–27. New York: Norton.

Hare, R., and Craigen, D. (1974). Psychopathy and physiological activity in a mixed-motive game situation. *Psychophysiology* 11:197–206.

Hare, R., Frazelle, J., and Cox, D. (1978). Psychopathy and physiological responses to threat of an aversive stimulus. *Psychophysiology* 15:165–172.

Hare, R., and Jutai, J. (1983). Criminal history of the male psychopath: some preliminary data. In *Prospective Studies of Crime and Delinquency*, ed. K. Van Dusen and S. Mednick. Boston: Kluwer-Nijhoff.

Hare, R., and McPherson, L. (1984). Violent and aggresssive behavior by criminal psychopaths. *International Journal of Law and Psychiatry* 7:35–50.

Hare, R., and Quinn, M. (1971). Psychopathy and autonomic conditioning. *Journal of Abnormal Psychology* 77:223–235.

Hartmann, H. (1924). Halluzinierte flachenfarben und bewegungen. *Mschr. Psychiatr. and Neurol.* 56:1–14.

———— (1939). *Ego Psychology and the Problem of Adaptation*. New York: International Universities Press.

Hartocollis, P. (1983). *Time and Timelessness*. New York: International Universities Press.

Haslam, D. (1967). Individual differences in pain threshold and level of arousal. *British Journal of Psychology* 58:139–142.

Heaven, T. (1988). The relationship between Hare's psychopathy checklist scores and Exner's Rorschach variables in an inmate population. Unpublished doctoral dissertation. United States International University, San Diego.

Heilbrun, A. B. (1979). Psychopathy and violent crime. *Journal of Consulting and Clinical Psychology* 47:509–516.

————— (1982). Cognitive models of criminal violence based upon intelligence and psychopathy levels. *Journal of Consulting and Clinical Psychology* 50:546–557.

Hellerstein, D., Frosch, W., and Koenigsberg, H. W. (1987). The clinical significance of command hallucinations. *American Journal of Psychiatry* 144:219–221.

Hellman, D., and Blackman, N. (1966). Enuresis, firesetting, and cruelty to animals. *American Journal of Psychiatry* 122:1431–1435.

Henderson, N. (1973). Brain weight changes resulting from enriched rearing conditions: A diallel analysis. *Developmental Psychobiology* 6:367–376.

Hereford, C., Cleland, C. C., and Fellner, M. (1973). Territoriality and scentmarking: a study of profoundly retarded enuretics and encopretics. *American Journal of Mental Deficiency* 77:426–430.

Hermann, I. (1934). Urwahrnehmungen, insbesondere augenleuchten und lautwerden des inneren. *International Journal of Psycho-Analysis* 20:553–555.

Hernandez-Peon, R., Scherrer, H., and Jouvet, M. (1956). Modification of electrical activity in cochlear nucleus during "attention" in unanesthetized cats. *Science* 123:331–332.

Herzog, A., and Van Hoesen, G. (1976). Temporal neocortical afferent connections to the amygdala in the rhesus monkey. *Brain Research* 115:57–69.

Hilgard, E. R. (1977). *Divided Consciousness: Multiples in Human Thought and Action.* New York: Wiley.

————— (1980). Consciousness in contemporary psychiatry. *Annual Review of Psychology* 31:1–26.

Hilgard, E. R., and Bower, G. (1975). *Theories of Learning.* Englewood Cliffs, NJ: Prentice-Hall.

Hoge, S. K., and Gutheil, T. G. (1987). The prosecution of psychiatric patients for assaults on staff: a preliminary empirical study. *Hospital and Community Psychiatry* 38:44–49.

Holcomb, W. R., and Adams, N. (1982). Racial influences on intelligence and personality measures of people who commit murder. *Journal of Clinical Psychology* 38:793–796.

Holland, H. (1963). Visual masking and the effect of stimulant and depressant drugs. In *Experiments with Drugs*, ed. H. Eysenck. London: Pergamon.

Holland, T. R., Beckett, G. E., and Levi, M. (1981). Intelligence, personality, and criminal violence: a multivariate analysis. *Journal of Consulting and Clinical Psychology* 49:106–111.

Holt, R. (1967). *Psychoanalytic Essays in Honor of David Rapaport.* New York: International Universities Press.

——— (1970). Manual for scoring of primary process manifestations in Rorschach responses. Unpublished manuscript. New York University Research Center for Mental Health.

——— (1985). The current status of psychoanalytic theory. *Psychoanalytic Psychology* 2:289–315.

Holzman, P. S. (1986). Thought disorder in schizophrenia: editor's introduction. *Schizophrenia Bulletin* 12:342–346.

Holzman, P. S., Shenton, M. E., and Solovay, M. R. (1986). Quality of thought disorder in differential diagnosis. *Schizophrenia Bulletin* 12:360–371.

Horney, K. (1945). *Our Inner Conflicts.* New York: Norton.

House, T., and Milligan, W. (1976). Autonomic responses to modeled distress in prison psychopaths. *Journal of Personality and Social Psychology* 34:556–600.

Howe, E. G. (1984). Psychiatric evaluation of offenders who commit crimes while experiencing dissociative states. *Law and Human Behavior* 8:253–282.

Hymer, S. (1986). The multidimensional significance of the look. *Psychoanalytic Psychology* 3:149–157.

Jacobson, E. (1957). Denial and repression. *Journal of the American Psychoanalytic Association* 5:61–92.

——— (1964). *The Self and the Object World.* New York: International Universities Press.

——— (1971). *Depression.* New York: International Universities Press.

James, W. (1884). What is emotion? *Mind* 9:188–205.

Janet, P. (1889). *L'Automatisme Psychologique.* Paris: Felix Alcan.

Johnson, A. M. (1949). Sanctions for superego lacunae of adolescents. In *Searchlights on Delinquency*, ed. K. Eissler, pp. 225–245. New York: International Universities Press.

Johnston, M., and Holzman, P. (1979). *Assessing Schizophrenic Thinking*. San Francisco: Jossey-Bass.

Joseph, B. (1960). Some characteristics of the psychopathic personality. *International Journal of Psycho-Analysis* 41:526–531.

Jung, C. G. (1907). The psychology of dementia praecox. *Collected Works* 3:3–151.

———— (1916). *Psychology of the Unconscious*. New York: Moffat Yard.

Karpman, B. (1941). On the need for separating psychopathy into two distinct clinical types: symptomatic and idiopathic. *Journal of Criminal Psychopathology* 3:112–137.

Kernberg, O. (1975). *Borderline Conditions and Pathological Narcissism*. New York: Jason Aronson.

———— (1976). *Object Relations Theory and Clinical Psychoanalysis*. New York: Jason Aronson.

———— (1980). *Internal World and External Reality*. New York: Jason Aronson.

———— (1982). Self, ego, affects, and drives. *Journal of the American Psychoanalytic Association* 30:893–917.

———— (1984). *Severe Personality Disorders: Psychotherapeutic Strategies*. New Haven: Yale University Press.

Keyes, D. (1981). *The Minds of Billy Milligan*. New York: Random House.

Khan, M. M. R. (1980). *Alienation in Perversions*. New York: International Universities Press.

King, D., and Appelbaum, J. (1973). Effect of trials on "emotionality" behavior of the rat and mouse. *Journal of Comparative Physiological Psychology* 85:186–194.

Kissen, M., ed. (1986). *Assessing Object Relations Phenomena*. New York: International Universities Press.

Klein, M. (1935). A contribution to the psychogenesis of manic-depressive states. *Contributions to Psychoanalysis: 1921–1945*. New York: McGraw-Hill, 1964.

———— (1946). Notes on some schizoid mechanisms. In *Envy and Gratitude and Other Works, 1946–1963*, pp. 1–24. New York: The Free Press, 1975.

———— (1957). Envy and gratitude. In *Envy and Gratitude and Other Works, 1946–1963*, pp. 176–238. New York: The Free Press, 1975.

———— (1964). *Contributions to Psychoanalysis: 1920–1945.* New York: McGraw-Hill.

Klopfer, B., Ainsworth, M., Klopfer, W., and Holt, R. (1954). *Developments in the Rorschach Technique.* Vol. 1. Yonkers-on-Hudson, New York: World Book.

Kluft, R. P. ed. (1985). *Childhood Antecedents of Multiple Personality Disorder.* Washington, DC: American Psychiatric Press.

Koch, J. L. (1891). *Die Psychopathischen Minderwertigkeiten.* Ravensburg: Maier.

Koehler, K. (1979). First rank symptoms of schizophrenia: questions concerning clinical boundaries. *British Journal of Psychiatry* 134:236–248.

Kohut, H. (1971). *Analysis of the Self.* New York: International Universities Press.

Kolb, B., and Nouneman, A. (1974). Frontolimbic lesions and social behavior in the rat. *Physiological Behavior* 13:637–643.

Kooi, K., Tucker, R., and Marshall, R. (1978). *Fundamentals of Electroencephalography.* 2nd ed. Hagerstown, MD: Harper & Row.

Kostowski, W., and Valzelli, L. (1974). Biochemical and behavioral effects of lesions of raphe nuclei in aggressive mice. *Pharmacology, Biochemistry, and Behavior* 2:277–280.

Kozol, H., Boucher, R., and Garofalo, R. (1972). The diagnosis and treatment of dangerousness. *Crime and Delinquency* 18:371–392.

Kraepelin, E. (1887). *Psychiatrie: Ein Lehrbuch.* 2nd ed. Leipzig: Abel.

———— (1889). *Psychiatrie: Ein Lehrbuch.* 3rd ed. Leipzig: Barth.

———— (1896). *Psychiatrie: Ein Lehrbuch.* 5th ed. Leipzig: Barth.

———— (1903–1904). *Psychiatrie: Ein Lehrbuch.* 7th ed. Leipzig: Barth.

———— (1915). *Psychiatrie: Ein Lehrbuch.* 8th ed. Leipzig: Barth.

Krafft-Ebing, R. von (1886). *Psychopathia Sexualis: A Medico-Forensic Study.* New York: Putnam, 1965.

Kreuz, L., and Rose, R. (1972). Assessment of aggressive behavior and plasma testosterone in a young criminal population. *Psychosomatic Medicine* 34:321–332.

Kris, E. (1952). *Psychoanalytic Explorations in Art.* New York: International Universities Press.

Kwawer, J. (1979). Borderline phenomena, interpersonal relations, and the Rorschach test. *Bulletin of the Menninger Clinic* 43:515–524.

———— (1980). Primitive interpersonal modes, borderline phenomena, and Rorschach content. In *Borderline Phenomena and the Rorschach Test*, ed. J. Kwawer, H. Lerner, P. Lerner, and A. Sugarman, pp. 89–106. New York: International Universities Press.

Kwawer, J., Lerner, H., Lerner, P., and Sugarman, A. (1980). *Borderline Phenomena and the Rorschach Test*. New York: International Universities Press.

Lacey, B., and Lacey, J. (1974). Studies of heart rate and other bodily processes in sensorimotor behavior. In *Cardiovascular Psychophysiology: Current Issues in Response Mechanisms, Biofeedback, and Methodology*, ed. P. Obrist, A. Blac, J. Breuer, and L. Dicara, pp. 538–564. Chicago: Aldine-Atherton.

Laing, R. (1976). *The Facts of Life*. Middlesex, England: Penguin Books.

Lange, C. (1885). *Om Sindsbevaegelser et psyko. Fysiolog. Studie*. Copenhagen: Kroner.

Laschet, U. (1973). Antiandrogen in the treatment of sex offenders: mode of action and therapeutic outcome. In *Contemporary Sexual Behavior*, ed. J. Zulbin and J. Money. Baltimore: Johns Hopkins University Press.

Lashley, K. (1938). The thalamus and emotion. *Psychological Review* 45:42–61.

Lehman, L. (1974). Depersonalization. *American Journal of Psychiatry* 131:1221–1224.

Lerner, H. (1986). An object representation approach to Rorschach assessment. In *Assessing Object Relations Phenomena*, ed. M. Kissen, pp. 127–142. Madison, CT: International Universities Press.

Lerner, H., Sugarman, A., and Gaughran, J. (1981). Borderline and schizophrenic patients: a comparative study of defensive structure. *Journal of Nervous and Mental Disease* 169:705–711.

Lerner, P., and Lerner, H. (1980). Rorschach assessment of primitive defenses in borderline personality structure. In *Borderline Phenomena and the Rorschach Test*, ed. J. Kwawer, H. Lerner, P. Lerner, and A. Sugarman, pp. 257–274. New York: International Universities Press.

Lester, D. (1986). Suicide and homicide on death row (letter). *American Journal of Psychiatry* 143:559–560.

Leura, A., and Exner, J. (1976). Rorschach performances of children with a multiple foster home history. Workshops Study no. 220 (unpublished). Rorschach Workshops.

Levin, J., and Fox, J. (1985). *Mass Murder.* New York: Plenum Press.

Levy, D. M. (1951). Psychopathic behavior in infants and children. *American Journal of Orthopsychiatry* 21:223–272.

Leyton, E. (1986). *Compulsive Killers: The Story of Modern Multiple Murder.* New York: New York University Press.

Lichtenberg, J., and Slap, J. (1972). On the defensive organization. *International Journal of Psycho-Analysis* 52:451–457.

Lilienfeld, S. O., Van Valkenburg, C., Larntz, K., and Akiskal, H. S. (1986). The relationship of histrionic personality disorder to antisocial personality disorder and somatization disorders. *American Journal of Psychiatry* 143:718–722.

Lindsley, D. (1951). Emotion. In *Handbook of Experimental Psychology,* ed. S. Stevens, pp. 473–516. New York: Wiley.

Lion, J. (1978). Outpatient treatment of psychopaths. In *The Psychopath: A Comprehensive Study of Antisocial Disorders and Behaviors,* ed. W. Reid, pp. 286–300. New York: Brunner/Mazel.

Lion, J., and Leaff, L. (1973). On the hazards of assessing character pathology in an outpatient setting. *Psychiatric Quarterly* 47:104–109.

Livingston, K., and Horneykiewicz, O., eds. (1978). *Limbic Mechanisms: The Continuing Evolution of the Limbic System Concept.* New York: Plenum Press.

Ljungberg, L. (1957). Hysteria: clinical, prognostic, and genetic study. *Acta Psychiatrica et Neurologica Scandinavica (suppl.) 122.*

Loeb, J., and Mednick, S. (1977). A prospective study of predictors of criminality: 3 electrodermal response patterns. In *Biosocial Bases of Criminal Behavior,* ed. S. Mednick and K. Christiansen. New York: Gardner.

Loewald, H. W. (1955). Hypnoid state, repression, abreaction, and recollection. *Journal of the American Psychoanalytic Association* 3:201–210.

Lombroso, C. (1872–1885). *L'Uomo Delinquente.* Bocca: Torino.

Lothane, Z. (1982). The psychopathology of hallucinations—a methodological analysis. *British Journal of Medical Psychology* 55:335–348.

Ludolph, P. (1983). Dissociative experience in borderline patients and normal individuals. Unpublished paper presented at the American Psychological Association, Anaheim, California, August 26.

Lunde, D. (1975). *Murder and Madness*. Stanford: Stanford Alumni Association.

Lykken, D. (1957). A study of anxiety in the sociopathic personality. *Journal of Abnormal and Social Psychology* 55:6–10.

Lynch, B. E., and Bradford, J. M. W. (1980). Amnesia: its detection by psychophysiological measures. *Bulletin of the American Academy of Psychiatry and Law* 8:288–293.

MacAndrew, C., and Edgerton, R. (1964). The everyday life of institutionalized idiots. *Human Organization* 23:312–318.

Maccoby, E., and Jacklin, C. (1980). Sex differences in aggression: a rejoinder and reprise. *Child Development* 51:964–980.

MacDonald, J. (1963). The threat to kill. *American Journal of Psychiatry* 120:125–130.

———— (1968). *Homicidal Threats*. Springfield, IL: Charles C Thomas.

MacLean, P. (1949). Psychosomatic disease and the "visceral brain": recent developments bearing on the Papez theory of emotion. *Psychosomatic Medicine* 11:338–353.

———— (1952). Some psychiatric implications of physiological studies on fronto-temporal portion of limbic system (visceral brain). *Electroencephalography and Clinical Neurophysiology* 4:407–418.

———— (1960). Psychomatics. In *Handbook of Physiology*. Washington, DC: American Physiology Society.

———— (1962). New findings relevant to the evolution of psychosexual functions of the brain. *Journal of Nervous and Mental Disease* 135:289–301.

———— (1964). Minor display in the squirrel monkey, Saimiri sciureus. *Science* 146:950–952.

———— (1972). Cerebral evolution and emotional processes: new findings on the striatal complex. *Annals of the New York Academy of Sciences* 193:137–149.

———— (1973). A triune concept of the brain and behavior; Lectures I, II, III. In *The Hincks Memorial Lectures*, ed. T. Boag and D. Campbell. Toronto: University of Toronto Press.

———— (1976). Sensory and perceptive factors in emotional functions of the triune brain. In *Biological Foundations of Psychiatry*, ed. R. Grenell and S. Gabay, pp. 177–198. New York: Raven Press.

Maddocks, P. D. (1970). A five year followup of untreated psychopaths. *British Journal of Psychiatry* 116:511–515.

Mahler, M. (1958). Autism and symbiosis, two extreme disturbances of identity. *International Journal of Psycho-Analysis* 39:77–83.

———— (1960). Perceptual dedifferentiation and psychotic "object relationship." *International Journal of Psycho-Analysis* 41:348–353.

———— (1967). On human symbiosis and the vicissitudes of individuation. *Journal of the American Psychoanalytic Association* 15:740–763.

———— (1968). *On Human Symbiosis and the Vicissitudes of Individuation. Vol. I. Infantile Psychosis.* New York: International Universities Press.

———— (1979). *Selected Papers of Margaret S. Mahler.* New York: Jason Aronson.

Mahler, M., Pine, F., and Bergman, A. (1975). *The Psychological Birth of the Human Infant.* New York: Basic Books.

Mailer, N. (1979). *The Executioner's Song.* New York: Little, Brown.

Maltsberger, J., and Buie, D. (1974). Countertransference hate in the treatment of suicidal patients. *Archives of General Psychiatry* 30:625–633.

Mason, B., and Exner, J. (1984). Correlations between WAIS subtests and nonpatient adult Rorschach data. Workshops Study 289 (unpublished). Rorschach Workshops.

Masur, J. (1972). Sex differences in "emotionality" and behavior of rats in the open-field. *Behavioral Biology* 7:749–754.

Mayman, M. (1962a). A multi-dimensional view of the Rorschach movement response: perception, fantasy, kinesthesia, self-representation, and object-relationships. In *Rorschach Psychology*, ed. M. A. Rickers-Ovsiankina, pp. 229–250. Huntington, NY: Krieger, 1977.

———— (1962b). Reality contact, defense effectiveness, and psychopathology in Rorschach form level scores. Unpublished manuscript. Ann Arbor: University of Michigan.

———— (1967). Object representations and object relationships in Rorschach responses. *Journal of Projective Techniques and Personality Assessment* 31:17–24.

Mednick, S., Gabrielli, W., and Hutchings, B. (1984). Genetic influences in criminal convictions: evidence from an adoption cohort. *Science* 224:891–894.

Mednick, S., Pollock, V., Volavka, J., and Gabrielli, W. (1982). Biology and violence. In *Criminal Violence*, ed. M. Wolfgang and N. Weiner. Beverly Hills: Sage.

Mednick, S., Volavka, J., Gabrielli, W., and Itil, T. (1981). EEG as a predictor of antisocial behavior. *Criminology* 19:219–231.

Megargee, E. (1976). The prediction of dangerous behavior. *Criminal Justice and Behavior* 3:3–21.

Meikle, S. (1970). Drug induced sympathetic arousal and neuroticism. *Canadian Psychologist* 11:269–280.

Meissner, W. W. (1970). Notes on identification I. Origins in Freud. *Psychoanalytic Quarterly* 39:563–589.

———— (1971). Notes on identification II. Clarification of related concepts. *Psychoanalytic Quarterly* 40:277–302.

———— (1972). Notes on identification III. The concept of identification. *Psychoanalytic Quarterly* 41:224–260.

———— (1977). Cognitive aspects of the paranoid process – prospectus. In *Psychiatry and the Humanities. Vol. 2: Thought, Consciousness, and Reality*, ed. J. H. Smith, pp. 159–216. New Haven: Yale University Press.

———— (1978). *The Paranoid Process*. New York: Jason Aronson.

———— (1981). Notes on the psychoanalytic psychology of the self. *Psychoanalytic Inquiry* 1:233–248.

———— (1983). Phenomenology of the self. In *The Future of Psychoanalysis*, ed. A. Goldberg, pp. 65–96. New York: International Universities Press.

———— (1986). Can psychoanalysis find its self? *Journal of the American Psychoanalytic Association* 34:379–400.

Meloy, R. (1984). Thought organization and primary process in the parents of schizophrenics. *British Journal of Medical Psychology* 57:279–281.

———— (1985). Concept and percept formation in object relations theory. *Psychoanalytic Psychology* 2:35–45.

———— (1986a). Rapid classification of the functionally psychotic individual in custody. *Criminal Justice and Behavior* 13:185–195.

———— (1986b). On the relationship between primary process and thought disorder. *Journal of the American Academy of Psychoanalysis* 14:47–56.

――― (1987). The prediction of violence in outpatient psychotherapy. *American Journal of Psychotherapy* 41:38–45.

――― (1988). Violent and homicidal behavior in primitive mental states. *Journal of the American Academy of Psychoanalysis* 16:381–394.

Meltzer, D. (1973). *Sexual States of Mind*. Perthshire, Scotland: Clunie.

――― (1975). Adhesive identification. *Contemporary Psychoanalysis* 11:289–310.

Meyer, A. (1908). The problem of mental reaction-types, mental causes and diseases. *Psychological Bulletin* 5:245–261.

Michaud, S., and Aynesworth, H. (1983). *The Only Living Witness*. New York: New American Library.

Miller, R. D., and Maier, G. J. (1987). Factors affecting the decision to prosecute mental patients for criminal behavior. *Hospital and Community Psychiatry* 38:50–55.

Millon, T. (1969). *Modern Psychopathology: A Biosocial Approach to Maladaptive Learning and Functioning*. Philadelphia: W. B. Saunders.

――― (1981). *Disorders of Personality DSM-III: Axis II*. New York: Wiley.

Minuchin, S., Montalvo, B., Guerney, B., Jr., Roseman, B., and Schumer, F. (1967). *Families of the Slums: An Exploration of their Structure and Treatment*. New York: Basic Books.

Modell, A. (1968). *Object Love and Reality*. New York: International Universities Press.

――― (1975). A narcissistic defense against affects and the illusion of self-sufficiency. *International Journal of Psycho-Analysis* 56:275–282.

Monroe, R. (1981). Brain dysfunction in prisoners. In *Violence and the Violent Individual*, ed. R. Hayes, T. Roberts, and K. Solway. New York: Spectrum.

Moorman, C. B. (1986). Peace officers murdered in California, 1980–1985. *Journal of California Law Enforcement* 20:85–93.

Moravesik, E. E. (1894). Das hysterische irresein. *Allg Z fur Psychiatrie* 50:117.

Morrison, H. (1978). The asocial child: A destiny of sociopath? In *The*

Psychopath: A Comprehensive Study of Antisocial Disorders and Behaviors, ed. W. H. Reid, pp. 22–65. New York: Brunner/Mazel.

Morse, S. (1982). Failed explanations and criminal responsibility: experts and the unconscious. 68 *Virginia Law Review* 971.

Moyer, K. (1968). Kinds of aggression and their physiological basis. *Commun. Behav. Biol. [A]* 2:65–87.

Murray, H. (1943). *Thematic Apperception Test.* Cambridge: Harvard University Press.

Neuman, G. G. (1987). Potential for transformation. In *Origins of Human Aggression*, ed. G. Neuman, pp. 174–188. New York: Human Sciences.

O'Brien, D. (1985). *Two of a Kind: The Hillside Stranglers.* New York: New American Library.

Ogden, T. H. (1983). The concept of internal object relations. *International Journal of Psycho-Analysis* 64:227–241.

———— (1985). On potential space. *International Journal of Psycho-Analysis* 66:129–141.

———— (1986). *The Matrix of the Mind.* Northvale, NJ: Jason Aronson.

Olweus, D. (1975). Bullies and whipping boys. In *Determinants and Origins of Aggressive Behavior*, ed. J. DeWit and W. W. Hartup. The Hague: Mouton.

Orne, M. T. (1961). The potential uses of hypnosis in interrogation. In *The Manipulation of Human Behavior*, ed. A. D. Biderman and H. Zimmer, pp. 169–215. New York: Wiley.

———— (1977). The concept of hypnosis: implications of the definition for research and practice. *Annals of the New York Academy of Science* 296:14–33.

Orne, M. T., Dinges, D. F., and Orne, E. C. (1984). On the differential diagnosis of multiple personality in the forensic context. *International Journal of Clinical and Experimental Hypnosis* 32:118–169.

Ornitz, E. (1969). Disorders of perception common to early infantile autism and schizophrenia. *Comprehensive Psychiatry* 10:259–274.

_____ (1970). Vestibular dysfunction in schizophrenia and childhood autism. *Comprehensive Psychiatry* 11:159–173.

Ornitz, E., and Ritvo, E. (1968a). Neurophysiologic mechanisms underlying perceptual inconstancy in autistic and schizophrenic children. *Archives of General Psychiatry* 19:22–27.

_____ (1968b). Perceptual inconstancy in early infantile autism. *Archives of General Psychiatry* 18:76–98.

Paluck, R. J., and Esser, A. H. (1971). Territorial behavior as an indicator of changes in clinical behavioral condition of severely retarded boys. *American Journal of Mental Deficiency* 76:284–290.

Pandya, D., Van Hoesen, G., and Mesulam, M. (1981). The corticocortical projections of the cingulate cortex in the rhesus monkey. *Experimental Brain Research* 42:319–330.

Papez, J. (1937). A proposed mechanism of emotion. *Archives of Neurology and Psychiatry* 38:725–744.

_____ (1958). Visceral brain: its component parts and their connections. *Journal of Nervous and Mental Disease* 126:40–56.

Partridge, G. E. (1927). A study of 50 cases of psychopathic personality. *American Journal of Psychiatry* 7:953–974.

Pavlov, I. P. (1927). *Conditioned Reflexes.* London: Clarendon Press.

Peebles, R. (1975). Rorschach as self-system in the Telophasic theory of personality development. In *Handbook of Rorschach Scales*, ed. P. Lerner, pp. 71–133. New York: International Universities Press.

Penfield, W., and Jasper, H. (1954). *Epilepsy and the Functional Anatomy of the Human Brain.* Boston: Little, Brown.

Persky, H., Smith, K., and Basu, G. (1971). Relation of psychologic measures of aggression and hostility to testosterone production in men. *Psychosomatic Medicine* 33:265–277.

Peto, A. (1969). Terrifying eyes: a visual superego forerunner. *Psychoanalytic Study of the Child* 24:197–212.

Piaget, J. (1954). *The Construction of Reality in the Child.* New York: Basic Books.

Piaget, J., and Inhelder, B. (1969). *The Psychology of the Child.* New York: Basic Books.

Pierce, G. (1978). The absent parent and the Rorschach "T" response. In

Children of Military Families, ed. E. Hunter and D. Nice. Washington, DC: U.S. Government Printing Office.

Pinel, P. (1801). *Traite medico-philosophique sur l'alienation mentale*. Paris: Richard, Caille et Ravier.

Post, J. (1984). Notes on a psychodynamic theory of terrorist behavior. *Terrorism: An International Journal* 7:241–256.

Prichard, J. C. (1835). *A Treatise on Insanity*. trans. D. Davis. New York: Hafner.

Pruitt, W., and Spilka, B. (1964). Rorschach empathy-object relationship scale. In *Handbook of Rorschach Scales*, ed. P. Lerner, pp. 315–323. New York: International Universities Press, 1975.

Quay, H. (1965). Psychopathic personality as pathological stimulation seeking. *American Journal of Psychiatry* 122:180–83.

Rachman, S. (1961). Effect of a stimulant drug on extent of motor response. *Perceptual Motor Skills* 12:186.

Racker, H. (1968). *Transference and Countertransference*. New York: International Universities Press.

Rada, R., Laws, D., and Kellner, R. (1976). Plasma testosterone levels in the rapist. *Psychosomatic Medicine* 38:257–268.

———— (1978). *Clinical Aspects of the Rapist*. New York: Grune & Stratton.

Rapaport, D. (1951). *Organization and Pathology of Thought*. New York: Columbia University Press.

Rapaport, D., Gill, M., and Schafer, R. (1946). *Diagnostic Psychological Testing*, ed. R. Holt. New York: International Universities Press, 1968.

Redl, F., and Wineman, D. (1951). *Children Who Hate: The Disorganization and Breakdown of Behavioral Controls*. New York: The Free Press.

Reich, A. (1951). On countertransference. *International Journal of Psycho-Analysis* 32:25–31.

Reich, W. (1945). *Character Analysis*. 2nd ed. New York: Farrar, Straus & Giroux.

Reid, W. H., ed. (1978). *The Psychopath: A Comprehensive Study of Antisocial Disorders and Behaviors*. New York: Brunner/Mazel.

Reid, W. H., Dorr, D., Walker, J., and Bonner, J. (1986). *Unmasking the Psychopath*. New York: Norton.

Reiser, M. (1984). *Mind, Brain, Body*. New York: Basic Books.

———— (1985). Converging sectors of psychoanalysis and neurobiology: mutual challenges and opportunity. *Journal of the American Psychoanalytic Association* 33:11–34.

Reiss, S., Levitan, G. W., and Szyszko, J. (1982). Emotional disturbance and mental retardation: diagnostic overshadowing. *American Journal of Mental Deficiency* 86:567–574.

Reiterman, T., and Jacobs, J. (1982). *Raven: The Untold Story of the Reverend Jim Jones and His People*. New York: Dutton.

Revitch, E., and Schlesinger, L. (1981). *Psychopathology of Homicide*. Springfield, IL: Charles C Thomas.

Richardson, L. (1960). *Statistics of Deadly Quarrels*. Pittsburgh: Boxwood Press.

Riedel, M., Zahn, M., and Mock, L. (1985). *The Nature and Patterns of American Homicide*. Washington, DC: U.S. Government Printing Office.

Rinsley, D. (1982). *Borderline and Other Self Disorders*. New York: Jason Aronson.

Ritzler, B., Zambianco, D., Harder, D., and Kaskey, M. (1980). Psychotic patterns of the concept of the object on the Rorschach test. *Journal of Abnormal Psychology* 89:46–55.

Robins, E., Purtell, J. J., and Cohen, M. E. (1952). "Hysteria" in men. *New England Journal of Medicine* 146:667–685.

Robins, L. N. (1966). *Deviant Children Grown Up: A Sociological and Psychiatric Study of Sociopathic Personality*. Baltimore: Williams & Wilkins.

Rogers, R. (1986). *Conducting Insanity Evaluations*. New York: Van Nostrand Reinhold.

Rorschach, H. (1921). *Psychodiagnostics*. Bern: Bircher, 1942.

Rosanoff, A. J. (1938). *Manual of Psychiatry and Mental Hygiene*. New York: Wiley.

Rosenfeld, H. (1964). On the psychopathology of narcissism: a clinical approach. *International Journal of Psycho-Analysis* 45:332–337.

Rothstein, A. (1980). *The Narcissistic Pursuit of Perfection*. New York: International Universities Press.

Rush, B. (1812). *Medical Inquiries and Observations upon the Diseases of the Mind.* Philadelphia: Kimber and Richardson.

Russell, P., and Williams, D. (1973). Effects of repeated testing on rats' locomotor activity in the open-field. *Animal behavior* 21:109–112.

Sagarin, E., ed. (1980). *Taboos in Criminology.* Beverly Hills: Sage.

Sandler, J., and Freud, A. (1985). Discussions in the Hampstead Index of "The Ego and the Mechanisms of Defense." In *Defense and Resistance: Historical Perspective and Current Concepts,* ed. H. Blum. New York: International Universities Press.

Satinover, J. (1986). Jung's lost contribution to the dilemma of narcissism. *Journal of the American Psychoanalytic Association* 34:401–438.

Scaramella, T., and Brown, W. (1978). Serum testosterone and aggressiveness in hockey players. *Psychosomatic Medicine* 40:262–265.

Scarr, S. (1965). The inheritance of sociability. *American Psychologist* 20:524.

Schachter, S., and Singer, J. (1962). Cognitive, social and physiological determinants of emotional state. *Psychological Review* 69:379–399.

Schachter, D. (1986a). Amnesia and crime: how much do we really know? *American Psychologist* 41:286–295.

———— (1986b). Feeling-of-knowing ratings distinguish between genuine and simulated forgetting. *Journal of Experimental Psychology: Learning, Memory, and Cognition* 12:30–41.

———— (1986c). On the relation between genuine and simulated amnesia. *Behavioral Sciences and the Law* 4:47–64.

Schafer, R. (1954). *Psychoanalytic Interpretation in Rorschach Testing.* New York: Grune & Stratton.

———— (1968). *Aspects of Internalization.* New York: International Universities Press.

———— (1976). *A New Language for Psychoanalysis.* New Haven: Yale University Press.

Schalling, D., Lidberg, L, Levander, S., and Dahlin, Y. (1973). Spontaneous autonomic activity as related to psychopathy. *Biological Psychology* 1:83–97.

Schmauk, F. (1970). Punishment, arousal, and avoidance learning in sociopaths. *Journal of Abnormal Psychology* 76:325–335.

Schmideberg, M. (1949). The analytic treatment of major criminals: therapeutic results and technical problems. In *Searchlights on Delinquency*, ed. K. Eissler, pp. 174–189. New York: International Universities Press.

Schneider, A., and Tarshis, B. (1975). *Physiological Psychology*. New York: Random House.

Schreiber, F. R. (1973). *Sybil*. Chicago: Regnery.

Schuckit, M. (1973). Alcoholism and sociopathy—diagnostic confusion. *Quarterly Journal of Studies in Alcoholism* 34:157–164.

Schulsinger, F. (1977). Psychopathy: heredity and environment. In *Biosocial Bases of Criminal Behavior*, ed. S. A. Mednick and K. O. Christiansen. New York: Wiley.

Searles, H. (1960). *The Nonhuman Environment in Normal Development and in Schizophrenia*. New York: International Universities Press.

———— (1965). *Collected Papers on Schizophrenia and Related Subjects*. New York: International Universities Press.

———— (1979). *Countertransference and Related Subjects*. New York: International Universities Press.

———— (1986). *My Work with Borderline Patients*. Northvale, NJ: Jason Aronson.

Selye, H. (1950). *The Physiology and Pathology of Exposure to Stress*. Montreal: Acta.

Senatore, V., Matson, J. L., and Kazdin, A. E. (1985). An inventory to assess psychopathology of mentally retarded adults. *American Journal of Mental Deficiency* 89:459–466.

Shapiro, D. (1965). *Neurotic Styles*. New York: Basic Books.

———— (1981). *Autonomy and Rigid Character*. New York: Basic Books.

Shapiro, D. L. (1984). *Psychological Evaluation and Expert Testimony*. New York: Van Nostrand Reinhold.

Shaw, E. D. (1986). Political terrorists: dangers of diagnosis and an alternative to the psychopathology model. *International Journal of Law and Psychiatry* 8:359–368.

Shields, J. (1962). *Monozygotic Twins*. Oxford: Oxford University Press.

Shipley, J., and Kolb, B. (1977). Neural correlates of species-typical behavior in the Syrian golden hamster. *Journal of Comparative and Physiological Psychology* 91:1056–1073.

Shute, C. C., and Lewis, P. R. (1967). The ascending cholinergic reticular system: neocortical, olfactory, and subcortical projections. *Brain* 90:497–520.

Siddle, D., Nicole, A., and Foggit, R. (1973). Habituation and over-extinction of the GSR component of the orienting response in antisocial adolescents. *British Journal of Social and Clinical Psychology* 12:303–308.

Silber, A. (1979). Childhood seduction, parental pathology, and hysterical symptoms: the genesis of an altered state of consciousness. *International Journal of Psycho-Analysis* 60:109–116.

Silverman, L. (1985). Mommy and I are one. *American Psychologist* 40:1296–1308.

Simon, R. I. (1977). Type A, AB, B murderers: their relationship to the victims and to the criminal justice system. *Bulletin of the American Academy of Psychiatry and the Law* 5:344–362.

Singer, M. (1977). The borderline diagnosis and psychological tests: review and research. In *Borderline Personality Disorders*, ed. P. Hartocollis, pp. 193–212. New York: International Universities Press.

Singer, M., and Wynne, L. (1965). Thought disorder and family relations of schizophrenics. IV: results and implications. *Archives of General Psychiatry* 12:201–212.

Sinha, S. (1964). Effects of GABA and metrazol on alternation of response. *American Psychologist* 534.

Skinner, B. F. (1953). *Science and Human Behavior.* New York: Macmillan.

Smith, K. (1980). Object relations concepts as applied to the borderline level of ego functioning. In *Borderline Phenomena and the Rorschach Test*, ed. J. Kwawer, H. Lerner, P. Lerner, and A. Sugarman, pp. 59–88. New York: International Universities Press.

Solnit, A. (1982). Developmental perspectives on self and object constancy. *The Psychoanalytic Study of the Child* 37:201–217.

——— (1986). Introduction. In *Self and Object Constancy*, ed. R. Lax, S. Bach, and J. Burland, pp. 1–7. New York: Guilford Press.

Sovner, R., and Hurley, A. D. (1983). Do the mentally retarded suffer from affective illness? *Archives of General Psychiatry* 40:61–67.

Spalt, L. (1980). Hysteria and antisocial personality: a single disorder? *Journal of Nervous and Mental Disease* 168:456–464.

Spiegel, H., and Spiegel, D. (1978). *Trance and Treatment.* New York: Basic Books.

Spiegel, L. (1959). Self, sense of self, and perception. *Psychoanalytic Study of the Child* 14:81–109.

Spohn, H., Coyne, L., Larson, J., Mittleman, F., Spray, J., and Hayes, K. (1986). Episodic and residual thought pathology in chronic schizophrenics: effect of neuroleptics. *Schizophrenia Bulletin* 12:394–407.

Stelmack, R., and Mandelzys, N. (1975). Extroversion and pupillary response to affective and taboo words. *Psychophysiology* 56:199–204.

Stewart, H. (1985). Changes of inner space. *International Journal of Psycho-Analysis* 66:255–264.

Stone, C. (1942). Maturation and instinctive functions and motivations. In *Comparative Psychology Revised Edition*, ed. F. Moss, pp. 32–97. New York: Prentice-Hall.

Stott, D. H., Marston, N. C., and Neill, S. J. (1975). *Taxonomy of Behavior Disturbance.* London: University of London Press.

Strasburger, L. (1986). Treatment of antisocial syndromes: the therapist's feelings. In *Unmasking the Psychopath*, ed. W. Reid, D. Dorr, J. Walker, and J. Bonner, pp. 191–207. New York: Norton.

Suarez, J. M., and Pittluck, A. T. (1975). Global amnesia: organic and functional considerations. *Bulletin of the American Academy of Psychiatry and Law* 3:17–24.

Sugarman, A. (1986). An object relations understanding of borderline phenomena on the Rorschach. In *Assessing Object Relations Phenomena*, ed. M. Kissen, pp. 77–88. New York: International Universities Press.

Sutker, F. (1970). Vicarious conditioning and sociopathy. *Journal of Abnormal Psychology* 76:380–386.

Svrakic, D. (1985). Emotional features of narcissistic personality disorder. *American Journal of Psychiatry* 142:720–724.

Szekacs, J. (1985). Impaired spatial structures. *International Journal of Psycho-Analysis* 66:193–199.

Szekely, L. (1954). Biological remarks on fears originating in early childhood. *International Journal of Psycho-Analysis* 35:57–67.

Tooley, K. (1974). Words, actions, and "acting out": Their role in the pathology of violent children. *International Review of Psycho-Analysis* 1:341–351.

———— (1976). Antisocial behavior and social alienation post divorce: the "man of the house" and his mother. *American Journal of Orthopsychiatry* 46:33–42.

Tucker, D. M. (1981). Lateral brain function, emotion and conceptualization. *Psychological Bulletin* 89:19–46.

Tustin, F. (1981). Psychological birth and psychological catastrophe. In *Do I Dare Disturb the Universe?* ed. J. Grotstein, pp. 181–196. Beverly Hills: Caesura Press.

Urist, J. (1980). The continuum between primary and secondary process thinking: toward a concept of borderline thought. In *Borderline Phenomena and the Rorschach Test*, ed. J. Kwawer, H. Lerner, P. Lerner, and A. Sugarman, pp. 133–154. New York: International Universities Press.

Vaillant, G. E. (1975). Sociopathy as a human process. *Archives of General Psychiatry* 32:178–183.

Valle, F. (1970). Effects of strain, sex, and illumination on open-field behavior of rats. *American Journal of Psychology* 83:103–111.

Valzelli, L. (1978). Clinical pharmacology of serotonin. In *Serotonin in Health and Disease. Vol. 4: Physiological Regulation and Pharmacological Action*, ed. W. B. Essman, pp. 295–339. New York: Spectrum.

———— (1979). *An Approach to Neuroanatomical and Neurochemical Psychophysiology*. Geneva: Granata Ed.

———— (1981). *Psychobiology of Aggression and Violence*. New York: Raven Press.

Venables, P., and Christie, M. (1975). *Research in Psychophysiology*. New York: Wiley.

———— (1985). Autonomic nervous system factors in criminal behavior. In *Biology and Crime*, ed. S. Mednick and T. Moffit. Cambridge: Cambridge University Press.

Volkan, V. (1973). Transitional fantasies in the analysis of a narcissistic personality. *Journal of the American Psychoanalytic Association* 21:351–376.

_____ (1976). *Primitive Internalized Object Relations.* New York: International Universities Press.

Von Domarus, E. (1944). The specific laws of logic in schizophrenia. In *Language and Thought in Schizophrenia,* ed. A. Kasinin, pp. 104–115. New York: Norton.

Wadsworth, M. (1975). Delinquency in a national sample of children. *British Journal of Criminology* 15:167–174.

Wasman, G., and Flynn, J. (1962). Directed attack elicited from hypothalamus. *Archives of Neurology* 6:220–227.

Watkins, J., and Stauffacher, J. (1952). An index of pathological thinking in the Rorschach. *Journal of Projective Techniques* 16:276–286.

Webbink, P. (1986). *The Power of the Eyes.* New York: Springer.

Wechsler, D. (1981). *WAIS-R Manual.* New York: Psychological Corp.

Werner, H. (1948). *Comparative Psychology of Mental Development.* New York: Harper & Row.

Werner, H., and Kaplan, B. (1963). *Symbol Formation.* New York: Wiley.

Wertham, F. (1937). The catathymic crisis: a clinical entity. *Archives of Neurology and Psychiatry* 37:974–977.

Whipple, D. (1986). Discussion of "The Merits and Problems with the Concept of Projective Identification" by J. Finell. *Psychoanalytic Review* 73:121–128.

Whitty, C. W. M., and Zangwill, O. L. (1977). *Amnesia.* Toronto: Butterworth.

Wilcock, J. (1968). Strain differences in response to shock in rats selectively bred for emotional elimination. *Animal Behavior* 16:294–297.

Willock, B. (1986). Narcissistic vulnerability in the hyper-aggressive child: the disregarded (unloved, uncared-for) self. *Psychoanalytic Psychology* 3:59–80.

Wilson, J., and Herrnstein, R. (1985). *Crime and Human Nature.* New York: Simon & Schuster.

Winnicott, D. W. (1953). Transitional objects and transitional phenomena. In *Collected Papers: Through Paediatrics to Psycho-analysis.* New York: Basic Books, 1958.

_____ (1960). Ego distortion in terms of true and false self. In *The*

Maturational Processes and the Facilitating Environment: Studies in the Theory of Emotional Development, pp. 140–152. New York: International Universities Press, 1965.

———— (1962). Ego integration in child development. In *The Maturational Processes and the Facilitating Environment*. Toronto: Clarke, Irwin, 1965.

———— (1964). Review of C. G. Jung's "Memories, Dreams and Reflections." *International Journal of Psycho-Analysis* 45:450–455.

———— (1965). *The Maturational Processes and the Facilitating Environment*. New York: International Universities Press.

Wittels, F. (1937). The criminal psychopath in the psychoanalytic system. *Psychoanalytic Review* 24:276–283.

Woerner, P. I., and Guze, S. B. (1968). A family and marital study of hysteria. *British Journal of Psychiatry* 114:161–168.

Yeudall, L. (1977). Neuropsychological assessment of forensic disorders. *Canadian Mental Health* 25:7.

Yeudall, L, Fedora, O., Fromm, D. (1984). A neuropsychological theory of persistent criminality: implications for assessment and treatment. *Alberta Hospital Education Research Bulletin no. 97*. Edmonton, Alberta.

Yochelson, S., and Samenow, S. (1977). *The Criminal Personality*. Vol. 1. New York: Jason Aronson.

Zillmann, D. (1984). *Connections between Sex and Aggression*. Hillsdale, NJ: Erlbaum.

Zuckerman, M. (1978). Sensation seeking and psychopathy. In *Psychopathic Behavior: Approaches to Research*, ed. R. Hare and D. Schalling, pp. 165–185. London: Wiley.

Index

Abraham, K., 275
Abrahamsen, D., 29, 65, 75, 77, 95, 101, 113, 226–227, 231
Acetylcholine, 26
Adams, J., 207
Adams, N., 301
Adler, G., 204
Adoption studies, 23–24
Affect block, 203–204
Affective aggression, 25–26, 192–212
  displacement of, 199–202
  and lowered self-esteem, 211–212
  and predatory aggression, 213–214
  and psychotic envelopment, 208–211
  and public ritual, 202–203
Affective discontinuity, 314–315
Aggression, 24–29, 187–191.

See also Affective aggression; Predatory aggression
  psychotic modes of, 292–293
  sexualization of, 135, 144–145
  and violence, 191–192
Aichorn, A., 9
Alarm state, 193, 202
Aleksandrowicz, D. R.,
Aleksandrowicz, M. K., 55
Alexander, F., 8–9
Allen, J., 332
Allison, R., 177–178
American Psychiatric Association, 6–7, 152–153, 245, 268, 279, 289
Amphetamines, 225, 280, 294
Andreasen, N. C., 263–265, 286
Andrew, J., 22
Anger, 81–91
"Apocalypse Now," 252
Appelbaum, J., 24

461

Predatory aggression, 25–26,
28–29, 212–241
and absence of conscious
emotion, 214–215
absence of threat in, 218
goals of, 219–223
minimal autonomic arousal
in, 213–214
minimal displacement in,
223–224
planned violence in, 215–218
and private ritual, 224–230
and reality testing, 233–234
self and object concepts in,
232–233
and self-esteem, 234
and sensory awareness,
230–231
time-unlimited nature of,
224

Premenstrual period, 28

Prichard, J. C., 7

Private ritual, 224–230

Projective identification and
object control, 141–148,
321

Psychoanalysis, and
psychopathy, 8–13

Psychopathic personality
organization, 19–20

Psychopathy, 5–7
biological substrates, 20–38
and conscious experience of
emotion, 74–113

denial and deception in,
120–132, 341–362
developmental origins of,
41–59
drug-induced psychosis and,
293–299
historical perspective on,
7–14
and hysteria, 161–170
imitation and simulation in,
132–141
mental retardation and,
299–303
and multiple personality
disorder, 170–181
paranoid schizophrenia and,
363–375
and predatory violence,
234–241
as process, 311
projective identification in,
141–148
psychosis and, 245–303
psychotherapeutic
treatment of, 309–340
reptilian states, 66–74
rorschach psychodiagnosis
of, 377–421
severity of, 311–322
splitting and dissociation in,
149–181
structure and function of,
17–20

Psychosis
drug-induced, 293–299